# China's Vulnerability Paradox

# China's Vulnerability Paradox

*How the World's Largest Consumer Transformed Global Commodity Markets*

PASCALE MASSOT

**OXFORD**
UNIVERSITY PRESS

Oxford University Press is a department of the University of Oxford. It furthers
the University's objective of excellence in research, scholarship, and education
by publishing worldwide. Oxford is a registered trade mark of Oxford University
Press in the UK and certain other countries.

Published in the United States of America by Oxford University Press
198 Madison Avenue, New York, NY 10016, United States of America.

© Oxford University Press 2024

All rights reserved. No part of this publication may be reproduced, stored in
a retrieval system, or transmitted, in any form or by any means, without the
prior permission in writing of Oxford University Press, or as expressly permitted
by law, by license, or under terms agreed with the appropriate reproduction
rights organization. Inquiries concerning reproduction outside the scope of the
above should be sent to the Rights Department, Oxford University Press, at the
address above.

You must not circulate this work in any other form
and you must impose this same condition on any acquirer.

Library of Congress Cataloging-in-Publication Data
Names: Massot, Pascale, author.
Title: China's vulnerability paradox : how the world's largest consumer
transformed global commodity markets / Pascale Massot.
Description: New York, NY : Oxford University Press, [2024]. |
Includes bibliographical references.
Identifiers: LCCN 2023043014 | ISBN 9780197771402 (paperback) |
ISBN 9780197771396 (hardback) | ISBN 9780197771426 (epub)
Subjects: LCSH: Commodity exchanges—China. | Mineral industries—China. |
China—Foreign economic relations.
Classification: LCC HG6051.C6 M377 2024 |
DDC 332.64/40951—dc23/eng/20231213
LC record available at https://lccn.loc.gov/2023043014

DOI: 10.1093/oso/9780197771396.001.0001

*To David, Mathilde, and Marguerite*

CONTENTS

*Tables* ix
*Figures* xi
*Acknowledgments* xiii
*Abbreviations* xvii

1. Introduction 1
    THE PUZZLES: VULNERABILITY, VARIATION, AND LIBERALIZATION 1
    THE ARGUMENT: MARKET POWER, MARKET VULNERABILITY, AND MARKET CHANGE 6
    BUILDING BLOCKS 13
    METHODOLOGY, DATA, AND CASE SELECTION 17
    PLAN OF THE BOOK 30

2. Global and Chinese Commodity Markets: Taking Variation Seriously 34
    GLOBAL AND CHINESE COMMODITY MARKETS 35
    THE POLITICAL ECONOMY OF GLOBAL COMMODITY MARKETS 39
    CHANGE IN GLOBAL COMMODITY MARKET PRICING REGIMES 43
    WHY DOES LIBERALIZATION NEED AN EXPLANATION? 46
    INTERNATIONAL POLITICAL ECONOMY OF NATURAL RESOURCES 52

3. Explaining Change in Global Market Institutions 55
    THE ARGUMENT: MARKET POWER, MARKET VULNERABILITY, AND MARKET CHANGE 56
    MARKET POWER, COORDINATION CAPACITY 63
    PRICES AND PREFERENCES FOR GLOBAL MARKET INSTITUTIONS 64
    COORDINATION IN DOMESTIC AND GLOBAL COMMODITY MARKETS 71
    BUILDING BLOCKS: HETEROGENEITY, VULNERABILITY, RESONANCE 75
    CONCLUSION 90

4. China's Impact on the Global Iron Ore Market   92
   MARKET POWER, MARKET VULNERABILITY, AND MARKET CHANGE   92
   THE GLOBAL IRON ORE MARKET AND PRICING REGIME PRIOR TO CHINA'S EMERGENCE   97
   THE DOMESTIC CHINESE IRON ORE AND STEEL MARKET   101
   THE FALL OF THE INTERNATIONAL IRON ORE BENCHMARKING REGIME   109
   CHINA'S IMPACT ON THE GLOBAL IRON ORE SHIPPING INDUSTRY   122
   JAPAN'S IMPACT ON THE GLOBAL IRON ORE MARKET FIFTY YEARS PRIOR   130
   CONCLUSION   136

5. China's Impact on the Global Potash Market   140
   MARKET POWER, MARKET VULNERABILITY, AND MARKET CHANGE   140
   CHINA AND THE GLOBAL POTASH MARKET   143
   THE GLOBAL POTASH PRICING REGIME PRIOR TO CHINA'S EMERGENCE   147
   THE DOMESTIC CHINESE POTASH AND FERTILIZER MARKETS   157
   CHINA'S IMPACT ON THE GLOBAL POTASH PRICING REGIME   170
   CONCLUSION   184

6. China's Impact on the Global Uranium and Copper Markets   187
   MARKET POWER, MARKET VULNERABILITY, AND MARKET CHANGE   187
   CHINA AND THE GLOBAL URANIUM MARKET   191
   THE URANIUM PRICING REGIME PRIOR TO CHINA'S EMERGENCE   193
   THE DOMESTIC CHINESE URANIUM MARKET AND CIVILIAN NUCLEAR INDUSTRY   197
   CHINA'S IMPACT ON THE GLOBAL URANIUM MARKET   204
   CHINA AND THE GLOBAL COPPER MARKET   210
   THE GLOBAL COPPER PRICING REGIME PRIOR TO CHINA'S EMERGENCE   213
   THE DOMESTIC CHINESE COPPER MARKET   216
   CHINA'S IMPACT ON THE GLOBAL COPPER MARKET   219
   CONCLUSION   228

7. Conclusion   232
   PUZZLES   232
   ARGUMENT   234
   BROADER LESSONS   238

*Appendix: Data*   249
*Notes*   255
*References*   261
*Index*   283

# TABLES

1.1 Market power, market vulnerability, and market change   7
1.2 Years of systemic significance for China in the iron ore, potash, uranium, and copper markets   22
1.3 Global potash and iron ore markets at the time of China's emergence as a dominant consumer, 2002–2003   24
1.4 Case studies distribution   27
1.5 Case studies list   29
2.1 Global commodity market concentration before and after China's emergence as dominant consumer   36
2.2 Liberalization of pricing regimes (dependent variable indicators)   45
2.3 Pricing regimes (dependent variable indicators), operationalization   47
2.4 Global pricing regime change after the emergence of China and Japan as dominant consumers   48
3.1 Two-level market power asymmetries   57
3.2 Change toward an asymmetric position of market power   58
3.3 Change toward a symmetric position of market power   59
3.4 Pricing regime preferences based on price levels   65
3.5 Number of domestic Chinese extractive enterprises, 2010   72
3.6 Domestic markets—coordination levels at time of China's emergence (independent variable)   73
3.7 Global commodity markets—coordination levels at the time of China's emergence (independent variable)   75
5.1 Comparative fragmentation of the iron ore and potash industries in China, 2007   158
5.2 A short history of potash import licenses   165
5.3 Chinese potash imports and prices paid, 2001   171
6.1 Global natural uranium production, 2009–2015   192

| | | |
|---|---|---|
| 6.2 | Reactors operable, under construction, planned, and proposed, and uranium requirements, 2007, 2015, and 2020 | 198 |
| 6.3 | Uranium mines in operation in Mainland China (2010) | 199 |
| 6.4 | Top four copper importers (1990, 2000, 2010, 2020) | 214 |
| A.1 | Workplaces, by interview (N=160 interviews) | 253 |

# FIGURES

1.1 World metals imports, China, India, Japan, and the United States, 1992–2021  2
1.2 Share of world seaborne iron ore production by firm, 1997 and 2007  25
1.3 Share of world potash exports by firm, 1995 and 2005  26
1.4 Chinese import dependence on the global iron ore, potash markets, 1990–2016  27
2.1 Share of large, medium, and small enterprises in China's mining sector, 2001–2016  39
2.2 Proportion of medium and large enterprises in the Chinese mining industry, 2007  40
2.3 Sales revenue by employee in the Chinese mining industry, 2001  40
2.4 Pricing regime change following the emergence of China (iron ore and potash) and Japan (iron ore) as dominant consumers  48
3.1 Proportion of medium and large enterprises in the Chinese domestic market  71
3.2 Proportion of top two Chinese importers in the iron ore, potash, copper, and uranium markets, 2000–2014  72
4.1 China's iron ore imports, 1960–2016  97
4.2 Shares of global iron ore imports: China and Japan, 1990–2016  98
4.3 World shares of iron ore exports by country, 2000 and 2015  99
4.4 China's iron ore imports by country, 2001 and 2016  99
4.5 China's iron ore production and imports, 1990–2016  102
4.6 China's iron ore import dependence, 1990–2016  103
4.7 Top four Chinese crude steel producers, 2000–2010  103
4.8 Number and share of large, medium, and small iron ore enterprises in China 2001, 2007, and 2015  104

## FIGURES

4.9  Proportion of enterprises, by size, in the Chinese mining industry, 2001 and 2015   105
4.10 Share of total iron ore imports by top two Chinese firms, 2000, 2005, 2010, and 2014   107
4.11 Iron ore prices, 1975–2022   115
5.1  Agricultural use of potash, 1990 and 2019   144
5.2  Agricultural use of potash for top four consumers (share of world total), 1980–2019   144
5.3  China's agricultural use of potash, imports and production 1961–2019   145
5.4  China's potash import dependence, 1961–2019   145
5.5  China's share of global potash imports, 1961–2019   146
5.6  Shares of world potash exports by country, 1995 and 2015   148
5.7  Potash prices, 1960–2023   149
5.8  China's potash imports by country, 2001 and 2015   151
5.9  Share of potash imports from the top two Chinese importers, 2000–2014   159
5.10 Share of potash and iron ore imports of the top ten Chinese importers, 2000–2014   160
5.11 Brazil imports as share of world imports, 1961–2019   183
6.1  China's share of world uranium imports, 2001–2020   192
6.2  Shares of world uranium exports by country, 2001 and 2015   193
6.3  Uranium prices, 1980–2019   196
6.4  Uranium imports, requirements, and production in China (tonnes), 2007–2020   200
6.5  China's uranium import dependence, 2007–2020   200
6.6  Share of China's total uranium imports by company, 2000–2014   203
6.7  China's uranium imports by country, 2005 and 2015   206
6.8  World shares of copper exports by country, 2000 and 2015   211
6.9  China's copper imports by country, 2001 and 2015   212
6.10 China's and Japan's share of world copper imports, 1990–2020   213
6.11 Share of copper mining enterprises in China by enterprise size, 2001 and 2015   217
6.12 Share of copper imports by the top two Chinese importers, 2000, 2005, 2010, and 2014   217
6.13 China's imports of raw copper and refined copper, 2000–2020   224
A.1  Nature of ownership   250
A.2  Workplaces   250
A.3  Language used in interviews   252

# ACKNOWLEDGMENTS

We can trace this book's origins to the bridge of a bulk cargo ship called *Mathilde*, which was transporting kaolin—and me—between Canada and South Korea, more than twenty years ago. On that ship was a captain named Andrej who announced to me that I would write a book one day. This is the first of what I hope will be many more. But the reason why the cargo voyage is at the origin of this book is that through sea routes, I ultimately made my way to China. It is a great *clin d'œil* to this journey that I ended up writing a book about China's impact on global commodity markets. The China I discovered, disembarking at the Port of Tanggu and through treks that took me to the Tibetan village of Xiahe in Gansu, a cotton and rice farming community in Hubei, the high-rises of Shenzhen, the southernmost tip of Yunnan, the mountainous passes of Sichuan, and down the Yangtze River, was already two decades into the profound economic roar that led to the most extraordinary rise in commodities consumption the world has ever seen. I knew then that I was witnessing a unique moment in the long arc of history that has led us to where we are. The curiosity and drive to understand and explain the deep workings of China's political economy have stayed with me since.

I started my academic journey at the University of Montréal, where David Ownby, a historian of religion in modern China, taught a mind-blowing undergraduate class on the modern political economy of China. I discovered what I thought were the most profoundly important and interesting questions I had encountered to date. To continue my training in this direction, David recommended I reach out to Yves Tiberghien at the University of British Columbia (UBC). That recommendation was one of the single most important inflection points of my life.

Yves Tiberghien is a scholar extraordinaire, a polymath, a deeply benevolent human being, and a phenomenal mentor. He knew before I did that I would pursue a PhD (a repeat pattern, it seems). He has been an inspiration for me ever since our first meeting in 2007. Alongside thoughtful and unfaltering mentors Brian Job and Paul Evans, he was the main reason I elected to pursue doctoral studies in the Department of Political Science at UBC. His unwavering belief in my potential and his encouragements have been the best incentive for me to work hard. He—and his family—have also made the experience truly enjoyable. Any measure of success I enjoy is in no small part the result of his kind and emphatic support.

At earlier stages, scholars at UBC and beyond were instrumental in supporting my work and offering constructive feedback or mentoring along the way, including my PhD committee member Lou Pauly, as well as David Zweig, Tim Cheek, Pitman Potter, Eric Helleiner, Herman Mark Schwartz, Amy Hanser, Ben Nyblade, Alan Jacobs, Richard Price, Max Cameron, Xiaojun Li, Kathleen Hancock, Derek Hall, Joe Wong, Gregory Chin, Randall Germain, Julian Gruin, Alexander Ebner, Robert Keohane, Tony Porter, Claude Comtois, Thomas Rawski, Jennifer Clapp, Sarah Martin and Kate Neville. At UBC, I was lucky to work with research assistant Haochen Li and Cary Wu. My PhD colleagues at the time Yingqiu Kuang and Linting Zhang also provided valuable help and camaraderie along the way. Out of the many PhD candidates and post-docs who shared my journey at UBC, two in particular have become lifelong friends, and their support through these years has been invaluable: Elena Caprioni and Şule Yaylaci. Many thanks go to Erin Williams, who edited earlier versions of the manuscript.

During my field research in China, I spent time as a visiting scholar in the World Energy Research Division at the Chinese Academy of Social Sciences' Institute for World Economics and Politics in Beijing. I am very grateful for the research team there for welcoming me as a peer. My thanks also go to colleagues at Peking University where I was a visiting PhD candidate at the Center of International Political Economy. The support of colleagues at the China Center for International Economic Exchanges (CCIEE) in Beijing was also invaluable. I also want to thank the research division of *China Business News* [第一财经] in Beijing for inviting me to publish and for their collegiality. I am grateful to the Chinese Ministry of Land and Resources Information Center for inviting me to speak at the China Mining Congress in Tianjin; the Potash Branch of the China Inorganic Salt Industry Association for inviting me to speak at their annual conference in Shanghai; as well as the Renmin University Department of Economics for inviting me to present my research. I am also grateful to the Natural Resources and Environment Security Research Centre at the Chinese Academy of Sciences, for their welcome. A special mention goes to Nicholas Martin, for his collegiality and friendship during our many months of field research in China.

My field research in China and beyond was a transformative experience—I conducted over 160 interviews with Chinese and international government officials, experts, journalists, industry insiders, and business leaders.

Among the dozens of interviews I conducted, a few stand out, including the time I spent with Brazilian diplomats, at the Brazilian Embassy in Beijing but also around the world. I am grateful for their time, feedback, and generosity. Current and former Vale executives also stand out for having been extremely gracious with their time and candid in their comments. Financial Times journalists were particularly generous with their time, insights and introductions. Folks at CRU Group are among the most knowledgeable about commodities out there and were incredibly open in sharing their expertise. There are so many others I do not have the space to list here and to whom I want to express my gratitude, from junior mining firm executives to government officials to busy consultants.

I am eternally grateful for my interviewees' time, openness, and candor. Your commitment to the pursuit of knowledge and your generosity in helping me along was invaluable. I often wonder why busy professionals would ever assent to give research interviews. I've asked and gotten a variety of responses. Many do it just to help out, or to pay it back, as they were helped along the way by others themselves; some do it to learn a little bit about what I do or think, and the conversation becomes an exchange; and some do it because they enjoy taking the time to articulate and make sense of their world. Many of my conversations lasted over an hour—sometimes several!—and have been some of the most pleasurable aspects of leading this research. I conducted all of the interviews myself, either in English, Chinese, or French, with a bit of Spanish thrown in along the way. I hope this work does them justice.

Although this book has grown out of my PhD dissertation, completed in 2015 at UBC in Vancouver, it has gone through extensive revisions since. Toward the end of the project, I was having difficulty accessing more recent Chinese government data. Loren Brandt provided a lifeline when he very kindly agreed to share with me one of his datasets of Chinese Customs data—his colleague Torsten Jaccard provided very gracious help sorting the data. One of Canada's most legendary players in the history of the Canada-China relationship, former minister and senator Jack Austin, kindly read sections of the manuscript and provided comments and encouragements. I am grateful for the feedback and support of A. Iain Johnston, who kindly read and commented on sections of the manuscript. Janice Stein provided support and inspiration.

At the University of Ottawa, I found an incredibly supportive community of colleagues who provided support one way or another while I was revising this manuscript. To mention a few, non-exhaustively: Jacqueline Best, Patrick Leblond, Ryan Katz-Rosene, Mark Salter, Roland Paris, Luc Turgeon, Jennifer Wallner, André Lecours, Janique Dubois, Robert Sparling, Éric Champagne, Daniel Stockemer, Chris Cooper, Hélène Pellerin, Kevin McMillan, Nisha Shah, Sophie Bourgault, Linda Cardinal, André Laliberté, Rita Abrahamsen and Monica Gattinger. I am also grateful for the stalwart support of our department chairs through the years, François Rocher, Christian Rouillard, and Frédéric Vairel, especially as I navigated my repeated *to and fro* between the University of Ottawa and the Government of Canada. Stellar research assistants, Chen Wang, Piers Eaton and Andrew Heffernan, provided precious fact-checking and feedback toward the end of the process. Many thanks to Glenna Jenkins who professionally edited the manuscript before its final submission.

I cherish Laurence Deschamps-Laporte's special collegiality and friendship, providing me with unswerving support as we both negotiate transitioning between and engaging with both the policy and academic worlds. I am thankful as well to many colleagues at the Government of Canada for their collegiality and dedication through my years of advisory work.

The project benefited from the financial support of the Social Sciences and Humanities Research Council of Canada, the Chiang Ching-kuo Foundation, and various UBC grants and fellowships as well as generous support from the Faculty of Social Sciences at the University of Ottawa.

I want to thank Taylor & Francis for allowing me to use in this book material I published in 2020 in *New Political Economy*, entitled "Market Power and Marketisation: Japan and China's Impact on the Iron Ore Market, 50 Years Apart."

I am grateful to my editor at Oxford University Press, David McBride, for believing in this project from the first and for steering it through the reviewing process, to two anonymous reviewers for their comments, which had a significant impact on the reframing of the project, and to OUP for welcoming this book as part of their collection.

I wanted a striking photo on the cover of this book. I am so pleased and grateful to Edward Burtynski and his team for allowing me to use a photograph from his marvellous *Anthropocene* series to this end.

I feel that this book could very well have never seen the light of day. Between the Covid pandemic, government service, and two babies, I really do think the cards were stacked against it. If I could find the strength and tenacity to bring this project to a close, my parents have certainly played a role, by instilling in me a capacity for deep all-encompassing determination, as well as a preoccupation for public service, the pursuit of knowledge, authenticity, and intellectual rigor. For knowing and respecting this, and for loving and supporting me through it all, I want to thank my partner David Needham, whom I met on the back of a truck in northern Laos twenty years ago and who has been my greatest supporter ever since. In the context of this decade-long project, he has been the far side of my moon, offering steadfast, mighty support, while making me whole. Our two little girls, Mathilde and Marguerite, will one day understand how much this book means to me—much less than they do.

# ABBREVIATIONS

| | |
|---|---|
| BHP | BHP Group (formerly BHP Billiton, and formerly Broken Hill Proprietary Company) |
| Big Three | BHP, Vale, and Rio Tinto |
| BPC | Belarusian Potash Company |
| BRI | Belt and Road Initiative |
| BRICS | Brazil, Russia, India, China, and South Africa |
| CANDU | Canada Deuterium Uranium |
| CBC | COSCO Bulk Carrier Co. |
| CBMX | China Beijing International Mining Exchange |
| CCCMC | China Chamber of Commerce of Metals, Minerals & Chemicals Importers & Exporters |
| CEO | Chief executive officer |
| CFR | Cost and freight |
| CGNPG/CGN | China General Nuclear Power Group, formerly China Guangdong Nuclear Power Group |
| CGN-URC | China Guangdong Nuclear Power Uranium Resources Co. |
| CIF | Cost, Insurance, and Freight |
| CIPEC | Intergovernmental Council of Copper Exporting States |
| CISA | China Iron and Steel Association |
| CMRG | China Mineral Resources Group |
| CNAMPGC | China National Agricultural Means of Production Group Corporation (Sino-Agri Group) |
| CNCCC | China National Chemical Construction Corporation, later a subsidiary of CNOOC |
| CNNC | China National Nuclear Corporation |
| CNOOC | China National Offshore Oil Corporation |
| CNPC | China National Petroleum Corporation |
| CNUC | China National Uranium Corporation Limited |

| | |
|---|---|
| COMEX | Commodity Exchange Inc., which is part of the New York Mercantile Exchange |
| COREX | Beijing Iron Ore Trading Center Corporation |
| COSCO | China Ocean Shipping Company |
| CPE | Comparative Political Economy |
| CPPCC | Chinese People's Political Consultative Conference |
| CSPT | China Smelters Purchase Team |
| CVRD | Companhia Vale do Rio Doce, now Vale |
| FAO | Food and Agriculture Organization of the United Nations |
| FOB | Freight on board |
| GDP | Gross Domestic Product |
| HHI | Herfindahl-Hirschman index |
| HKEX | Stock Exchange of Hong Kong Limited |
| HST | Hegemonic Stability Theory |
| IAEA | International Atomic Energy Agency |
| ICL | Israel Chemicals Group |
| IODEX | Platts Iron Ore Index |
| IPC | International Potash Company |
| IPE | International Political Economy |
| $K_2O$ | Potassium oxide |
| KCl | Potassium chloride |
| LME | Liberal market economy |
| LME | London Metal Exchange |
| LNG | Liquefied natural gas |
| MITI | Ministry of International Trade and Industry (Japan) |
| MOFCOM | Chinese Ministry of Commerce |
| MOP | Muriate of Potash, or potassium chloride |
| MOU | Memorandum of understanding |
| Mt | Million metric tons (million tonnes) |
| NDRC | National Development and Reform Commission |
| NFSRA | China National Food and Strategic Reserves Administration |
| NNSA | National Nuclear Safety Administration |
| NYMEX | New York Mercantile Exchange |
| OPEC | Organization of the Petroleum Exporting Countries |
| PPC | Petro-political cycle |
| RMB | Renminbi |
| SASAC | State-owned Assets Supervision and Administration Commission |
| SHFE | Shanghai Futures Exchange |
| SOE | State-owned enterprise |
| SPIC | State Power Investment Corporation |

| | |
|---|---|
| t | Metric ton (tonne), 1000kg |
| TC/RC | Treatment and refining charges |
| UN Comtrade | United Nations Commodity Trade Statistics Database |
| UNCTAD | United Nations Conference on Trade and Development |
| VLOC | Very large ore carrier |
| VOC | Variety of capitalism |
| WISCO | Wuhan Iron and Steel Corporation |
| WTO | World Trade Organization |

# 1

# Introduction

## The Puzzles: Vulnerability, Variation, and Liberalization

### Vulnerability

In the summer of 2022, the Chinese government announced the creation of a $3 billion state-owned iron ore giant, the China Mineral Resources Group, whose mission is to manage the multifaceted undertakings of iron ore imports, processing and trading, as well as overseas investments. This was an extraordinary announcement and in many ways the culmination of at least fifteen years of frustrations on behalf of leading Chinese iron ore market stakeholders.

There is something paradoxical about China's relationship with and impact on global commodity markets. On one hand, within a short period of time, China emerged from being an almost complete outsider to becoming the principal player in most commodity markets. It has risen to become the number one consumer of main metals and, in many cases, also one of the top, if not the top, player in the global supply chain, particularly the processing segment. Between 1995 and 2020, China rose from consuming 7 percent of the world's main metals to 69 percent (see Figure 1.1). By 2005, it had been ranked first in the world in terms of main metals consumption; in 2011, it became the world's largest energy consumer. But despite this growing market clout, over the past twenty years China has not been able to consistently impose itself onto global commodity markets, either by setting the rules of the game, or through planning ahead and inducing stable global market conditions and prices (as Japan had done decades earlier).

In fact, in the case of China's impact on the global iron ore market, the largest Chinese market stakeholders were not able to get their preferred global market outcome. Worse, the fall of the decades-old iron ore benchmark pricing system in 2010, triggered by China's rise, was the opposite of what major Chinese market stakeholders had wanted. In fact, these stakeholders actively tried to

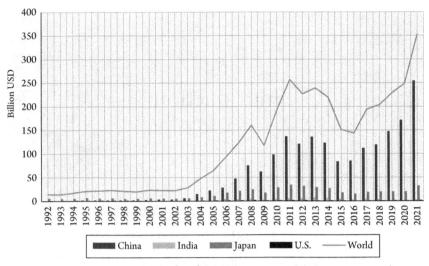

Source: UN Comtrade data by trade value (USD) for iron ore, copper, nickel, aluminium, zinc, and tin (HS codes: 3601, 3603, 3604, 3606, 3608, 36090).

Figure 1.1 World metals imports, China, India, Japan, and the United States, 1992–2021

*prevent* this from occurring (and in some ways, they still are, as the creation of the China Mineral Resources Group illustrates). So here you had what was by far the world's largest iron ore importer and market player having a significant impact on the principal global iron ore market pricing institution, which was the opposite of what key Chinese market players had been trying to achieve. Despite their market size, Chinese importers were in a position of deep *vulnerability*, not strength. China was the largest stakeholder, yet it lacked the power to effect change in its preferred direction.

This vulnerability paradox—how a county can be the largest player in a market and yet feel vulnerable—is, I suggest, the result of at least four interrelated dynamics. First, in the cases selected in this book, China is import dependent for more than (or close to) 50 percent of its domestic needs. This plays an important role in informing Chinese positions of vulnerability and reduces China's room for maneuver in commodity procurement.

Second, another paradox perhaps is that China's rise was too fast for its own good. Whereas Japan was able to invest in iron ore production to make sure there was adequate supply to meet its demand, China's rise in consumption was simply too fast to handle for Chinese and international commodity producers alike. Many commodity insiders were surprised by the speed and scale of China's rise in the early 2000s. This in turn had an impact on price levels and volatility, leading into the 2007–2008 commodities supercycle. The resulting landscape was not to China's benefit.

Third, a related vulnerability is that whereas there are some advantages to relative backwardness (Gerschenkron 1962), for China, in the case of commodities procurement, this was not the case. China's rise met with global commodity markets that were already dominated by major global mining giants (Nolan 2012). By the time China emerged, at the turn of the twenty-first century, as the world's number one consumer of most commodities, the global commodities marketplace had already evolved a set of market institutions and certain patterns of exchange. This does not mean that China could not transform global markets—it did; it means that in meaningful ways, China was a latecomer and, as a result, certain options were not available to it. For instance, some of the best mineral deposits had already been discovered and were already owned by powerful global mining companies. This led China to invest in more risky endeavors, and some of those investments have yet to come to fruition, many years down the line.

Finally, there is a fourth way in which China is vulnerable when it comes to global commodity procurement, which I refer to in this book as market power vulnerability. There are distinct market power differentials between domestic and global market stakeholders in each of the commodity markets studied in this book. Given China's industrial and development history, in some of the cases studied in this book, the political economy of certain domestic Chinese markets is particularly messy; iron and steel come to mind. In the iron ore market, there are thousands of market stakeholders, along with bureaucratic infighting, and important clashes over interests between larger and smaller steel enterprises, and there is a profound lack of coordination capacity. On its own, domestic fragmentation would be bad enough, and on this note the Chinese domestic iron ore and copper markets share some traits. But it is the combination of China's domestic iron ore market fragmentation and the concentrated and coordinated nature of the global iron ore market that has resulted in a position of market power vulnerability for China.

China experienced at least two types of vulnerability in each of the four cases presented in this book. High import dependence and a rapid rise in consumption were present in all cases, including the uranium market. In the potash and copper markets, China experienced one more vulnerability: its late arrival in global commodity markets. China's iron ore market was home to all four types of vulnerabilities: high import dependence, a rapid rise in consumption, its late arrival, and relative market vulnerability.

This vulnerability paradox—the tension between China's market size and its state of vulnerability—has been a common thread in Chinese commodities consumption over the past two decades. Understanding how China navigates its double identity of being a powerful-yet-vulnerable global market player is one of the principal anchors of this book. It is key to explaining how global markets have changed (or not) since the early 2000s and can shed light on the future of China's interaction patterns with the world more generally.

## Variation

There is another important aspect of China's interaction with global commodity markets that warrants our attention: variation. Despite considerable similarities, China's behavior, its interaction with global market stakeholders, and the resulting changes in global market institutions have varied in significant ways across commodity markets. These variations are puzzling. Why would China behave differently, and how would this lead to significantly different outcomes in markets that were otherwise similarly structured before China's rise?

The explanation I advance goes back to the domestic roots of China's global economic behavior and focuses on the variation in the political economy of each commodity market at the Chinese domestic level. Given distinct industrial histories and the various ways each commodity market inserts itself into the broader Chinese economy, Chinese domestic commodity markets vary in their configurations. In characterizing each market's domestic political economy, I consider the role of a wide range of Chinese market stakeholders, both state and private.[1] Next, I consider the variation in the political economy of commodity markets at the global level. I focus on the various market institutions that have evolved over the past decades in distinct markets: chiefly, the relevant pricing regimes.

This book goes further than acknowledging variation at both domestic and global levels and draws attention to variation in the resonance dynamics between the two. There are patterns of variation in the interaction between Chinese domestic market stakeholders and market stakeholders at the international level. I pay particular attention to Chinese market stakeholders' behavior at various stages of interaction with global markets and the resulting unequal patterns of success and failure they have experienced in the pursuit of their preferences at the global level.

## Liberalization

This book addresses a third puzzle. In the dramatic case of iron ore, China's rise led to one of the most disruptive events in the history of the iron ore market: the abrupt fall of the decades-old benchmark pricing regime, in 2010, and the emergence of a global spot market. The collapse of the iron ore benchmark pricing regime is a fascinating and understudied event in the recent history of China's relations with the global economy. Here, you have a concrete empirical example of a decades-old market institution falling apart and of a spot market emerging in its stead, ostensibly as a result of China's emergence as the number one iron ore importer just seven years prior, in 2003. This outcome represents, in fact, the sudden liberalization of a commodity market.

In the case of the global potash market, the global benchmark pricing system has survived until now, at the time of writing. But China's rise led to the fall of one of the world's largest producers' marketing cartels in 2013. Liberalization dynamics are also present in the potash case, but the timing and the mechanism through which they are occurring are distinct. As we will see, China's emergence initially led to some liberalization dynamics in the copper market as well, but attempts to halt these and to better coordinate behavior were also deployed. The uranium market has also been undergoing some liberalization trends, especially financialization; but here, China's role is less prominent. In other words, I observed different kinds of liberalization dynamics in all markets, some of which were directly the result of China's interactions in the commodities space, other less so. Equally important, these were not the same kinds of liberalization dynamics. Some involved increased competition among large producers, some involved the emergence of spot pricing. They did not happen at the same time or via the same mechanisms. Liberalization patterns following the emergence of China as number one consumer require an explanation.

The idea that China would lead to the liberalization of commodity markets is counterintuitive. It is not as if even the most optimistic analysts—those who argued in the 2000s that China would continue on a path toward deepening market reforms and who expected China to fully integrate into global economic institutions without disrupting their functioning—expected China to go around the world *liberalizing* global markets. In fact, liberalization was not at all conceptualized as a likely outcome of China's rise. One of the reasons this possibility was not built into the debate on China's integration in the global economy, as it were, is because of a blind spot in this very debate: there is not enough problematization, in the global China literature, of the global markets that China rose to disrupt. Global markets are often characterized, in the China debate, as having been *liberal* or *open* at the time of China's emergence in the global economy, in the 1990s and 2000s. But at least in the case of commodity markets—and elsewhere, I would suggest—this was not the best way to describe these markets prior to China's rise in the early 2000s. In fact, the markets for iron ore and potash were highly concentrated, home to decades-old negotiated pricing institutions, and spot markets were a negligible component of the global market. The finding that China has led to the liberalization of some commodity markets over the past twenty years turns some liberal arguments on their heads; that is, instead of China being coopted into the existing liberal international order, China has, at times, led to the liberalization of global markets that were not very liberal to start with.

I hasten to add two elements to this discussion. First, in many of the instances of liberalization I uncover in this book, the major Chinese market stakeholders did not intend for these outcomes to occur. So, the argument here is not that these trends were part of some master plan for the liberalization of global markets. In each case, the unequal and partial liberalization outcomes in the various markets studied here were the result of particular market power configurations between domestic and global market stakeholders, as we will see in more detail below. In a way, here China played the role of a market disruptor, as other large emerging economies have done in the past. I theorize further below about the conditions under which the emergence of an economy the size of China's is likely to disrupt established ways of market organizing.

Second, I am not arguing that the liberalization trends I observed in some commodity markets over the first two decades of the twenty-first century are representative of China's impact on the global economy in general. We have seen a return of the state (and the party) in China's domestic political economy, and China's impact abroad does continue to entail key roles for both. We are also seeing a return of economic nationalism more broadly in the global economy. Ultimately, the best analyses of China's impact abroad must contend with both the presence of Chinese party-state and private stakeholders globally as well as the combination of conforming and disruptive patterns of interaction with global markets they have displayed over the recent past.

Solving the following three puzzles is thus the core motivation behind this book: Why, despite China's rising salience in global commodity markets, are Chinese actors often in a position of vulnerability and unable to shape market institutions in their preferred direction? What explains the variation in China's impact on global markets? In other words, why have some global commodity markets undergone fundamental changes in the way they operate as a result of China's emergence while other similar markets have been more resilient? Finally, how can we explain the (uneven) liberalization dynamics across commodity markets, following China's rise? My goal in this book is to explain the diverging global market outcomes resulting from the dramatic contemporary expansion of China's economy.

## The Argument: Market Power, Market Vulnerability, and Market Change

In this book, I trace key variation in China's behavior and its impacts on global market institutions to the market power differentials between Chinese domestic and international market stakeholders. In so doing, the full picture is unveiled, from domestic variables to international-level outcomes. I argue that there is a causal relationship between relative market power—or the relative capacity of consumers and producers to coordinate behavior—and market institutional change at the global level. China's impact on global market institutions and Chinese stakeholders' capacity to influence global market outcomes are the result of the particular configurations of market power at Chinese domestic and international levels in each given market.

At the time of China's emergence, its domestic commodity markets varied: some were coordinated, others were fragmented. Likewise, global commodity markets significantly varied. This book's argument builds on the variation in the market power of Chinese and global market stakeholders as it investigates the resonance dynamics between the domestic political economy of large emerging economies and the political economy of global markets.

The book develops a two-level framework that identifies the circumstances under which global market institutional change is more likely to occur following the emergence of a new player (Table 1.1). Indeed, global market outcomes cannot be explained exclusively as the result of domestic or international dynamics but by their interaction.

This argument consists of both static and dynamic components. The former suggests which side can wield influence more effectively, while the latter explains the likelihood of global market institutional change. First, I argue that an asymmetric distribution of market power in general provides dominant players with more powerful tools with which to actualize their preferences for global market institutions. Asymmetry in market power provides dominant stakeholders with

*Table 1.1* **Market power, market vulnerability, and market change**

| | *International market (producers)* | |
|---|---|---|
| *Domestic market (consumers)* | **Fragmentation** | **Coordination** |
| **Fragmentation** | 1 **Symmetry** Low likelihood of change No dominant preferences | 2 **Asymmetry** High likelihood of change Dominant preferences: producers |
| **Coordination** | 3 **Asymmetry** High likelihood of change Dominant preferences: consumers | 4 **Symmetry** Medium likelihood of change No dominant preferences |

influence over global pricing regimes and affects preferences and behavior. In turn, market stakeholders with low market power, or coordination capacity, have more difficulty influencing outcomes. As we will see in the case studies presented in this book, careful attention to the relative coordination capacity of market stakeholders at the export/import interface of a given market can give us clues as to who will have a determining influence on global market institutions.

In a dynamic sense, I argue that the emergence of a new dominant player, such as China, is more likely to lead to changes in global market institutions when existing power relations are disrupted. One could say that a "transformative window" opens as a result of disruptions to the global balance of power in a given market. In other words, status quo disruptions, when one dominant consumer rapidly displaces another (say, China replacing Japan), are most likely to lead to global market institutional change if they involve a significant transformation in relative market power between consumers and producers.

In addition, I argue that perceptions of market vulnerability, which are influenced in important ways by positions of market power vis-à-vis a market stakeholder's own peers, play a role in global market institutional preference formation: domestic positions of weakness lead to preferences for disruption and/or more competitive markets while domestic positions of power lead to preferences for stability and/or more strategic or negotiated markets.

In other words, I argue that one of the keys to explaining patterns of market change as a result of China's emergence lies in understanding and tracing the relative market power dynamics, from the domestic level all the way to the international level.

Market power is understood as market stakeholders' capacity to influence outcomes (Strange 1996). In operationalizing this concept, I focus on what I argue is one key component of market power: coordination capacity. Coordination capacity is the capacity of various state and non-state market stakeholders to overcome collective action problems and work together effectively. Coordination capacity is important because coordination is one of the key ways through which market stakeholders can affect institutional change (Ostrom 1997; Hall and Soskice 2001; Gereffi et al. 2005; Wilson 2013; Radetzki 2013). Effective coordination facilitates cohesion, the pursuit of certain procurement goals, and also increases bargaining power. Maintaining (or changing) pricing regimes requires coordination, including between public and private actors.

The literature on China's rise has seen—understandably so—a focus on the role of the state in China's interactions with the global economy, including that of state-owned enterprises (SOEs) (Wang 2002; Alden and Davies 2006; Blanchard 2011; Norris 2016; de Graaff and van Apeldoorn 2017). SOEs are undoubtedly central in the story of Chinese economic development and its interaction with the global economy. But a focus on SOEs obscures the complex ecosystem of market stakeholders that are at work in China today (Huang 2017). This book's case studies are attentive to the relationships between different state and non-state actors. In fact, not only did non-state actors play a determining role in the fall of the iron ore benchmarking regime, but Chinese state actors who wanted to prevent this outcome from occurring were unable to do so. In other cases, Chinese state organs actually disagreed on the course of action to take, similar to how Jones and Hameiri argue that "Chinese foreign ... policy is shaped by these ongoing complementary or competitive interactions between actors within the transformed party-state, which are never decisively resolved" (Jones and Hameiri 2021, 13).

In a way, this book runs against both treatments of China as unitary and of expectations of a strong Chinese state: China's transformative impacts on global market institutions were at times the result of a Chinese position of vulnerability. In some cases, they were unexpected or, even worse, ran in the opposite direction to the preferences of major Chinese market stakeholders, including state organs. Allowing for global markets and Chinese behavior to vary across cases and relaxing the strong Chinese state assumption allow us to conceive of possibilities that have been otherwise overlooked.

This is a study about the deepest sort of economic interdependence, that of institutional resonance and complementarity between global markets and their largest emerging stakeholders. China's divergent impacts on the global markets of iron ore, potash, and uranium cannot be explained from either a uniquely international or a uniquely domestic perspective. The interaction of domestic and international-market stakeholders and, specifically, their coordination capacity, or market power, combined to create the conditions for market change to occur at the global level.

## To Be Explained: Pricing Regime Change

This book focuses on the variation in one set of global market institutions: pricing regimes. Before China's rise, global commodity markets presented a concurrent variety of pricing regimes. In some cases, market institutions had evolved closer to the competitive end of the spectrum, where the pricing was driven by global commodity exchanges; other market institutions had evolved at the managed, or strategic, end of the spectrum—in some cases, formal cartels regulating marketing and price negotiations. Copper, for instance, was financialized and traded on spot and futures markets. Iron ore or potash were home to long-term negotiated benchmark pricing systems. Others still, such as uranium, were home to negotiated prices and long-term contracts, where only a small percentage of trades occurred on the spot market and there was no annual benchmarking system.

The pricing regimes discussed in this book are conceptualized along a "competitive–strategic" continuum (Hall and Soskice 2001; Hall and Gingerich 2004). A movement toward more competitive interaction is conceptualized as "liberalization," and a movement toward more strategic interaction is conceptualized as "de-liberalization." Liberalization is understood here as a multifold process, which includes financialization dynamics and can be conceived as a movement away from strategic interaction between market actors. Here, I am less interested in the level of state ownership, although I do note it where relevant, but more in the type of market interaction that occurs between different market stakeholders, competitive or strategic. In some ways the binary conception of state vs. private ownership has become more difficult to discern in the Chinese political economy, as minority stakes are common and other forms of state control become prevalent across the board. In concrete terms, the liberalization of a pricing regime entails a movement toward a higher number of firms, higher frequency of pricing signals, shorter-term contracts, the presence of multiple pricing signals, less importance of long-term relationships between firms, inclusion in major commodity indices, the emergence of spot-trading platforms, and the importance of the spot price as a price signal. The de-liberalization (strategic end of the spectrum) of a pricing regime is a movement in the opposite direction.

Given the conceptualization of markets as institutional systems, where power relations play a significant role and where multiple equilibria are possible, by definition, every change in a pricing regime needs to be explained. A movement toward either end of the spectrum entails trade-offs, changes in power relations, and winners and losers. The conceptualization of global markets along a competitive-strategic continuum allows us to conceive of China's emergence as potentially leading to liberalization, to de-liberalization, or to no significant change in global pricing regime dynamics.

## Empirical Narratives

Before China's emergence as the world's number one consumer, the era of Japanese iron ore import dominance in the second half of the twentieth century had seen the establishment of stable, predictable global iron ore market institutions. Here, Japanese iron ore importers acted as part of a coordinated purchasing group, while Japanese financiers invested upstream in the mining industry to guarantee adequate supply. The Japanese spearheaded the establishment of an annual benchmark pricing regime, which consisted of closed-door negotiations between Japanese importers and global producers for a price that remained valid for the global market that year. In 2003, China emerged as the number one importer of iron ore in the world, and, in 2005, it replaced Japan as the lead negotiator in the benchmark system for the first time. Within five years, the decades-old benchmark system fell apart and a spot market surfaced in its stead. Why did the benchmark system fall? What was China's role in this event? Was the fall of the iron ore benchmark pricing regime an outlier event, or could we expect more of the same?

In the iron ore case, China emerged in the 2000s as a fragmented consumer that faced coordinated global market stakeholders. The lack of coordination of Chinese iron ore consumers disrupted global benchmarking negotiations and gave producers the opportunity to push for the liberalization of the iron ore pricing regime. This went against the will of the largest Chinese market stakeholders, including state-owned firms and the lead industry association. In this case, the preferences of smaller, private Chinese iron ore importers aligned with those of the three largest global iron ore exporters, at least temporarily. Counterintuitively, Chinese market stakeholders' failure to coordinate, or a Chinese position of market vulnerability, enabled this major change in the global iron ore market pricing regime, despite the fact that China was by far the world's largest iron ore consumer. Fifty years earlier, Japan had emerged as the number one consumer. However, its consumers had been coordinated in the face of a fragmented global market. This situation had allowed large Japanese firms to actualize their preferences for a stable benchmark pricing regime (de-liberalization). The transition from Japan to China as the world's number one consumer disrupted established power relationships and entailed a shift from one extreme asymmetric position of power to another. This profound shift in market power asymmetries increased the likelihood of a transition that would lead to an institutional change in the market at the global level.

At the time, I decided to go on the hunt for other commodity market candidates for a comparison with the iron ore market. I set off looking for a market that presented similar features to the global iron ore market prior to China's emergence. This meant finding a market that was highly concentrated, geographically and by firm, and that had developed similar pricing institutions, in which China had quickly become a dominant player and toward which China had developed a similar relationship of heavy import dependence, while at the same time not knowing what kinds of impacts China would turn out to have over the coming years.

A few months after the fall of the iron ore benchmark pricing regime in 2010, BHP Billiton made a $US38.6 billion hostile takeover bid for Canada's Potash Corp (now Nutrien). In a move that shocked the global investment community, the Canadian government blocked the deal. But not before a flurry of concerned commentaries flooded the Chinese internet. In a later interview with a Chinese industry association executive, I was told that the Chinese government did not see BHP's bid as being at all a good development for China and that a lot of concern was expressed at the time. The Chinese industry association executive mentioned that the central government even held an emergency meeting, in Beijing in September 2010, with many interested parties, to discuss possible strategies in response (Interview 95, Industry association executive, 2012).

Unfamiliar with fertilizer markets at the time, and with my interest piqued, I was surprised to find many similarities between the global potash and iron ore markets, both in terms of their global structure and also in terms of China's positioning toward them. The overwhelming proportion of global potash production is concentrated in two locales, one a developed Anglo-Saxon economy (Canada) and the other a BRICS economy (Russia, though Belarus is also a major producer). The global seaborne iron ore production is also overwhelmingly concentrated in two locales, one a developed Anglo-Saxon economy (Australia) and the other a major BRICS economy (Brazil). Before China's emergence as key importer, both markets were home to long-term contracts and regular, closed-door benchmarking negotiations between major producers and consumers. As a result, relationships between producers and consumers were rich and institutionalized. In both cases, spot markets and spot pricing were negligible features of the global market, if they existed at all. Finally, China had rapidly developed a major import dependence toward both global markets. In 2010, China had import dependence levels of 47 percent in the potash market and of 63 percent in the iron ore market.[2] Comparisons between the iron ore and potash cases form the core of this book. Over the course of the following decade, I followed the evolution of each market's domestic political economy in China, their global political economy and the interactions between the two, until 2022.

It turns out that despite the original similarities, China's impact on the global iron ore and potash markets differed in significant and interesting ways. In the potash case, China became the dominant consumer and importer in the late 1990s and early 2000s. As in iron ore, China also emerged as the world's number one potash consumer in the face of a highly concentrated and coordinated global potash market. In this case, it was constituted of two powerful producer cartels: Canada's Canpotex and Eurasia's Belarusian Potash Corporation. Contrary to the iron ore case, however, the Chinese domestic potash market presented a significantly more coordinated interface with the global market. This relative symmetry of market power led to bargaining patterns and incremental change and allowed Chinese stakeholders more opportunity to actualize their preferences at the global level. By the early 2000s, Chinese importers had established themselves as the lead benchmark negotiator. Over the years, Chinese negotiators were able to extract significant concessions in their favor, be it in terms of price or changes in the frequency of the benchmark negotiations, which at times doubled from annually to biannually and at other times lapsed for more than eighteen months, to suit the Chinese importers. China's actions and interactions led to the emergence of new smaller players globally and to the breakdown of the Russia-Belarus producers' cartel in 2013. These changes notwithstanding, the global benchmark pricing regime, although fraying, survives until today.

Whereas the global iron ore market saw rapid, decisive change toward liberalization and financialization, the global potash market displayed higher levels of continuity in its pricing institutions. Over the past few years, as Brazil, another major consumer, became more and more dominant, the delicate balance in the global potash market was disrupted once more. The overall direction of change in the potash market following China's emergence has been toward moderate liberalization, in a more restrained fashion than in the iron ore case, but the mechanisms that led to it were different.

The argument I put forward in this book may be relatively straightforward—that strong relative positions of market power are more likely to enable a market player to influence global market institutions and that changes in relative positions of market power are more likely to be disruptive and lead to global market institutional change. Yet the theoretical building blocks required to get there and the implications of the argument for our understanding of China's relationship with the global economy are significant.

## Building Blocks

### Markets as Institutional Systems

The theorization of global markets as institutional systems is the first building block underpinning this investigation of China's impact on global commodity markets. I argue that a critical precondition to correctly diagnosing China's impact on global markets is to proceed from a thicker conceptualization of global market institutions. If one defines global markets as arenas, empty spaces where the forces of supply and demand meet, the arrival of a new player does not change the rules of the game, it simply affects aggregate demand (and/or supply) and, eventually, prices.

In the comparative and global political economy literatures, the tendency has been to think of national markets as mediated by national-level structures and dynamics and, thus, as being inherently prone to divergence, whereas global markets, being located beyond national borders, have been less conceived as likely to diverge from one another and are often treated as "free." The distributional impacts of changes in market institutions at the sub-national level have received more attention; the distributional impacts of changes in global market institutions, less so.

The assumption that global markets became free, especially after the fall of the Soviet Union, and theorizing them as open, or liberal, as China rose and formally entered the world economy with its accession to the WTO in 2001, is so commonplace that singling out examples feels unfair. Let me take two from each side of the China debate: "China has already discovered the massive economic returns that are possible by operating within this open-market system" (Ikenberry 2008, 29), and "[c]reating a liberal international order involved . . . creat[ing] an open and inclusive international economy that maximized free trade and fostered unfettered capital markets" (Mearsheimer 2019, 22). It must be said here that huge pans of the heterodox economics and political science and political economy literatures conceptualize global markets as imperfect and hierarchical, but these analyses have not taken a significant place in the debate on China and the global economy to date, with a few exceptions (Porter 2018).[3]

Only when one problematizes markets as non-neutral institutional systems, replete with power dynamics and distinctively path-dependent, do the various ways in which they change over time become apparent. Only with a thicker conceptualization of markets does the dependent variable, global market pricing institutions, take on the many dimensions that will be investigated in this book, from the competitive to the strategic end of the spectrum. In other words, theorizing about China potentially leading to the liberalization of certain global market institutions and, I would argue, whether we can *see* this outcome at all, hinges on how one defines global markets. The approach I propose looks at markets qualitatively, with an interest in observing changes over time in the market institutions themselves, and will be expanded on further in Chapter 2. It is critical to have a deeper appreciation of the variety of global markets that exist simultaneously to fully be able to theorize China's impact on them. Seeing markets as institutional systems transforms the question from "Will China integrate or disrupt open markets?" to "How will China impact various global market institutions?" This approach helps us move beyond binary assessments of China's impact on the global economy.

## China as a Heterogeneous Power

The literature on global China has often attempted to characterize China's international posture as a whole; most famously, as either a revisionist or status quo power, with the former becoming more prevalent in recent years. But one of the reasons this debate is so vigorous is that we find quite divergent descriptions of international Chinese postures. As Jones and Hameiri put it, "Chinese behaviour actually displays both status quo and revisionist behaviour simultaneously" (Jones and Hameiri 2021, 7). The second building block underpinning my argument in this book is attention to variation in China's international behavior.

This book is a contribution to a growing body of research that is interested in mapping and explaining *concurrent variation* in Chinese behavior across different global areas (say, climate change vs. development finance) (Johnston 2019; Foot and Walter 2010; Weiss and Wallace 2021; Tiberghien 2020; Jones and Hameiri 2021, Nathan 2016; Wang and French 2014). I call this emerging area of scholarship the *China as heterogeneous power literature*. This new literature has at least five emergent characteristics. First, it is firmly grounded in empirical research in Chinese politics, political economy, or foreign policy. Second, it is attuned to the relationship between domestic and international dynamics. Third, it tends not to view China as *sui generis* and beyond comparison with other large states. Fourth, it is interested in explaining the *concurrent* variation in Chinese behaviors and in their impacts internationally. Fifth, this emerging literature tends to frame the debate about China's impact on the global economy not as *whether or not* China may cause change but why, how, and when it does so.

Authors in the *China as heterogeneous power* literature have theorized about simultaneous variation in Chinese behavior and impacts across distinct, broad global issue areas (commonly, international trade, climate change, nonproliferation, development assistance, etc.). It should be intuitive enough to expect China (or any other large power) to behave differently in the climate change issue area than in areas touching on territorial integrity, for instance. But in this book, I am looking within a smaller issue area subset: commodity markets.

At first, the extent and attributes of the cross-case variation I observe were not a given. Once I proceeded further in the project, and the extent of the variation became apparent, the value of zooming in on one subset of the global economy also became apparent. Focusing on one type of market allows me to hold constant a whole host of variables. For a start, the four commodity markets studied here do share similarities by virtue of their being raw commodities. China's posture with regard to global commodities also has a certain number of shared objectives, such as increasing domestic production and reducing reliance on imports. In addition, the two main commodities investigated in this book, iron ore and potash, were selected because their general global structures were similar prior to China's rise as dominant consumer. In fact, I would argue that the variation in Chinese behavior observed in the two main case studies in this book was even more unlikely than the variation in its behavior in fundamentally different areas of the global economy.

## Broader Debates

Here are a few implications of the framework presented in this book for our understanding of China's impact on the global economy. The debate on the political economy of China's rise and impact on the global economy has evolved from one where liberals argued that China should integrate into the global economy and realists argued that it would disrupt it, to one where both liberals and realists argue that China threatens open markets but they disagree on what to do about it. The evolution of this debate has hidden from view the very real ways in which power manifests in global markets, with and without China's involvement. Positions of market power are the variegated terrain on which any emerging market stakeholders must operate.

Being attuned to considerations of market power is also important when market power is lacking. Too often it is assumed that China's largest impacts globally will result from a position of strength, whereas being in a position of vulnerability would lead China to have little impact or to integrate into existing global economic institutions. The cases studied in this book unveil a more complex array of possibilities. In the iron ore case, China's position of market vulnerability led to the disruption of a long-lasting global market institution. Some of the largest impacts of China's rise may be the unintended global consequences of domestic market power dynamics. In the potash case, China's rise led to the unsettling of existing positions of market power. The argument here is not that China's rise is replacing established positions of market power with something more benign. In the potash case, levels of concentration in the Chinese domestic potash market are high, and smaller potash stakeholders in China complain about the domestic oligopoly controlling the market. The point is that market power configurations are a fundamental feature of all global markets, that they vary from market to market, and that the emergence of a large new player will unsettle these power configurations in different ways, leading to unique patterns of global institutional change.

This book tackles fundamental questions about the role of market power differentials in explaining global market institutional change as a result of the emergence of a significant new player. In doing so, it sheds new light on the political economy of global commodity markets, why they operate the way they do, and how they have evolved as a result of China's rapid emergence as the number one commodities consumer in the 2000s. Explaining the variation in China's impact on global markets can shed light on ongoing debates about the systemic resilience of global market structures and the domestic determinants of global economic power.

The sheer size of China's push and pull on the global economy and the rapidity of its growth have had tremendous impacts on global commodity markets. For many commodity producers, this has been great news. But China's rise has also created new uncertainties, including for policymakers concerned about its dominance over global markets, from supply crunches (rare earths) to overproduction (steel). At a time of crucial debates about the future of the global economy, this book provides an alternative lens through which to think about international Chinese economic behavior.

Changes in market configurations have significance beyond price trends or even commodities. These shifts in market power relationships can offer a glimpse into the future of China's relationship with the global economy. China's capacity to have impacts on global market institutions depends as much on the particulars of its domestic political economy in each market as it does on the existing structures of global market power in each global market. Refining our understanding of China's impact on global markets, or more accurately, the joint outcomes of China's rise and the subsequent response of major global market stakeholders is of critical importance to rethinking the future of global economic relations and the pursuit of policy dialogues with Chinese counterparts on such topics as competition, fair access, or the role of the state in the economy.

In trying to understand Chinese preferences and behavior in the global economy, there is value in looking at global markets from the perspective of an emerging economy. During a time of increasing US-China tension and contestations of the legitimacy of the liberal international order, this book provides an alternative framing of Chinese preferences and behaviors and likely impacts on the global economy. Many global markets function under very high levels of industry concentration and coordination, and this can create power-relation asymmetries and market vulnerabilities for emerging economies. This assessment acknowledges the widespread Chinese perception of some global market institutions as skewed against their interests. In the cases of the global commodity markets studied in this book, toward all of which China had an important import dependence, Chinese stakeholders did not see a level playing field.

The framework developed in this book provides insight into the role of market power in global market institutional change, the importance of the plurality of global markets and of Chinese global behavior, and the role of Chinese domestic market fragmentation and positions of market vulnerability leading to unintended outcomes at the global level, including market liberalization.

## Methodology, Data, and Case Selection

> For social scientists who enjoy comparisons, happiness is finding a force or event which affects a number of societies at the same time. Like test-tube solutions that respond differently to the same agent, these societies reveal their characters in divergent responses to the same stimulus. (Gourevitch 1977, 281)

## Why Commodities?

Extractive commodity markets are defined here as markets for primary commodities or materials in their raw or unprocessed state. These products' status as commodities is partly defined by the fact that they are, in their refined form, indistinguishable from one another (i.e., copper is copper is copper, and it is measured by concentration). This gets more complicated, however, in many extractive commodity markets, as different moisture contents, grades, or overall quality of the resources play a role in differentiating one commodity's source from another. However, it remains that the boundaries between commodity markets are easily identifiable and distinguishable from one another. Furthermore, it is difficult, if not impossible, to find a substitute for most commodities. This provides us with a degree of conceptual clarity. China's rapid emergence as a commodities consumer also offers an opportunity to study how these global markets evolved as a result.

One of the trends that is true across most global commodities is the rapidity with which China's imports grew as a share of world imports. In the iron ore market, China's imports as share of global imports grew from 14 percent in 2000 to 67 percent in 2015. In the potash market, imports grew from 11 percent in 1995 to 19 percent in 2015. China's share in the uranium market grew from 1 percent of global imports in 2001 to 34 percent in 2015. In the copper market, China's share of global imports went from 16 percent in 2000 to 46 percent in 2015 (see Table 2.1, Chapter 2). China became the dominant consumer of iron ore, potash, uranium, and copper at various points in the 2000s. In fact, China emerged as a systemically relevant market stakeholder in most global commodity markets at that time. This means that Chinese market stakeholders' behaviors in global commodity markets have become a determining feature that will continue to have impacts on long-term trends in these markets for the foreseeable future.

China's rise is not the only major event in the world of commodities in the first two decades of the twenty-first century, but I make the argument that its impact on commodity markets is large enough to be systemic. This means that changes in global commodity markets during this period are likely to have had something to do with China's rapid emergence as a dominant consumer. The accuracy of that statement and the process by which China is having an impact on global commodity markets can be empirically evaluated and traced over time. This book uses a qualitative comparative case study methodology to explain variation at the global level.

## Methodology and Data

This book presents a unique application of a comparative political economy methodology to study China's impact on global commodity markets over the past twenty-five years or so. As such, this study bridges comparative and international political economy by leveraging the comparative method to study global-level market institutional change. As will be detailed below, a method of difference case selection strategy is applied to the two main case studies, iron ore and potash, which were structured very similarly before China's emergence yet experienced diverging outcomes. Thereafter, two further case studies are added to increase the variation on the independent variables, uranium and copper. In addition, I leverage within-market case studies in the iron ore market, including over time, by investigating Japan's impact on the same market, fifty years prior, to build robustness and investigate the generalizability of my findings.

One of the advantages of a comparative strategy in studying China's impact internationally is that it is by design inclined to explain variation, and this brings a healthy dose of nuance in a debate that can at times portray Chinese government behavior as coherent and consistent across a range of issue areas.

China's emergence as the dominant commodity consumer over the course of the first decade of the twenty-first century was so rapid and so deep that investigating this phenomenon can be fruitfully conceived of as a quasi-natural experiment in investigating China's impact on the global economy. By this I mean that as the shock of China's emergence was felt across all mineral markets at roughly the same time and as it was so large as to be of systemic significance across the board, this allows us to use that moment to evaluate and compare China's impact on global markets in a systematic way.

The methodological approach adopted in this study includes building rich empirical causal narratives and tracing the process of change in each market to establish the mechanisms and sequencing at play. Through a triangulation of multiple sources of data, I trace the process of change in four global commodity-pricing regimes, placing an emphasis on English- and Chinese-language interviews (over 160 interviews, see Appendix) and analyses of official documents. I also trace regulatory changes, analyze corporate documents, and perform comparative/descriptive statistical analyses, with the objective of tracing the causal pathways between market stakeholders' positions of market power, their subsequent behaviors, and institutional market changes at the global level. At the domestic level, mainly in the iron ore and potash cases, a process-tracing analysis of the history of import licensing in China is conducted.

A defining feature of this book is the attention paid to the positions of market power and subsequent interactions between domestic and international-market players. At each level, an attempt is made to characterize positions of market power for domestic- and international-market stakeholders, their preferences and behaviors, and their capacity to coordinate these behaviors. Next, in each of the case studies, particular attention is paid to characterizing the patterns of interactions at the interface between Chinese domestic and international-market stakeholders over time and, ultimately, the amplitude and direction of the changes in market institutions at the global level.

The universe of the cases relevant to this book is the emergence of a systemically significant economy's impact on global market pricing institutions. This book considers each "emerging economy–commodity market" dyad as one case and evaluates the changes that occurred within a given commodity market. As a result, I argue that the argument presented in this book is directly relevant to other cases where a systemically relevant economy is in a relationship of dependence on a particular market. The dynamics unveiled in this book also allow us to draw deeper insights about China's relationship with the global economy.

I take the view that evaluating one country's impact on specific global market institutions is justified in cases where that country's impact on a given market has become systemic. There are many ways to measure systemic significance, but in the markets selected in this book, I assess China's overall importance by tracking its imports as shares of global imports as well as its shares of global consumption.

## Moment of Systemic Significance

China's emergence and rise as the dominant consumer has been of such scale and speed that it can fruitfully be conceived of as having been a systemic shock to the global economy. In turn, its impact on the global commodity market institutions that had been established before its emergence can, thus, be conceived of as a "quasi-natural experiment." In a way reminiscent of comparative studies of the various ways in which national systems of political economy reacted to global economic crises, in this book I observe and compare China's rapid emergence as the world's dominant consumer and the impact it has had across markets.

The quasi-natural experiment approach means that I pay particular attention to the years before and after China reached a position of systemic significance in each market as I assess institutional change over time. To structure my inquiry, for each market, I select a key "turning point" year that I conceptualize as the "moment of systemic significance" for that particular market. I define this turning point as the year in which China became the world's number one importer. I also look at the year in which its share of global imports first exceeded 20 percent. The reason for looking at two measures of systemic significance is that I pay attention to the shape and pace of the rise in Chinese consumption and I try to take into account, as much as possible, both measures of systemic significance. As you will see, in the markets I study, these two moments of systemic significance come within a few years of each other.

This characterization is somewhat arbitrary, of course, but it nevertheless allows us to temporally frame China's relationship with each market. It is clear that China's impact had been felt in the years prior to its becoming the number one consumer. The research undertaken in this book is comparative and qualitative in nature and includes process tracing and interviews, which allows me to take this temporal framing exercise as more of a guidepost and less of a hard limit. In other words, I do not ignore China's impacts on commodity markets in the years immediately prior to the "moment of systemic significance." It simply has given me a sense of where to look (the early 2000s for iron ore and potash, the late 2000s for copper, and the early 2010s for uranium). All this being said, and acknowledging the fact that the particular year of systemic significance is not cut and dried (was it 2002 or 2003 for iron ore?), I do argue that the years I identified for each commodity come close to capturing moments of deep significance for global commodity markets: the arrival of China as the world's dominant consumer, compared to a not-so-distant past when China was either almost completely absent from the global commodities trade or a very minor stakeholder. These moments of systemic significance are the moments that I argue can be construed as shocks to global commodity markets, each one constituting a turning point for a comparative analysis of the variation in China's impacts across different commodities.

In the iron ore market, China became the number one importer in 2003, with 26 percent of global imports (it first imported more than 20 percent of global imports in 2002, with 21 percent of total imports) (UNCTAD). In the potash market, China first became the number one importer in 2002, with 18 percent of global imports (it imported more than 20 percent for the first time in 2005, at 21 percent) (UN Comtrade by value). The same year, China also became the number one potash consumer in the world, in terms of total agricultural use of potash (FAO).[4] In the uranium market, China became the number one importer in 2010 (with 31 percent of world imports), importing more than 20 percent of global uranium imports (UN Comtrade). In the copper market, China became the number one importer in 2008, with 28 percent of world imports, but it had already been importing more than 20 percent of global copper imports in 2003 (UN Comtrade) (see Table 1.2).

China became the world's number one importer and, as I argue, systemically significant in each of the commodities studied here at some point between 2002 and 2010. In comparing the statistical data, I do my best to select data a few years prior to and after the "turning point" in each market. This temporal focus also explains why, despite the fact this book is published in the 2020s, I nevertheless remain interested in the years that immediately precede and follow China's "arrival" as dominant consumer in each of the markets under study. In concrete terms, this means that I am particularly interested in characterizing international and Chinese domestic markets in the early 2000s, prior to China's becoming the dominant consumer, and in the late 2000s and early 2010s, as the initial impacts of China's rise as dominant consumer were being felt. Nevertheless, in each case,

*Table 1.2* **Years of systemic significance for China in the iron ore, potash, uranium, and copper markets**

| Commodity | Year China became the world's number one importer | Year China's share of global imports exceeded 20% |
| --- | --- | --- |
| Iron ore | **2003** | 2002 |
| Potash[a] | **2002** | 2005 |
| Uranium | **2010** | 2010 |
| Copper | **2008** | 2003 |

[a] I used UN Comtrade data by value for these datapoints (HS 3104). Global potash data are tricky to assess for a variety of reasons. If we look at UN Comtrade data by weight, China started importing more than 20 percent of global imports in 2005, but there appear to be issues with the US data for the years 2000–2005, with data by net weight dropping to a level a thousand times lower than the years immediately before and after. The US import numbers come back up to numbers in the million tonnes in 2006 (whereas the data by value follow a coherent trendline throughout). Conversations with industry analysts suggest this is more likely a mistake. If we adjust the data, China started importing more than 20 percent of global imports in 2003. Based on FAO data, China's potash imports stood at 3 percent of global imports in 1980. Chinese imports went through a steep rise until they reached 20 percent of global imports in 2002 (looking at FAO data, they remain slightly below the US level, so China does not become the number one importer). A second key element to note is that the role of US imports in the global market is unique. US imports have been important throughout the period under study, until today, many years coming slightly above Chinese imports. However, the United States imports almost all of its potash from Canada via direct relationships with Canadian producers. In fact, Canpotex, the Canadian potash export marketing agency, sells potash to countries around the world except the United States. Since 1991, the share of US potash imports coming from Canada has never dipped below 75 percent and reached a high of 93 percent in the 1990s (UN Comtrade, by trade value). In this way, some argue that the US potash market is somewhat closed off from the global potash market. If we were to subtract US imports from the overall numbers, China started importing more than 20 percent of global potash imports in 1997. The last element to note in the potash market is the emergence of Brazil as the number one importer in recent years. In the markets for iron ore, copper, and uranium, China's share of global imports continued to rise for years after becoming the number one importer. In 2016, for instance, China imported 69 percent of global iron ore imports. In the potash market, Chinese imports as a share of global imports, after a steep rise through the 1990s, have remained stable or even decreased slightly in the 2010s before coming back to their 2000 levels and then decreasing slightly again. This separates the potash case from the other cases, where to this day China remains the number one importer. Brazil started importing larger quantities of potash in the 2010s, and since 2016 it has consistently imported a larger share than China. In 2019, China accounted for 16 percent of global imports, whereas Brazil accounted for 18 percent (FAO). The impacts of this transition will be covered in Chapter 5.

Source: For iron ore, UNCTAD; for potash, UN Comtrade and FAO; for Uranium, UN Comtrade; for copper, UN Comtrade. Author's calculations.

I continue to trace the process of China's impacts on global commodity markets until today.

## Case Selection Strategy

The comparative case selection strategy in this book is based on Mill's method of difference,[5] where the divergent impacts of China's emergence are compared across global markets that had been similarly structured prior to its emergence (see Table 1.3). The two principal cases are the iron ore and potash market pricing regimes.

The market for iron ore, the raw material necessary to produce steel, is the second largest commodity market in the world, after oil. The market for steel is the largest metals market in the world, by far, and accounts for 95 percent of global metal production (The Lore of Ore 2012). The global iron ore and steel manufacturing markets were valued at $US498bn in 2019 (Global Steel Market Overview 2019). The iron ore market was chosen among other global commodities for its size and central importance to economic development, as well for China's importance in it. "Iron ore may be more integral to the global economy than any other raw material or commodity, other than perhaps oil" (Waldmeir and MacNamara 2010). Iron ore is a core component of the political economy of the Asia Pacific and has been central to China and Japan's growth pathways. China consumed 69 percent of global iron ore imports in 2016 (UNCTAD). China's import dependence has increased markedly in recent years: Chinese iron ore imports as a share of total Chinese iron ore imports plus its domestic production was 90 percent in 2016 (UNCTAD data; see Figure 1.4).

The potash[6] market was chosen from among other global commodities for its importance, for the fact that it is understudied in the political economy literature, and for its comparative fit with the iron ore market. In 2015, the global fertilizer industry had annual sales of about $US175bn (Terazono 2015). China is responsible for 14 percent of global potash production (2019, FAO), consumes 28 percent of global potash production (2019, FAO), and imports the equivalent of 58 percent of its annual consumption needs (imports as a share of agricultural use, 2019 FAO data; see Figure 1.4). Two characteristics make potash a critical resource. First, potash (potassium) is one of three essential plant nutrients, or basic elements, in commercial fertilizers, alongside phosphate (phosphorus) and nitrate (nitrogen). As such, the main driver of potash consumption around the world is the demand for food, especially food that contributes to higher-protein diets (biofuel crops, such as palm trees, are also a potassium-intensive crop) (Stone 2008). But also important is the increase

*Table 1.3* **Global potash and iron ore markets at the time of China's emergence as a dominant consumer, 2002–2003**

|  | Iron Ore | Potash |
|---|---|---|
| **Market shape** | | |
| Nature of the commodity | Extractive, essential to economic development, low substitution potential, high barriers to entry | Extractive, essential to economic development, low substitution potential, high barriers to entry |
| Geographical concentration | High, with 74% of global exports coming from Brazil, Australia, Canada, and Ukraine (2000)[b] | High, with 86% of global exports coming from Canada, Germany, Belarus, and Russia (2000)[c] |
| **Market governance** | | |
| Pricing regime | Long-term contracts and annual benchmarking pricing system | Long-term contracts and annual benchmarking pricing system |
| **Chinese dependence on trade** | | |
| Import dependence | High level of import dependence (46% in 2001)[d] Essential to China's economic development | Very high level of import dependence (between 81% and 92% in 2000)[e] Essential to China's food security |

[b] UN Comtrade, by trade value.
[c] UN Comtrade, by trade value.
[d] *China Mining Yearbook 2002* [中国矿业年鉴], 76.
[e] From 1961 to 2002, according to FAO data, China's import dependence, calculated as the share of agricultural use not fulfilled by domestic production, was very high. It stood at 94 percent in 1970, increased to 98 percent by 1990, and was still at 92 percent in 2000. Starting in the early 2000s, domestic Chinese production increased and levels of import dependence came down to 47 percent in 2010 and 41 percent in 2019. According to China's Ministry of Land and Resources, China's potash import dependence stood at around 80 percent in the early 2000s and decreased to around 50 percent in the early 2010s.

in demand for high-quality products, as potash use improves the taste, color, and texture of agricultural products. More than 95 percent of potash is mined for agricultural purposes (Grant et al. 2010). Second, potash has no substitutes and cannot be manufactured synthetically. It is mined or harvested as salt that contains potassium in water-soluble form. Given the centrality of fertilizers to the global food industry and China's central impact on global fertilizer markets, this is a critically understudied empirical area.

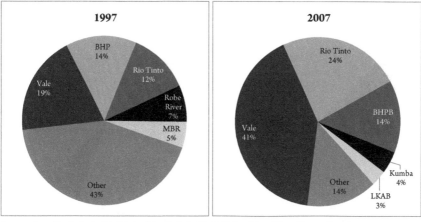

Source: Iron Ore Industry Trends and Analysis. 2009. *Baffinland Iron Mines Corporation*, August 31.

*Figure 1.2* Share of world seaborne iron ore production by firm, 1997 and 2007

The global iron ore and potash markets shared many characteristics at the time of China's emergence as a systemic consumer, yet were transformed differently by China. First, both markets were bulk commodities extractive markets with capital-intensive requirements and continued to have long lead-time horizons and high barriers to entry (Komesaroff 2013). Iron ore and potash are both essential to economic and agricultural activity, respectively, as they have very low potential, if at all, for substitution.

In addition, both the global iron ore and potash markets have very high concentrations of reserves in just two or three countries. This was true at the time of China's emergence as the dominant consumer. In 2000, fully 74 percent of global iron ore exports came from Brazil, Australia, Canada, and Ukraine,[7] and 86 percent of global potash exports came from Canada, Germany, Belarus, and Russia (see Table 1.3). Both markets' dominant producers include one developed economy in the Asia Pacific (Australia for iron ore and Canada for potash) and one BRICS economy (Brazil for iron ore and Russia for potash). Before China's emergence as a systemically significant consumer at the beginning of the 2000s, both markets were controlled by a few large companies (Vale, BHP Billiton, and Rio Tinto for iron ore; Potash Corp., Mosaic, Ukalkali, and Belarukali for potash) (see Figures 1.2 and 1.3).

China's initial positioning toward the global iron ore and potash markets was also comparable, inasmuch as levels of import dependence were (and continue to be) high in both cases. We will see in Chapters 4 and 5 that import dependence trends have in some ways mirrored each other over the past twenty years. In 2000, import dependence stood at 46 percent in the iron ore market and 92 percent in the potash market. Whereas domestic iron ore production

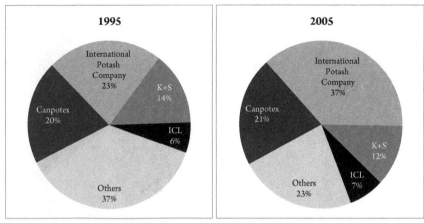

Source: Fertilizer industry data, from personal communication with retired senior fertilizer industry analyst (Interview 174, August 2022) (others include Jordan, Uzbekistan [from 2011] and Laos [from 2013], as well as sales by Canadian producers [not Canpotex] to the US market).

Figure 1.3  Share of world potash exports by firm, 1995 and 2005

has played a decreasing role in overall use, over time, for environmental reasons among others, domestic potash production saw an important increase in the 2000s, until it plateaued in the 2010s. In 2016, import dependence levels stood at 90 percent for iron ore, while they stood at 43 percent for potash (see Figure 1.4). For case selection purposes, the important criterion is import dependence, which was and continues to be high in both cases.

In addition, both markets' pricing regimes were comparable before China's rise, with a long history of closed-door annual benchmarking pricing negotiations, long-term contracts, low prices, and low volatility. Despite these similarities between the global iron ore and potash markets, China's impact on these markets diverged significantly. As we will see in Chapter 3, whereas the markets for iron ore and potash both exhibited high levels of coordination at the global level, the most striking difference is in the variation in Chinese domestic coordination levels, high in the potash case and low in the iron ore case (see Table 1.4). This comparison allows us to focus on the role of Chinese domestic market coordination levels in explaining the variation in outcomes.

In order to increase the variation on the independent variables (variation in coordination levels at the domestic and international levels), to refine the book's argument, and to evaluate the potential for generalization beyond the two main cases under study here, this book investigates China's impact on two further cases, the global uranium and copper markets. Despite China's vast civilian nuclear power ambitions, there has been little attention devoted to the political economy of China's uranium procurement. One could make the same argument for copper. Given the importance of copper as an industrial commodity and

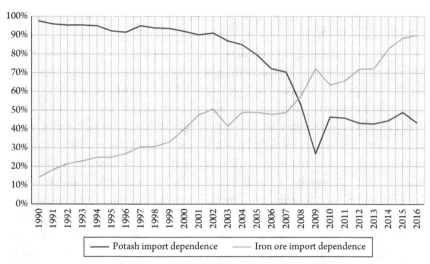

Source: For iron ore, UNCTAD (share of iron ore imports on the sum of imports and domestic production); for potash, FAO (share of agricultural use net of domestic production), author's calculations.

*Figure 1.4* Chinese import dependence on the global iron ore, potash markets, 1990–2016

*Table 1.4* **Case studies distribution**

| | *Global market (producers)* | |
|---|---|---|
| **Domestic market (consumers)** | **Fragmentation** | **Coordination** |
| **Fragmentation** | Copper | Iron ore |
| **Coordination** | Uranium | Potash |

for the world's green transition, and China's dominant role in the global copper market, the relatively low level of attention paid to the political economy of China's copper consumption is surprising.

The uranium and copper cases offer many similar characteristics to the iron ore and potash cases at the time of China's emergence as a systemic consumer. To begin, uranium and copper both have low substitutability, and China has a high level of import dependence in both markets. China is heavily dependent on uranium imports, from 51 percent in 2007 to 81 percent in 2020. If we consider copper ores, refined copper, and scrap copper, in 2001 China was 70 percent import-dependent (*China Mining Yearbook 2002* [中国矿业年鉴] 2002). In terms of geographic concentration, in the global market for uranium the top four exporters were responsible for 88 percent of global exports. The copper market has relatively more moderate levels of geographic concentration, although the top four exporters were responsible for more than 60 percent of global exports in 2000 (see Table 2.1).

The uranium and copper cases allow us to investigate China's impact on global pricing regimes in situations where the global market was not home to negotiated benchmarks prior to China's rise (see Table 1.4). In the uranium market, levels of coordination at the domestic level are relatively high, with some similarities to the potash case, but they are lower at the global level than in the iron ore or potash cases. Indeed, as we will see in Chapter 6, despite its high levels of concentration, the global uranium market can be thought of as segmented among relatively distinct regions (Central Asia, Africa, North America) and as having less institutionalized coordination among producers. In the copper market, coordination levels are relatively low, at a level comparable to the domestic iron ore market. To illustrate, in 2001, the proportion of small enterprises and small mines in the overall copper industry amounted to 94.4 percent, while it amounted to 97.8 percent in the iron ore industry (*China Mining Yearbook 2002* [中国矿业年鉴] 2002). However, at the global level, at the time of China's emergence, the copper market was one of the most financialized metals markets, with inclusion in major commodity indices, a large role for traders, liquid spot markets, and spot market pricing being dominant in the industry. The inclusion of such a case is important for us as we investigate a market that was liberalized before China's emergence, contrary to the three other cases.

The addition of the uranium and copper cases allows us to refine the book's argument. Looking at the potash and uranium cases side by side contrasts situations where Chinese domestic coordination levels are high but global market coordination levels vary. Despite similar levels of success in coordination domestically, the impact of China's emergence on the global uranium market is more subdued than in the potash case. Looking at the copper and iron ore cases side by side also allows us to "hold constant" Chinese domestic coordination levels (both low) while global coordination levels vary. These comparisons allow us to look more closely at the role global market stakeholders play in determining global market institutional change (or stability) but also at how variation in global market coordination levels is felt among Chinese consumers, what these consumers' preferences are regarding global market outcomes, and their ensuing behavior.

Conversely, just as was the case for the two main case studies, iron ore and potash, looking at the copper and uranium cases side by side allows us to focus on the variation in domestic coordination levels, as global market coordination levels are more comparable (although there are more significant differences between the global markets for copper and uranium than for iron ore and potash).

In short, a two-by-two case selection matrix helps us investigate variation at the domestic and global levels while holding one level constant. The exercise highlights the fact that explanations situated exclusively either at the domestic or international levels are not sufficient to explain the outcomes. First, there is meaningful variation between the iron ore and copper cases and between the potash and uranium cases (despite both pairs exhibiting similar levels of domestic coordination, being fragmented in the first pair and coordinated in the second). Second, there is meaningful variation between the copper and uranium cases and between the iron ore and potash cases (again, despite both pairs exhibiting similar levels of international coordination and being fragmented in the first pair and coordinated in the second).

In addition to the four commodity market case studies, another comparative strategy is employed (see Table 1.5). In order to look more deeply into the domestic mechanisms at play, and to control for variables that are specific to one commodity market, I dive further into the iron ore case study in two ways. First, I consider China's impact on a second set of market institutions within the iron ore market: the global iron ore bulk shipping regime. Here, China's impact on the global market diverges in interesting ways and, with them, the causal pathways. The selection of this contemporaneous "within-market" comparison allows us to observe variation in Chinese domestic dynamics within one commodity market and to trace the parallel—related but distinct—causal relationships,

*Table 1.5* **Case studies list**

| *Main case studies (across markets)* | *Across time* |
|---|---|
| ***Iron ore*** | |
| 1. China's impact on the global iron ore market (pricing)—2000s/2010s | 3. Japan's impact on the global iron ore market (pricing and shipping regimes)—1960s/1970s |
| 2. China's impact on the global iron ore market (shipping)—2000s/2010s | |
| ***Potash*** | |
| 4. China's impact on the global potash market (pricing regime)—2000s/2010s | |
| *Minor case studies (across markets)* | |
| ***Uranium*** | |
| 5. China's impact on the global uranium market (market shape)—2000s/2010s | |
| ***Copper*** | |
| 6. China's impact on the global copper market (market shape)—2000s/2010s | |

all the way to the global level. This strategy allows us to make inferences while holding the "country values" and the "commodity values" constant, thereby maximizing the leverage offered by the comparative method. It also allows us to answer questions such as: Was there something specific at play in the iron ore market that prevented effective coordination in China? What would effective coordination look like and what effect would it have at the global level in the broader context of the iron ore market?

Finally, still working within the global iron ore market, a plausibility probe is conducted to determine the generalizability of the findings, over time and space, as they apply to the rise of another systemically significant consumer, decades earlier. China's impact on the iron ore pricing and shipping regimes is compared with Japan's impact at the time of its emergence fifty years prior, in the 1960s and 1970s. The Japanese and Chinese cases take extreme values on the independent variables. Allowing the country to vary, but not the commodity market, allows us to more fully leverage the comparative method by holding constant the variables that are specific to the iron ore market while focusing on the impact of another emerging dominant consumer. Japan emerged as dominant consumer with higher domestic coordination levels, facing at the time an international market that was much more fragmented. This comparison allows us to answer questions such as: Was there something specific to the iron ore market at play? Should we expect to find an "emerging country pattern?" What kinds of impacts could the emergence of a coordinated consumer have on global iron ore market institutions?

This book's comparative strategy allows us to carefully consider the impact of variation in coordination capacity at both the domestic and international levels, across commodities, within the same commodity markets, and across time. The results constitute an encouraging assessment of the generalizability of the argument beyond the iron ore and potash cases as well as beyond China. Focusing on market power, or coordination capacity, at both domestic and international levels, and on the interaction patterns that ensue between market actors at both levels allows us to garner deep insights into the resonance dynamics between systemically significant economies and changes (or lack thereof) in global market institutions.

## Plan of the Book

The rest of this book is organized as follows. Chapters 2 and 3 present the theoretical building blocks in more detail. Chapter 2 discusses the dependent variable, global commodity market pricing institutions. Before doing so, it discusses commodity markets and their variation, both at the global level and at the

Chinese domestic level. It also introduces an institutional conceptualization of the global market, based on four premises: markets as created, embedded, contested, and plural. This conceptualization of global markets allows us to think about global market change in a thicker, more qualitative way, by looking at its shape, concentration levels, power relations between stakeholders, governance mechanisms and regulatory specificities, history, and embedded assumptions shared by stakeholders or price determination mechanisms. This thicker conception of markets gives us leverage to describe the changes occurring in global commodity markets beyond prices or volatility levels.

Chapter 3 presents the argument in more detail, both its static and dynamic components, and delineates five hypotheses. It then provides a discussion of the independent variables, domestic and international configurations of market power and their differentials, operationalized here as the capacity to coordinate market behavior. I then discuss the way this framework differs from an approach that would be mainly focused on price levels, as well as the question of market stakeholders' preferences for global market institutions. Then, I provide an overview of market coordination levels, in each case studied in this book, at the domestic and international levels. Finally, the chapter provides a longer discussion of the ways in which it engages and contributes to the literature on global China, the global and comparative political economy literature on the resonance between the domestic and global political economy, and the classical political economy literature on the role of market power.

Chapter 4 examines China's impact on the global iron ore market. China emerged as the number one importer of iron ore in the world in 2003, overtaking Japan. At the time, for fifty years until 2010, the global iron ore market had operated under a negotiated benchmark pricing regime. Prices were determined in annual benchmarking negotiations between the three main iron ore producers, BHP Billiton, Rio Tinto, and Vale, on one hand, and the Japanese importers, on the other. The pricing regime had enjoyed decades of stability. In 2006, Baosteel, the lead Chinese importer, took over the Japanese importers to negotiate the benchmark price with global suppliers for the first time. Over the next four years, prices saw a dramatic rise. By 2010, the negotiations had collapsed and the big three iron ore producers ushered in a quarterly and then a spot-pricing regime. Within five years from China taking over negotiations, the decades-old global iron ore benchmark pricing regime met a dramatic end. The position of market vulnerability on behalf of the Chinese iron ore market stakeholders in the face of powerful iron ore exporters led to chaotic behavior and the unintended liberalization of the global pricing regime.

A comparison is conducted with a concurrent event in the iron ore shipping industry—the Valemax saga. Here, coordinated behavior on behalf of Chinese market stakeholders led to patterns of bargaining behavior with the main global stakeholder, Vale. Finally, in contrast with China's chaotic behavior in the main iron ore case, when Japan emerged as the number one importer of iron ore in the 1960s, high levels of market coordination enabled it to successfully establish a stable long-term negotiated pricing regime, the very benchmarking system China would rise to disrupt fifty years later.

Chapter 5 examines China's impact on the global potash market. At the time of China's emergence as dominant consumer and importer of potash, the global potash market presented many similarities with the global iron ore market. It was heavily concentrated, had been stable for decades, and was home to a negotiated benchmark pricing regime. In the potash case, the emergence of China was followed by the fall of one of the two largest global marketing cartels, the Belarusian Potash Company, in 2013, and by some changes in the frequency of annual benchmark pricing negotiations. Overall, however, the benchmark pricing system survives until today (2023), with China as the lead benchmark price negotiator. The global pricing regime saw some liberalization movement but has shown more resilience than in the iron ore case. This chapter argues that the explanation lies in the balance of market power between Chinese domestic and global market stakeholders, especially the high level of market coordination by Chinese importers, at the interface with the global market. Indeed, China is home to a powerful group of importers, three (but really two) key state-owned entities control close to half of all imports, and it has carefully coordinated its procurement strategy, including its negotiation strategy with the world's main potash exporters.

Chapter 6 evaluates China's impact on two minor case studies, the global commodity markets for uranium and copper. In the uranium case, China's emergence as the dominant consumer came toward the end of the 2000s. It increased its uranium imports from around 1 percent to 31 percent of world imports between 2001 and 2010, the year it became the world's number one importer. There were no international benchmarking negotiations per se in the uranium market prior to China's emergence, but the pricing regime relied on closed-door negotiations between key producers and importers. In the uranium case, China emerged as a dominant consumer in the face of a concentrated global market that displayed lower levels of coordination. On the domestic side, however, the Chinese uranium and civilian nuclear industries were highly coordinated. In this case, China was less constrained in fulfilling its procurement needs and was able to operate more comfortably in this market, which led to the emergence of the world's new dominant exporter—Kazakhstan. China has not used accusatory rhetoric against global uranium suppliers in the same way that it has in the iron ore and potash markets. In the uranium case, China supported the continuation of the existing long-term pricing mechanisms, made full use of opportunities to create direct, long-lasting relationships with producers, and showed a willingness to be a meaningful participant in various international initiatives for civilian nuclear safety. Interestingly, this is arguably the case where China had the most room to maneuver globally. At the same time, global uranium market institutions have seen a high degree of continuity, with some movement in the direction of de-liberalization insofar as Chinese market stakeholders are concerned and some movement in the direction of liberalization insofar as the parallel rise of uranium trading companies are concerned.

In the copper case, China emerged as the number one importer in 2008, with 28 percent of global copper imports. Between 1998 and 2020, China increased its share of global copper imports from 11 percent to 57 percent (by net weight) (UN Comtrade). In this case, both the Chinese and global market stakeholders were in a more fragmented position, while the global market had already been financialized prior to China's emergence. Here, China's emergence, given its chaotic nature at the interface with the global market, initially pushed market institutions further in the direction of liberalization. Subsequently, Chinese stakeholders attempted to increase market coordination, with limited results. This is a case where change in market pricing institutions was unlikely, given the fragmented nature on both sides of the equation.

The empirical focus in this book is global commodity markets and their systemically relevant consumers, but the conclusions point to broader patterns we can expect as China attempts to carve out a position of market power that is commensurate with its size in the global economy.

# 2

# Global and Chinese Commodity Markets

*Taking Variation Seriously*

Over the course of the 1990s, and culminating in the early 2000s, China's commodities consumption patterns went from a Chinese domestic issue to a global one. In other words, insofar as commodities are concerned, China has very quickly risen from a level of minor international relevance to systemic relevance. What is true in the commodities world is also true more broadly. Starting with China's entry into the WTO in 2001 and, perhaps, more strikingly since the 2008 global financial crisis, when China's massive stimulus directly contributed to recovery in global growth, it has become clear that domestic Chinese dynamics are having direct impacts on the global economy. This is what is meant by global systemic significance here; that is, when domestic changes, even those not intended to affect global markets and institutions, can have a direct, significant effects internationally.

China's impact is often measured in quantitative terms, whether on global GDP growth, or on the demand and supply of raw materials and goods and services and, as a consequence, on price levels. Instead, this book is interested in China's qualitative impact on global markets, specifically, on the ways in which global commodity market institutions were transformed (or not) by China's rapid emergence as the world's dominant consumer.

This chapter discusses the outcomes that are explained in this book: China's impact on global commodity market pricing institutions for iron ore, potash, uranium, and copper markets. One of the key premises of this book is that there are variations at all levels. Despite important similarities, global and Chinese domestic commodity markets vary meaningfully in their configurations. As a result, these markets have evolved differently as China rose to the number one consumer of minerals in the world during the 2000s. In Chapter 3, I will argue that there is a relationship between changes in Chinese domestic and international markets and I will characterize their patterns.

In this chapter, I will first provide an overview of the state of affairs in global and Chinese commodity markets as China emerged as dominant consumer in the 2000s. Second, I will discuss contributions to relevant literature on the political economy of commodities. Third, to support my investigation into the variations in global institutional market changes, I present the conceptualization of global markets that is employed in this book. Fourth, I describe and explain the variation in global market outcomes that I observe. Finally, I cover the case selection rationale and the methodological approach employed.

## Global and Chinese Commodity Markets

The rapidity and magnitude of China's rise as dominant consumer of commodities has given us the opportunity to study China's impacts on global commodity markets and, specifically, to trace and compare the processes of institutional change in different commodity markets across time.

Before we delve into the variation that exists between commodity market institutions, we must acknowledge common trends. Extractive commodity markets are high entry cost, high volume, and capital intensive. Many have argued that these markets lend themselves to high degrees of market concentration (see Table 2.1). Rodrik explained in 1982 that "mineral industries are a far cry from [an] idealized world" of perfect competition: "There are high barriers to entry in almost all stages of mining and processing due to technology and large capital costs. Transport costs and differences in the types of ore mined further segment the market. Consequently, there tend to be high degrees of concentration both upstream and downstream" (Rodrik 1982, 543). Many commodity markets have a history of formal oligopolistic practices and attempts at price controls (Zacher 1993; Krasner 1974).

Several commodity markets have gone through a period of consolidation, through mergers and acquisitions, and have seen their levels of concentration rise over the latter part of the twentieth century. In 1965, the four largest iron ore exporters (by country) controlled 50.5 percent of global exports (Brantley 1966), compared to 78.2 percent in 2003 (Jorgenson and Kirk 2004). The top three firms were responsible for almost 70 percent of the seaborne iron ore trade in 2003 (Jorgenson and Kirk 2004). In fact, all of the commodities studied in this book, as well as many others, have levels of concentration exceeding that of the oil and gas industry (2022).

Depending on whether one looks at concentration levels at the country or firm level, many markets have seen their concentrations continue to increase as

Table 2.1 Global commodity market concentration before and after China's emergence as dominant consumer

| Commodity | Oil[a] | | Copper | | Coal | | | Potash[b] | | Iron ore | | Uranium | |
|---|---|---|---|---|---|---|---|---|---|---|---|---|---|
| Year | 2000 | 2015 | 2000 | 2015 | 2000 | 2020 | 1995 | 2015 | 2000 | 2015 | 2000 | 2015 |
| Chinese imports as a share of global imports | 3.6%[c] | 17%*[d] | 16%* | 46%* | 0.4%[e]* | 18%[f]* | 11%* | 19%* | 14%[g] | 67%[h] | 1%[i]* | 34%* |
| Geographical dispersion (% of top four exporting countries) | 44%[j]* | 46%* | 62%* | 53%* | 62%* | 79%[l] | 71%[k] | 77%[l] | 74%* | 85%* | 88%[m]* | 90%* |
| Firm concentration (% of production or exports by the four largest firms)[n] | 26%[n] | 27%[o] | 40%[p] | 36%[q] | 31.4%[s] | 15.14%[t] | 63%[u] | 80%[v] | 70%[w] | 63%[x] | 54%[y] | 59%*[z] |

[a] China has not reached dominance in the global oil market as per this book's measure.
[b] HS3104 (UN Comtrade: Fertilizers, mineral or chemical, potassic), by net weight.
[c] US Department of Energy.
[d] Qty (net weight). (*) denotes data from UN Comtrade.
[e] HS 2701 (UN Comtrade: Coal, briquettes, ovoids, and similar solid fuels manufactured from coal), includes metallurgical coal and bituminous coal.
[f] Net weight.
[g] UNCTAD.
[h] UNCTAD.
[i] By trade value for 2001 (UN Comtrade data are available from 2001 only).
[j] HS2709 (UN Comtrade: Petroleum oils and oils obtained from bituminous minerals; crude), by trade value.
[k] FAO data, by net weight.
[l] FAO data, by net weight.
[m] HS284410 (UN Comtrade: Uranium; natural uranium or compounds), by trade value.
[n] A note of caution here, as industry concentration numbers are extremely difficult to collate and compare. Where possible, I indicate concentration numbers for exports. Otherwise, as indicated, I include concentration numbers for production (which leads to lower numbers). For instance, firm concentration numbers for coal are production numbers, whereas for iron ore they are seaborne production (or export) numbers.

o For 1996. Top four oil-producing companies were Saudi Aramco, National Iranian Oil Company, Petróleos Mexicanos, and Petróleos de Venezuela (Al-Moneef 1998), from Petroleum Intelligence Weekly data.

p Top four oil-producing companies were Saudi Aramco, National Iranian Oil Company, China National Petroleum Corporation, and Exxon Mobil, from Petroleum Intelligence Weekly data and OPEC Annual Statistical Bulletin (Petroleum Intelligence Weekly 2016; OPEC Annual Statistical Bulletin 2016).

q Top five companies, share of total production (Boliden Annual Report 2002).

r Top five firms, copper output, 2012 (Basov 2013).

s The top four producers of coal were Coal India Limited, Peabody (US), Rio Tinto (UK), and BHP Billiton (Australia) (Breaking New Ground 2002; Kirkby 2001).

t The following top four producers of coal, Coal India Limited, China Shenhua Energy Company Limited, Yanzhou Coal Mining Company, and Peabody, accounted for 1,127 million tonnes of coal production, over a total world coal production of 7,438 million tonnes for 2020. Total world production numbers from the International Energy Agency (Global Coal Production 2022). Production numbers from each company's annual report.

u Fertilizer industry data, from personal communication with retired senior fertilizer industry analyst (Interview 174, August 2022).

v Fertilizer industry data, from personal communication with retired senior fertilizer industry analyst (Interview 174, August 2022).

w Almost 70 percent for the world's top three companies: Vale, Rio Tinto, and BHP Billiton (Ericsson 2004).

x 62.5 percent for the world's top three companies: Vale, Rio Tinto, and BHP Billiton (Löf et al. 2016).

y To note that this reflects production share and not market share, for 1999 (Vance 2000).

z The top four exporting companies are KazAtomProm, Cameco, Areva, and ARMZ–Uranium One (*Uranium Enrichment* 2013).

China emerged as dominant consumer in the 2000s. This was the case for the oil, potash, and uranium markets (both country and firm concentrations increased). The iron ore market has seen its geographic concentration increase and firm concentration decrease somewhat, probably due to the emergence of Fortescue Metals Group, the fourth largest producer of iron ore in the world. The copper market has seen both geographic and firm-level concentration levels decrease somewhat; however, overall levels remain relatively high.

General trends toward concentration in commodity markets mirror that of the global economy in general, as we continue to observe a momentum toward concentration in many other areas (Gilpin 1977; Ostrom 1997; Nolan 2012; Stiglitz 2017). Today, many markets are home to extensive degrees of market concentration and established firms that occupy positions of power, be they in the resource or the technology sectors (Kurz 2017; Hearn and Tepper 2018).[1]

There is a storied debate in the political economy literature about whether there is a "natural convergence" toward oligopolistic or competitive markets. Streeck (2009), to highlight one of many researchers, argues that there is a natural tendency toward competition in markets. Along the same line of argument, Krasner (1974) argues that if there is tension between competitive and cooperative behavior in markets that offer an opportunity to restrain trade, there is nevertheless a natural tendency toward the breakup of cooperative arrangements such as cartels. On the other side of the debate, scholars argue that the natural tendency in capitalist markets is toward concentration and coordination (Strange 1996; Nolan 2012). Fligstein argues that when legal frameworks allow it, cartel arrangements become the major strategy for coping with competition (1990, 23), such as in Europe in the nineteenth century. He also argues that "the social structures of markets and the internal organizations of firms are best viewed as attempts to mitigate the effect of competition with other firms" (Fligstein 1996, 657).

For the purpose of this book, the extent to which I observe concentration and coordination in global commodity markets is an empirical question, the answer to which I do not take for granted. The key insight of interest, and the one on which this book builds, however, is that despite high concentration levels across the board, important differences across markets remain in coordination levels, market behavior, and pricing institutions. Even within one commodity market, key actors respond differently to the same event. The significant variance found across global commodity markets predates China's emergence as a dominant global consumer in the twenty-first century. China's impact on these various markets also varies. It is this variation that most interests us.

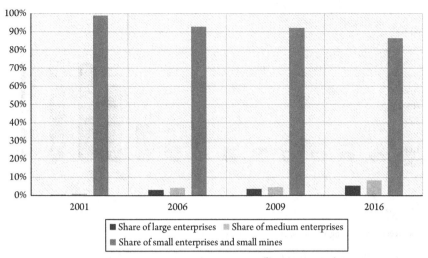

Source: China Mining Yearbooks (2002, 2007, 2010 and 2017). To note, the total number of enterprises includes entries for Hong Kong and Macao, as well as Taiwan and foreign invested enterprises.

*Figure 2.1* Share of large, medium, and small enterprises in China's mining sector, 2001–2016

Just as global markets vary, commodity market institutions, coordination levels, and the behavior of stakeholders also vary at the Chinese domestic level: some are concentrated, some are fragmented, some are very sensitive to price signals, and others are less so. If we look at the share of large, medium, and small enterprises in the Chinese mining sector, we can see that the overwhelming majority are small enterprises or small mines, at 86.4 percent in 2016 (see Figure 2.1). Yet the proportion of large- and medium-sized enterprises operating in a given commodity market in China, or the sales revenues per employee, varies across commodities (see Figure 2.2 and Figure 2.3). Whereas the major extractive industries in China—iron ore, coal, and copper—are more fragmented, a few industries have higher levels of concentration, potash among them.

## The Political Economy of Global Commodity Markets

This book takes as a core premise that market configurations vary in ways that are analytically important.[2] Attention to institutional variation is at the core of one of the puzzles animating this book: Why does China have different impacts on global commodity markets? I take the view that answering this question

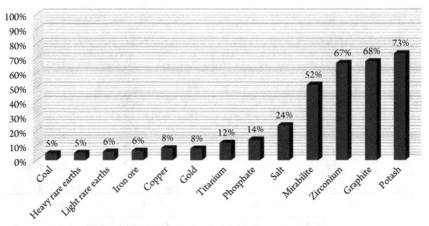

Source: China Mining Yearbook 2008. Author's calculations.

*Figure 2.2* Proportion of medium and large enterprises in the Chinese mining industry, 2007

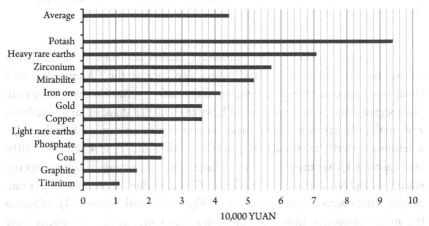

Source: China Mining Yearbook 2002. Author's calculations.

*Figure 2.3* Sales revenue by employee in the Chinese mining industry, 2001

satisfactorily requires a thicker conceptualization of global markets than the common liberal atomistic definition.

I see markets as complex institutional ecosystems. Looking at a broad array of market institutions and features, being attuned to the variety of actors that constitute everyday markets and their evolution over time, and tracking the manifestations of power in global markets and the ways in which it is wielded allow me to characterize China's impact on global markets in a way that I hope is analytically richer.

The definition of global markets adopted here is informed by a broadly conceived institutional tradition that is rooted in Polanyi's notion of markets as being "created" and "embedded" (Polanyi 1944). This definition is also sensitive to classical political economy concerns about the entwined nature of wealth and power and to comparative political economy's attentiveness to the concurrent divergence in national systems of political economy.

Markets are defined here as *institutional systems—material, institutional, normative, and power architectures—that enable, connect, and constrain stakeholders— individuals, firms, states, organizations—and channel them toward distinctive patterns of repeated exchanges, of which modes of competition and value or price formation can be critical regulating features.*

This definition moves away from the "market-as-arena" metaphor, which I argue has had too powerful an influence on common "thin" ways of thinking about markets (see Watson 2005 for a discussion). Markets occupy "spaces," but these spaces are not empty. The architecture that shapes the space and the institutions that constrain and enable behavior are very much indissociable from the markets themselves and, indeed, constitute them.

The conceptualization of markets this book adopts builds on four propositions: markets are created (and not spontaneous); markets are embedded (and not autonomous); markets are disputed (and not devoid of power relations); and markets are plural (and not uniform).

First, markets here are understood as having been "created," as opposed to being "natural" phenomena. The idea of a spontaneous, self-regulating market is a myth (Gilpin 1977; Polanyi 1944; Fligstein 2001, 2008; Watson, 2018). This position contrasts with the view that markets naturally converge toward competitive forms of exchange. Just as markets are not "natural," neither is liberalization a "natural" process. Liberalization trends are no more apolitical than de-liberalization trends. What some see as natural trends are, in fact, the reorganization of power hierarchies. It follows that liberalization occurs to the benefit of some actors and at the expense of others, and, as such, must always be explained.

Second, markets are embedded. Market stakeholders' behaviors are embedded in micro, meso, and macro dynamics that can be fruitfully analyzed using a wide array of approaches and tools, from "calculus" to "cultural" (Ebner and Beck 2008; Hall and Taylor 1996). We should not assume that market behavior is different from other human behaviors; that is, in terms of being closer to "calculus" and further from "cultural" patterns of behavior. This book takes seriously the embeddedness of markets in their broader sociopolitical environments.

Third, markets are disputed. Both power relations and exchange relations are constitutive features of markets because individuals, firms, industry associations, or states—all market stakeholders—negotiate these two fundamental forces concomitantly (List 1909; Carr 1939; Viner 1948; Gilpin 1977; Kirshner 2003). The point, here, is that markets are not simply subjected to varying degrees of political distortion. This would imply that if markets were free from politics, they would tend toward an ideal of competitiveness (Duina 2011). This conceptualization is in line with the view that "markets by themselves are neither morally nor politically neutral; they embody the values of society and the interests of powerful actors" (Gilpin 2000, 50).

Fourth, markets are plural. Distinct global markets that exhibit different characteristics, dynamics, and complementarities can be conceived of as distinct institutional architectures that coexist concurrently in the global economy. In the political science literature, there is a tendency to consider national markets as being subjected to national political dynamics and institutions—and thus prone to divergence—and international markets as being subjected to international dynamics and institutions—and thus less likely to diverge from one another.[3] This book's comparative analysis of global markets is motivated by the recognition of persisting *sequential* and *concurrent* variation among distinct global markets.

For this, I build on the comparative impulse found in the varieties of capitalism (VOC) literature, which asks why qualitatively different types of market economies can and do coexist under the broader umbrella of a capitalist world economy and are not necessarily converging toward one ideal type (Hall and Soskice 2001; Katzenstein 1985; Esping-Andersen 1990; Zysman 1983). I also draw from the "divergence" school in the international political economy (IPE) literature (Keohane and Milner 1996; Tiberghien 2007; Dore and Berger 1996), which focuses on the divergence that persists between national systems of political economy despite powerful globalization forces.

A comparative frame of analysis allows us to take seriously the variations in the dynamics across global markets, even within the same industry, by allowing for global markets to vary along different institutional features.

The features of the global commodity markets investigated in this book include the behavior of relevant market stakeholders (state, private, national, and international); the geographical shape of markets, including their dispersion, corporate concentration, and other physical characteristics that shape markets, such as transportation patterns; coordination capacity, including the alignment of expectations; governance mechanisms, such as import/export licensing or other regulatory features; price determination mechanisms, including the presence or absence of benchmark negotiations or trading platforms; market power relations between key market stakeholders; and social embeddedness features, such as levels of trust and shared values, a market's history, and its systemic stability (Massot 2021, 549).

# Change in Global Commodity Market Pricing Regimes

## Defining Pricing Regimes

This book seeks to explain the variation in China's impact on one specific dimension of global commodity markets: their pricing regimes. Pricing regimes are understood as *sets of market institutions that comprise the necessary features for the establishment of dominant and durable patterns of price determination.* In other words, pricing regimes constitute a system of market institutions of which price levels are simply one of many observable manifestations. There are relationships between pricing regimes and patterns in price variations. For instance, administered pricing regimes tend to be less volatile than competitive pricing regimes. However, this book's focus remains on the market institutions themselves rather than their relationship with price levels. The goal here is to characterize, in as rich and constructive a way, the features of different pricing regimes in global commodity markets and how they have evolved over time.

There are a variety of pricing regimes in existence in global commodity markets today. Some commodities, such as copper, are more financialized and liquid, and include large traders, such as Glencore, as dominant market actors; they are also traded in a variety of financial forms and their sales are based on spot prices (as opposed to longer-term benchmark prices). Other commodities, such as potash, are home to long-term negotiated benchmark pricing regimes in which prices for important shares of global volumes are negotiated between producers and consumers and are valid over longer periods of time. Pricing regimes matter for reasons of efficiency and distributional consequences. Every pricing regime is an ecosystem that is home to different positions of power—and, as a result, pricing regime changes create winners and losers.

## Measuring Liberalization

In characterizing changes in pricing regimes as a result of China's (and Japan's) emergence as dominant consumer of commodities, I draw from the comparative political economy (CPE) literature that is interested in the variation among and institutional complementarities within national systems of political economy: the variety of capitalism (VOC) literature (Katzenstein 1985; Hall and Soskice 2001).

I draw from the VOC literature in two ways. First, I argue that it is useful to compare distinct international markets by leveraging comparative tools that are traditionally used to compare national economies. It is commonly accepted in the comparative political economy literature that national economies that are in similar categories when it comes to GDP per capita, for instance, can be home to meaningfully different systems of political economy. Applying this insight to global markets has not been common practice. Doing so allows us to look further than price levels and to delve into meaningful institutional variation across global markets, some of which are more "liberal" than others. It is understood that global markets are not as neatly separated from each other by national boundaries, compared to national economies—the parallel can only go so far. However, it is proposed here that global markets constitute, to a certain degree, distinct institutional ecosystems with their own recognizable patterns of exchange, behaviors, relationships, and regulatory environments and attendant institutional complementarities. Thinking of markets as distinct market ecosystems and systematically comparing their evolution over time can yield important insights that are missed when we evaluate commodities (or other global markets) as a group.

The second way in which I draw from the VOC literature is in conceptualizing change in global commodity pricing regimes alongside a continuum from competitive to strategic market interactions. This conceptualization is, in part, inspired by the "market-strategic" continuum developed by Hall and Soskice (2001) and further developed in Hall and Gingerich (2004). Hall and Soskice characterize types of national political economies when they conceptualize two ideal types: liberal and coordinated market economies. In the former,

> "firms coordinate their activities primarily via hierarchies and competitive market arrangements . . . characterised by arms-length exchange of goods and services in a context of competition and formal contracting." In the other modality, "firms depend more heavily on non-market relationships to coordinate their endeavours with other actors and to construct their core competencies. . . . These non-market modes of coordination generally entail more extensive relational or incomplete contracting, . . . and more reliance on collaborative, as opposed to competitive, relationships. . . . In contrast to liberal market economies (LMEs), where the equilibrium outcomes of firm behaviour are usually given by demand and supply conditions in competitive markets, the equilibria on which firms coordinate in coordinated market economies are more often the result of strategic interaction among firms and other actors." (Hall and Soskice 2001, 8)

This allows us to conceptualize markets on a range of positions on the competitive-strategic continuum. This in turn makes clear the fact that many commodity markets were not very liberal, or competitive, prior to China's rise— case in point, the two main case studies in this volume were home to negotiated benchmark pricing regimes in the 2000s. An important consequence of this insight is that one can appreciate, conceptually, the possibility that China has had a *liberalizing* effect on some global commodity markets, an insight that has not been adequately theorized, or highlighted, in the literature.

Finally, I draw from the VOC literature in taking into consideration a variety of market actors, including but beyond firms, such as various government departments, industry associations, or other international bodies, where relevant. In this book, a movement toward more-competitive market interaction is labeled "liberalization," and a movement toward more-strategic market interaction is labeled "de-liberalization" (see Table 2.2).

The liberalization of pricing regimes is measured along the following eight indicators: the number of firms; the frequency of pricing signals; the predominant length of contracts; the presence or absence of a benchmark or other system that sets the price for longer periods of time; the type of relations between firms; the presence or absence of a commodity in major commodity indices;[4] the presence or absence of spot trading platforms; and the role of the spot price as a price signal in the global market. The liberalization of pricing regimes thus includes financialization dynamics, defined as "the increasing role of financial motives, financial markets, financial actors and financial institutions in the operation of the domestic and international economies" (Epstein 2005, 3); and as a "strengthening interaction of commodities markets with the financial system . . . [and where] returns from commodities are increasingly pooled with returns from pure financial assets ('pooling effect')" (Valiante 2013). It

*Table 2.2* **Liberalization of pricing regimes (dependent variable indicators)**

*Liberalization*

| *Competitive* | *Strategic* |
|---|---|
| High number of firms | Low number of firms |
| Higher frequency of pricing signals | Lower frequency of pricing signals |
| Shorter-term contracts | Longer-term contracts |
| Multiple prices | Benchmark |
| Lack of long-term relations between firms | Long-term relations between firms |
| Included in major commodity indices | Not included in major commodity indices |
| New spot trading platforms | No new spot trading platforms |
| Large role of spot price as price signal | Minor role of spot price as price signal |

also includes broader liberalization dynamics, such as higher volatility, higher number of firms, or the lack of long-term relations between market actors.[5]

In short, the liberalization of a commodity market pricing regime is operationalized as a movement toward a higher number of firms playing an important role in the market; pricing signals happening more frequently (say, a move from annual to quarterly pricing); the prevalence of short-term contracts; the lack of a price benchmark; the lack of longer-term relations between producers and consumers; the inclusion of a commodity in major indices; the appearance of new spot trading platforms; and a larger role of spot prices as price signals. A movement in the other direction is a movement toward more-strategic interactions. Among other things, such a movement can be characterized by the presence of fewer firms in the market (e.g., via mergers and acquisitions); a lower frequency of pricing signals (e.g., via annual negotiations); the presence of longer-term contracts; the presence of a benchmark pricing regime; the presence of long-term relationships between firms; the exclusion of commodities from major commodity indices (a common reason mentioned is a lack of liquidity in particular commodity markets, including all of the markets studied in this book, to the exception of the copper market); the absence, or low share, of total trading on spot trading platforms; as well as a minor role for spot prices in global price signals.

Moving along the market-strategic continuum is a political economic process. In both directions, changes in pricing regimes consist of disrupting existing power relations in global markets. This book takes the position that a movement in one direction, say toward liberalization, is no more "natural" than a movement in the other direction. Both movements constitute displacing and reorganizing existing power hierarchies. A movement along the continuum occurs to the benefit of some actors, at the expense of others, and as such, needs to be explained in both directions.

Table 2.3 illustrates the operationalization of the outcome of interest—a pricing regime change—alongside eight components. Table 2.4 summarizes the overall results, along with a summary of the pricing regime changes for each main case study. Figure 2.4 illustrates the extent and direction of these pricing regime changes.

## Why Does Liberalization Need an Explanation?

It feels as though we should pause for a second here and ask ourselves whether liberalization outcomes are surprising in this context. I argue that they are. But there are four reasons these trends require an explanation, above and beyond whether one expects such an outcome. First, the most powerful Chinese actors

*Table 2.3* **Pricing regimes (dependent variable indicators), operationalization**

| Competitive (0) | Strategic (10) | Operationalization | Iron ore (China) Prior[a] | Post | Iron ore (Japan) Prior | Post | Potash (China) Prior | Post |
|---|---|---|---|---|---|---|---|---|
| Multiple firms | Monopoly/Monopsony | Presence of monopoly/monopsony (2)/Multiple firms (0) | 1 | 1 | 1 | 1 | 1 | 1 |
| High frequency of pricing signals | Low frequency of pricing signals | High frequency (0)/Low frequency (2) | 2 | 0 | 1 | 2 | 2 | 1 |
| Short-term contracts (30-day, quarterly) | Long-term contracts (annual, multi-annual) | Shorter-term contracts (0)/Longer-term contracts (2) | 2 | 1 | 1 | 2 | 2 | 2 |
| Multiple prices | Benchmark | Multiple prices (0)/Benchmark (2) | 2 | 0 | 1 | 2 | 2 | 1 |
| Lack of long-term relations between firms | Long-term relations between firms | Lack of long-term relations (0)/Presence of long-term relations (2) | 2 | 1 | 2 | 2 | 2 | 1 |
| Included in major commodity indices | Not included in major commodity indices | Yes (0)/No (2) | 2 | 2 | 2 | 2 | 2 | 2 |
| New spot trading platforms | No new spot trading platforms | Yes (0)/No (2) | 2 | 0 | 2 | 2 | 2 | 1 |
| Large role of spot price as price signal | Minor role of spot price as price signal | Role of spot market as price signal Large (0)/Small (2) | 2 | 0 | 2 | 2 | 2 | 1 |
| Total | | | 15 | 5 | 12 | 15 | 15 | 10 |
| **Liberalization (0–10, where 0 is liberalized)** | | | **9** | **3** | **8** | **9** | **9** | **6** |

[a] Prior and post-China's (or Japan's) emergence as dominant consumer.

*Table 2.4* **Global pricing regime change after the emergence of China and Japan as dominant consumers**

| Market change | 1. China—iron ore 2000s–2010s | 2. Japan—iron ore 1960s–1970s | 3. China—potash 2000s–2010s |
|---|---|---|---|
| **Pricing regimes** (Benchmark versus spot, short-term versus long-term contracts, volatility, role of spot pricing) | Fall of the benchmark, opening of new spot trading platforms, quarterly contracts, increase in price volatility and frequency of trades | Increased role of state, annual benchmarking pricing regime, long-term contracts, regime stability | Increase in frequency of negotiations and price volatility, fall of a producer cartel, increased role of spot pricing, benchmarking system survives |
| **Liberalization (Competitive 0– Strategic 10)** | Significant movement toward competitive interactions 9 → 3 | Moderate movement toward strategic interactions 8 → 9 | Moderate movement toward competitive interactions 9 → 6 |

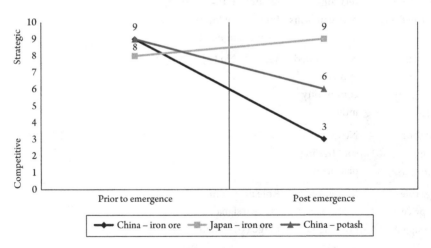

*Figure 2.4* Pricing regime change following the emergence of China (iron ore and potash) and Japan (iron ore) as dominant consumers

in both the potash and iron ore cases had no intention of achieving outcomes that liberalized the pricing regimes for these commodities. Second, liberalization impacts are not a direct expression abroad of the nature of the Chinese domestic political economy. Third, liberalization processes are political processes and, as such, they deserve an explanation. Fourth, liberalization outcomes vary in important ways across cases, whether in timing, speed, or depth, which in itself warrants careful analysis.

If China's rise as dominant consumer of commodities led to liberalization impacts on global markets, this is not simply because "Chinese actors are powerful, and they get what they want." In fact, a thread running through this book is one of Chinese vulnerability toward the global commodity markets it is so dependent on. The cases in this book show that, at critical moments, dominant Chinese stakeholders do not get their preferred outcomes internationally. In this particular light, whether China is actually in a powerful position at all is not something we should take for granted, despite the country's market size.

The argument here is not that a vulnerable China will have no impact on global markets. China's size means that it will have an impact, one way or another. The impact varies, but it can indeed be profoundly disruptive, as the iron ore case illustrates. The argument is rather that China's liberalizing impact is surprising because it was unintended. Worse, it was the *opposite* of what the most powerful Chinese actors wanted. In the iron ore case, the fall of the benchmark pricing regime in 2010 was not in the interests of China's large steel SOEs or import license holders. This was not a policy or goal of the relevant Chinese state organs, such as the NDRC, the State Council, or the lead negotiator, the China Iron and Steel Association (CISA). Yet it was Chinese behavior, its lack of coordination, and its position of market vulnerability, combined with the big global iron ore producers' stronger market power and their willingness to push in the direction of liberalization, that led to this outcome.

For those who may argue that China's domestic markets were undergoing a process of liberalization and that this is why we observe liberalization impacts globally, suffice it to say that in the case where we observe the most rapid and decisive liberalization of pricing regimes, the iron ore market, we also find a domestic market that was replete with power politics, transport frictions, and other features of non-competitive markets. These factors were also mediated by subnational provincial and local politics and were in many ways out of the reach of top-level Chinese regulators, which makes the symmetry argument difficult to follow through. The Chinese government first reacted to what they perceived as a coordination problem in the iron ore industry by encouraging its consolidation and constraining access to import licenses, only to then reverse tack and liberalize the licensing process altogether, in 2013. The recent creation of the China Mineral Resources Group, in July 2022, was the latest effort on behalf of the central government to effect control over the interface between the domestic and global iron ore markets. This new state-owned entity's purpose is explicitly to better coordinate China's interface with the global iron ore industry. It remains to be seen how effective this new entity will be. In other words, the political economy of China's domestic iron ore industry is not best characterized as undergoing a seamless process toward liberalization; quite the contrary.

On the other side of the debate, but following a similar logic, there are observers who are surprised to see liberalization outcomes because they expect China to have a statist effect on the global economy. That is, some analysts expect to see China's illiberal market characteristics "exported" at the global level. The empirical stories unveiled in this book show that this intuition has not been borne out. First, "exporting statism" is not a stated government objective, certainly not one shared by all of the Chinese market stakeholders represented in this book. In addition, we just saw that national-level Chinese state organs have a limited capacity to have their preferences expressed at the global level. Where this argument may have more traction is in conceiving of Chinese stakeholders' market behaviors as being informed by different, non-Western-centric views of how markets work. This in turn is bound to affect market behaviors and ultimately global outcomes. This is a promising area of research.

What I can say at this point is that the cases under review in this book show that there is no direct mirroring of domestic market dynamics on global market behaviors and their impact. In fact, in more than one case, we have a non-liberal, hybrid economy (China), where the state plays a dominant role (Eaton 2015), leading to liberalization impacts at the global level. A given country's foreign economic policy and global impacts are not simply a reflection of the nature of its domestic economic system. A liberal market economy can conduct illiberal foreign economic policies and vice versa. The kind of impacts Chinese actors may have, globally, or even if they decide to advocate for the state to have a larger/smaller role in global markets need not be a reflection of the situation within their borders. This point is derived from the case studies contained in this book and is an important insight. If anything, we need to be careful in assuming the direction of major economies' impacts on global market institutions. The variation in the impacts China has on the global commodity markets on which it depends challenges us to think more carefully about the relationship between major international markets and the domestic political economies of these markets' major national stakeholders.

Liberalization, and market change more generally, is always and everywhere a political economic process. In other words, I argue here that just as markets are not "natural," neither is liberalization a "natural" process. Just as the fall of Bretton Woods requires an explanation (Helleiner 1994; Best 2004), the liberalization and financialization of commodity markets requires one. What some see as a natural trend is in fact the displacement or reorganizing of existing power relations in global markets and not a tendency toward more-apolitical markets. Liberalization occurs to the benefit of some actors and at the expense of others. A change occurring in a particular direction is the result of a win by certain interest groups and, as such, needs to be explained. Explaining liberalization's occurrence—*how* and *why* it occurs, who plays the dominant roles, who benefits, and who loses—must be done whether or not one had expected it to happen (I did not).

Finally, one may argue that the liberalization trends I observe in the second decade of the twenty-first century were one part of the broader process of global convergence following the rise of neoliberal economic policymaking in the 1980s and the fall of many cartelized commodity pricing arrangements in the 1970s. Interestingly, contrary to the oil market, this broader context, from the 1980s onward, also coincided with a period of price stability and a lack of deep financialization in most of the cases under study here (except for copper), until China's rise in the 2000s. Only after the global financial crisis and the retreat of the global momentum toward liberalization have the iron ore and potash markets experienced financialization. This timing needs to be explained.

But if we assume for a second that the general trend in global commodity markets is one of liberalization and financialization, questions still arise. China did not have a uniform impact on global markets and displayed a sufficient amount of variation in behavior to be puzzling and warranting careful analysis. In fact, the liberalization trends are far from overwhelming (oligopolies are hard to displace).

Inasmuch as the commodities studied in this book have liberalized, they have done so at different speeds, with different depths across cases, and have accelerated and slowed down at different times over the past two decades. Why do markets liberalize at different speeds? What causes the variation in the resilience of some global market institutions over others? As we see de-globalization and de-liberalization trends picking up speed over the past few years, should we expect equivalent reversals in the world of commodities? What are the limits of financialization and liberalization in different commodities, if any? The burden of explanation remains relevant and necessary from the moment we recognize that liberalization is not unavoidable, or equal, across cases. Indeed, the tracing of the process through which liberalization happens unveils a fascinating story.

It may be that at certain times in history, outcomes resonate across markets and toward a certain horizon, at least for a period of time. But if we do not carefully trace the process of liberalization (and its reversals), not only will the causal mechanisms behind the particular types of institutional change remain obscured but within-case reversals (such as the liberalization–de-liberalization–liberalization pathway in the iron ore market, following Japan's and then China's emergence), may remain hidden from view.

The final comment I will make here is that many industry insiders persist in saying that some commodity markets are not fungible enough to ever become fully commodified and financialized (some include iron ore in this category and some include potash or uranium). The reasons are specific to each market and include the physical reality of the resource (humidity levels, differentiated iron content for iron ore, different grades for potash, or logistical transporting requirements), which makes different sources significantly differentiated and non-fungible; the role of international security and safety standards; restrictions or agreements in the uranium market; or the role of governments in agricultural production for the case of potash. The potential existence of certain "limits" to financialization and liberalization, which bring to mind Polanyi's discussion of the inherent limits to the commodification of land, labor, and money (Polanyi 1944), plays a background role in the empirical stories recounted here, as each market dances back and forth toward its own "liberalization frontier."

## International Political Economy of Natural Resources

How does this book situate itself in the international political economy (IPE) of resources literature?[6] The field of IPE itself is deeply intertwined with the political economy of natural resources. IPE arguably emerged in part as a reaction to the oil crisis of the early 1970s, which brought back to the fore the inescapable relevance of power in the study of the international economy (Lake 2009; Hancock and Vivoda 2014). Many early IPE scholars were interested in global extractive markets, including through the lens of resource oligopolies (Moran 1973; Bergsten 1974; Zacher 1987; Krasner 1978; Krasner 1974; Katzenstein 1977). These scholars were attentive to the diversity of market arrangements and even debated the normative value of cartelized markets.[7]

This book's approach is inspired by early IPE of resources scholars Dani Rodrik (1982) and Stephen Krasner (1974), who developed multifaceted indicators to evaluate global extractive commodity markets. Krasner identified the conditions that make durable cartel behavior more likely: the price inelasticity of demand, high barriers to entry, high market concentration, shared experience among producers, lack of consumer resistance, the ability to work with extended time horizons, and shared values. Rodrik defined global commodity markets along four variables: their degree of concentration, vertical integration, state ownership, and trade and price-formation modes.

Krasner and Rodrik's respective theorizations of market variables were instrumental for me in the development of a thicker conceptualization of global commodity markets. Rodrik focuses on three markets—copper, iron ore, and bauxite—on which the United States and Japan were both heavily import dependent and frames the article as a study of Japan's procurement strategies as it emerged to take over from the United States as dominant commodities consumer. Rodrik also takes the time to specify the different market structures at the global level and proceeds to draw from the domestic industrial structure of Japan and the United States to explain the variation in procurement strategies between the two countries. Rodrik concludes that, paradoxically, Japan was more successful than the United States in procuring raw materials during the 1960s and 1970s despite an initial reluctance to use vertical integration as main procurement strategy, as the United States had done. This article, covering the transition from the United States to Japan as leading commodities consumer in the second half of the twentieth century begged for a rejoinder: What about the transition from Japan to China as dominant consumer? How did China's approach differ from that of Japan, and was it able to a successfully implement a distinct procurement strategy? This provided fertile ground on which to grow the framework developed in this book.

The fading away of cartels and the stabilization of global commodity prices, which began in the 1980s and continued until the early 2000s, led IPE scholars to turn away from the study of extractive markets (Hughes and Lipscy 2013). In 2013, Hughes and Lipscy plotted the percentage of journal articles, published in top political science journals since the 1970s, that addressed energy politics. They found that the rate of publications increased from 1 percent to 4 percent of total publications during the 1970s and then gradually declined over the next twenty years as oil prices also declined. More important, the end of the Cold War and the period of US hegemony that followed led to the neglect of some of the core concerns of early scholarship on the IPE of resources, including the study of the diversity of global market arrangements and the political impulses behind the emergence of non-classical or non-liberal market arrangements (for an exception, see Bates 1997).

This was true perhaps until China's rapid emergence as dominant resource consumer in the 2000s[8] and the commodities supercycle that preceded the global financial crisis of 2008 and the return of commodity price volatility. In the 2010s, review articles began calling for the return of the IPE of resources, identifying China as a transformative actor and one of the key drivers behind resurgent empirical activity in extractive commodities (Goldthau and Witte 2009; Dubash and Florini 2011; Rudra and Jensen 2011; Helleiner and Clapp 2012; Hughes and Lipscy 2013; Hancock and Vivoda 2014; Van de Graaf and Colgan 2016).

This book contributes to the literature on the international political economy of resources in the following three ways. First, the resurgence in the literature on the IPE of resources has predominantly concentrated on the global governance of energy, chiefly oil, gas, and renewables.[9] This book concentrates on three key non-energy resources: iron ore, potash, and copper, as well as one less studied energy commodity: uranium. Despite some recent work on the subject, the IPE of resources literature has not matched the intense empirical activity non-energy extractives have seen since the turn of the century, given their importance to global economic activity. Just to take fertilizers as an example, the recent sanctions against Belarus and Russia's invasion of Ukraine brought to the fore the importance of potash to the global agriculture industry, yet few analyses can be found of the resource in the literature.[10]

Similarly, this book builds on the emerging literature on China's impact on the global iron ore market (Sukagawa 2010; Wilson 2012, 2013, 2015; Humphreys 2013, 2015; Economy and Levi 2014; Hurst 2015a, 2015b, 2016). Contributions include theorizing differentials in market power at the domestic and global levels and developing a framework to explain the consequences of these market power differentials beyond the iron ore market. In addition, this book zeros in on China's role in the significant liberalization of the global iron ore market (Wilson 2012, 2013; Economy and Levi 2014) and puts this surprising outcome in dialogue with the current debates on China's impact on the global economy.

Second, within the IPE of non-energy resources, this book places renewed emphasis on power dynamics that go beyond resource security or resource-curse questions that have occupied much of the literature (Rosser 2006; Nem Singh 2013). This book adopts a classical political economy focus on market power relationships between Chinese and global market stakeholders, going beyond unitary state conceptualizations. This book also purposely focuses on Chinese positions of vulnerability in resource procurement, a reality that is not well accounted for in the literature on Chinese consumption of global commodities. This focus on the not-always-intuitive relationship between market size, market power, market behavior, and global market change provides a fresh outlook on the political economy of global commodity markets in the era of dominant Chinese demand.

Third, this book focuses on the dynamics that exist at the interface between national and international markets. This was identified as a pertinent angle of study that lacked scholarly attention (Dubash and Florini 2011; Van de Graaf and Colgan 2016). Specifically, building on Peter Katzenstein (1977) and Robert Putnam (1988), the book focuses on interactions between a variety of global, national, and subnational actors, both state and non-state, and teases out the resonance patterns between domestic and global market institutional change.

# 3

# Explaining Change in Global Market Institutions

In its simplest form, this book examines the variation in China's impact on global commodity markets over the past twenty years, focusing on positions of market power and vulnerability at the domestic and global levels. China went from an outsider to the number one importer of most global commodities within a decade or less. However, despite China's size, it has often found itself in a position of market vulnerability. The vulnerability paradox—the combination of China's heft in market size and its market vulnerability—is a thread that runs through the book. This reality stems from the fact that China emerged as the largest market player in a whole class of global markets without having developed the concurrent hegemonic power to shape global market institutions to its liking. Not only do dominant Chinese stakeholders not always get what they want, but their behavior can also lead to unexpected global outcomes, which include liberalization trends. This, I argue, is counterintuitive.

This book presents an answer to three puzzles: Why, despite China's rising salience, are Chinese stakeholders often not able to shape markets in their preferred direction? What explains the variation in China's impact on global commodity markets? And lastly, how can we explain the uneven liberalization dynamics across markets?

In the case of the iron ore market, China's emergence as number one importer led to the rapid fall of a decades-old global negotiated pricing institution and the emergence of a spot market. In this case, uncoordinated Chinese behavior played a determining role in the liberalization of a global market. In the case of the global potash market, China's rise led to the fall of a cartel of global producers and the partial liberalization of this market, yet a global benchmark pricing regime survives to this day. In the global uranium and copper markets, China's rapid emergence as the dominant consumer did not lead to major changes in global market institutions. In short, China's impact has not been uniform across markets, either in the direction, type, or intensity of change.

This chapter builds an inside-out interactive framework rooted in the variation in market power at the domestic and global levels. I argue that Chinese preferences, behaviors, and the global outcomes that are the results of the interaction between Chinese and global actors vary in large part because of relative positions of market power and vulnerability.

## The Argument: Market Power, Market Vulnerability, and Market Change

In this book I argue that the balance of market power between domestic and international market stakeholders and the way it evolves over time explains the behavior of market stakeholders as well as the likelihood of change in global market institutions. I also argue that market power dynamics play a role in the formation of Chinese domestic and global market stakeholders' preferences for global market institutions.

I look at three aspects of relative market power and their relation to market institutional change: the relative position dominant market stakeholders find themselves in relative to either producers or consumers (as determining who wields more influence), the change in relative market power between dominant producers and consumers (as a catalyst for change in global market institutions), and the relative position of market power market stakeholders occupy vis-à-vis their own peers (as a determinant in the development of preferences for pricing regimes at the global level). Let me discuss each one in turn.

In terms of the relative positions of market power and their consequences, I argue that asymmetric positions of market power affect domestic and global market players' incentives and also their capacity to act. In other words, in terms of the behavior of the dominant consumers (at the Chinese domestic level) and the producers (at the global level), market power asymmetries provide the dominant side more potential to wield influence over market institutions. Market stakeholders with the most relative market power at the export/import interface of a given commodity market have a higher capacity to influence global market institutions (see Table 3.1). Significant attention is thus concentrated on characterizing the evolution of market power, operationalized here as coordination capacity at both the Chinese domestic level and the global market level in each case study.

Positions of asymmetry afford the dominant side more leeway to influence outcomes in their preferred direction; in the table, they work in favor of

*Table 3.1* **Two-level market power asymmetries**

| Domestic market (consumers) | International market (producers) | |
|---|---|---|
| | **Fragmentation** | **Coordination** |
| **Fragmentation** | 1<br>**Symmetry**<br>No dominant position of influence<br>Dynamic: competitive<br>*Case: Copper pricing regime in 2000s–2010s (China)* | 2<br>**Asymmetry**<br>Dominant position of influence: producers<br>Dynamic: oligopolistic<br>*Case: Iron ore pricing regime in 2000s–2010s (China)* |
| **Coordination** | 3<br>**Asymmetry**<br>Dominant position of influence: consumers<br>Dynamic: oligopsonistic<br>*Cases: Iron ore pricing and shipping regimes in 1970s–1980s (Japan)*<br>*Uranium 2000s–2010s (China)* | 4<br>**Symmetry**<br>No dominant position of influence<br>Dynamic: strategic bargaining<br>*Cases: Iron ore shipping regime in 2000s–2010s (China)*<br>*Potash 2000s–2010s (China)* |

producers in Quadrant 2 and consumers in Quadrant 3. There are positions of symmetry where market power is evenly matched either because both sides are fragmented (Quadrant 1), which is likely to lead to competitive dynamics, or because both sides are coordinated (Quadrant 4), which is likely to lead to more-conflictual dynamics or strategic bargaining dynamics. A situation in Quadrant 1 is more likely to lead to continuity in global market institutions because of the diffuse nature of the power relations. There is a debate on whether tendencies toward competition or consolidation will emerge. Quadrant 4, where there is a symmetry of market power, as coordination capacity is high on both sides, can be unpredictable. In this case, it becomes difficult to predict the outcome, given the lack of dominance and the likelihood that patterns of conflict or strategic bargaining will emerge.

The second component of this argument is dynamic. Market power asymmetries between domestic and global market stakeholders affect the conditions for global market institutional change at the global level. Two possible scenarios follow the emergence of a new dominant market player: either two-level relations of power are maintained or they are transformed.

An example of the former would be a fragmented consumer taking over as the number one consumer, usurping another fragmented consumer, while both face a fragmented global market. Here, we would have a transition that maintains the market power asymmetries (a transition that takes place within the same quadrant). All else being equal, I argue that this is less likely to lead to changes in global market institutions compared to situations where two-level power relations are deeply transformed.

A second scenario would be that of an emerging new market player that causes more profound shifts in the two-level relations of market power, amounting to a change between quadrants. Since holding a position of market power puts market stakeholders in advantageous positions of influence regarding global market institutions, assuming that different consumers and producers have different preferences regarding global market institutions, it follows that shifts in relative market power in a given market increase the likelihood of change occurring in global market institutions. I argue that the emergence of a new dominant market player that causes deep change in consumer-producer power relations (leading to a movement from one quadrant to another) is more likely to lead to change occurring in market institutions at the global level. The greater the change in the relative positions of market power, the greater the likelihood of change occurring in global market institutions, all else being equal.

As we will see in more detail below, this means that changes toward an asymmetric position of market power (Quadrants 2 and 3, Table 3.2) are more likely to lead to global institutional market change than would changes toward a symmetric position of market power (Quadrants 1 and 4, Table 3.3).

*Table 3.2* **Change toward an asymmetric position of market power**

| Domestic market (consumers) | International market (Producers) | |
| --- | --- | --- |
| | **Fragmentation** | **Coordination** |
| **Fragmentation** | 1<br>**Symmetry**<br>Dynamic: competitive | 2<br>**Asymmetry**<br>Dynamic: oligopolistic<br>**High likelihood of change** |
| **Coordination** | 3<br>**Asymmetry**<br>Dynamic: oligopsonistic<br>**High likelihood of change** | 4<br>**Symmetry**<br>Dynamic: strategic bargaining |

*Table 3.3* **Change toward a symmetric position of market power**

|  | *International market (producers)* | |
|---|---|---|
| **Domestic market (consumers)** | **Fragmentation** | **Coordination** |
| **Fragmentation** | 1<br>**Symmetry**<br>Dynamic: competitive | 2<br>**Asymmetry**<br>Dynamic: oligopolistic |
|  | **Low likelihood of change** | |
| **Coordination** | 3<br>**Asymmetry**<br>Dynamic: oligopsonistic | 4<br>**Symmetry**<br>Dynamic: strategic bargaining |
|  | | **Medium likelihood of change** |

Movement toward Quadrant 4 entails a medium likelihood of change because evenly matched positions of market power can lead to conflict and strategic bargaining with unpredictable outcomes. Such shifts in two-level market power relations can be caused by a variety of phenomena, including the emergence of a new dominant consumer in a global market, which is the focus of this book. In the way it approaches change, this model is coherent with Colgan, Keohane, and Van de Graaf's conception of a regime change in the energy sector following a pattern of punctuated equilibrium (Colgan et al. 2012; Krasner 1984). This is to say that periods of major change are understood to be interspersed with periods of greater stability. As we saw in Chapter 2, this book conceptualizes China's emergence as a shock and a critical juncture in the evolution of global commodity markets. This book uses this shock as an opportunity to compare global market institutional change across different markets.

The third component of the argument has to do with the formation of preferences toward international market institutions. As we will see below, here, I tentatively argue that at the domestic level, strong (weak) positions of market power relative to a market stakeholders' own peers will lead to preferences for the de-liberalization (liberalization) of global market institutions. At the global level, I argue that strong (weak) positions of market power relative to domestic counterparts lead to preferences for the liberalization (de-liberalization) of global market institutions.

In summary, positions of market power provide influence over global market institutions. Profound changes in relative positions of market power are more likely to lead to global market institutional change, and this is especially true of transitions toward asymmetric quadrants. Transitions from one extreme position of asymmetry to another bring with them the highest likelihood of global market institutional change, especially given the fact that preferences for global market institutions are also influenced by positions of market power and vulnerability.

## Hypotheses

The argument developed can be summarized into the following five hypotheses:

(1) An asymmetric distribution of market power affords the dominant side with more influence over global market institutions and, in times of change, more likelihood to actualize its preferences (producers in Quadrant 2 and consumers in Quadrant 3).

(2) In cases where there is relative symmetry of market power (Quadrants 1 or 4), the outcomes are likely to be the result of competition (Quadrant 1) or strategic bargaining (Quadrant 4) between market stakeholders.

(3) Change in global market institutions is more likely to occur when the emergence of new, dominant market players disrupts the existing power relations between producers and consumers. In other words, a movement from one quadrant to another is more likely to be disruptive than a movement within the same quadrant, all else being equal.

(4) The emergence of a dominant consumer that entails a change toward asymmetric positions of power (Quadrants 2 or 3) is more likely to be disruptive than the emergence of a consumer that entails a change toward symmetric positions of power (Quadrants 1 and 4). The most disruptive movement is one that entails the most profound change in relative power, that is, transitions from Quadrant 2 to 3 or Quadrant 3 to 2. A change toward Quadrant 1, where there is a large number of uncoordinated players, is more likely to lead to an incremental change in market institutions. The impact of a change toward Quadrant 4 is the least predictable, as it can either lead to a deadlock or conflict between equally powerful market players.

(5) This book does not develop a theory of preference formation toward competitive or strategic pricing regimes. However, I do propose tentative ones, or at the very least provide avenues for further investigation. For domestic market stakeholders, I argue that positions of market power *vis-à-vis their own peers* (at the domestic level) are key to understanding their global pricing regime preferences. Weak (strong) positions of market power at the domestic level vis-à-vis their own peers tend to favor preferences toward liberalization (de-liberalization). At the global level, it is more delicate to articulate predictions, given the supranational nature of interactions.[1]

Positions of market power *vis-à-vis their own peers* matter, as a strong position of market power may afford global market stakeholders with better positions from which to act decisively and effect change. But here, I argue that the determinant variable is the position of market power *relative to the major consumers* (symmetry or asymmetry). A strong (weak) position of market power vis-à-vis the dominant consumers is more likely to lead to the emergence of liberalization (de-liberalization) preferences.

Empirically, this is how the hypotheses play out: in the case of Japan's emergence as the top consumer of iron ore in the second half of the twentieth century, we saw coordinated domestic players face a relatively fragmented global market (Quadrant 3), or market power asymmetry in favor of Japanese consumers. This situation afforded large Japanese firms (consumers) leeway to actualize their preferences for a strategic pricing regime. The establishment of the benchmark pricing regime was a movement toward the de-liberalization of the iron ore pricing regime and was in line with Japanese market stakeholders' preferences. Japanese iron ore market stakeholders on the steel industry and financing sides enjoyed strong positions of market power vis-à-vis their own peers and had strong preferences for a negotiated, stable pricing regime. Japan's emergence in the second half of the twentieth century illustrates the de-liberalization impact a dominant, coordinated consumer can have on global markets.

We have seen that the highest likelihood of a global pricing regime change follows a movement from one asymmetric position of market power toward the opposite position of market power. The emergence of China as the world's top consumer of iron ore in the 2000s saw a fragmented consumer facing a global iron ore market that had seen its consolidation and coordination levels rise significantly (Quadrant 2). This transition from a Japanese-dominated market (Quadrant 3) to a Chinese-dominated one (Quadrant 2) illustrates a movement from one extreme asymmetric position of market power to another, opening a window of instability and increasing the probability of market institutional change at the global level. Given the fragmented nature of the Chinese domestic iron ore industry, larger market stakeholders benefiting from the possibility of extracting rents at the import interface had preferences for a strategic pricing regime. Smaller Chinese firms in a position of market vulnerability had a preference for the liberalization of the global benchmark pricing regime.

Whereas Japanese consumers' preferences held more sway during Japan's tenure as the dominant consumer of iron ore, the preferences of global iron ore suppliers became more determinant as China rose. The combination of a shift in dominance from consumers to producers and the fragmented nature of Chinese customers explains why the transition to a China-dominated iron ore market had the potential to be disruptive. The coordination failure and the fragmented procurement behavior of Chinese consumers enabled the actualization of the preferences of minor Chinese market stakeholders and dominant global iron ore producers for trade liberalization.

The case of China's impact on the global iron ore shipping regime and, more specifically, that of the Valemax saga are also situated in Quadrant 4. Here, bold moves from global iron ore shipping stakeholders were met by bold moves from Chinese domestic market stakeholders. Chinese market stakeholders, in a position of market power domestically, expressed preferences for de-liberalization. In that case, as the Chinese stakeholders were better able to coordinate market behavior across multiple interest groups, they were able to have more influence over the outcomes and successfully countered Vale's strategy. The interaction was conflictual but the deadlock was resolved through strategic bargaining. The result was incremental change in favor of Chinese stakeholders.

The potash case illustrates a transition toward a symmetric position of market power between domestic and international market stakeholders (Quadrant 4). In this instance, following the model developed here, change in global market institutions is still possible. However, change is likely to be incremental, and the result of strategic bargaining, because consumers and producers are both in positions of power. As this position involves equally powerful positions in both market realms, it can lead to stability in market institutions over time, in case of an alignment of preferences at the two levels, but it is also unpredictable because of the possibility of a deadlock or conflict between the dominant players if their preferences are misaligned. The potash case illustrates this scenario. Here, Chinese market stakeholders had a preference for a strategic pricing regime, given the strong position of market power they occupied vis-à-vis their own peers (domestic level). For the whole period of China dominance, until 2018 or so, this was also the preference of major global potash market stakeholders. The resulting pricing regime experienced continuity and strategic bargaining patterns.

The copper market provides a case located in Quadrant 1, where both consumers and producers are in relative positions of market fragmentation. This is not to say that there are no powerful players on either side of the copper market; it is simply that on the Chinese side they are much less concentrated and coordinated than in other markets, such as potash and uranium, and on the global side, copper market stakeholders are also more numerous and the market is more diffuse relative to other cases, such as for potash or iron ore. Here, given the more vulnerable positions of market power on both sides and, thus, the low capacity for influence, this situation is the least likely to lead to rapid change in global market institutions. Indeed, we have seen at most incremental change, with Chinese stakeholders unable to have much influence on global market institutions.

Finally, the uranium case is located in Quadrant 2, with Chinese market stakeholders in a position of market power on one side and relatively fragmented market stakeholders on the producer side. Here, China's emergence did not lead to a transition from one quadrant to another but it occurred within Quadrant 2, as uranium consumers prior to the 2010s (and until today) are also large civilian nuclear companies, often state-owned, that had established a pattern of large multiannual negotiated contracts prior to China's emergence. In this case, the Chinese market stakeholders have been agents of stability rather than change, with a continued preference for a negotiated pricing regime. Until now, they have fallen short of pushing for a more fully consolidated global pricing regime (in the fashion of others such as the potash pricing regime) but have also resisted financialization trends and expressed a clear preference for multiannual, longer-term contracts.

## Market Power, Coordination Capacity

The framework presented in this book only fully comes to life when grounded in a relational, multilevel, and multidimensional definition of market power (Baldwin 1980; Strange 1996).[2] Market power is defined here as market stakeholders' capacity to influence outcomes, at both the domestic and international levels, and coordination capacity is conceived as one key manifestation of market power. Asymmetry in market power provides influence over global pricing regimes and is at the root of global institutional market change.

I argue that coordination capacity is one of the key ways through which market stakeholders affect institutional change (Ostrom 1997; Hall and Soskice 2001; Hall and Gingerich 2004; Gourevitch and Shinn 2005; Gereffi et al. 2005; Wilson 2013; Radetzki 2013). Coordination capacity is the capacity of market stakeholders to work together effectively to facilitate the pursuit of common goals, and it increases bargaining power. In this book, I focus on market stakeholders' differential wielding of coordination capacity at the domestic and international levels, or the "differential ability of actors to solve their collective action problems" (Lake 2009, 224; Ostrom 1997), as the key variable we use to measure market power.

Coordination is not the only component of market power, but it is a key way through which market stakeholders can influence institutional change at the global level. Concentration is neither necessary nor sufficient to successful market coordination; indeed, coordination capacity does not depend solely on group size. However, this book adopts the (common) view that high levels of market concentration facilitate coordination and that market fragmentation increases the challenges to collective action (see, e.g., Olson 1965). Vivoda (2009b) provides a review of the literature on the relationship between (low) industry concentration and (low) bargaining power of multinational corporations. Among other authors who have identified concentration as a variable of interest, we find Rodrik (1982), Krasner (1974), Hughes and Long (2014) and Radetzki (2013). Hughes and Long (2014) investigate the link between (higher) market concentration and the potential for coercion. One of the ways in which firms can achieve a position of market power is by consolidating their market position (Gilpin 1977; Fligstein 1996). Concentration levels remain quite high in global commodity markets, and attempts at coordination have taken many forms over the past decades, even as the golden era of formal cartel arrangements has faded away.

An important conceptual characteristic of this framework is its specific focus on the differential between the coordination levels at the intersection of domestic and international markets. As a result, and throughout the case studies, particular care is devoted to assessing the capacity and quality of the coordination that takes place among global producers and Chinese stakeholders, not generally, but at the import/export interface. This is inspired by Putnam's concept of the "area of entanglement"; however, building on Putnam, I focus on a different range of relevant actors at the junction between domestic and international markets and I do not exclusively focus on the state presence at the international level (Putnam 1988). In this book, the focus is on coordination capacity on both the producer and consumer sides, among market and non-market entities that have a stake in a given market's pricing regime. Relevant market stakeholders include large, medium, and small firms, private and state-owned, government departments, industry associations, and/or the relevant international organizations. Maintaining pricing regimes—and changing pricing regimes—requires coordination, including between public and private actors.

The goal here is always to understand and explain the dynamics that have led to variation in China's impacts on global market institutions following its rise as dominant consumer in the 2000s.

## Prices and Preferences for Global Market Institutions

Price levels are without a doubt an important indicator of the state of affairs in each commodity market, given their relationship to supply and demand conditions. They influence market stakeholders' preferences and behaviors and, in turn, are influenced by them.

Price levels usually figure front and center in analyses of China's impact on commodity markets. A plethora of analysts have debated, for instance, on the importance of China's rapid rise in commodities consumption leading into the commodities price boom of the second half of the 2000s (Cuddington and Jerrett 2008; Radetzki 2012, 2006; Heap 2005), with many concluding that other factors were also behind the surge, such as capacity issues (Radetzki et al. 2008) or, in the case of grains, biofuels (Wright 2014). Many in the political science literature have also based their analysis of market stakeholder's behaviors on price levels (see the petro-political cycle model (PPC) (Wilson, 1986)). As Vivoda explains, "The PPC model posits that... in rising markets, sellers... gain leverage; in falling markets, buyers . . . gain leverage" (Vivoda 2009b, 518). Colgan, Keohane, and Van de Graaf argue that the timing of an institutional innovation in the global oil market depends on the levels of dissatisfaction, which, in turn, depend on the price—when prices rise above a certain level, consumers are dissatisfied and when prices fall below a certain level, producers are dissatisfied (Colgan et al. 2012).

Indeed, relying on deductive reasoning based on price levels, it would follow that large producers should have an interest in the liberalization of pricing regimes when supply is tight and prices are rising and in a movement toward strategic coordination, or de-liberalization, when prices are falling. On the other hand, it would follow that large consumers should have an interest in a movement toward strategic coordination when prices are rising and in liberalization when prices are falling (see Table 3.4).

This book acknowledges that the balance of supply and demand, and prices, shape the environment in which market stakeholders find themselves and, in turn, has an impact on behavior (and vice versa). However, I have chosen to not make price levels the principal focus of my inquiries for two reasons: a theoretical one and an empirical one.

First and foremost, this book is interested in global market dynamics that go beyond price levels. I am not focusing on price levels as an explanatory variable or as a possible outcome of Chinese procurement behavior—the question I ask requires that I look at other indicators and dynamics. Price levels alone cannot illustrate how China's rise has transformed market institutions; this is because market institutions themselves manifest beyond price levels. Prices do not tell us enough about market behavior or changes, given the definition of markets I adopt

*Table 3.4* **Pricing regime preferences based on price levels**

|  | **Producers** | **Consumers** |
|---|---|---|
| **Tight supply** (Prices trend up) | Competitive | Strategic |
| **Abundant supply** (Prices trend down) | Strategic | Competitive |

in this book. I define markets as multifaceted institutional ecosystems, and their analysis requires attention to qualitative institutional change (see Chapter 2). Too great of a focus on prices here would have flattened our analysis. Market institutions, whether in the presence of annual benchmarking negotiations at the global level or the resilience of relationships between producers and consumers, matter in their own right and for reasons not entirely related to price levels.

This is true for price levels as cause or consequence of a disruption such as China's rise. Market institutional changes lead to a whole host of consequences, in terms of who wins, who loses, who has power, and who has not, beyond what price levels can tell us. One can have different kinds of market institutional arrangements that lead to higher or lower price levels. One can focus on the price rises and eventual adjustments to supply levels that China's demand shock has engendered, but this misses the deeper changes in global market institutions that may accompany China's rise. On the flip side, there are dynamics aside from price levels that lead to preferences for different types of market institutions. In other words, a choice of analytical focus on price levels is not a bad one; it simply shines a light on some dynamics and obscures others. These choices have analytical consequences, as a focus on prices to the detriment of other market dynamics can make it seem as though the underlying constitutive structure of markets remained unchanged following China's rise (some say that there is no such structure, as markets are empty spaces). In other words, how global markets are understood can influence whether one thinks China is integrating into existing global market arrangements without changing the ways in which things are done. I argue that a focus on broader market institutions can unveil the deeper changes that have occurred in global commodity markets as a result of China's rise. As these changes have been unequal across markets, we need to explain them and their variation, despite the presence of similar price variations across many markets.

The second reason I chose to focus on indicators and variables other than prices is an empirical one. I study a variety of market stakeholders, which, given their varied size, structure, and positioning toward the global market, display a synchronous heterogeneity of preferences and behaviors despite a given global supply/demand/price scenario. In other words, the evidence I have gathered puts into relief market stakeholders' behaviors and preferences that do not align with the expectations outlined in Table 3.4.

At times, of course, market stakeholders do display preferences that are in line with a price-determined logic. For instance, a price-determined logic would indicate that major global iron ore producers should indeed have been keen on seeing the liberalization of the global iron ore pricing regime in 2009–2010, given the expectations of rising iron ore prices at the time. But, here, it is necessary to point out that global iron ore producers markedly differed in terms of their timing and willingness to act. Rio Tinto saw this move as short-sighted and also saw the volatility that accompanies liberalization as not being desirable. The company also wanted to maintain the stable and privileged relationship they had built with European and Japanese consumers. BHP Billiton and Vale saw things differently. The very fact that different major producers in the same market, facing the same price levels, did not have the same preferences should tell us that price levels are an insufficient determinant of preferences and ensuing behaviors.

In many more of the cases studied here, market stakeholders' preferences did not align with a price-determined logic. The simplest illustration of this state of affairs is that price movements displayed similar trends across commodities over the past twenty years, yet market stakeholders' behaviors differed in major ways across and within markets. This was true of consumers located in different countries but in the same commodity market, facing the same price trends and sharing many interests. Indeed, consumers in the same global market who face the same price trends do not always have the same preferences, given their different domestic positions as well as their relative positions toward global market stakeholders. Some market stakeholders continue to hold the same preferences despite significant changes in price trends, such as the Japanese iron ore importers who kept the same preferences for a negotiated global iron ore benchmark pricing regime during the 2000s and 2010s. Large Chinese and Japanese iron ore consumers have routinely behaved differently and expressed different preferences concurrently despite facing the same global price trends. Indeed, Japanese consumers continued to hold a strong preference for the benchmarking regime even when prices were falling.

This is also true of different consumers in the same domestic market. On the domestic side, for reasons that I argue have to do with relative market power, larger Chinese SOEs and smaller private firms have held different preferences toward the global iron ore benchmarking regime, at the same time (i.e., facing the same global prices). This variation is puzzling and suggests that sectoral or factor endowment-based explanations (Frieden and Rogowski 1996; Hiscox 2001) are not quite adapted to the study of within-market variation in preferences for global pricing regimes (not the least because they are outside-in arguments instead of inside-out).

It is important to also point out that many market actors, especially of the type this book focuses on, which includes very large state-owned and private firms as well as government entities, do not see supply or price levels as exogenous variables. In other words, market stakeholders have displayed clear and at times successful plans to alter supply/demand and/or price levels directly in their favor. What then becomes more interesting is whether and when these stakeholders are successful in doing this. In any case, the position taken here is that market stakeholders' preferences for global pricing regimes are not satisfactorily explained by focusing on price trends alone.

## Preferences

As mentioned earlier, this book does not have the space to develop a full-blown theory of preference formation in the context of two-level market power asymmetries (it focuses on behavior and outcomes). However, it does pay attention to how market stakeholders' preferences vary and it has generated a tentative hypothesis about one key driver of this variation.

Various scholarly traditions have weighed in on preferences toward the global economy. In this book, the state is not considered the main unitary actor (though state organs do play a role). However, some theories of the state as the main unitary actor serve as inspiration here. Notably, work by development economists has shown that positions of weakness (or developmental backwardness) tend to lead to preferences for economic nationalism (or, one could argue, de-liberalization), whereas positions of strength have led to preferences for liberalization (List 1909; Chang 2002). Along another line of reasoning, Lake referred to Gilpin's contribution to hegemonic stability theory when he argued that "large dominant states possess strong preferences for free and open international exchange, and, in turn, coerce, induce or persuade other states into opening their markets to foreign trade and investment" (Lake 1993, 224). Leaving aside for a moment the fact that these works were looking at a small subset of large states (the United Kingdom and the United States), and that this book does not look at unitary states, the inspiration drawn here is that there may be a relationship between positions of power or vulnerability and preferences for global economic regimes.

This book goes to a different space in two ways. First, many contributions mentioned above theorized about the preferences of great powers that were home to a liberal, Anglo-Saxon model of a capitalist economy. What are we to make of Chinese actors' preferences toward the global economy, given a different national system of political economy? Second, the contributions mentioned above tend to conceive of the state of the global economy at the apex of each great power (the UK or United States) as liberal, or open. This book problematizes the nature of global markets as being liberal by looking at global markets as institutional ecosystems that are the locus of power relations (Chapter 2). I seek to theorize about a dominant economy the size of China, home to a statist capitalist system and facing a globalized marketplace that is home to embedded relations of power.

Looking at scholarly work that has theorized about subnational preferences and disaggregated global preferences for global market institutions, we can turn to economic theories of firm behavior under situations of monopoly and oligopoly or monopsony and oligopsony. This book's argument on market power contains parallels with the work of economists and political scientists who have focused on monopolies and oligopolies (Sweezy 1939; Stigler 1947; Washburn 1978)[3] and particular firms' capacities to coordinate pricing and extract rent (or the capacity to charge above marginal cost).[4] On the political science side of things, the literature on "fragmented" preferences and foreign economic engagement is useful, specifically that in the context of Chinese politics (Mertha 2009; Shambaugh 2011; Oksenberg and Lieberthal 1988; Jones and Hameiri 2021).

This book views relative positions of market power as key to understanding preference formation. The tentative hypothesis developed here, as stated in Hypothesis (5) above, is that a stakeholder's position of market power relative to that of their peers (at the domestic and global levels) affects their preferences for global market institutions. Domestic market stakeholders are more likely to have preferences for the *liberalization* of pricing regimes when they are occupying a vulnerable position of market power relative to their own peers, in terms of their access to the global market. They are more likely to have preferences for the *de-liberalization* of pricing regimes when they occupy a strong position of market power relative to their own peers, again in terms of their access to the global market. Indeed, when key commodities consumers occupy domestic positions of power with rent-extracting privileges, this provides them with disincentives to push for the liberalization of global pricing regimes, regardless of the price levels, since they can extract benefits from their privileged access. At the global level, this is more difficult to theorize, but I shall make two points. First, having a dominant position of market power relative to *their own peers* certainly gives global market stakeholders' more leeway to influence global market institutions. Second, a position of market power relative to the dominant consumer may lead to stronger preferences for the *liberalization* of pricing regimes, whereas a more vulnerable position of market power relative to the dominant consumer may lead to stronger preferences for the *de-liberalization* of a pricing regime (this was the case of iron ore producers during the Japanese era).

This is consistent with the fact that in the case of the global iron ore pricing regime in the 2000s, large Chinese iron ore importers with positions of market power relative to their domestic peers preferred *de-liberalization*, while small- and medium-sized importers in positions of vulnerability relative to their domestic peers preferred *liberalization*. The preferences of domestic Chinese consumers do not follow a price-determined logic. Despite falling prices in the wake of the global financial crisis, large Chinese market stakeholders continued to prefer the benchmarking regime. Large Chinese consumers' positions of power relative to other Chinese consumers provided them with rent-extracting privileges and, thus, with disincentives to push for the liberalization of global pricing regimes, regardless of the price levels. Smaller Chinese consumers' positions of vulnerability relative to other, larger Chinese consumers provided them with an incentive to push for the liberalization of global pricing regimes, also quite independently from price levels. This explains small- and medium-sized Chinese consumers' preferences for a global spot market in 2010, despite rising prices. At the time, smaller Chinese iron ore consumers disregarded the Chinese Iron and Steel Association's appeals for restraint and coordination and directly contributed to the fall of the global benchmarking regime. We also know that the preferences of dominant Japanese consumers remained skewed toward the benchmarking regime, or *de-liberalization*, over time, despite huge variations in price trends.

In the case of dominant producers, I argue that they are influenced by the positions of market power they occupy relative to their own peers (a strong position provides more room to maneuver), but I make the argument that they are predominantly influenced by positions of market power relative to dominant consumers. This hypothesis is consistent with the fact that BHP Billiton is said to have been the lead mover in pushing for the fall of the iron ore benchmark pricing regime in 2009–2010, given BHP's dominant position relative to its own peers (as well as relative to Chinese consumers). It is also consistent with BHP Billiton and Vale's (and eventually Rio Tinto's as well) preference for liberalization when prices were surging, prior to the fall of the benchmarking regime, and their continued preferences for this system even when prices subsequently began to fall.

Looking at the potash case, the dominant Chinese consumers' preferences for the global benchmarking regime is consistent with the fact that they are in a position of power relative to other domestic potash consumers. Because of the licensing system and the leading small group's role in determining who negotiates with global producers, the top Chinese potash importers extract rents by reselling imported potash to other domestic consumers. Rent-extracting privileges provide dominant Chinese consumers with incentives to continue to sustain a strategic global pricing regime, despite wide variations in the price over the past twenty years. Following a price-determined logic, falling global potash prices in the mid-2010s could have been a window of opportunity for Chinese potash importers to push for the liberalization of the global potash pricing regime but, on the contrary, these importers have continued to be staunch supporters of the benchmark pricing regime. In turn, the fall of the Russia-Belarus potash cartel does not make sense from a price-determined logic. This is because in an era of rapidly falling prices, producers should have preferred a movement toward strategic pricing institutions. This development put producers in a disadvantageous position in relation to Chinese consumers.

This will not be the final word on preferences for global market institutions, but at the very least, I argue that attention to relative positions of market power yield precious insights into the ways in which market stakeholders perceive themselves in relation to global markets and that this influences their preferences and subsequent behaviors. In my view, this insight is underdetermining and simply provides the conditions under which leading market stakeholders choose to act. From this perspective, neither liberalization nor de-liberalization trends can be taken for granted and they should be explained.

## Coordination in Domestic and Global Commodity Markets

The fundamental market conditions at the Chinese domestic level—the fragmented or concentrated structure of Chinese domestic markets—are the result of path-dependent historical trajectories, the analysis of which is beyond the scope of this study (see Figure 3.1 and Table 3.5).

It is likely the case that more-fragmented domestic markets are likely more difficult to coordinate than more-concentrated ones. Yet, as is the case for global markets, levels of concentration and coordination do not perfectly covary in domestic markets (see Figure 3.2). For instance, the Chinese domestic potash market is relatively concentrated but not as much as the uranium market. However, at the interface with the international market, the potash market is more strongly coordinated—a "small group" is tasked with coordinating behavior and agreements occur to limit competition among importers. In this case, Chinese potash importers have exhibited higher coordination capacity than have uranium importers, despite the lower levels of concentration in the domestic industry (see Table 3.5).

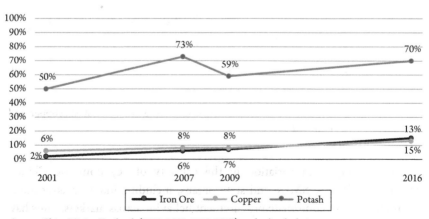

Source: China Mining Yearbook (2002, 2008, 2010, 2017), author's calculations.

*Figure 3.1* Proportion of medium and large enterprises in the Chinese domestic market

*Table 3.5* **Number of domestic Chinese extractive enterprises, 2010**

| Iron ore | Copper | Potash | Uranium |
|---|---|---|---|
| 4250 | 823 | 16 | 1[a] |

[a] Note that the article lists seven uranium mines in operation in 2010, all of which are revealed (after a search of online open sources) to be affiliated in one way or another with the China National Nuclear Corporation.

Source: *China Mining Yearbook 2011*. For uranium, (Hou et al. 2010).[a]

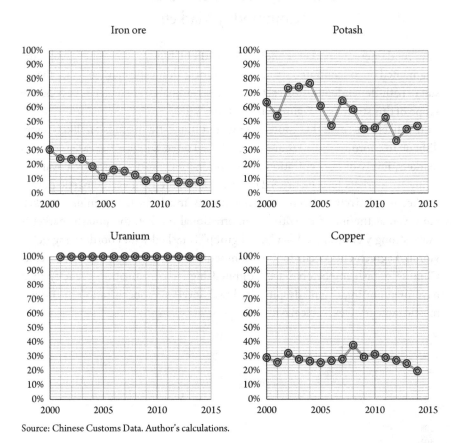

Source: Chinese Customs Data. Author's calculations.

*Figure 3.2* Proportion of top two Chinese importers in the iron ore, potash, copper, and uranium markets, 2000–2014

There is important variation in the capacity of key domestic Chinese stakeholders (SOEs, SMEs, and state organs, including industry associations and ministries) to coordinate procurement behavior across markets. They have done so with varying degrees of success, at times surmounting problems associated with collective action and at times succumbing to them.

Some of the elements that are examined to characterize the level of domestic coordination in each market at the import interface with global markets include the number of import licenses, the number of companies actually importing the resource despite the absence of a license, the share of imports by the top domestic companies, industry associations or groups of importers' capacity for control in pricing negotiations, the role of small leadership groups, and the level of preferences alignment (see Table 3.6).

Pointing out and investigating the reasons for the divergences in Chinese procurement behavior across commodities does not mean that one should be oblivious to the overall Chinese policy environment operating in the background. It is important to note that the Chinese government has issued a variety of national-level policies and regulations and developed conceptual language with a goal to, depending on the instance and with variable success on the ground, offer guidance, coordinate behavior, provide a regulatory frame, incite, detract, or punish. I will mention two of the higher-level policy frames that are particularly relevant to the procurement of commodities: the "One Third, One Third, One Third" policy and the "Two Markets, Two Resources"[5] policy.

The Two Markets, Two Resources policy was coined in the 1990s and came before and is related to the Going-Out policy (Xiao and Gao 2009; Gu and Wang 2005). The framework emphasizes the need to leverage both domestic supply sources (this includes increased investment in prospecting and mining) and international supply sources (through an array of options, including foreign acquisitions, investment, and short- and long-term purchasing

*Table 3.6* **Domestic markets—coordination levels at time of China's emergence (independent variable)**

| Domestic market | Coordination levels (at interface with global market) | |
|---|---|---|
| **China iron ore (pricing)** | Fragmented behavior, collective action problems, weak industry association, failed coordination | Low |
| **China iron ore (bulk shipping)** | Successful coordination between various stakeholders | High |
| **Japan iron ore** | Successful coordination among importers, establishment of benchmark pricing regime | Very high |
| **China potash** | Coordination between actors at interface, presence of coordinating "small groups" among key importers | Very high |
| **China uranium** | Very few actors, state involvement, some competition | High |
| **China copper** | Many importers, some attempt to coordinate | Medium |

contracts) (China—Measures Related to the Exportation of Various Raw Materials 2010, 8). As recently as April 2022, China's National Development and Reform Commission published an article extolling the potential of a Two Markets, Two Resources framework to achieve the country's development goals (*Leverage the Two Markets and Two Resources to Cultivate New Advantages in Cooperation and Competition* [利用两个市场两种资源培育合作和竞争新优势] 2022).

The One Third, One Third, One Third policy provides a similar frame, yet with a further degree specification. It has been applied to the procurement of natural resources and is more precise in its prescription. The policy frame prescribes that one-third of Chinese resource needs shall come from domestic production, one-third from direct procurement contracts, and one-third from overseas investments and acquisitions in the natural resources sector. As applied to uranium procurement, the following provides an indication of the use of both frames by analysts: "The basic principle of China's uranium policy is 'Two Markets, Two Resources,' that is, the simultaneous development of both domestic (including the development of advanced nuclear power systems or alternative nuclear power to save fuel) and international resources (through cross-border acquisitions, investments and long-term contracts). In 2020, China's natural uranium supply situation will be one-third from domestic production, one-third from direct procurement from foreign suppliers, and one-third from the production of uranium mines held overseas by China" (*How China Should Deal with Overseas Uranium Dependence* [中国如何应对海外铀依赖] 2012).

The precision of the policy prescription also arguably made procurement strategies more likely to fall short of the One Third, One Third, One Third policy frame. In some markets, China has been able to approach this framework a little more closely, for example in the potash market, where domestic production has fulfilled close to 50 percent of overall demand for nearly a decade. In other markets, such as iron ore or indeed uranium, China's insufficient domestic resource endowments coupled with a difficult international investment environment have made this a difficult goal to achieve.

These policy frames, just like the Going-out policy, have offered important macro guiding sets of incentives in policy and regulatory tools that have provided informal and formal framing and incentivized the behavior of Chinese market stakeholders in each of the markets studied here. However, despite these common general frames, and despite many important similarities in the general governance of commodity markets in China, the divergences in Chinese behaviors and in the global outcomes remain significant. The goal of this book is to explain why.

*Table 3.7* **Global commodity markets—coordination levels at the time of China's emergence (independent variable)**

| International market | Coordination levels | |
|---|---|---|
| **Iron ore** | Strong oligopoly<br>Annual benchmarking negotiations | High |
| **Iron ore (Japan era)** | Fragmented | Low |
| **Potash** | Two formal cartel-like organizations, annual benchmarking negotiations | Very high |
| **Uranium** | Few producers, but low coordination, no annual benchmarking negotiations | Low |
| **Copper** | Presence of many actors, competitive market dynamics | Very low |

At the global level, similar to the domestic level, concentration and coordination do not always covary. Equally concentrated markets, or oligopolies, do not necessarily coordinate behavior in the same way or successfully at all. The case studies in this book paint a portrait of the varying market ecosystems in place and the varying coordination capacities present among global market stakeholders, despite relatively high levels of concentration across the board. As a case in point, the market for uranium exhibited relatively high levels of market concentration (in 2000, four countries contributed 88 percent of global uranium production)[6] and the potash market was also highly concentrated (in 2000, four countries contributed 73 percent of global potash production)[7]. However, global uranium market players had not developed institutionalized cooperative relations. Hence, in the uranium market, we saw the characteristics of a relatively concentrated yet segmented global market. However, in the global potash market, we see higher levels of coordination in the form of highly institutionalized export arrangements among major suppliers. Table 3.7 presents levels of coordination in global markets, for all four commodities, at the time of China's (or Japan's) emergence.

## Building Blocks: Heterogeneity, Vulnerability, Resonance

The argument in this book builds on three strands of the literature that have something to say about China's impact on the global economy: the literature on global China, the global and comparative political economy literatures on the resonance between the domestic and global political economy, and the classical political economy literature on the role of market power. Let me take each in turn.

## The Literature on Global China

An ongoing, lively debate is occurring on the ways in which China will transform the global economy and the international order, at the confluence of the literature on global and comparative political economy, international relations, and Chinese politics.

Earlier iterations of this debate, especially in the 2000s and particularly in the international relations literature, have tended to characterize China's rise in dichotomous terms; in other words, whether China was likely to integrate or disrupt the global economy, international institutions, or the (liberal) international order. This framing was deeply influenced by Iain Johnston's 2003 article "Is China a Status Quo Power?" (despite the author problematizing the concept of revisionism and concluding with a nuanced assessment of China's foreign policy). Subsequent arguments have often fallen on one or the other side of the debate, with caveats.

Revisionist scenarios, which have gained ground in recent years, foresee China's rise, its illiberal preferences, assertive behavior, state-centered economic development, and thirst for resources as leading to destabilizing behavior on the global stage and conflict (Economy 2010; Vivoda 2009a; Mearsheimer 2010; Mearsheimer 2014; Jacques 2009; Calder 1996; Bremmer 2010; Kane and Serewicz 2001; Ellis 2009; Leonard 2013). As this position has become dominant, it has assembled a wide variety of arguments and assumptions, some liberal, some realist.[8] We find here the whole gamut of approaches, from more-structuralist, hegemonic transition arguments to more-liberal normative assessments of the weakening of the liberal international order. In the political economy literature, some argue that China's impact will be destabilizing because of the nature of the Chinese domestic economic model—its state-centered economy—and the likelihood that it will project these dynamics abroad. Delineated specifically in the case of China's impact on global resource markets, the revisionist argument goes as follows, enunciated—and then refuted—by Economy and Levi:

> Chinese investment in overseas resources is transforming the commodities world from one governed mainly by free markets to one in which China locks up reserves and creates its own mercantilist system for trade. Western companies, previously used to competing with each other on commercial terms, now face Chinese state-owned

behemoths that secure resource deals by using every level of the Chinese government—and availing themselves of ultra-cheap loans—to beat the competition, shifting the balance of economic power from free markets to state capitalism in the process. (Economy and Levi 2014, 5–6)

As we have seen and will cover again below, this book takes the view that this frame is not useful in assessing the positioning of China vis-à-vis the global economy.

On the other side of the debate as traditionally framed, status quo scenarios have predicted that China is more likely to integrate into existing international economic institutions (Ikenberry 2008; Johnston 2003; Steinfeld 2010; Buzan and Cox 2013; Nolan 2012; Bergsten et al. 2008; Andrews-Speed et al. 2002; Houser 2008). This side of the debate has seen a marked deflation in recent years as a new consensus emerged in the Western literature on global China. More than a decade ago, in an oft-quoted piece, Ikenberry argued that "China [would] integrate into the liberal international order" because it has "already discovered the massive economic returns that are possible by operating within this open-market system" (Ikenberry 2008, 29–30). At the time, instead of emphasizing China's rationale for pursuing status quo options, some scholars in the liberal tradition instead highlighted the post-hegemonic endurance of global liberal economic institutions (Ruggie 1982; Ikenberry 2012) as well as the constraining forces of economic interdependence (Keohane and Nye 1977; Nye 2019). Here, proponents argued that China would continue to (predominantly) integrate into the global economy either because it is in China's interest and Chinese stakeholders are making a conscious choice to do so or because China is too weak in the face of entrenched global liberal institutions. Some in the realist tradition have argued that, at this point, it is simply not in China's interest to challenge United States hegemony. I would argue that, in recent years, this side of the debate has shifted its emphasis to calling out what are perceived as exaggerated claims made by others on the China as revisionist power side of the debate.

But as has already become apparent, characterizing the debate in these dichotomous terms is not constructive and severely limits our discussion. Many authors have made this point. Johnston argues that "the current status quo versus revisionist binary . . . makes no conceptual sense in a world of multiple and often inconsistent orders" (Johnston 2019, 58). As Jones and Hameiri explain, "the IR literature on China's rise is enormous, but the debate has consolidated and stalled around two basic positions. . . . Unfortunately, ample evidence exists to support both positions. . . . Chinese behavior actually displays revisionist and status quo orientations simultaneously" (Jones and Hameiri 2021, 4–7).

Indeed, dividing the debate into these two categories cannot satisfactorily illustrate the evolution in Chinese behavior over the past two decades. The international context is changing fast, uniform Chinese preferences seem elusive, and, in addition, there is too much variation to neatly fit into an either/or scenario.

## The China as Heterogeneous Power Literature

Over the years, global China scholars have developed a nuanced understanding of the variation in China's behavior internationally. This emerging body of literature has been built on one foundational notion: the concurrent heterogeneity of Chinese behaviors and impacts abroad. For this reason I shall call it the *China as heterogeneous power literature*.

Iain Johnston undertook one of the most exhaustive efforts to characterize this variation. In his 2019 article, he provides a rich analysis of the variation in China's behavior across global orders (constitutive, military, political and social development, trade, finance, environment, and information) occurring at the same time (Johnston 2019). Johnston argues that "there is no single international order that defines whether a state is a challenger/revisionist or not" (2019, 25)—this is consistent with Colgan's recent book on partial hegemony (Colgan 2021)—and finds that China's support for different orders goes from low (political development order), to medium (global financial and trade orders), to high (constitutive order—sovereignty, territoriality) (2019, 57). In sum, he notes "that there is less to the liberal international order than many believe, and ... China's challenge to order is less deep and/or wide than the current narrative suggests" (2019, 12).

The *China as heterogeneous power literature* has five emergent characteristics. First, it is firmly grounded in empirical research in Chinese politics, political economy, or foreign policy. Second, it is attuned to the relationship between domestic and international dynamics. Third, it tends not to view China as *sui generis* and beyond comparison with other large states. Indeed, as Nathan argues, it "see[s] all actors (including Western actors) as engaged in a contest to shape such norms and institutions" (Nathan 2016, 167). Fourth, it is interested in explaining the variation in Chinese international behaviors and their impacts on global institutions. Fifth, it tends not to think of the debate about China and the global economy in binary terms, or as *whether or not* China may cause change, but as how, when, and why it does so.

The heterogeneous power literature is one of the most important and stimulating bodies of recent research in the literature on global China. Before going further, I offer a note on sequential versus concurrent variation: the novelty of this literature has been to focus on the simultaneous presence of fundamentally different international behavior on behalf of China. However, a few authors who may identify with the spirit of this literature have instead focused on the variation in Chinese behavior *across time* (Fung 2016; Wuthnow 2012). For the purposes of this discussion, I chose to focus here on authors who more directly discuss *concurrent* variation in Chinese behavior.

In this literature, we can see the contours of three interrelated approaches to the study of variation in Chinese behavior. All of the authors work to delineate Chinese behaviors—and their variations—in different issue areas, but the types of explanations offered for this variation differ. First, there are authors who trace these variations back to variations in domestic interests and argue that the Chinese have been able to act coherently on these interests (Kennedy and Cheng 2012; Wang and French 2014; Nathan 2016; Mazarr et al. 2018; Weiss and Wallace 2021).

An early effort to characterize the variation in Chinese behaviors across a range of issue areas was provided by Scott Kennedy in the introduction to his coedited volume (Kennedy and Cheng 2012). Kennedy argues that "the Chinese government approaches global governance through the lens of China's own development priorities" (Kennedy and Cheng 2012, 14). The volume provides an overview of eleven different Chinese approaches to different issue areas internationally, from the governance of global health to climate change and the World Trade Organization.

Wang and French (2014) examine China's behavior across distinct areas within global economic governance (trade, foreign direct investment, finance, and development aid). They find that Chinese behavior varies from the conservative, that is, mostly following existing rules (for trade and foreign direct investment), to the "anti-status quo" (for finance and development aid governance), and they argue that this is due to China's divergent economic interests in each of these areas.

In 2016, Andrew Nathan asked how China behaved with respect to the international system, with an eye for the logic of Chinese preferences in different regimes. He did not find "a pattern of promoting a distinctive 'Chinese model'" (Nathan 2016, 189). He argued that China is more compliant than not in a broad range of international regimes, from international finance to arms control and UN peacekeeping, in a way that is consistent with its interests.

Mazarr, Heath, and Cevallos argue that China's approach to UN-centric global orders (such as the UN system, the global trade order, or the multilateral security order) has been mostly conciliatory, whereas China's approach to the U.S.-centric global security order, much less so.

Finally, in their 2021 article, Weiss and Wallace ask, "How do the domestic politics of an authoritarian state such as the PRC affect whether it seeks to engage or reshape the international order as it grows in power and influence?" (2021, 639). The authors identify areas where China has worked within the confines of established norms (WTO, IMF, UNSC) and others where it has sought to undermine these norms (International Tribunal for the Law of the Sea, ITLOS). They also identify two domestic variables as shaping China's behavior across the constitutive components of international order: centrality and heterogeneity. In interesting ways, the argument developed in this book, which focuses on market power as measured by the capacity for coordination versus fragmentation, overlaps with Weiss and Wallace's concept of heterogeneity, which they define as the "degree of domestic division and contestation over government policy regarding a given international issue" (Weiss and Wallace 2021, 651). However, whereas the authors effectively conclude that "low heterogeneity" leads to more-assertive behavior, and "high heterogeneity" leads to more-conciliatory behavior/partial implementation, I find a more counterintuitive, contingent relationship between Chinese coordination capacity, or market power, and global outcomes. In the cases studied here, where there was low coordination capacity, or when the Chinese stakeholders could not "get their act together" very effectively, we have one case where the impact on global institutions was very disruptive (if unintended), and another one where the impact on global market institutions was very small. On the other hand, in cases where there was high coordination capacity, where Chinese stakeholders had more market power, we also find one case where the impact on global institutions was less disruptive and one where it was more disruptive. The argument made in this book is that a key variable necessary to explain China's behavior is the particular international context present in each case. In other words, Chinese coordination capacity does not tell us enough on its own. It needs to be comprehended in relation to the coordination capacity present at the global level. In other words, the determination I make of Chinese stakeholders' market power is relational.

A second category of authors in the *China as heterogeneous power* literature have developed more-complex explanations for the variation in Chinese behavior across issue areas that focus either on the interaction of domestic and international variables or on the fragmented nature of Chinese preferences. Here, I would include the pioneering work of Foot and Walter (2010), as well as the more recent work of Kastner, Pearson, and Rector (2018); Tiberghien (2020); and Jones and Hameiri (2021).[9]

One of the earliest exemplars of the China as heterogeneous power literature was Foot and Walter (2011), who sought to understand the extent to which China and the United States' behaviors were consistent with global norms in distinct issue areas. The research question propelling their book was innovative for at least two reasons: (1) it compared the behavior of the United States and China without assuming certain trends a priori; and (2) it took seriously the variation in behavior on behalf of both countries across different global issue areas and over time. Three causes were identified as explaining the variation in the United States and China's behavioral consistencies with global norms: levels of domestic significance, legitimacy and fairness, and effect on the global distribution of power. In their book, Foot and Walter characterized the consistency of Chinese norms as anywhere from low (Responsibility to Protect, or R2P), to "gradually higher with some areas of inconsistencies" (financial regulation), while the evaluation of the United States found levels of consistency from low to high. The authors concluded that "neither China nor the United States exhibit consistently high levels of behavioural conformity across a range of global normative frameworks.... The stances of both countries towards such frameworks often differ substantially, though not inversely.... There is also a broad tendency for both countries to exhibit lower levels of behavioural consistency in areas of high domestic social and political significance" (Foot and Walter 2010, 279).

Kastner, Pearson, and Rector also take as a point of departure the fact that "China's behavior in global governance, and in particular with regard to regime creation and maintenance, has exhibited considerable variation across cases and, often, over time within cases" (Kastner et al. 2018, 5). They see China as one example of a rising state in its relationship to preexisting multilateral regimes. The argument they put forward is that China will tend to "invest" in either existing or new international regimes when its options are seen as unfavorable. Conversely, when the balance of outside options is seen as favorable, China will tend to either "accept" existing regimes (when it is not seen as indispensable) or "hold-up" its participation (as leverage, when it is seen as indispensable to the regime in question).

Yves Tiberghien has also theorized about concurrent variations in Chinese behavior across international issue areas (climate, trade, development finance, cyber and energy governance, etc.). Tiberghien argues against a reading of Chinese behavior as being the result of a coherent grand strategy and instead argues that China's behavior is the result of gradual, interactive, and hybrid dynamics, which lead to variation in its behavior across policy areas. Tiberghien roots his explanation, of this variation in domestic dynamics and frames, in the status of each global space and in the mediated interactions that occur between powerful states in each area. As domestic dynamics and frames vary across domains, global outcomes also vary across domains (Tiberghien 2020).

In their book *Fractured China*, Lee Jones and Shahar Hameiri (2021) weigh in on this debate and argue that the variation in Chinese international behavior is the outcome of contestation between the central party-state and a variety of subnational actors that can influence, interpret, or ignore central attempts at shaping behavior: "Chinese behaviour abroad is often not the product of a coherent grand strategy, but results from a sometimes-chaotic struggle for power and resources among contending politico-business interests" (Jones and

Hameiri 2021, abstract). The authors zero in on the "coordinated/fragmented behaviour on China's part" (18).

I similarly take issue with common characterizations of coherent and unitary Chinese behavior. In ways that are coherent with Jones and Hameiri, but that are applied to the field of global commodity markets, I argue that Chinese economic behavior abroad is the result of "sometimes-chaotic" and not always successful attempts at coordination among different Chinese market actors.

Third, a smaller group of scholars has made efforts to trace and explain the varying *impacts* on global institutions that Chinese behavior abroad causes as well as the role of global stakeholders in responding to Chinese actions. Because global institutional change is difficult to trace, given its interactive nature, and because (until recently) we had more limited empirical evidence of institutional change as a result of China's rise, few authors have concentrated on the outcomes of Chinese behavior (as opposed to the behavior itself). In their book *Fractured China*, Jones and Hameiri build an argument to explain the outcomes of Chinese foreign policy behaviors. They argue that these outcomes are "shaped both by China's state transformation processes in particular policy domains, and by how these dynamics interact with struggles for power and resources in recipient societies" (Jones and Hameiri 2021, 14).

This book is a contribution to the emergent *China as heterogeneous power* literature I characterize here, especially the second and third categories. It belongs to the second category because the explanation I develop considers the fragmented nature of the Chinese domestic political economy as well as the interaction of domestic and international variables. This book also belongs to the third category, as it focuses at least an equal part of its efforts on tracing the changes in global market institutions as a result of China's rise and the significant role global stakeholders play in shaping these outcomes.

Authors in this body of literature have mostly theorized about the variation in Chinese behavior and its impacts across distinct, broadly conceived areas of international affairs (trade, climate change, international trade, non-proliferation, development assistance, etc.). This book applies similar insights to the study of one area of the global political economy, global commodities. Few authors theorize about China's impact on the global economy from the perspective of heterogeneity. I go even further and focus on the variation in Chinese stakeholders' behavior within one single global commodity market. The equivalent in another area of global affairs would be to compare Chinese stakeholders' behavior across different environmental regimes and also to parse out the variation in distinct Chinese stakeholders' behaviors within each regime, for instance. By investigating Chinese behavior in the same area of the global economy (commodities), I have been able to, in effect, control for certain dynamics that are prevalent in this specific area and zoom in with greater granularity on the domestic and international determinants of the variation I observe.

## China's Market Vulnerability

I identify a paradox in this book—it is that China, as large and dominant its economy is in the world of commodity markets, finds itself at times in a position of vulnerability. This position of vulnerability manifests itself in at least four ways. China is vulnerable in the markets I study because it is import dependent for more than (or close to) 50 percent of its domestic needs. China is also vulnerable because of the fact that its rise was so rapid and on such a scale that it was more challenging for it to invest in global mining production to ensure market stability, as Japan had done in the decades prior. The speed and scale of China's rise was simply too much to handle for global mining production and this led to a price volatility that was not in China's favor.

Third, at the time of its rise, China entered a global commodities space already dominated by other large companies, with the most productive mining assets having already been discovered and exploited (Nolan 2012). In turn, certain market institutions were already entrenched, which meant China had to navigate the lay of the land as a latecomer.

There is a fourth aspect to China's vulnerability, which I label "market power vulnerability" in this book. This refers to the market power differentials experienced by Chinese stakeholders in given markets, given China's domestic political economy. Indeed, given China's particular industrial and development history, some of its domestic markets, such as the iron ore and copper markets, are more fragmented than those of other rising economies before it, such as the United States or Japan. When this fragmentation is coupled with a global market that is particularly concentrated and coordinated, this puts Chinese market stakeholders in a position of vulnerability. In the case of iron ore, China experienced all four types of vulnerability. This has hamstrung China's capacity to manage its procurement strategy and has led to outcomes that were the opposite to what key Chinese stakeholders had wanted to achieve. In two of the other cases studied in this book, the potash and copper markets, China is home to the three first types of vulnerabilities: high import dependence, rapid rise, and late arrival in global commodity markets, but less to the fourth type: relative market vulnerability. In the case of the uranium market, China experienced high import dependence and rapid rise but was much less exposed to the two other kinds of vulnerability: late arrival and relative domestic fragmentation.

What does the broader literature have to say about the relationship between vulnerability and international behavior?[10] One can find arguments for and against the fact that large states' positions of vulnerability are linked with more-assertive behavior on the global stage. Similarly with positions of strength.[11] A number of approaches, including some realist ones, associate rising relative power in a large state (and a disrupted global balance of power) with the likelihood of more-assertive behavior (Waltz 1959; Mearsheimer 2001). Power transition theorists have also argued that a rise in a large state's power would increase the likelihood of disruptive behavior (Organski 1958). This assumption of a relationship between the rising power of a large state and more-assertive behavior in the global economy finds itself in government policy documents. In one of many examples, the U.S. Department of State argues that "the PRC wields its vast economic power globally to bring countries under its sway" (Policy Planning Staff 2020).

In an important effort to nuance these arguments, Keohane, while discussing realist theory, explained that, in fact, states did not seek to maximize power at all times, but only when they are vulnerable. "States concerned with self-preservation do not seek to maximize their power when they are not in danger. . . . [T]hey moderate their efforts when their positions are secure. Conversely, they intensify their efforts when danger arises, which assumes that they were not maximizing them under more benign conditions" (Keohane 1989, 47). Similarly, Kupchan argued that heightened perceptions of vulnerability led states to adopt self-defeating behaviour (Kupchan, 1994).

This is more consistent with another important frame in international relations. Scholarship on the security dilemma suggests that perceptions of relative insecurity lead states to adopt behavior that may in turn increase the insecurity of their peers (Hertz 1950).[12] In a political economy context, one could extrapolate to say that perceptions of market vulnerability may lead to cycles of defensive economic measures that would result in the other side responding in kind with similar measures, whereas those dynamics would be less likely in contexts where there are fewer concerns about relative market insecurity. Following a parallel logic, authors have argued that when vulnerabilities emerge as a consequence of economic interdependence, because of either opportunity costs (Baldwin 1980) or negative expectations (Copeland 2015), states may be more assertive or disruptive. Some authors have also theorized about the insecurity of great powers and its relationship with grand nationalist projects (Musgrave and Nexon 2018).[13] Here, the authors argue that periods of vulnerability may lead states to invest in projects that would not otherwise make sense economically or militarily, to accrue or confirm their global status.

A number of China scholars have in fact followed this line of reasoning when discussing the notion of vulnerability (variously labeled fragility, weakness, or incapacity). Most famously, Susan Shirk argued in her 2007 book *China, Fragile Superpower* that China has faced the following paradox: "The more developed and prosperous the country becomes, the more insecure and threatened they feel" (5). She reminds us that "China may be an emerging superpower, but it is a fragile one" (6). But what are we to make of the consequences of fragility or insecurity on China's behavior? Speaking about Taiwan, Shirk argues that "[T]he more confident a leader feels of his power, the better able he is to take a restrained, flexible approach" (2007, 18). Here, a relationship is posited between confidence, or the lack of vulnerability, and more conciliatory behavior.

Other China scholars have theorized about the relationship between domestic constraints or fragility and China's behavior abroad. In her study of Chinese nationalism, Jessica Chen Weiss elaborates on the linkages between "state incapacity" and foreign policy stances in the context of a government's ability to contain nationalist protests (Weiss 2014, 36). Weiss's rationale is that a state with weaker capacity to suppress protests will find itself constrained on the international stage. In other words, protests in the context of state incapacity, or vulnerability, are linked with reduced flexibility and more uncompromising or hawkish foreign policy stances.[14] Along the same lines, Ross argues that the source of "strident Chinese diplomacy ... reflects the regime's spiraling domestic confidence and its increasing dependence on nationalism for domestic stability" (Ross 2011, 46). Many others have also argued that China's domestic dynamics constrain its behavior internationally (Gill 2007; Gries 2020). Here again, positions of vulnerability are understood to lead to less-conciliatory behavior.[15]

The China scholars reviewed in the two preceding paragraphs tend to articulate a rationale for the use of more-assertive behavior based on domestic variables. In this book, I argue that a more complete picture of China's vulnerabilities and resulting behavior should take into account dynamics that are based on a more relational and contextualized understanding in each case—or the specific configuration of domestic-global market vulnerability in a particular market. This is to say, trying to understand China's behavior based on domestic variables alone gives a partial picture of the dynamics that underpin it.

Other scholars of China have also adopted a more interactive framework, where China's position and preferences are understood to derive from the relative position it occupies vis-à-vis other dominant powers. Taylor Fravel, in his 2008 book *Strong Borders, Secure Nation*, explains that "China has been more likely to compromise in its territorial conflicts and less likely to use force than many policy analysts assert, theories of international relations predict, or scholars of China expect" (Fravel 2008, 286). Fravel argues that in situations of domestic insecurity, states may be more likely to compromise. But China has been most likely to use force in situations where its bargaining power relative to another state was threatened or weakened. Here, overall insecurity (arising from domestic or international threats) may have led to compromise with bordering states, whereas relative insecurity vis-à-vis other large powers in the specific context of a border dispute has led to the use of force. Yves Tiberghien also adopts an interactive framework, paying attention to the varying characteristics of the external environment in which China operates. Tiberghien argues that "Where China finds significant systemic space in a permissive global order, it may act as a systemic stabilizer or systemic balancer, depending on the domestic frames. Where China faces limited space or even threatening actions by a traditional power, it acts either as a systemic innovator or as a systemic disruptor" (Tiberghien 2020). Tiberghien argues that China is most likely to adopt disruptive behavior in situations of vulnerability at both the domestic and international levels.

Much of this scholarly work addresses vulnerability in the broader context of international affairs and security. In this book, I claim that consideration of relative market vulnerability in the context of China's rise as major commodities consumer also leads to important insights. If we can deduce a general argument from the various strands of the global China literature covered above, it is that for a large power, positions of vulnerability may decrease the likelihood of conciliatory behavior on the global stage. This book's findings indeed suggest that market power vulnerability may be one determinant of disruptive behavior. For instance, in the iron ore case, I argue that positions of market vulnerability toward global market players have led Chinese market stakeholders to have a more disruptive impact than was the case when Chinese stakeholders were in a position of market power, such as in the uranium market.

What we can theorize about relative positions of market power is less clear. In the cases studied in this book, positions of market power have resulted in a range of behaviors, including assertive but also rule-taking behavior. The presence of more room to maneuver for Chinese stakeholders at the global level does seem compatible with more-conciliant or at least institution-preserving (if not less self-interested) behavior. More research is needed, in a greater diversity of cases, to specify exactly under which conditions a position of market power will lead to more- or less- conciliatory behavior.

More work remains to be done to further theorize about China's vulnerability in the global political economy. How can we think about vulnerability in a disaggregated way, looking at subnational actors with diverging interests? In this book, I take some steps in this direction and theorize about the effect of positions of market vulnerability relative to one's own peers, on preferences for global market arrangements. In the Chinese iron ore market, there are more-vulnerable and less-vulnerable market stakeholders. Differentiating between their preferences and behaviors is critical to explaining outcomes. Indeed, both groups exhibit some vulnerability toward global producers but also have different relations of market power among each other. I argue that this leads to distinct preferences and behaviors toward market institutions at the global level, where domestically powerful—yet globally vulnerable—stakeholders may be more likely to prefer noncompetitive market solutions but have little capacity to actualize their preferences.

One last note on the notion of vulnerability is in separating China's market size and its capacity to effectively organize to wield power, relative to other global players. As has become clear by now, Chinese positions of vulnerability do not mean an absence of, or a reduced impact on, global market institutions. In fact, it is a reality of China's market heft that it may have large impacts on the global economy *whether Chinese stakeholders want it or not* and, I may add, whether this impact goes *in their preferred direction or not*. Many of the impacts I investigate in this book are the *unintended* consequences of Chinese behavior, in the context of market power differentials.[16]

## Resonance between the Domestic and Global Political Economy

This book's argument builds on the global political economy literature that has sought to theorize about the relationship between domestic and international phenomena.[17] Contributions to this literature have often been focused in one of two directions: the role of domestic politics in explaining foreign policy or international behavior ("inside-out") (Katzenstein 1976) and the role of international dynamics in explaining domestic political (economy) outcomes ("outside-in") (Rogowski 1989; Hiscox 2001). Discussing this relationship, Peter Gourevitch argued that, in this regard, international relations scholarship is mainly interested in domestic politics as an explanatory variable ("inside-out" or "second image"), while the comparativist scholarship is mainly interested in international politics as an explanatory variable ("outside-in" or "second image reversed") (Gourevitch 1978).

While this book is in many ways closer to the "inside-out" than the "outside-in" tradition and builds on the work of scholars who have theorized about the domestic foundations of international (economic) behavior (Seabrooke 2007; Bates 1997; Gourevitch and Shinn 2005), it also conceives both dependent and independent variables and their relationship in ways that are slightly different from these traditions.

First, given the range of stakeholders considered in the causal narratives at both the domestic and international levels, the approach here goes beyond unitary states. This book also seeks to explain more than "the determinants of the foreign economic policies of states" (Katzenstein et al. 1998). Indeed, the dependent variable, global pricing regimes, is located at the global level, beyond national boundaries.

More important, beyond strictly outside-in or inside-out arguments, this book focuses on interactive features between domestic and international stakeholders and institutions. In this way it builds on the legacy of Robert Putnam's two-level games (Putnam 1988; Mo 1994). This book thus theorizes about the mutual influence of domestic- and global-level variables. In doing that, it focuses on a key space of interaction: the interface of domestic and international markets.

Efforts that go beyond the inside-out–outside-in divide in studying China's impact on the global economy are few and far between (Chin 2007). I argue that China's impact on global markets cannot be fully understood by looking at either the domestic or international dynamics. The interrelation of domestic and international variables reveals the full picture (Buthe 2014). In other words, the explanatory variables identified in this book are situated at both the domestic and international levels.

In one of the most theoretically rich political economy analyses of a non-energy global commodity market, the coffee market, Bates argues that nations' policies toward the global coffee market are defined domestically in processes structured by institutions (Bates 1997). In his book, Bates studied the relationship between one global commodity market and the varying domestic politics of producer countries. This setup did not allow him to evaluate whether there was something about this particular global market that also had causal power. In this book, the selection of cases that vary at both the international and domestic levels allows us to evaluate the causal dynamics at both levels.

In her book *Disaggregating China, Inc.*, Yeling Tan engages with this literature. Tan argues that "WTO entry provoked a divergence of policy responses within the state. Moving beyond frameworks that organize responses to globalization in binary terms such as protectionism or liberalization, I show that these responses draw from three competing state strategies, or philosophies of economic governance: market-substituting (directive), market-shaping (developmental) and market-enhancing (regulatory)" (Tan 2021).

In interesting ways, this book is like a mirror to Tan's. I write a story about the divergence of China's impacts on global markets, while she writes about the divergence of Chinese domestic responses following its entry into the WTO. Tan argues that globalization is mediated by fragmented state structures in China. I argue that varying political economic structures—in China and in global markets—mediate China's impact abroad. Here, I emphasize the resonance dynamics between domestic Chinese markets and international markets. Again, instead of adopting a purely inside-out perspective, I focus on the interaction of domestic and international actors in each market.

Another recent book on China's overseas aid and lending programs, including the Belt and Road Initiative (BRI), delves into profound domestic economic roots of China's economic and policy behavior globally (Dreher et al. 2022). The authors find that contrary to the speculation, much of which argues that the

BRI represents China's intention to reshape the global order, the fundamental motivation of the BRI is to manage structural domestic economic issues. More specifically, the motivation is to overcome challenges of the oversupply of foreign currency and the high level of industrial overproduction and to secure the natural resources needed for continued economic growth. Overall, the authors argue that the BRI and China's lending activities internationally are less about foreign policy goals and more about solving domestic challenges, an argument that dovetails with this book's argument.

## Role of Market Power in the Political Economy

The notion of market power is critical to this book's argument. In this sense, the book builds on three topics in the literature. First, the classical political economy literature grounds the analysis and focuses on market power relations in domestic and global markets (cf. Carr 1939; Gilpin 1977; Kirshner 2003). As mentioned in Chapter 2, the work of Susan Strange is important in this regard, in terms of both the conceptualization of power and in being attuned to the presence of power relations in global markets in the first place. As such, classical political economy provides the foundations of this manuscript's core argument: relative market power is key to explaining global market change.

This book is cognizant of the role market power plays in market change and it builds on the various strands of the political economy literature that have theorized about the relationship between great powers and the nature of the global economy, including the literature on the "infant industry" theory (List 1909; Chang 2002) or even hegemonic stability theory (HST) (Krasner 1976; Keohane 1980). Various "infant industry" or HST scholars have argued that dominant powers will tend to prefer open markets: "[L]arge dominant states possess strong preferences for free and open international exchange, and, in turn, coerce, induce or persuade other states into opening their markets to foreign trade and investment" (Krasner 1976; Gilpin 1987, in Lake 2009, 224). This scholarship is important because there are few places to look for power-centric discussions of the relationship between large states and global economic market structures. Nevertheless, HST contains within it the seeds of an important insight: there exist power relations in all markets, whether competitive or managed, and periods of increasing openness by some measures (such as reduction in tariffs) have not resulted in "open fields," even in the heyday of the last wave of globalization in the 1990s or 2000s. This was especially the case in global commodity markets, where levels of concentration were high and where the fact that most high-quality mines were in many cases already in operation limited the options of any new market entrants of the size of China.

The literature on neomercantilism and economic nationalism is also germane to this book (Helleiner 2021; Baldwin 2020; Humphreys 2013), and much attention is devoted to Chinese state policies and attempts to consolidate the mining industry or to increase market power at the global level. Two caveats are in order: this book pays attention to the variation in the power and interests of the various Chinese and international market stakeholders beyond the state. Second, the Chinese state may have had some ambitions for its place in global markets, but a sufficiently large number of stakeholders with different interests, as well as positions of market vulnerability have blunted its capacity to actualize its preferences at the global level

Indeed, a central argument in this book is that Chinese state (and other) actors were not always able to effect change in their preferred direction. As indicated above, many scholars have highlighted the ways in which China has been able to use its growing size and power abroad. It is doing some of that in global commodity markets as well. But this book also shows that, in fact, at key moments and in different markets, the dominant sentiment on the part of Chinese commodity market stakeholders was one of frustration and disadvantage. Whether China is actually in a powerful position despite being the dominant consumer is not something we should take for granted.

## Conclusion

This chapter presented a framework that explains the diverging global commodity market outcomes resulting from the dramatic and contemporary expansion of China's economy and the variation in Chinese market stakeholders' capacity to shape global commodity markets in their preferred direction. Much has been written on Chinese positions of power. But this work argues that we have to focus more of our attention on Chinese and global market stakeholders' relative positions of market power and vulnerability, their interactions, and the consequent variation in global market outcomes. A focus on market power asymmetries at both the domestic and global levels unveils the full chain of interactions, from the domestic to the international level. This is an argument in favor of understanding the resonance between the global economy and its systemically significant players. The framework developed traces global outcomes from the determinants of Chinese foreign behavior, the interaction of Chinese stakeholders with their global counterparts, and the eventual market changes.

In doing so, and in highlighting the variation in how this change manifests itself, this book's framework builds on an emerging strand of the global China literature, labeled here the literature on *China as a heterogeneous power*, which seeks to characterize and explain the variation in Chinese behavior internationally.

Together with this growing body of literature, it pushes our understanding of China's interaction with the global economy by problematizing perceptions of uniformity both at the level of global markets and at the level of Chinese behavior.

Reconceptualizing global markets as diverse institutional ecosystems, and being attuned to variation in Chinese behavior, contributes needed nuance to debates about the resilience of global economic institutions to the arrival of China as a systemically relevant economic actor.

# 4

# China's Impact on the Global Iron Ore Market

> China is the largest iron ore importer, and it thought that this would provide it with a strong hand to influence the market, but it found itself in a position of weakness, and it doesn't know what to do about it. (Interview 7, Academic at a Chinese university, 2012)

## Market Power, Market Vulnerability, and Market Change

In 2009, the China Iron and Steel Association (CISA), a powerful industry association that represents the interests of its member companies—many of them state-owned—and coordinates policy with central government organs, was leading benchmark pricing negotiations with the "Big Three" global iron ore producers (Rio Tinto, BHP Billiton, and Vale), as it had done two years prior. China had only recently overtaken Japan as the world's number one consumer of iron ore (in 2003) and had only just replaced Japan as the lead benchmark pricing negotiator (in 2006). The benchmark pricing regime had been a stable market institution established by the Japanese and had been willingly respected by the major iron ore producers for the preceding four decades. Iron ore prices had hovered around $20/tonne for over twenty years (and were even lower before that; "only sand was cheaper!" as one of my interviewees noted).

The global environment had been disrupted in the aftermath of the global financial crisis, as well as the Beijing Olympics, which had led to a fall in Chinese steel production. The prices generated on the Chinese domestic iron ore market had been dropping significantly below the previous year's negotiated benchmark price. CISA had a lot riding on these negotiations. The tone it used to express frustration at the Big Three producers for exerting their "monopoly power" was accusatory, indicative of the pressure it was under to negotiate big price reductions, given the environment. In October 2010, CISA's secretary general, Shan Shanghua, noted that "[T]he association will try to establish a new pricing model for iron ore imports in order to negotiate on China's own terms rather than 'blindly' following agreements made between foreign steelmakers and leading miners BHP, Rio Tinto and Vale" ("Iron Ore Price Talks Reach a Crossroads: Can China Get What It Wants?" 2009). CISA adopted a tough negotiating strategy by refusing to agree to a benchmark price in 2009, refusing to honor the price agreed to by Japanese and Koreans importers, who had moved ahead with their own negotiations, and asking for significant markdowns. While the negotiations were ongoing, CISA demanded that its members and iron ore import license holders refrain from buying on the global iron ore market. However, the industry association's strategy backfired. A multitude of small- and medium-sized Chinese firms ignored the request and purchased iron ore on the global market through individual "spot" contracts, delivered to China by BHP and then by Vale. The iron ore benchmark pricing system was China's to lose. None of the large Chinese market stakeholders wanted it to fall apart. In fact, they had wanted to accomplish just the opposite. Yet by March 2010, headlines around the world were announcing its final demise. The *Financial Times* ran the following title: "Annual Iron Ore Contract System Collapses" (Blas 2010). Only seven years after China had become the world's top iron ore consumer, the behavior of its iron ore importers disrupted the decades-old benchmark pricing regime and a spot pricing regime emerged in its stead. The Chinese position of market vulnerability and its lack of capacity to coordinate procurement behavior, combined with some key decisions on behalf of key global iron ore producers, had led to the liberalization of the decades-old benchmark pricing regime.

The emergence of China as the world's number one iron ore consumer was effectively one of the most formidable thrusts a rising economy can have on a global market. The scale and speed of China's growth in steel consumption was nothing the world had ever seen, and it took many seasoned market participants by surprise. The iron ore case is fascinating because it combines extremes of market power, market vulnerability, and market change. As the number one iron ore and steel producer in the world, China had enormous market size and no doubt felt it should have been in a position to wield market power. As the world's number one iron ore importer, China was massively import-dependent and vulnerable to the vagaries of global iron ore suppliers. The fall of the iron ore benchmark pricing regime in 2010 remains, to this day, as one of the most striking examples of market institutional change to come as a result of China's emergence.

In 2003, when China emerged as the world's top iron ore consumer, the global iron ore market exhibited higher levels of coordination, while the opposite was true of China's domestic iron ore industry. This placed Chinese importers in a position of market vulnerability. The pricing regime the Chinese rose to disrupt had been established by the Japanese decades earlier and had enjoyed a long period of stability. It is instructive to compare the impact of China's rise as the number one iron ore consumer with that of Japan, fifty years earlier. Indeed, an almost completely opposite scenario existed in the 1960s, when Japan emerged as the world's top iron ore consumer. At the time, the global iron ore market had been more fragmented, while the domestic Japanese industry exhibited high levels of coordination. This put Japanese importers in a position of market power and gave them leeway to influence global iron ore market institutions in their preferred direction.

Table 2.4 and Figure 2.4 (Chapter 2) illustrate the variation in the pricing regime change that resulted from Japan's (1960s–1970s) and China's (2000s–2010s) emergence as the world's top iron ore consumers. As noted in Chapter 2, a movement toward more-competitive market interaction at the global level is labeled "liberalization," and a movement toward more-strategic market interaction is referred to as "de-liberalization."

A further within-market case study has been added to this chapter to increase the variation on the explanatory variables. The iron ore shipping industry is an interesting case since it is closely related to the iron ore market. This allows us to control for certain iron ore market-specific variables, and it results in additional variation in outcomes. In the case of Japan, the dynamics observed in the iron ore and shipping markets parallel each other. In China's case, however, they do not. Contrary to China's impact on the iron ore benchmark pricing regime, its impact on the pricing regime of iron ore shipping was a movement toward strategic interaction, or relative de-liberalization. The empirical narrative will show that the main difference between the Chinese iron ore industry and its iron ore shipping industry is that the latter was more successfully coordinated and was therefore in a stronger position of market power compared to its cousin.

In the late 2000s, as the benchmark pricing regime was falling apart, which also led to a shift in shipping-pricing conventions, the Brazilian firm Vale built a fleet of very large ore carriers (VLOCs) to ship iron ore to China. The Chinese response was bold. In 2011, a government edict blocked Vale's supertankers from docking and unloading their cargo in Chinese ports. The impasse was only solved two years later when Vale agreed to a series of lease-back agreements with the China Ocean Shipping Company (COSCO). This is not best understood as a top-down central government policy; rather, the impetus came from Chinese ship owners and operators, chiefly COSCO. This Chinese behavior amounted to successful coordination between the relevant Chinese market stakeholders (COSCO, the Ministry of Transport, China Shipowner's Association) acting against other competing national priorities—namely, in this case, China's steelmakers.

These empirical dynamics raise a series of puzzles. Why, given the size of Chinese iron ore demand, had Chinese actors failed to translate this position into influence on global iron ore market institutions? Why were Chinese stakeholders not able to organize their behavior and commodity procurement strategies as effectively as Japan had done and maintain the benchmark pricing regime, which they had explicitly stated was their goal? And how do we make sense of the liberalization of a commodity market as a result of China's rise?

None of the outcomes described above—the fall of the benchmarking regime, the blocking of Valemax cargoes from docking at Chinese ports, or Japan's emergence and the creation of a stable pricing regime in the second half of the twentieth century—can be explained from either an exclusively international or domestic perspective. At the time of their emergence, the domestic iron ore industries in Japan and China varied: it was coordinated in one and fragmented in the other. Likewise, the global iron ore market significantly varied.

The argument presented in this book is that market power dynamics between consumers and producers affect the type and direction of market change at the global level. In Chapter 3, I elaborated on my argument that the causal relationship connects the relative coordination capacity—or relative market power—of domestic/consumer (Chinese or Japanese) and international/producer market stakeholders and market institutional change at the global level.

Four hypotheses are derived from the argument developed in Chapter 3. First, the market stakeholders with the most relative coordination capacity at the export/import interface of a given market have a determining influence on global pricing regimes—the Japanese consumers in the late twentieth century, and the global iron ore producers in the early twenty-first century. Second, when power relations are disrupted, the emergence of new market players is more likely to lead to changes in global market institutions. The more dramatic the shifts, the more likely the change. Third, movement toward an asymmetric position of power (as the transition between Japan and China as lead consumers) is more likely to be disruptive than a movement toward a symmetric one. Fourth, movement toward a symmetric position of market power (Quadrant 1 or 4) will lead to competition or strategic bargaining between market stakeholders. In this case, change can be incremental. Quadrant 4 is the least predictable, as it can lead to a deadlock or conflict between equally powerful players (as we will find in the Valemax saga).

In the case of Japan's emergence as the number one consumer in the second half of the twentieth century, we saw coordinated domestic players face a fragmented global market (Quadrant 3). This situation afforded large Japanese firms (consumers) a position of market power from which they could actualize their preferences for a stable benchmark pricing regime (de-liberalization) at the global level. This illustrates the impact a coordinated consumer can have on global markets when in a dominant position of market power.

The transition from Japan to China as the top iron ore consumer was likely to be disruptive for two reasons. First, it involved a transition toward an asymmetric position of power (Quadrant 2). The emergence of China in the 2000s saw a fragmented consumer facing a global market characterized by higher levels of coordination. Second, it involved a transition from the opposite configuration of market power and, thus, a profound change in relative market power from being the dominant consumers (who had the upper hand under Japanese tenure) to being the dominant producers (a movement from Quadrant 3 to Quadrant 2). This transition from Quadrant 3 to Quadrant 2, from one extreme asymmetric position of market power to another, is arguably the most disruptive (in one direction or the other). In China's case, it gave global iron ore producers more opportunity to influence change in their preferred direction. This is how China's rise, despite its heft, led to change in the opposite direction from its key market stakeholders' preferences: the rapid liberalization of the global iron ore market pricing regime.

This rapid liberalization is surprising and interesting for several reasons. First, as I just made clear, the most important Chinese iron ore market stakeholders—the large state-owned steel enterprises (SOEs), as well as CISA, the powerful industry association—did not want this to occur. This outcome was the result of a coordination failure and market vulnerability on the part of the Chinese stakeholders. The Chinese position of market vulnerability, or weakness, may be surprising to the external observer, on the face of it, because China is by far the largest consumer of iron ore in the world. However, Chinese market stakeholders have been abundantly clear about their frustrations with the situation over the past twenty years. The rapid liberalization of the iron ore pricing regime is also surprising because it is a movement in the opposite direction from the "advance of the state" in China's domestic economy (Eaton 2015), an outcome that is not usually discussed as a likely consequence of China's rise. The causal logic behind these dynamics, I argue, is not to be found in a symmetrical resonance between domestic and international markets. In other words, it appears that a statist economy can have a liberalizing effect abroad, and vice versa. The dynamics can be explained by paying attention to the balance of market power (or vulnerability) between domestic and international market stakeholders in a given market and, more specifically, to changes in their relative market power or coordination capacity over time.

The first part of this chapter provides an overview of the global iron ore industry and pricing regime prior to China's emergence. It then provides an overview of the domestic Chinese iron ore and steel industries, including tracing government policy toward importing licenses until just after the fall of the benchmark, when the government abandoned the policy. The discussion then turns to the causal narrative around the fall of the iron ore benchmark pricing regime. Finally, I conduct a review of China's impact on the iron ore shipping regime, focusing on the saga of the Valemax cargoes. The final section is devoted to a comparison with Japan's impact on the global iron ore market, fifty years prior.

## The Global Iron Ore Market and Pricing Regime Prior to China's Emergence

### China and the Global Iron Ore Market

China is home to large deposits of iron ore but it is generally of poor quality, with lower iron content than deposits in other large iron ore–producing countries such as Brazil or Australia. Throughout the 1960s and 1970s, China started importing very small quantities of iron ore (see Figure 4.1). In the 1960s, it imported on average 0.74 million tonnes of iron ore or 0.4 percent of global exports and, in the 1970s, 2.9 million tonnes annually on average, or 0.8 percent of world exports (Sheng and Song 2012).

China's imports as share of world imports remained below 10 percent until 1996 (see Figure 4.2). In the 2000s, the ratio of China's iron ore imports to world imports started rapidly increasing. The year 2003 was the first time China's iron ore imports surpassed those of Japan, the number one iron ore importer until then. China went

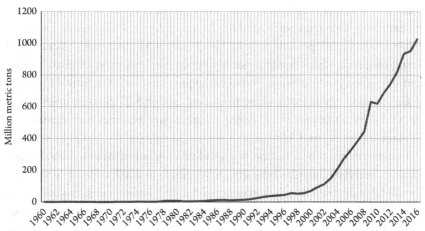

Source: CISA and Iron and Steel Institute data for years 1960–1989, in Sheng and Song (2012); UNCTAD for years 1990–2016.

*Figure 4.1* China's iron ore imports, 1960–2016

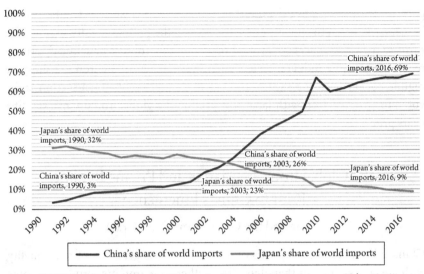

Source: UNCTAD (Chinese production of iron ore has been recalculated to be comparable), author's calculations, accessed April 2022.

Figure 4.2  Shares of global iron ore imports: China and Japan, 1990–2016

from importing 3.5 percent of global iron ore imports in 1990 to 25.6 percent in 2003 and 68.9 percent of global iron ore imports in 2016 (UNCTAD).

When China emerged as the world's top iron ore consumer, it faced a global iron ore market that was particularly highly concentrated. The market was dominated by two producing countries—Australia and Brazil—and three producing companies—Rio Tinto, BHP Billiton, and Vale, or the Big Three. In 2000, before China's emergence as the number one consumer, the top four iron ore exporting countries accounted for 74 percent of global exports, a number that increased to 85 percent in 2015 (see Figure 4.3). That year, Australia and Brazil, on which China remains heavily import-dependent, controlled 75 percent of the world's iron ore exports (see Figure 4.3). In 2001, fully 41 percent of China's iron ore imports came from Australia and 27 percent from Brazil. By 2016, China's import dependence on these two countries had increased to 84 percent (see Figure 4.4).

Looking at firm concentration, Magnus Ericsson, one of the iron ore industry's leading observers, described the iron ore industry in 2002 as being "one of the few metal industries that has experienced a continuous consolidation trend since the 1970s" (Ericsson 2002). Looking at seaborne iron ore exports (since much global iron ore production is captive), in 2003 the three largest exporters, or the Big Three, controlled 70 percent of the market (Ericsson 2003). In 2015, the Big Three's share was 64.4 percent (Lof and Ericsson 2017). In 2017, it stood

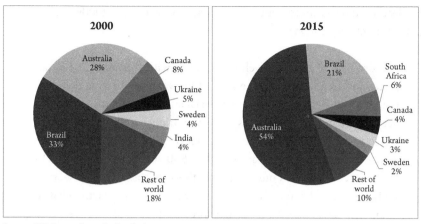

Source: UN Comtrade, author's calculations.

*Figure 4.3* World shares of iron ore exports by country, 2000 and 2015

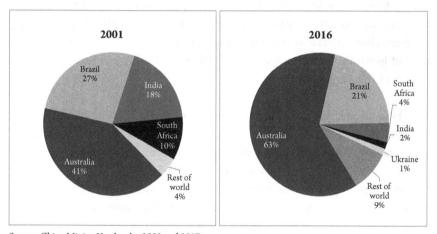

Source: China Mining Yearbooks, 2002 and 2017.

*Figure 4.4* China's iron ore imports by country, 2001 and 2016

at 60.6 percent (Lof and Ericsson 2018). The Big Three producers are particularly dominant in terms of low-cost production (Hurst 2015a).

## Global Iron Ore Pricing Regime Prior to China's Emergence

In the early 2000s, the global iron ore market operated under a negotiated benchmark pricing regime. Prices were determined as a result of annual benchmarking negotiations between the three main iron ore producers and the leading international importers, which until the early 2000s had been the Japanese (Zhang, 2009a).

> The ore market did very well for 50 years with the annual negotiated prices and L/T contracts. The contact between producer and end-user was direct and intense with commercial and technical discussions and data exchanges. The pricing system was transparent for both groups but less so for financial institutions, but they did not care as the commodity sold for typically around $20–$30 mt FOB load port. Only sand was cheaper! . . . I often read that these discussions were secretive. Only for the outsiders, the sellers and buyers knew exactly what was going on! (Interview 126, Former director at several iron ore mining companies, 2013)

Many have pointed to the Big Three's market power and coordination of behavior, beyond the fact that some price competition was also present during benchmark negotiations until the end of the 2000s (Hurst 2015a). The industry has been characterized as one consisting of a "small number of firms with a record of institutionalized cooperation" (Wilson 2013, 173). A leading iron ore industry expert argued that

> [t]he three large iron ore producers don't have to collude in order to exercise considerable control over the market and ensure that they are pursuing mutually consistent strategies. Their objective is obvious—to maximise profits—and their method of achieving the objective equally so: keeping prices high enough to pay for new investment but low enough so that new entrants do not become realistic alternative sources of product. (Ericsson et al. 2011)

Another way to evaluate market power and the potential for coordination is to look at the big producers' marginal costs of producing iron ore and the difference between these and export prices. In 2014, Hurst estimated each of the Big Three producers' iron ore costs delivered to China (CFR) at US$47/t for Rio Tinto, US$50/t for BHP Billiton, and US$62/t for Brazil's Vale, whereas global iron ore prices were above US$100/tonne.

Supranational regulatory gaps have given established multinational corporations more leeway to operate. As one Chinese academic noted, "The problem with global markets is that there is no regulatory oversight on market actors' behaviour . . ., at the WTO for instance, there is nothing regulating the oligopolistic behaviour of the three big iron ore companies. This is a problem" (Interview 7, Academic at a Chinese university, 2012).

A senior Chinese journalist commenting on informal cartels in commodity markets and oligopolies said, "Speaking of the dynamics among the major producers, even if iron ore is not controlled by a government-to-government cartel, we think it is just a different type, with private companies involved" (Interview 8, Senior journalist at a Chinese media outlet, 2012). Some interviewees went even further. A Chinese official and industry insider exclaimed that "Price making is in Western hands! By monopolies! But the demand is in emerging countries! And [we have] no price making power! Very frustrating!" (Interview 65, Senior researcher at a Chinese government think tank, 2012).

Major Chinese market stakeholders certainly perceive producers' behavior as being collusive. The China Iron and Steel Association (CISA), an industry association established in January 1999, which represented 161 members and accounted for 93 percent of domestic steel output and 75 percent of industry employees in 2001 (*China Mining Yearbook 2002* [中国矿业年鉴] 2002, 400), has long accused global miners of collusion ("CISA Plans Domestic Iron Ore Pricing Mechanism" 2013). In 2010, the then vice chairman of CISA, Luo Bingsheng, said, "The three giant miners have been using their position to control prices at unreasonably high levels . . . it is not price negotiations, it's that they fixed a price and you have to accept, if not, they cut off the supply" (Zhang and Lan 2010). In March 2013, China's powerful economic planning and price-setting agency, the National Development and Reform Commission (NDRC), also released a report wherein the big iron ore mining companies were accused of "artificially inflating the price of iron ore, by delaying and controlling shipments, delaying sales, and causing a temporary illusion of shortage in the market" (Zhong 2013).

This assessment has continued until now, even after the fall of the benchmarking system. In a 2019 notice, the China Iron Ore and Steel Association stated that "Although my country is the world's largest importer of iron ore, the international pricing power of imported iron ore has long been held in the hands of four major mines including Vale in Brazil and Rio Tinto, BHP Billiton and MFG in Australia" (Li 2019). A former mining industry executive commented, however, that there has been a softening of the tone over the past few years, since the emergence of Chinese traders who have grown to play a dominant role in the iron ore market (Interview 160, Former senior mining industry executive, 2022).

## The Domestic Chinese Iron Ore and Steel Market

China became the world's largest steel producer in the late 1990s. By 2015, it accounted for 49.6 percent of world steel production (Brandt et al. 2022). To understand the scale of China's domestic iron ore production and imports, it

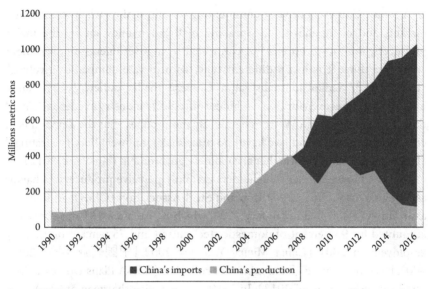

Source: UNCTAD (Chinese production of iron ore has been recalculated to be comparable), accessed April 2022.

*Figure 4.5* China's iron ore production and imports, 1990–2016

helps to ponder the fact that when China became the world's largest iron ore importer in 2003 (with 148.2 Mt), its domestic iron ore production (at 208.2 Mt) (UNCTAD) still exceeded its iron ore imports. As Chinese steel production skyrocketed, domestic iron ore production ramped up in the early 2000s as China tried to reduce an emerging import dependence (see Figure 4.5). But conflicting national goals of industry consolidation, higher productivity, and pollution reduction clashed with the goal of reducing import dependence on iron ore. Global price fluctuations in the 2010s also had an impact on the profitability of some Chinese iron ore producers (given the low iron ore content, some Chinese mines are only profitable above a certain threshold). The Chinese domestic production of iron ore peaked in 2007 at 402 million tonnes. In 2008, China began importing more iron ore than it produced (see Figure 4.5), that is, if we exempt the year 2002 (when imports were only slightly above domestic production). Chinese import dependence, calculated as the proportion of imports to the sum of imports and domestic production, has increased ever since, reaching 90 percent in 2016 (see Figure 4.6).

The domestic iron ore and steel industry in China is so fragmented that it is difficult to get a clear picture of the number of companies that are operating at any one time (Li and Li 2011; Sukagawa 2010; Su 2012).

In 2005, just as Baosteel was taking over as the lead benchmark negotiator for Chinese importers, the top four crude steel producers accounted for 18 percent

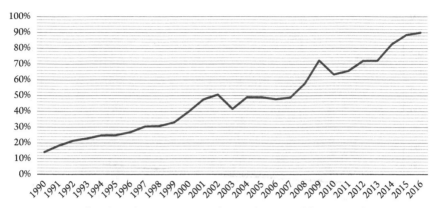

Source: UNCTAD data, share of iron ore imports on the sum of imports and domestic production, author's calculations.

*Figure 4.6* China's iron ore import dependence, 1990–2016

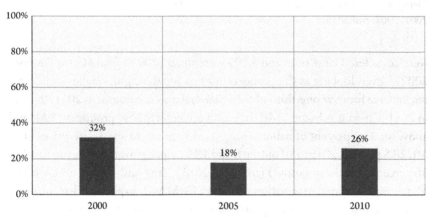

Source: Chinese Steel Statistical Yearbook (2001–2011). Author's calculations.

*Figure 4.7* Top four Chinese crude steel producers, 2000–2010

of total steel production, and Baosteel, just 6 percent (see Figure 4.7), whereas the three largest steelmakers occupied only 14 percent of total domestic production in 2005 in China, compared to 70 percent in Japan and 60 percent in the United States (Bergsten et al. 2008). The China Metallurgical Press cited a total number of 7,373 steel-producing enterprises in 2007, an increase from 6,999 enterprises in 2006; and in 2000 there were 2,997 steel producers in the country (Yang 2010). In 2008, 93.6 percent of those enterprises were small- or medium-sized (*China Mining Yearbook 2008* [中国矿业年鉴] 2009).

The Chinese iron ore industry is equally fragmented (see Figure 4.8). In 2006, there were 3,933 iron ore mining enterprises, among which only 73

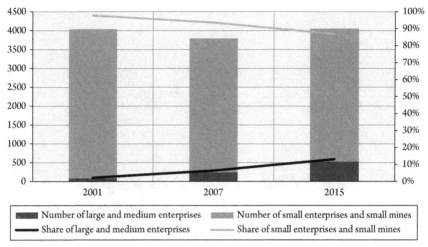

Source: China Mining Yearbook (2002, 2008, 2016).

*Figure 4.8* Number and share of large, medium, and small iron ore enterprises in China 2001, 2007, and 2015

were considered large ones and 3,709 were small (*2007 China Mining Yearbook* 2007).[1] Even looking at the proportion of national output, smaller firms were responsible for over one-third of total national iron ore output in 2011. Indeed, in 2011, China was home to 40 large iron ore enterprises (producing 5 Mt and above, or 35.3 percent of national output), 187 medium-sized enterprises (1–5 Mt, 28.8 percent of national output), and 1,171 small private mines (up to 1 Mt, 36 percent of national output) (Mayfield 2013). Yang Jiasheng, chairman of the Metallurgical Mines Association of China (MMAC), explained that, in 2015, large-scale mines still made up only around 3 percent of the country's 4,037 mines (Stanway 2015). Looking at steel- and iron ore–producing enterprises together, in 2010, the country's total number was 12,143 enterprises (*China Steel Yearbook 2011* [钢铁工业年鉴] 2012). An impressive number of interviewees described the Chinese domestic iron ore industry as "fragmented" or "chaotic" [乱], including Chinese government officials (Interview 111, Chinese state-owned enterprise employee, 2012).[2]

Consolidation efforts in the Chinese steel industry have been laborious and fall short of stated targets. As one Chinese industry insider commented in 2012, "One of the great failings of the last five years is that China could not reach its objectives of consolidation in the iron ore market. The objective was to reach 50% of the market for the 10 biggest steel companies by 2010, and 70% in 2020. In 2010, they were only at 42%" (Interview 98, Industry consultant, 2012). This number stood at 34 percent in 2015 (Ng 2016). The Chinese government has continued to promote the consolidation of the domestic steel industry, with the recent merger of Shanghai Baosteel with Wuhan Iron & Steel, in 2016 (Wildau 2017), but half the country's output is still accounted for by small private firms (Shepherd 2016).

Comparing these trends in the Chinese iron ore industry is all the more striking when put in perspective with the rest of the Chinese mining industry. Whereas the total number of mines decreased from 153,723 to 83,648 between 2001 and 2015, the total number of iron ore mines increased from 4,036 to 4,052 over the same period (see Figure 4.9). The overall proportion of small enterprises and small mines in the overall Chinese mining industry went from 99 percent to 87 percent during that time (see Figure 4.9.).

Trendlines are moving in the direction of a higher proportion of large- and medium-sized enterprises on the total number of enterprises over time, even if absolute numbers remain overwhelmingly skewed toward small enterprises and small mines. But notice that the absolute number of total iron ore enterprises, if it saw a small decrease between 2001 and 2007, increased again between 2007 and 2015.

These numbers give an indication of the overall fragmentation of the domestic iron ore and steel industry, but this book is more specifically concerned with the capacity for coordination at the interface between the Chinese and the global iron ore market. Hence, the following section will look at the number of Chinese companies that have imported iron ore over the past two decades. Indeed, prior to the collapse of the iron ore benchmarking regime, the Chinese government had deployed various strategies to reduce this number, although it was largely unsuccessful.

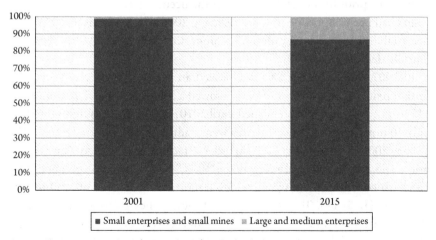

Source: China Mining Yearbook (2002 and 2016), author's calculations.

*Figure 4.9* Proportion of enterprises, by size, in the Chinese mining industry, 2001 and 2015

## Iron Ore Importing Licenses—A Brief History

In the early 2000s, Chinese regulators were concerned with issues regarding the iron ore import process, including the fact that large steel-producing enterprises often hoarded ore and resold it at higher prices to small and medium-sized enterprises. In an effort to remediate the situation, a series of largely unsuccessful measures was implemented, beginning with the "automatic import licensing system" for iron ore, which the Chinese Ministry of Commerce (MOFCOM) and the General Administration of Customs announced on March 1, 2005 (Provisional Procedures, 2005).[3] Pertaining to the new licensing system, only companies that conformed to the various criteria outlined by MOFCOM could obtain an import license.

One of these criteria stipulated that companies needed to conform to the qualification standards established by the China Chamber of Commerce of Metals, Minerals & Chemicals Importers & Exporters (CCCMC, a unit of China's Ministry of Commerce) and CISA that were issued on February 28, 2005 (Provisional Procedures 2005). These standards included the need for companies to have, among other things, imported a minimum of 300,000 tonnes of iron ore the previous year. It also required firms to conform to a notice the General Office of the State Council sent out to the NDRC and other departments, on December 23, 2002, entitled "Ideas on How to Put a Stop to Blind Investments in the Steel, Aluminium and Cement Industries." This notice included a directive to strictly enforce market access and consolidate the industry in order to avoid excessive competition and a waste of resources.

In 2004, prior to the establishment of the license system, 523 companies in China had been importing iron ore (Zhuang 2006). In 2005, MOFCOM's notice established the number of iron ore importing licenses at 118, more than a fourfold decrease.

In 2007, CISA and the CCCMC issued an announcement that they were further reducing the number of firms allowed a license to import iron ore from 118 to 112 (a number that remained until 2010) (Liang 2007). Of this number, only 40 firms accorded these licenses were trading companies, down from 250 (Zhang 2009b). In February 2008, in order to tackle the issue of soaring iron ore prices and consolidate and reorganize ["整顿"] domestic iron ore importers, CISA issued a notice that would see even more stringent controls on iron ore importers (Li 2011). The consequence of these policy reforms was to gradually decrease the number of enterprises with access to official import licenses. The objective of these efforts was framed as an attempt to reduce China's dependence on a foreign iron ore export "monopoly" ["垄断"] (Zhao 2013) by strengthening the hand of Chinese importers.

These efforts were largely unsuccessful. First, the share of the volume of imports for specific Chinese domestic steel companies continued to decrease over the same period. Data from the China Customs Department indicate an increasing level of fragmentation at the industry's interface with the global iron ore market (among companies officially licensed to import iron ore). In 2001, China's two largest importers of iron ore (Baosteel and WISCO) imported 24 percent of total imports. By 2011, the proportion of imports of the two largest importers (now Baosteel and Hebei Iron & Steel) had dropped to only 10 percent (Figure 4.10). Note that the relative size of the number one importer, Baosteel, is quite small. Second, the introduction of the license system led to the widespread (and illicit) practice of more than one company using the same license.

In April 2010, CISA and the CCCMC established a "joint office of iron ore imports" specifically to "control the flow of iron ore imports and curb speculative behavior" and issued three further notices (Li 2010).[4] Among the newly tightened "Iron Ore Import Qualifying Guidelines," the minimum quantity of iron ore imported increased from the previous year's import quota of 300,000 tonnes to 1,000,000 tonnes. And again, the number of firms granted an import license dropped from 112 to 105 (Zhao 2013).

Interviewees confirmed that this was in response to the illicit, widespread use of official licenses by more than one company. The number of companies

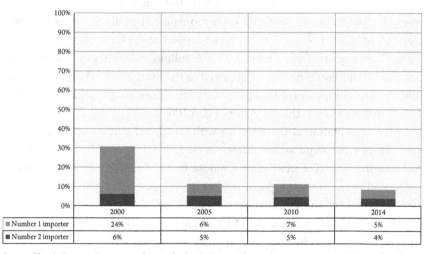

Source: China's Customs Department data, Author's calculations. The number one importer in 2000 was Shanghai Baosteel, in 2005 and 2010 was Baosteel and in 2014, RGL Group, a trading company. The number two importer in 2000 was Wuhan Iron and Steel (WISCO), in 2005 was Shanghai Baosteel, in 2010 was Sinosteel (now Baowu Iron and Steel) and in 2014 was Hesteel Group (formerly Hebei Iron and Steel).

*Figure 4.10* Share of total iron ore imports by top two Chinese firms, 2000, 2005, 2010, and 2014

purchasing iron ore on the global market was well in excess of the number of official licenses that permitted companies to do so, and this was creating a problem that was referred to as "stir-fry ore" behavior ["炒矿行为"] (speculating behavior in the iron ore industry).

Despite the legal efforts to curb the number of domestic companies importing ore, many companies, including those without licenses, continued to bypass China's domestic regulatory system. Evidence shows that, in 2010, at least 200 companies were importing iron ore when, in fact, there existed only 112 official import licenses. A journalist interviewed a Beijing-based iron ore company that, at the time, had been selling between 500,000 and 2 million tonnes of iron ore a year on the Chinese market for three years, not with an official license but with a "purchased license." The process was very simple: a company without a license would arrange the contact, price and delivery with a foreign seller, then it would ask a domestic license holder to apply their own official seal on the contract, in exchange for a fee. As per the journalist's interview, fees ranged from 0.1 to 0.7 percent of the value of a 50,000-tonne cargo, which would be worth upward of 20 million RMB. In some cases, the fee could reach 140,000 RMB (Zhao 2013). Another senior journalist confirmed that if only a few steel companies had the required permit to import ore, other politically connected companies were still managing to import ore and resell it domestically. As such, he explained that "many companies in China have an interest in iron ore prices going up. This is a problem" (Interview, 8, Senior journalist at Chinese media company, 2012). Large SOEs benefited from the benchmarking system. As one researcher put it, "Some steel mills make more profit by selling ore to small ones than selling steel" (Zhang 2009b). News reports at the time indicated that "in 2004, Shougang imported a total of 13.336 million tonnes of iron ore, of which only 9.8158 million tonnes were supplied to the head office, while the rest was sold to other companies at the spot price . . . [the company] realized a profit of 140.43 million yuan in this operation" (Cao 2009).

This fragmentation at the interface with the global iron ore market made it very difficult for large stakeholders—including CISA and Baosteel—to coordinate the behavior of smaller Chinese firms. Relations of market power influenced preferences for global market openness. Large SOEs with licenses clearly wanted the continuation of the benchmark because of the advantageous position it would allow these firms to maintain toward their domestic peers. For smaller firms without licenses, the rationale was the opposite.

At the time of China's emergence as the world's largest iron ore importer, the country was firmly situated in Quadrant 2, where fragmented domestic consumers were facing coordinated global producers.

After the fall of the benchmark, on July 1, 2013, MOFCOM abolished the iron ore import license system that had been established in 2005. A senior

CISA official was quoted as saying that removing the qualifying restrictions on import licenses was a positive step for the Chinese steel industry (Zhao 2013). He then went on to say that the licensing system had not only failed to fulfill its original goals, either by weakening what many in China labeled a "resource monopoly" or by reducing China's dependence on Australia or Brazil, but it had also resulted in the "reselling issue" (Zhao 2013).[5] A Chinese industry insider added that the licensing system "did not restrain the price of iron ore, but instead created a domestic monopoly. There is no need to perpetuate such conditions" (Zhao 2013).

## The Fall of the International Iron Ore Benchmarking Regime

By 2003, China had become the world's leading iron ore importer, but Nippon Steel, the leading Japanese firm, continued to negotiate the benchmark with global suppliers and settle the annual benchmark until 2005. Following the significant price increase of 71.5 percent Nippon Steel had agreed to in 2005, the Chinese side appointed Baosteel to lead the annual benchmarking negotiations (Wilson 2012). In 2006, for the first time, Baosteel led these negotiations with global suppliers, ahead of the Japanese. At the time, the iron ore benchmark was a little above US$40 a tonne (Figure 4.11). Baosteel had negotiated a price increase of 19 percent over the previous year, which at the time was below expectations (Wilson 2012). Baosteel continued to lead negotiations in 2007, resulting in a 10 percent price increase (Craze and Blount 2006). In 2008, Baosteel agreed to a 65 percent price rise with Vale after the latter had first agreed to the same price increase with Japanese and South Korean consumers (Baosteel 2008) and then to an 80 percent increase with Rio Tinto (Hurst 2015a). This time around, the increase was significant, with the benchmark sitting above US$90 a tonne and, in 2009, the Chinese government appointed CISA to replace Baosteel as the lead negotiator (Wilson 2013).

In 2009, in the midst of the global financial crisis and the Stern Hu affair,[6] CISA took a tough negotiating stance toward the Big Three iron ore producers and asked for a 45 percent markdown ("China: Lessons" 2009; Wilson 2012). CISA also asked all domestic steel companies to refrain from buying iron ore on the global market while negotiations were ongoing. However, it was unable to enforce this strategy and it backfired. Many small Chinese steel firms ignored the China Iron and Steel Association's request and began purchasing iron ore through spot contracts. Despite the association's having urged its national steel makers to not negotiate directly with the iron ore producers, the major Chinese steel companies had broken ranks with CISA and signed contracts of their own with foreign suppliers.

In the early 2000s, a spot price had already emerged, in China, to facilitate the allocation of iron ore between the thousands of iron ore and steel market players in the country. At the time, Chinese firms used the spot price domestically—there were no traders yet—whereas international prices were negotiated. "The main market was in Hebei. If you looked at internal publications in China, you could see the spot price" (Interview 160, Former senior mining industry executive, 2022). The sudden emergence of India as a non-insignificant iron ore exporter also played a role in the emergence of a spot price, as the supply sat outside benchmark negotiations and much of it found its way to China (Llewellyn-Smith 2013). India's iron ore exports rose above 50 million tonnes a year between 2003 and 2009, only to go back down again subsequently (Ahmed and Rai, 2019). At the time, however, the spot price remained marginal.

In 2009 and 2010, two events set the stage for bold moves on the part of smaller Chinese consumers and the Big Three international producers. First was the global financial crisis and the fall of commodity prices that followed, coupled, in the case of iron ore, with the Beijing Olympics. In the lead-up to the Olympics, the Chinese government, in the hope of achieving blue skies, had ordered a dramatic cut in iron ore production. For the first time, in quite a dramatic fashion, the iron ore spot price was lower than the benchmark price.

> The Chinese government cut iron ore production! So, suddenly there was a lot of iron ore available. A lot. At the price of the old benchmark system. So, then what happened? Vale and Rio Tinto tried to keep the benchmark system. But who is going to buy? The Japanese are buying much less and the Europeans much less. . . . Even the Chinese are buying less. The Chinese steel industry took the opportunity to try to buy more on the spot market. (Interview 160, Former senior mining industry executive, 2022)

As an academic at a Chinese university put it at the time, "The fragmentation of the iron ore market explains a lot. It is so difficult for China to have an iron ore strategy, since all the iron ore companies don't listen!" (Interview 60, Academic at a Chinese university, Beijing, 2012). During the 2009–2010 benchmark negotiations, CISA did not have enough sway over Chinese importers. In addition, CISA had overestimated the Three Big suppliers' need to sell (Gu 2009), compared to the Chinese mills' need to buy iron ore.

Interviews with global iron ore industry executives point us to a few critical decisions that were made by key individuals working at the Big Three iron ore suppliers, taking advantage of the emerging opportunity to disrupt the long-standing practice of annual negotiations, which accelerated the fall of the benchmark pricing regime.

Of the Big Three, BHP Billiton was most clearly in favor of a transition toward a quarterly and eventually a spot market system, whereas Rio Tinto's management took a more traditional approach, in part because their long-standing Japanese and South Korean clients had a clear preference for the stability of the benchmarking pricing system. A high-level executive in the iron ore industry, speaking about BHP and its interest in having the benchmarking system fall apart, said, "Yes, they were very vocal about it" (Interview 69, Senior mining industry executive, 2012). At the time, the CEO of BHP (Marius Kloppers) is said to have been "pretty keen on seeing the fall of the benchmark," according to a longtime iron ore industry insider (Interview 127, Former director at several iron ore mining companies, 2013), because he estimated that the spot price would rise above the contract price after the industry recovered from the global financial crisis. He was right. "[Kloppers] was always talking against a benchmark system. He said it's a very murky system. You go to a restaurant and sit at a table, and then you start discussing.... He thought that if you change the system, the Brazilians would lose because they were further away. So, if you sell at the same price, it's to the Brazilians' disadvantage. His idea was if you finish with the benchmark system, Vale will sell in Europe and Australia will sell in Asia. But it wasn't that way in the end" (Interview 160, Former senior mining industry executive, 2022). In 2009, Kloppers was quoted in the Chinese press as saying, "Small ore buyers favor fluctuating prices, while large steel mills want stable prices.... BHP would like to see the market be more transparent when it comes to pricing, thus avoiding the likelihood of pricing impasses that we are currently in the midst of" ("Iron Ore Price Talks Reach a Crossroads: Can China Get What It Wants?" 2009).

Vale also played a leading role in the fall of the benchmark. Back in 2009, as the global financial crisis and the Beijing Olympics were bringing the spot price below the benchmark and CISA was trying to enforce a tough negotiating stance to obtain price reductions, there was a period of sharp iron ore oversupply in Brazil. A former senior mining executive commented, "Vale had to shut down mines, you couldn't use the railway because the railway was full of wagons full of iron ore." What follows is his fascinating account of internal decision-making at Vale:

> At Vale, we decided to send the ore to China. We started hiring ships and put the ore on the ships and sent it to China. The decision to go CNF was made at the beginning of 2009. There was a lot of ore available and nobody was fulfilling their commitments. So, we started filling the ships and sending them to China. We were joking internally; we

were calling this the great Armada! I can tell you April, May 2009, I had more than a hundred ships going to China full of ore, without any orders. I think in one month we sent 40 million tonnes to China without any orders. To sell there at the market price. Then two things happened. First, we went to spot. Second, we moved from FOB to CNF. This was a tremendous change. Because Vale never did that before. I can tell you; it was a very difficult decision to make. I remember one of my guys who worked with me said we cannot do this. If you send the ore there and we don't find customers to buy it ... we have to bring it back! I said look if the freight is too high, we'll throw it in the ocean! It's a way to say we have to do it. It took 45 days to make the trip. In 45 days, I moved all my commercial team to China. I have more than 10 guys in China to sell these ships. They went to Shanghai and there you had a guy with the table and all the ships coming, the ore, the quality, the quantity, who could be the customers. ... All the ships were sold ... [to] smaller companies. We took advantage of the fragmentation. We went to the middle of China, looking for people who wanted to buy. (Interview 160, Former senior mining industry executive, 2022)

The situation was such that on Tuesday, March 30, 2010, BHP Billiton and Vale, provided with a window of opportunity due to uncoordinated Chinese procurement behavior and enough willing Chinese consumers, ushered in a new era (Blas and Smith 2010). This came a day after Baosteel had finally acknowledged that the system needed to go through "some changes and adjustments." The *Financial Review* reported that this comment had "drive[n] the final nail into the coffin of the 40-year-old benchmark pricing system" (Wyatt 2010). Spot pricing took over and, thus, the decades-old benchmarking system came to an end. On March 30, 2010, the *Financial Times* reported: "The benchmark system has ended. There is no comeback" (Blas and Smith 2010).

On April 9, 2010, Rio Tinto is said to have been last to follow BHP and Vale's lead, when it finally agreed to enter talks with iron ore consumers about the ore being priced on a quarterly instead of an annual basis ("Rio Tinto Joins Steel Reform as Local Costs Mount" 2010). And thus, the quarterly contract price was introduced. A senior iron ore industry insider who was close to Rio Tinto said, "During the fall of the benchmark, was Rio more reticent? Yes, BHP was the early mover. But now they wonder if they shouldn't have made the move earlier! Why? They figured out that it was indeed a profitable move. BHP saw it before, and now Rio has come to the realization that it was indeed beneficial and could have moved earlier" (Interview 134, Senior iron ore industry insider, 2014). When I asked why Rio might have been more reticent, the industry insider explained that, at the time, Japanese and Korean consumers were more important to Rio Tinto than the Chinese consumers, who were growing in importance but had not displaced the other two. Rio Tinto had also developed long-term relationships with buyers who were more comfortable with the benchmark system.

In 2010, a final twist in the story of the fall of the benchmark is that the Japanese realized the inevitable and began to move toward quarterly pricing. This was probably the final straw for the large Chinese state-owned steel mills. "The Chinese recognised their intransigence in the face of Japanese pricing flexibility would probably result, yet again, in the Japanese setting the contract iron ore price for the world" (Wyatt 2010).

On the Chinese side, the lead negotiator's lack of capacity to coordinate domestic iron ore importers was compounded by infighting that took place between two key market stakeholders, CISA and the Ministry of Commerce. CISA had unsuccessfully tried to block the importation of ore by Chinese importers who were paying well above the previous year's negotiated price (Bunker and Ciccantell 2007). It then proposed canceling the licenses from the renegade Chinese steel mills and traders, a move the Ministry of Commerce opposed for fear of endangering China's resource security (Zhang 2009b).

In the midst of the upheaval, on April 5, 2010, CISA and the CCCMC held a closed-door meeting to discuss "regulating an orderly iron ore market,"[7] where the two government entities expressed disagreement about the path ahead. In the midst of the deadlock in the international benchmarking negotiations and the Stern Hu affair, CISA and the CCCMC attempted to regain control over the domestic iron ore importing situation and make peace. Media reports hinted at previous infighting and efforts at "making peace" [安内], a news article commenting on the meeting declared that "making internal peace is necessary before resisting foreign aggression!" [攘外必先安内!] (Li 2010). Newspaper reports mention a "joint petition" being submitted to the upper levels of government by the leaders of Chinese steel SOEs, asking that the difficulties in the iron ore negotiations be raised to a "national-level issue."

CISA and CCCMC eventually established a "Joint Office for Iron Ore Imports"[8] to control imports of iron ore resources, collect all import contract information, and monitor iron ore flows, in an attempt to curb speculative iron ore behavior (Li 2010).[9] However, the attempts to put an end to license-holding companies reselling iron ore to smaller domestic companies had little effect.

CISA faced "harsh criticism... for mishandling the 2008–2009 negotiations as an out-of-touch government entity with no experience in the world of trade" ("China: Lessons" 2009). "Executive Deputy Chairman Luo Bingsheng, General Secretary Shan Shanghua, and Chen Xianwen, the director of CISA's market investigation department who was lead negotiator during the failed 2009 price negotiations, all submitted their resignations at the organization's annual meeting Feb. 20 [2011]" ("Chinese Dependence on Foreign Iron Ore: A Special Report" 2011).

As one Chinese industry insider explained, "The first step was the market evolving from a benchmark to a quarterly contract system. But the Chinese walked from the contracts and the pricing system evolved increasingly close to a spot system" (Interview 112, Iron ore industry analyst, 2012).

Multiple interviewees, coming from inside the Chinese decision-making structure, from the perspective of the Big Three producers, as well as from the perspective of other market participants and observers not directly working for either consumers or suppliers, confirmed to me that CISA and the large SOEs did not want the benchmarking system to fall. As late as 2010, Baosteel was quoted as saying, "Baosteel supports the long-term annual contract system. This system is beneficial for steel mills and raw material suppliers to build a long-term and stable relationship based on co-operation" (Wyatt 2010). We are looking here at a very concrete and rarely considered example of China's rise directly causing a radical change in international-level market institutions in a direction opposite to what the lead Chinese government and industry players (SOEs) desired.

One high-level international industry insider commented that "There is a saying in Chinese, 'you lift the rock and it falls on your foot'; this was the situation with iron ore.... The fall of the benchmarking system is particularly bad for the purchasers. The Chinese had no intention of making the benchmarking system fall! ... So, the benchmark system fell down, and this was a big blow to the Chinese steel companies. So short-sighted" (Interview 86, International mining industry executive, 2012). This was confirmed by a former executive in the global mining industry, who said, "The big state-owned companies, they always supported the benchmark system" (Interview 160, Former senior mining industry executive, 2022).

A Chinese government official with intimate knowledge of the events confirmed the fact that the Chinese negotiators had not intended to cause the benchmark pricing system to fall. When asked whether CISA wanted to end the benchmarking system when it was leading the negotiations in 2009–2010, the interviewee responded, "No, CISA did not want to end the benchmarking system at that point. They just thought that the price was too high. It wasn't their intention to see the end of the benchmark, nor was it Baogang's" (Interview 111, Chinese state-owned enterprise employee, 2012). From another Chinese government official's point of view, "CISA supported the benchmarking system, they were conservative, and it was Australia who wasn't willing" (Interview 59, Executive, Chinese state-owned enterprise, 2012).

In 2010, when the negotiations fell apart and Chinese SOEs were forced to fend for themselves on the spot market, prices had already risen above US$100/tonne (Figure 4.11). "One executive estimated that the profits of the Big Three

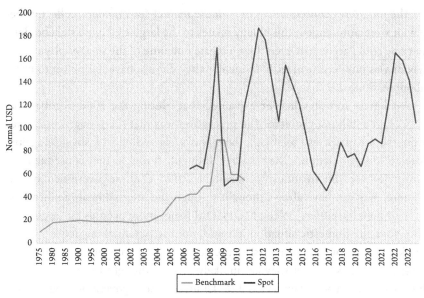

Source: Komesaroff, 2010; Tan, 2012; The Financial Times, 2022. Benchmark prices: Tan 2012; spot prices, until 2010: Tan 2012 and Komesaroff, 2010; from 2010 to 2022: The Financial Times data.

Figure 4.11  Iron ore prices, 1975–2022

producers, Vale, Rio Tinto and BHP Billiton, would be boosted by at least $5 billion this year" (Blas and Smith 2010). The shift in the iron ore pricing regime "gives major producers more leverage.... The control exercised by the Big Three will, to some extent, counteract the tendency to greater price instability that will result from the new pricing methods" (Ericsson et al. 2011).

Why did CISA and the large SOEs not want the benchmark pricing regime to fall? The answer to this question is that this system had put the association and the large SOEs in a position of market power relative to other, smaller Chinese iron ore consumers. Large state-owned steel companies benefited from the benchmark pricing regime in combination with the import licensing system. Given the presence of limited import licenses, they were able to extract rents from Chinese firms with no access to the import interface by reselling the ore domestically at a profit. The smaller mills preferred fending for themselves on the spot market. As the director of a Chinese industry consultancy put it, "On the one hand, some Chinese steel companies would rather import ore bought on contract and then resell it for more money on the spot market, pocketing the difference.... On the other hand, although the Chinese are definitely large enough as purchasers, the import market remains very chaotic because it has so many importers with different interests and goals" ("Iron Ore Price Talks Reach a Crossroads: Can China Get What It Wants?" 2009).

The long-term consequences of Chinese market stakeholders' collective behavior were unintended; this chiefly relates to the largest Chinese stakeholders, but one could argue that even the aggregate outcome of the smaller players' behavior was unintentional as, individually, they did not have the power to bring about institutional change.

A Chinese industry insider explained that "during the 2008 negotiations, CISA had a cultural problem. The perception was that the foreign companies were there to trick us [骗我门], there was a big feeling of a struggle against foreign discrimination. They hadn't thought through the consequences" (Interview 46, Iron ore industry consultant, 2012). Chinese government organizations may not have always thought through the international ramifications of their policies, either: "When MOFCOM issues more licenses for importing, they have the domestic situation in mind, not the potential impacts on global market institutions . . . some issues they consider . . . competition among domestic providers . . . but they are unlikely to have thought through the likely international impacts" (Interview 128, Chinese central government agency official, 2012).

Iron ore consumers around the world were affected by the fall in the benchmark pricing regime. A longtime iron ore industry insider explained, "The traditional consumers of iron ore (European and Japanese steel mills) detest the development as it appears not to be in their interest and has severed the relationship between producer-consumer" (Interview 126, Former director at several iron ore mining companies, 2013). Even the World Steel Association, which in 2010 represented 180 steelmakers, was not in favor of the fall of the benchmark and the move toward spot pricing. As the director general, Ian Christmas, said at the time: " 'The benchmark system may have imperfections but it has the merit of supporting long-term relationships between the steel industry and raw materials suppliers leading to beneficial medium-term investment decisions. The implied move to spot pricing will be volatile and benefit neither side in the medium to long term.' He added that the move will lead to an oligopoly between the three miners and he urged the competition authorities to investigate the matter" ("Rio Tinto Joins Steel Reform as Local Costs Mount" 2010).

Until today, "Vale continues to have long-term contracts with customers. BHP and Rio Tinto also. But part of the iron ore is sold on the stock market because we need to have a price. The reference for the contracts is the spot price. I would say that 30 percent or 40 percent of iron ore is sold on the spot market. In the spot market, a big part of the buyers are the traders" (Interview 160, Former senior mining industry executive, 2022).

The fall of the iron ore benchmark pricing regime had an immediate impact on another closely related market, that for coking coal. From 2010 onward, the annual pricing system in that market was also replaced by a quarterly pricing mechanism. BHP Billiton is understood to have pushed for this transition with the aim for it to move toward a monthly pricing system. "Following this transition to shorter pricing mechanisms that are either based on or influenced by spot prices for iron ore and coking coal imports to China, price dynamics generally have experienced shorter cycles and greater volatility" ("Management's Discussion and Analysis of Financial Condition and Results of Operations for the Six Months Ended June 30, 2011" 2011).

## Launch of the Iron Ore Price Index, the Iron Ore Trading Platform, the Emergence of Traders, and the Launch of China Mineral Resources Group

Major Chinese importers, CISA, and other Chinese government organs have remained frustrated and concerned about the market and pricing power of the large global iron ore producers despite the arrival of spot market pricing. The often-unsuccessful attempts to assert more control over the benchmark system in the 2000s evolved into various attempts to regulate, control, or design more-financialized market relationships with global iron ore market stakeholders in the 2010s and 2020s.

In January 2012, China launched its own iron ore spot trading platform, CBMX, in Beijing. The platform went live on May 8, 2012. CISA publicly backed the platform. At the time, I asked a few iron ore industry insiders in China why China was so keen to launch an iron ore trading platform. I posed the following question: "In some ways, it shouldn't matter where the trading platform is located, right? Why does China want an iron ore trading platform on Chinese soil?" More than one interviewee said that there may have been domestic market control objectives (Interview 46, Chinese consultant and iron ore industry expert, 2012; Interview 69, Senior mining industry executive, 2012). Both agreed there may also be long-term RMB internationalization objectives.

The public backing of a China-based iron ore trading platform came years after CISA had blocked an earlier attempt to create one in 2008–2009, one year prior to the fall of the benchmarking regime. Interviewees confirmed that CISA was not supportive of the establishment of a spot trading platform at the time, before the fall of the benchmark, whereas other Chinese stakeholders had tried to push the project forward, including some port groups (Interview 46, Chinese consultant and iron ore industry expert, 2012). This indicates that, at the time, CISA was still invested in the benchmark system. Others, such as the National Development and Reform Commission, were also not pushing for the establishment of a trading platform in the early days. "In January 2010, the NDRC said 'a what platform?' Once the benchmark system fell apart, CISA and other government bodies backed the iron ore trading platform" (Interview 59, Chinese state-owned enterprise official, 2012). The platform was created by CISA, China Chamber of Commerce of Metals, Minerals & Chemicals Importers & Exporters (CCCMC), and the China Beijing International Mining Exchange. A year after the launch, the volume of transactions on the CBMX platform amounted to about 13 million tonnes.

Next, GlobalOre, a rival platform backed by BHP, was launched in Singapore on May 30, 2012, only three weeks after the launch of the Chinese platform, as the two vied to fill the gap left by the fall of the benchmark pricing regime. GlobalOre's founding members included BHP Billiton, Vale, and Rio Tinto, as well as Glencore and China's Baosteel and Minmetals (Serapio Jr, 2012). An interviewee indicated at the time that "Australian ore is closer to a commodity. Because of that, GlobalOre works best for BHP, since it is listed as groups [meaning wider categories, groups of ore quality]. [On the other hand,] Vale is CBMX's biggest supporter, and on CBMX, you can list specification of the vessel [Vale's ore varies from vessel to vessel]" (Interview 69, Senior mining industry executive, 2012).

In September 2014, only two years after the launch, ownership of the CBMX platform was transferred to a Sino-foreign joint venture, the Beijing Iron Ore Trading Center Corporation (COREX). Ownership was now broadened to the Big Four producers,[10] the four largest Chinese steel mills, including Baosteel, and trading houses, as well as the original owner, CISA. Transaction volumes reached 30 million tonnes in 2015 and 100 million tonnes by 2016 ("China CBMX Transfers Iron Ore Trading Platform Ownership to JV of Mill, Miners, Traders" 2014).

In the aftermath of the fall of the iron ore benchmarking system, in 2011, Platts[11] launched what became the global iron ore market's main iron ore price index, IODEX (62% Fe CFR China), playing a determining role in the pricing of quarterly and spot contracts. That same year, a series of announcements of new, based-in-China iron ore pricing indices were also made, including the CSI Index, a new index by Custeel (led by CISA and other major Chinese steel firms). "Luo Bingsheng, deputy party secretary of China Iron and Steel Association (CISA), said . . . that 'China has always had doubts on IODEX'" (Park 2011). The China Iron Ore Price Index (CIOPI) was also launched not long thereafter.

In 2013, the NDRC went as far as to say that the Platts iron ore index could not be fully trusted because it uses opaque and unrepresentative pricing systems, which push prices higher, and because these inflated prices were the basis for its calculations (Zhong 2013). BHP and Platts immediately issued a rebuttal (Riseborough 2013). "From a China point of view, the Platts index is really opaque; they can't explain how they come up with the price, and its links with the three big iron ore companies and with companies such as Goldman Sachs and Merrill Lynch are evident!" (Interview 59, Chinese state-owned enterprise official, 2012). Another Chinese industry insider concurred: "People here do not think that Platts is transparent or objective" (Interview 111, Chinese state-owned enterprise employee, 2012).

In 2018, Reuters reported that Chinese import contracts were incorporating Chinese domestic iron ore index prices into their formula, a move that was encouraged by Chinese steel companies (Dai et al. 2018). Zhou Tao, an analyst at the CITIC, one of the largest Chinese state-owned financial conglomerates, was quoted as saying, about the development, that "China has been working to expand its pricing clout in resources" (Dai et al. 2018). The article continued, "While this may not have much of an impact on prices, it will give Chinese buyers confidence that prices reflect domestic demand and are in line with China's desire to increase its influence on commodity pricing." The report indicates that BHP had agreed to incorporate Mysteel prices, a Chinese index, and that Fortescue had agreed to incorporate Custeel and Mysteel prices into their formula.

Key Chinese market stakeholders continued to frame the ongoing liberalization and financialization of the global iron ore pricing regime as a market power struggle with international market stakeholders. From the perspective of CISA, the Platts iron ore index was still characterized as unfair, in 2019:

> Since 2009, with the end of the international iron ore long-term negotiation mechanism, the four major foreign mines have launched a pricing mechanism based on the Platts index in order to capture higher monopoly profits. The Platts index is a price indicator of iron ore imported into Chinese ports compiled by overseas agencies, which does not have the characteristics of openness, fairness and equity, and is not conducive to fair and mutually beneficial price negotiations between Chinese steel enterprises and the Big four miners. The excessively high iron ore prices caused by the extreme monopoly of foreign miners have not only put increasing pressure on the production and operation of Chinese steel enterprises, but also constitute an important threat to national industrial security. (Li, 2019)

Over the past two decades, a new iron ore market player slowly emerged in China, the traders. In the early 2000s, interviewees confirmed that although there was a spot market emerging in Hebei, traders were nonexistent. This changed with the financialization of the iron ore market from the 2010s onward. One interviewee put it this way:

> Who makes money speculating with price trends? The traders. They move the price down, the price up.... Iron ore traders in China also trade steel. They trade slag. They do a lot of things with the steelmakers, they do not only sell iron ore to them but also buy steel slag, ferroalloys.... There is a big link between Chinese traders and the steelmakers. Almost the same as what you have in Japan, with Mitsubishi who is close to Nippon Steel, and Mitsui who is close to JFE... it is similar, but much more aggressive because it is very China-centric. Japanese traders are everywhere, in Europe, etc. Chinese traders are only in China.

The interviewee continued by explaining what had been occurring with the dozens of traders in China:

> [They] are becoming really big. I know some of them that started trading two or three ships and are now trading probably a hundred or two hundred ships from Brazil, from Australia, from everywhere in the world. They blend. There is a big business in blending. You buy good iron ore here, and then this price is very low, this price is very high, but to blend iron ore you need a port and huge installations, so the Chinese ports today are becoming an iron ore blending system. (Interview 160, Former senior mining industry executive, 2022)

Many in China perceived the fall of the benchmark as an "own goal." Feelings of frustration linger until today and can explain the creation, on July 19, 2022, of the state-owned China Minerals Resources Group, a US$3 billion giant with the mandate to coordinate the global procurement behavior of Chinese iron ore market stakeholders, including iron ore purchases and overseas investments. As articulated by a Bloomberg piece breaking the news:

> The goal is to tackle what Beijing says is a power imbalance between a clutch of global mining giants on the one hand and China's vast but fragmented steel industry on the other. China imports 1.1 billion tonnes of iron ore annually, at a cost in 2021 of about $180 billion. There are about 500 steel mills in China, of which the top 10 companies only contribute 40% of the national output production. Each of the individual steel plants are responsible for buying their own raw materials, while iron ore supply by contrast is highly concentrated. By centralizing purchasing, China aims to gain more clout with suppliers over pricing.... People familiar with the matter have told Bloomberg that the company's creation was encouraged and closely monitored by top leaders in Beijing. They see a consolidated platform for buying

resources as a way to strengthen the country's negotiating position in an unfriendly international environment. (Cang, 2022)

It remains to be seen whether this attempt by the Chinese government to tighten up control of the domestic iron ore industry at the import interface will bear fruit. We have seen that previous consolidation attempts by the Chinese iron ore mining industry were not very successful. But this is the first time the effort has been concentrated at the import interface with the global iron ore market. In a way, the Chinese government is trying to replicate the successful Japanese model of the latter half of the twentieth century. Time will tell whether it is coming two decades too late. A former senior mining industry executive commented on this Bloomberg article, in an email exchange:

> There is a certain irony in this given that it was China who did [sic] for the benchmark system in the first place. And BHP only "spearheaded the move to floating prices" when the benchmark system had already effectively been destroyed and its [sic] had become apparent that this was the only possible way forward. A centralised buying arrangement is not going to be easy to pull off. As the article points out, there are 500 steel mills in China. This is not a Japan/RoK situation. . . . I can't see a full return to a benchmark system. This is a mature market with more players than was the case in the benchmark's heyday. But I don't think either we can rule out that this Chinese initiative will be without consequence. As you suggest, we may be looking towards a two-tier pricing system with annual contract pricing and spot pricing working in tandem. (Interview 169, Former senior mining industry insider, 2022)

## Conclusion

The global iron ore market saw rapid change toward the liberalization of the pricing regime. This was brought forward by the transition from Japan to China as the world's largest consumer, which disrupted established power relationships. Whereas the Japanese purchasers had spearheaded a stable regime by effectively coordinating procurement, the Chinese consumers suffered from excessive fragmentation and lack of coordination capacity. The move from a Japanese-dominated to a Chinese-dominated global market entailed a shift from one asymmetric position of market power to another—dominant consumers, Quadrant 3, to dominant producers, Quadrant 2—which made a change in global market institutions more likely and created opportunities for global iron ore producers to actualize their preferences regarding the iron ore pricing regime.

While global suppliers, led at first by BHP and Vale, actively pushed for spot pricing, the opening for them to do so was made possible by Chinese market stakeholders, who disrupted a long-standing pricing system. The fall of the decades-old international benchmarking regime was a consequence of Chinese consumers' lack of coordination capacity and, effectively, their weak position of market power compared with global producers. The fact that China had little control over the global iron ore pricing regime was painfully felt by Chinese stakeholders, given that China was by far the largest consumer of iron ore globally (Wu and Wu 2009). CISA Secretary General Shan admitted that "over the past few years, I wasn't able to better co-ordinate the Chinese steel industry and the iron ore price negotiations became disorganised. I had intended to encourage mergers, but the sector became more fragmented. I had planned to get rid of out-dated mills, but in fact steel capacity increased" (Tang, 2011).

## China's Impact on the Global Iron Ore Shipping Industry

### The Global Iron Ore Shipping Industry at the Time of China's Emergence as the Top Importer

The global iron ore shipping industry is relatively concentrated, with most tonnage controlled by either the exporters or the importers of the resource (Asariotis et al. 2011). Prior to China's emergence as the world's top iron ore importer, Japan had established its preferred stable system, where iron ore was priced prior to shipping, or FOB (free on board). Japanese steel mills dominated the bulk cargo shipping business and chartered the ships themselves as shipping costs were low. China's emergence disrupted these dynamics.

Iron ore was and continues to be the largest dry bulk commodity worldwide by volume. China's emergence as the largest iron ore consumer has transformed incentive structures in the global shipping market. The rapid increase in Chinese demand in the first decade of the 2000s led to the highest increase in dry bulk shipping freight rates in fifty years (Lu and Li 2009, 359). These price increases created opportunities that Australian and Brazilian producers seized upon differently than did the Chinese.

In 2008, the difference in freight costs to China between Brazil and Australia was around US$55/mt. Unlike Japan's emergence as the number one seaborne iron ore consumer, Chinese firms were not able to take control of the shipping market. As an iron ore industry insider explained, "The Australians were underpricing . . . FOB was based on low freight rates, and then they thought, 'Why should you save $20 by buying my stuff!!!' Spot CFR was a freight equalizer" (Interview 112, Iron ore industry analyst, 2012). During deadlocks in the iron ore pricing negotiations, Australian iron ore exporters began to shift to a CFR (cost and freight) pricing regime, in order to benefit from the increasingly significant differentials in shipping costs ("Iron Ore: A History" 2012). "In 2008 there were two key developments. For the first time, the Australian miners negotiated a different settlement than Vale to account for the significant freight differential that had started to develop over the previous 24 months.... Some entrants in the space, including Fortescue Metals Group Ltd., pushed for freight to be incorporated in pricing contracts" (China Blocks Large Ore Carriers from Ports 2012).

By 2007, "62% iron ore content CFR China" had become the pricing standard. Thus, the end of the era of Japanese influence on the iron ore pricing regime also heralded the end of the decades-long Japanese-led FOB pricing system for shipping. The emergence of China, and the rapid rise of shipping rates, coupled with Australian iron ore exporters' pathbreaking behavior and opportunism caused the pendulum to swing back in the other direction. Indeed, iron ore prices had also been settled "CFR," or "delivered," under the market's European tenure prior to Japan's emergence. "Before, shipping was the problem of the buyer, now it is the problem of the seller!" (Interview 69, Senior mining industry executive, 2012).

In stark contrast with the gradual evolution of the shipping-pricing regime under Japan's tenure as the dominant market player (which will be discussed below), China's impact on the shipping market was much more concentrated in time and there was an absence of careful planning and coordination between the Chinese steelmakers and the ship owner-operators. This allowed the big international iron ore suppliers to push for their preferred outcome.

Vale's reaction was as distinctive as was the result of China's arrival, which was a disruption to incentive structures. In 2008, to compensate for the swift increase in freight rates that benefited the Australian producers, Vale commissioned a new line of very large ore carriers (VLOCs), which it named "Valemax." Valemax carriers are the largest bulk carriers ever built: over twice the size of Capesize carriers (400,000 deadweight tonnage [dwt]).

## The Domestic Chinese Shipping Industry

In stark contrast with the above iron-ore-pricing-regime case, the Chinese shipping industry has undergone more successful consolidation. In 1999, COSCO and China Shipping controlled 60 percent of total Chinese tonnage (Flynn 1999). In December 2011, COSCO, already the second largest bulk shipping company in the world, launched COSCO Bulk Carrier Co. Ltd. (CBC). This new subsidiary owned 420 vessels and further consolidated three of its other subsidiaries in Tianjin, Qingdao, Shenzhen, and Hong Kong (Wu 2011). In 2016, COSCO merged with China Shipping, thereby continuing to consolidate its position domestically and in the global shipping market (Goh and Miller 2017).

In the early days of China's tenure as the largest consumer of iron ore, there were unsuccessful coordination attempts, between stakeholders of the Chinese steel and shipping industry that went counter to Japan's successful coordination of its domestic steel and shipping industries in the second half of the twentieth century. Initially, this gave international iron ore suppliers the opportunity to push for their preferred outcome (a "CFR China" pricing regime). However, following Vale's commissioning of a new line of extra-large ships, players in the Chinese shipping market were able to coordinate and organize a powerful response. This resulted in a stalemate in bargaining and, ultimately, in incremental changes that followed Chinese preferences for de-marketization. The key difference between the Chinese iron ore pricing and shipping cases is that China's interface with the global shipping market was much more concentrated and its coordination capacity here was greater (Table 3.2, Quadrant 4).

## China and the Valemax Shipping Impasse

Vale initially commissioned thirty-five Valemax cargo ships and had twenty-four of them built in China for a total cost of US$2 billion, of which US$1.3 billion was financed by the Export-Import Bank of China and the Bank of China (Murphy 2012). Chinese shipbuilders were some of the direct beneficiaries of this change in Vale's shipping strategy; these shipbuilders included China Rongsheng Heavy Industries Group and Bohai Shipbuilding Heavy Industry. The Chinese government and the large SOEs had been aware of this development for years (confirmed by various interviews with industry insiders, Beijing, 2012). Vale was confident that its shipping strategy would be in the interests of Chinese iron ore consumers because it would bring the price of Brazilian iron ore down (Interview 69, Senior mining industry executive, 2012).

The arrival of Vale-owned-and-controlled iron ore bulk carriers was unsettling for one group of Chinese stakeholders, however, mainly shipowners and chiefly COSCO, which stood to lose a share of the global iron ore bulk shipping business. The first Valemax ship, the *Vale Brazil*, was delivered to Vale in November 2011. A ship almost as large as the Valemax, the *Berge Everest*, a 388,000-tonne ship commissioned by the Singaporean company Berge Bulk, was delivered a month earlier and chartered by Vale. The *Berge Everest* had docked in Dalian in December 2011 without incident, and "the head of China's steel industry association said the ships would help lower costs" (Murphy 2012). At the time, this was how Vale's move was framed: "Vale SA, the world's largest iron ore producer by volume, took a significant step toward its goal of controlling all its shipping to China" (Wright et al. 2012). As a shipping industry expert explained, "If one owns the ships, one has better control on prices" (Interview 132, Academic at a Canadian university, 2013). This is exactly how COSCO perceived it.

Stunning the shipping world and beyond, on January 29, 2012, the Chinese Ministry of Transport, citing safety concerns, issued a notice specifying that cargo ships with a capacity greater than 350,000 dwt could not dock in Chinese ports. The China Shipowners Association also voiced its opposition to 400,000 dwt cargoes ever docking in Chinese ports (Rust 2014).

The rupture of one of the Valemax's hulls (the *Vale Beijing*) in early December 2011 may have provided the impetus for the ban. But the *Wall Street Journal* quoted shipping engineers as saying that safety concerns cited by the Chinese Transport Ministry were "insufficient to cast serious doubt on the safety of Valemax ships. Valemax vessels have docked at ports in such places as Japan, Italy, the Netherlands and the Philippines" (Murphy 2012). Jia Dashan from the China Waterborne Transport Research Institute confirmed, in the 2012 China International Steel and Raw Materials Conference Proceedings, that "in 2011, there were 45 wharfs capable of receiving VLOC and Capesize ships" in China (Jia 2012). An interview with a senior international executive in the iron ore industry confirmed that "at least three ports are equipped [to deal with the berthing of VLOCs]: Dalian, Qingdao and Majishan. The first two are public, the third one is private, Baosteel owns it, and it is near Shanghai" (Interview 69, Senior mining industry executive, 2012).

Several interviews confirm that Vale was taken aback, as were many Chinese iron ore industry insiders: "On the Valemax story, Vale feels cheated. Some of the Valemax cargoes were built here! China knew about it! And then turns around and blocks them!" (Interview 38, Diplomat posted in Beijing, 2012). A former senior mining industry executive with intimate knowledge of the matter said that "The first name of the ship was not Valemax, it was Chinamax! Then [Vale] saw there was difficulty to put the Chinamax there, [and] changed the name" (Interview 160, Former senior mining industry executive, 2022). A senior executive and iron ore industry insider confirmed Vale's response: "Was Vale surprised? Of course! It was even a surprise for the Chinese!!" (Interview 69, Senior mining industry executive, 2012). As one interviewee put it, "Vale sold the Valemax idea to China when the pricing system was FOB. In the FOB system, they could say they were then sharing costs... but by the time the ships got built, the market had shifted to CFR. Savings all belong to the seller! Vale makes more profits! Not fair!" (Interview 112, Iron ore industry analyst, 2012). But as in the iron ore benchmark case, interests diverged among different market stakeholders. Some, including large steel mills, were pleased about the ships' arrival on the market. As one stakeholder asserted, "Yes, about Valemax, the SOEs were happy. It was the shipping companies that weren't" (Interview 128, Chinese central government agency official, 2012). One senior international organization employee with knowledge of the matter confirmed that the decision to block Valemax cargoes was made at the very highest levels of the Chinese decision-making apparatus (Interview 135, Senior International organization employee, 2014). This makes sense given the various interest groups involved.

The ban was extremely costly for Vale, as the company had to shift carriers in the Philippines at an additional cost of between $US2 and $US7 per tonne (Vale mega ship, 2013; "Iron Ore: A History"). One iron ore industry insider put it at $US3–$US4 per tonne (Interview 112, Iron ore industry analyst, 2012). This meant Vale was forced to unload its Valemax cargoes at docking stations in the Philippines and South Korea before loading the ore onto smaller vessels for the remainder of the journey to China.

There was no consensus among all of the interested parties, just as in the iron ore case, and the impetus for the blocking came from one powerful state-owned firm in response to specific developments abroad. The key difference between the iron ore benchmark case and the shipping case is that China's interface with the global shipping market in that particular industry was much more concentrated and the capacity for coordinating behavior was much greater. The strongest opposition and lobbying came mainly from Chinese ship owner-operators, led by COSCO. They feared they were going to lose shipping business but held enough sway over the Chinese Shipowners Association, the port authorities, and the Transport Ministry to make a ban happen. Another interviewee noted that "COSCO owns shares in Chinese ports" (Interview 132, Academic at a Canadian university, 2013). A senior international iron ore company executive confirmed that "[t]he whole Valemax saga . . . actually the main perpetrator is COSCO!" (Interview 69, Senior mining industry executive, 2012). This was confirmed by a former Brazilian mining executive close to Vale:

> We started building the Valemax in 2008. We went to China and looked at all the ports that could receive the ship. . . . And the 400 thousand tonnes . . . we could build 500, 600, but why 400? Because those vessels could berth in existing ports in China. We went to every port, and talked to all the ones responsible for the port and everybody was ready because it would be good for them. . . . And then I start to hear about the fact that the Chinese would not let us berth. And the main reason was COSCO. COSCO made a very bad deal two years prior, during the global financial crisis. COSCO tried to monopolize all the ships in the world. So, . . . they went to the other ship owners and hired all the ships based on something like 60$/tonne and started charging 80 or 90$/

tonne. But after the market collapsed, what happened, the freight went down very sharply. So, they had big losses with their contracts.... They put their finger to us. Vale with their big ships ... destroying COSCO. Then the Chinese government decided to put the limit to 300 thousand tonnes. (Interview 160, Former senior mining industry executive, 2022)

Around the time of the announcement that Valemax ships would be blocked from docking at Chinese ports, Mr. Shouguo Zhang, vice executive chairman of China Shipowners Association, was quoted as saying the following:

Vale is an iron ore producing corporation that obviously lacks experience in ship safety management, ship pollution prevention and ship operation and management. It is difficult for them to run ships as good as professional shipping companies and thus tend to arouse safety and environment risks.... Vale holds the cargo to itself and now intends to control shipping tonnage. It is a matter of monopoly and unfair competition, which not only harms the shipping interest [sic] of mainland China but also that of South Korea, Japan and the Taiwan area. (2011)

"It is obvious and natural that a company like COSCO will be upset that a former client now becomes a competitor" (Murphy 2012). It is worth noting that the president of the Chinese Shipowners Association at the time, Wei Jiafu, who also happened to be the president of COSCO, "used his influence as head of the China Shipowners Association to start a vocal campaign against Vale's vessels. Wei lobbied the NDRC, as well as the Ministry of Transportation" (Fabi and Lian 2011). The vice executive chairman of the China Shipowners Association was quoted as saying, "Vale holds the cargo to itself and now intends to control shipping tonnage. It is a matter of monopoly and unfair competition which ... harms the shipping interests of mainland China" (China Shipowners 2011).

The blocking of the Valemax cargoes is best understood in the context of China's large iron ore importers' perceptions of vulnerability to one of the largest iron ore suppliers in the world, combined with their domestic position of strength. "Valemaxes could give the miner complete monopolization of the iron ore supply to China," said an iron ore official in Northern China, echoing the complaints of several steelmakers (Fabi and Lian 2011).

The blocking of the global iron ore giant Vale's carriers was due to the successful coordination that took place among key Chinese stakeholders and resulted in a deadlock. The only way out for Vale was for it to agree to charter some of the ships back to Chinese shipping companies and, thus, to "share" some of the shipping business. Indeed, as early as 2011, "Vale [had] offered to sell or lease the fleet as it look[ed] to appease foreign shipowners" (Fabi and Lian 2011).

In 2013, a few reports emerged of a quiet docking by the Vale Malaysia, which arrived in Lianyungang, in Jiangsu, on April 14 of that year. The Chinese media company Caixin reported that "The China Shipowners Association (CSA), the powerful industry organization, which has long opposed the entrance of Vale's ships in Chinese ports, said it reported the issue to the National Development and Reform Commission, the Ministry of Transport and the Lianyungang Port Authority" (June 2013). Then, in December 2013, there was news of one such "sharing agreement" by José Carlos Martins, executive director of ferrous and strategy, Vale:

> More details of a controversial charter arrangement have come to light as Brazilian miner Vale continues to struggle with access to Chinese ports. . . . Qingdao-based Shandong Shipping Alliance took the four ships on five-year bareboat charters at the end of October but has not so far said which ones. . . . "We have just concluded this operation this year with Shandong Shipping. And we believe that in the future we will also complete other agreements with other shipping companies, preferably from China," Martins told investors and journalists. . . . Despite the hush-hush, two of the ships have quietly begun to trade under their new charter names. They are the 402,000-dwt Shandong Da De (ex–Rio de Janeiro, built 2011) and Shandong Da Zhi (ex–Vale Minas Gerais, built 2012). ("Shandong Valemax Secrets Slipping Out" 2014)

On September 12, 2014, in a groundbreaking announcement that heralded the resolution of an almost three-year impasse, Vale revealed that it had reached a "framework agreement for strategic cooperation in iron ore shipping" with COSCO. Following the terms of the agreement, Vale transferred four VLOCs to COSCO and chartered them back from the shipping giant for the next twenty-five years (Vale and COSCO signed a co-operation agreement on VLOCs in 2014). It agreed to similar terms regarding ten more VLOCs to be built by COSCO to transport iron ore from Brazil, as well as two more cooperation agreements with Chinese shipping companies. As the former Brazilian mining executive explained,

> China Merchants were the first to make an agreement with us to build Valemax. Then others came. Other companies, not steel makers, but shipping companies. Then even COSCO made an agreement with us. At that point in time, the ports started to become more flexible to welcome the ships. Here and there. One ship here, one ship there.

And then today [Vale] has more than fifty Valemax operating. [The Chinese government] understood this was for real. [Vale is] delivering the ore at lower cost. In Japan, in Korea. Chinese steelmakers started going to the government and said look, Vale built these ships, they are delivering at much lower freight to Japan, Korea, and you are not taking any of them. So, a movement started inside China to allow [Valemax ships] to berth. . . . [Vale] had a very good meeting with someone at the Ministry of Communications and Transportation. He [said] a very simple thing, he said, "Big ships are the future no doubt about that. But now, you know, China is the mother, and she has a lot of children. And one of the children is not performing the way we would like to see, but it is our child. It continues to be our child. We are not going to take a decision against our child." He used this metaphor to say to us that he understood the movement, but it was something they couldn't do against COSCO. COSCO had those huge losses because of these bad contracts. The guy was very strong politically. As some customers started to get interested in the ships, things started moving. (Interview 160, Former senior mining industry executive, 2022)

In 2015, the Chinese Ministry of Transport lifted the ban on the Valemax ships. Later the same year, COSCO bought a further four Valemax ships and, in 2016, COSCO, China Merchants and ICBC purchased a further thirty Valemax ships (2016).

## Conclusion

The broader context that led to COSCO's successful coordination of the Chinese domestic market interface was the disruption of the iron ore shipping industry that followed China's emergence as the world's top importer of iron ore. The shift toward a spot pricing regime in the iron ore market that occurred in 2009–2010 was accompanied by a shift from FOB pricing to CFR China pricing. This led to a dramatic shift in the relative position of Brazilian and Australian producers. Since iron ore was suddenly priced as "delivered to China," and since Brazil is further away from China than Australia is, this put the Brazilians at a clear disadvantage. This situation led Vale's move to commission the larger Valemax ships. Key Chinese shipping industry stakeholders, led by COSCO, were able to coordinate behavior in response to this move by Vale. Higher coordination capacity in the Chinese iron ore shipping industry was partly the result of more-successful restructuring in China's shipping industry in the 1990s, compared to its iron ore and steel industries.

Ironically, many of Vale's ships were built in China and the reductions in the price of delivered iron ore were clearly in the interests of various powerful Chinese market stakeholders, including the shipbuilding companies, the Export-Import Bank of China (which financed the deal), and the large consumers of iron ore that would benefit from the lower costs. Yet these stakeholders did not control the interface between the Chinese shipping industry and the global shipping market.

This position of strength enabled COSCO to match the market power of the global iron ore giant Vale and resulted in a deadlock of almost three years and ensuing bargaining dynamics (Quadrant 4). Ultimately, the dominant stakeholders in the Chinese shipping industry were able to actualize their preferences towards de-liberalization and to force Vale's hand into the freight-sharing arrangements.

## Japan's Impact on the Global Iron Ore Market Fifty Years Prior

### Market Power and Market Change

At the time of Japan's emergence as the number one iron ore consumer in the world, in the second half of the twentieth century, the Japanese consumers were in a favorable asymmetric position of market power relative to global iron ore suppliers, given their high levels of coordination at the interface with the global market and the relative fragmentation of global market stakeholders (they were situated in Quadrant 3). This enabled them to actualize their preferences for global pricing regimes. The Japanese import ecosystem had a significant impact on the global iron ore pricing and shipping regimes over the course of subsequent decades. Major players included large steelmakers such as Nippon Steel and corporate groups (Keiretsu) such as Mitsubishi. The preference of Japanese importers for the de-liberalization of the global iron ore pricing regime, a movement toward the strategic end of the spectrum, can be explained given the domestic position of market power they occupied. Japanese iron ore consumers dominated the iron ore market for decades and oversaw the establishment of the very negotiated annual benchmark pricing regime Chinese consumers would rise to disrupt in 2010.

### Global Iron Ore Industry and Pricing Regime Prior to Japan's Emergence

Immediately following World War II, reconstruction efforts in Europe lent momentum to the global steel industry, particularly in Germany, which occupied a price-leading role in negotiations with Swedish iron ore producers (Pnovolos 1987). "The annual price negotiations as existed after World War II were for the longest time between the German mills' buying agent (Rohstoffhandel) and mainly the Brazilian miner CVRD, now Vale" (Interview 126, Former director at several iron ore mining companies, 2013).

When Japan emerged as one of the largest players in the 1960s, it was considered a latecomer to the iron ore market, similar to China in the 2000s, when it emerged as the world's largest iron ore importer Japanese steelmakers were paying a 50 percent premium over European steelmakers (Rodrik 1982, 549).

> Post–World War II, iron ore pricing was dominated by Europe via the Rotterdam pricing mechanism and prices were settled from the start of January to coincide with the European financial year. ThyssenKrupp, and latterly the predecessors of ArcelorMittal, settled annual deals with miners in Canada, Sierra Leone, Liberia and Brazil for ore on a CIF Rotterdam basis. ("Iron Ore: A History" 2012)

Contrary to the state of affairs in the 2000s at the time of China's emergence, however, global iron ore suppliers were geographically dispersed and not coordinated. In the 1950s, the Japanese were importing under short-term contracts and relied on eighty-six suppliers in fourteen countries (Hurst 2015b). The pricing regime was much less institutionalized; the global market was decentralized and fragmented, with many domestic needs being fulfilled domestically or regionally (Sukagawa 2010). Before Japan's emergence, iron ore was priced CIF Rotterdam (Banks 1979).

In addition, when Australia gradually emerged as a leading producer in the 1960s, not only was the Australian iron ore industry underdeveloped but also high levels of inter-provincial infighting weakened the hand of Australian iron ore exporters (Wilson 2013; Rodrik 1982).[12] "The three largest exporters of iron ore to Japan—Australia, Brazil and India—have always been more dependent on the Japanese market than Japan has been dependent on them" (Rodrik 1982, 550).

## The Japanese Domestic Steel Industry

The Japanese domestic steel industry has historically exhibited high levels of domestic concentration and coordination (Rodrik 1982; Sukagawa 2010; Wilson 2012, 2013). In the 2000s, Japan's three biggest steel makers still produced 70 percent of total domestic steel (Bergsten et al. 2008) and Nippon Steel, the leading Japanese negotiator during the benchmark years, controlled about a third of Japanese production ("The Lore of Ore" 2012), or 26 percent in 2000 (Rapp 2002).

The core characteristic of the Japanese model revolved around the critical role the state played in successfully steering the country's development path (Johnson 1982; Katzenstein 1985). Japan relied on a mixture of policies that included the formation of cartels and a financial architecture that encouraged the socialization of risk (Katzenstein 1985). Following the emergence of Australia as a major iron ore exporter in the 1960s, the largest Japanese steel firms formed a buying cartel in 1964 (the Committee of Ten). The cartel, led by Nippon Steel, provided the Japanese with a consolidated negotiating position in the face of a fragmented Australian position. Japanese firms displayed coordination in another way: They sustained a long-term view of their iron ore and coal demand over the coming decades and carried out "pre-emptive investments" to stimulate iron ore supply and stifle the consolidation of the iron ore suppliers in both industries in Australia (Banks 1979; Sukagawa 2010; Rodrik 1982).

"Japan got its act together much more than China. When it could see its demand was going to go up, it encouraged producers to build new mines, and faced a very stable market over time, regardless of the increase in demand" (Interview 112, Iron ore industry analyst, 2012). As Rodrik describes, following Australia's emergence as a major iron ore exporter in the 1960s,

> There was a rush of American and European capital to mine the vast deposits of the country. Finance for these ventures was obtained in large part with the assurance provided by the long-term contracts signed between the Australian mines and Japanese steel producers. In these initial long-term contracts Japan exhibited a strategy which has paid off quite well to this day. Japan's largest steel companies formed a buying cartel in 1964 when the vast extent of Australian deposits became evident. Called the Committee of Ten, the cartel allowed the Japanese to negotiate as a single unit while the Australian mining companies and the different states competed with each other on the terms of contracts. (Rodrik 1982, 549)

Rodrik continues, "Despite frequent renegotiations of these [long-term] contracts . . ., the superior bargaining position of the Japanese deriving from their monopsony power over their suppliers, ensured that the contracts would work to the advantage of the Japanese" (Rodrik 1982, 550). One iron ore industry insider with decades of experience, including at the negotiation table, said that "Japanese iron ore companies in the '80s and '90s used to have joint ventures with Australian companies and then sit at the negotiation table on the side of the Japanese ... the Australians were naive" (Interview 87, Private sector mining executive, 2012).

This level of coordination also extended to the shipping sector. In 1963, Japan's Ministry of International Trade and Industry (MITI) pushed through with the successful rationalization of the Japanese shipping industry, which consolidated from eighty-eight firms down to six (Hurst 2015b). So at the time of Japan's emergence as the world's leading iron ore importer, the country was firmly situated as a highly coordinated domestic consumer (Quadrant 3) facing fragmented global producers. This coordination capacity enabled the Japanese players to actualize their preferences toward the de-marketization of global iron ore pricing regimes.

## Japan's Impact on the Global Iron Ore Pricing and Shipping Regimes

Japan's iron ore consumption rose rapidly after the end of World War II, as the country embarked on a path of reconstruction and intensive industrial development. In the 1960s, pricing conventions began to shift after Japan began importing the bulk of all global iron ore imports. In 1964, Japanese steel mills negotiated their original long-term iron ore contract with Australian suppliers (Barndon 2016; Hurst 2015b). This contract was the precursor to the annual benchmark regime, which evolved to include Australian and Brazilian companies leading on the suppliers' side (BHP, Amax, and Rio Tinto, as well as Vale[13]) and Nippon Steel on the Japanese side (Sukagawa 2010).

The 1970s and 1980s saw the continuation of the leadership transition from German to Japanese consumers in the annual price negotiations. By the late 1970s, the Japanese mills were procuring 96 percent of their iron ore on long-term contracts, and the benchmarking system had been stabilized, with annual negotiations, ten-year supply arrangements, and terms that ran in line with the Japanese financial year (April to March) (Banks 1979).

The Japanese mills were procuring iron ore at prices that were 20–50 percent below United States prices (Rodrik 1982) and eventually came to determine prices for the rest of the global industry, including European purchasers ("Iron Ore: A History" 2012).

A former senior mining executive with intimate knowledge of the benchmarking system recounted the story of the role the Japanese consumers played in the establishment of the benchmarking system as follows:

> It was done between January and April every year. Because everything was following the Japanese system. If you look at the corporate year

in Japan, the year is April to March. So, the benchmark system was negotiated for one year, April to March. Because of the way they negotiate with the car industry. . . . The benchmark system itself was a creation of the Japanese steel industry. They did it because there were direct negotiations between the Europeans and the Australians and the Brazilians . . . but the Japanese created this model. They put it in place and also did this very interesting thing, they kind of, they created the commoditization of iron ore. Because iron ore is not a pure commodity. Every mine has a different characteristic, different quality. They created a price for dry metric tonne units. They created a price for every percent of iron ore content. By doing that they commodified the product. This is very, very interesting, they were clever. You can see that they were very well prepared for this. And they always managed to create overcapacity. They came to Brazil and helped to build a big mine. Then they went to Australia and helped to build a big mine. . . . The combination of Australian ore and Brazilian ore was very good for the Japanese. Australia is very close to them, and Brazil is very far. Brazil has high quality and, in Australia, to develop new mines, they had to go for the low-quality ore. Today the majority of the product on the market is Australian. But at the time, it was not developed. The Japanese did it with the help of high-quality Brazilian ore and Canadian ore. They could mix it. They were always developing very interesting things, to control the price of iron ore. (Interview 160, Former senior mining industry executive, 2022)

The Japanese tenure as lead negotiator heralded an era of stable prices: "The market was very, very stable. Long-term contracts, one year price, FOB and no traders. It was a kind of agreement between the [Japanese] steel makers and the iron ore producers. They agreed on it. The Japanese were able to convince people that that was better. . . . The Koreans followed the same Japanese style, the Taiwanese also" (Interview 160, Former senior mining industry executive, 2022). In the 1980s, iron ore prices rarely fluctuated by more than a few dollars annually and remained close to US$20 a tonne until China's emergence. Over time, Japanese consumers established an intricate institutional system that underpinned the pricing regime and included practices that aimed to avoid supply disruptions, such as cooperation in case of hardship and provisional pricing in case annual negotiations were not concluded on time (Sukagawa 2010). By the 1980s, the iron ore benchmarking system had been centered on Japanese purchasers, which held annual talks with the three big miners—BHP, Rio, and Vale—and determined prices for the rest of the global industry, including European purchasers ("Iron Ore: A History" 2012). "The Japanese signed long-term contracts of a decade or more to ensure Australians could secure mining investment. Contract periods shortened with the arrival of competition from Brazilian ore, resulting in a one-year benchmark-price system that lasted for 40 years" ("The Lore of Ore" 2012). The investments and financial assistance for mining iron ore that the Japanese firms provided to their suppliers also helped shape the industry: "So widespread was the form of assistance that by the end of the 1960s almost all (96%) of Japanese imports of iron ore came from sources which had received long-term Japanese loans or other types of financial commitment (including direct foreign investment)" (Rodrik 1982, 551).[14]

Parallel trends were at play in the iron ore shipping sector. In the 1960s, following industrial consolidation, the Japanese shipping companies invested in large bulk vessels. Japanese policies had an impact on overall shipping costs (Banks 1979), which was fundamental to the emergence of Australia and Brazil as leading iron ore producers.

When Japan emerged as one of the largest iron ore importers in the world in the 1960s, the accepted shipping convention was CFR (delivered to) Rotterdam. The Japanese eventually insisted on paying the Rotterdam CFR price as well. Despite the fact that from the perspective of the Atlantic suppliers the freight cost to Japan was higher, Japanese consumers were able to reach an arrangement, with these suppliers (the Brazilians and the Canadians), that allowed Japan to pay a recalculated price. The system was called freight sharing, but it was essentially a theoretical calculation that led to Japan paying a lower FOB price that reflected the fact that the suppliers were paying the difference in the shipping costs (Interview 127, Former director at several iron ore mining companies, 2013). The Japanese initiative, led by Nippon Steel, included the establishment of a freight-sharing system with Brazilian producer Vale to account for freight cost differentials between Brazil and Japan and Europe and Japan (Sukagawa 2010), reminiscent of the arrangement the Chinese had struck with Vale in the mid-2010s. In close coordination with the Japanese government, the Japanese steel mills negotiated a transition to FOB pricing with Australian producers. This worked to the benefit of the Japanese shipping industry, but it went against the will of the Australian suppliers, which preferred delivering the iron they produced (Hurst 2015b).

"Despite the insistence of the Australians for CIF prices, the contract prices were stipulated in FOB terms, which allowed the Japanese to reap the benefits of future declines in freight costs" (Rodrik 1982, 550). In other words, the Japanese steelmakers, knowing that they would have more control over costs and the industry in general if they shipped the iron ore themselves, slowly inflicted price reductions on iron ore suppliers and, eventually, through a coordinated industrial policy, also gained control of the shipping part of the equation. To do so,

> [t]he Japanese pioneered the construction of large bulk vessels and highly efficient unloading and port facilities. As a result, freight charges as a share of the landed cost of Japanese iron ore fell by more than 50% between 1956 and 1976, although the average shipping distance increase [sic] by almost 1000 miles in the same period. (Rodrik 1982, 550)

Japanese preferences for a stable benchmark pricing regime continued well into the 2000s. As the benchmark pricing regime was falling apart, Japanese steel mills continued to prefer longer-term contracts to support the benchmarking regime (Interview 98, CEO, Iron ore industry consultancy firm, 2012). "'It is against our creed that we break contracts and shift to spot buying when the market is not good,' [said] Eiji Hayashida, chairman of the Japan Iron and Steel Federation" (Blas 2011).

## Conclusion

In the end, as a former senior mining industry executive explained, the Chinese iron ore importers may have attempted to model their industry's interaction with global markets on that of the Japanese, but the combination of domestic and international circumstances did not enable a parallel outcome:

> The biggest iron ore and steel producer in China, Baosteel, they had a technical agreement with the Japanese. They tried to bring all the same ideas, long-term contracts, development of new mines, because if you want to increase your steel production, at the same time you have to increase mine output. . . . But first, the pace of growth in China was much quicker than in Japan. Second, fragmentation. I think the combination of fast growth and the fragmentation helped to bring an end to the benchmark system. (Interview 160, Former senior mining industry executive, 2022)

In the three within-market case studies under review in this chapter, deep transformations in market power relations between consumers and producers led to instability in global market institutions and increased the likelihood of market institutional change. When consumers found themselves in a position of relatively superior coordination capacity, a type of market power, like the Japanese in the second half of the twentieth century, this enabled them to have more influence on the global pricing regime, which they pushed in their preferred direction. When, in the late 2000s, the Chinese iron ore consumers found themselves in a position of market vulnerability, global suppliers had a window of opportunity within which to influence change in their preferred direction.

In the case of the fall of the iron ore benchmarking regime, the combination of two dynamics led to the fall and liberalization of the decades-old iron ore benchmark pricing regime. First, a market power transition between Japan and China as the number one consumer disrupted the established power relationships between consumers and producers. This movement from one extreme position of market asymmetry to another saw a significant transfer of market power from Japanese consumers to global producers and increased the likelihood of institutional market change at the global level (a movement from Quadrant 2 to 3). Second, the fact that Chinese iron ore market stakeholders had low market power (or coordination capacity), compared to global iron ore market stakeholders (which were highly concentrated and better coordinated), led to disorganized and destabilizing procurement behavior on behalf of Chinese consumers. An advantageous position of market power gave global market stakeholders more influence in pushing for their preferred outcome at the global level. The fragmented domestic situation in China also meant that Chinese domestic market stakeholders expressed different preferences and behaviors, including some (by the smaller Chinese steelmakers) that overlapped with the preferences of global iron ore suppliers.

Decades earlier, Japanese consumers had established a benchmark pricing regime that was in the mirror opposite situation: coordinated Japanese consumers facing fragmented global market producers. In that scenario, the transition to a Japanese-dominated global market was less disruptive, given that the transition occurred within the same quadrant, Quadrant 3 (market power relations between previously dominant and coordinated key consumers [Europeans] and relatively fragmented global producers were maintained). An advantageous position of market power gave Japanese consumers more influence in pushing for their preferred global pricing regime, which, in this case, was in the direction of de-liberalization.

The case of the shipping-pricing regime allows us to investigate a closely related market situation where China's rise also disrupted established conventions, but where leading Chinese market stakeholders—COSCO, port authorities, and the Ministry of Transport—were able to successfully coordinate Chinese behavior and influence the outcomes in their preferred direction, in this case, de-liberalization.

This chapter demonstrates the importance of studying the impacts of emerging economies on global markets from the perspective of the resonance and complementarity between leading domestic and global market stakeholders. The fall of the benchmarking regime, the blocking of Valemax cargoes from docking at Chinese ports, or Japan's emergence and the creation of a stable pricing regime in the second half of the twentieth century cannot be explained from either a uniquely international or domestic perspective. The interaction of domestic and international market stakeholders and, specifically, their relative market power combined to create the conditions for market institutional change at the global level.

This chapter highlights the need to look beyond the national level and to take variation seriously. By tracing international procurement behavior back to their domestic roots, even within one commodity market, within-country variations in market dynamics are apparent. In the case of iron ore procurement, Chinese market stakeholders were fragmented and had a weak capacity to coordinate behavior; in the case of the shipping industry, Chinese stakeholders were able to coordinate behavior and exert influence. We cannot presume unitary Chinese patterns of behavior. In these two within-case studies, the source of variation in Chinese behaviour globally can be traced to domestic dynamics.

Being attentive to domestic realities does not mean that Chinese behavior abroad will simply be an extension of the character of its domestic markets. The argument that China will bring an increased role of the state into global markets because of the statist nature of its economy does not hold true, at least not across all cases. This book argues that domestic market structures matter especially in relation to their global market counterparts. In other words, Chinese market actors do not enter neutral global markets. Global market configurations matter equally to our understanding of institutional change. We need to pay attention to variation at the global level as well. Analyses that are more sensitive to variations in global market dynamics would bring much needed nuance to ongoing debates about the future of the global economy. The argument presented in this chapter, in fact, turns a classical liberal argument (Ikenberry 2008) on its head: Instead of China integrating into the existing liberal international order, I argue that China has led to the liberalization of a global market. Underproblematizing global (open) markets—one of the pillars of the liberal international order—can obscure the existing power relations embedded in global market institutions, a key variable in explaining relations between Chinese and global market stakeholders and the resilience of global market institutions.

Finally, this chapter calls for increased attention to the notion of Chinese market vulnerability and its multiple incarnations and consequences at the global level. Counterintuitively, fragmented Chinese domestic stakeholders, in a weak position of market power, can have large impacts on global markets. We cannot assume that China's largest impacts internationally are the result of a position of strength, whereas a position of weakness would lead China to be a "rule-taker" or to seamlessly integrate into international markets. The relationship between Chinese domestic dynamics and institutional change at the global level is more nuanced. Given China's size, positions of vulnerability and strength can be associated with large global impacts. It is essential that we pay attention to internal Chinese dynamics to better understand the nature of Chinese behavior, as well as the likelihood for it to change over time. In the iron ore benchmark pricing case studied here, a Chinese position of market vulnerability led to the disruption of a long-lasting global market institution. Indicating awareness of the impact of fragmentation on the capacity for Chinese market stakeholders to influence global market institutions, in the summer 2022 the Chinese government announced the creation of a "macro-coordinator" of the iron ore industry, the China Mineral Resources Group. Its mission explicitly includes the coordination of the various Chinese iron ore market stakeholders at the interface with global markets.

# 5

# China's Impact on the Global Potash Market

## Market Power, Market Vulnerability, and Market Change

Due to the intense monopoly of international potash fertilizer resources and production capacity, in order to ensure domestic potash supply and price stability, and to enhance China's foreign procurement bargaining power, at the instruction of the State Council, the Ministry of Commerce established in 2005 a potash import price joint negotiating mechanism, which . . . took the lead in coordinating domestic potash importers to negotiate prices with a united outward front, to achieve the purpose of "one voice to the outside world" and to strive for maximum national benefits. . . . Know oneself and know your enemy, you will never lose a hundred battles. Sinochem notice, 2020. (Zhu 2020)

In 2010, when I started investigating China's impact on the global iron ore and potash markets, the global iron ore benchmark pricing regime was literally falling apart before our eyes. In the story that unfolds, the potash market experienced very different global market outcomes as a result of China's emergence. Many of my interviewees, especially those operating in China, would readily compare the cases of potash and iron ore, often without being prompted. The Chinese iron ore market stakeholders who were frustrated with China's market vulnerability in that market would find that the potash case offered an unattainable exemplar of unity of purpose and coordination.

The potash market stakeholders would find that the iron ore case offered a ready cautionary tale. As one interviewee commented, "the domestic markets for potash and uranium are very concentrated. We were successful in those markets. The market for iron ore is another story" (Interview 8, Chinese media executive, 2012). Even state-owned companies publicly compared the relative power of potash importers to the relative vulnerability of iron ore importers. In 2015, Sinochem published the following note on its website: "Experts involved in the negotiations said that China is the largest importer of iron ore, but we also pay the highest price, and have almost no say; while the situation is different for potash imports, the country clenches a fist from top to bottom, so that we can effectively release our power" (Yin 2015).

These diverging global outcomes happened despite the fact that the potash and iron ore markets presented similar global characteristics prior to China's emergence as dominant consumer. Indeed, in the early 2000s, both markets were highly concentrated, geographically and by firm,[1] and global prices were determined by annual benchmarking negotiations between producers and consumers, which set prices for the following year. China had also developed high levels of import dependence toward both markets. Yet the Chinese domestic political economy of the two markets varied significantly, including at the interface with global markets.

This chapter tells the story of the evolution of the global potash market following China's emergence as a dominant consumer in the late 1990s and early 2000s. In the case of iron ore, we saw the abrupt fall of the decades-old iron ore benchmark pricing regime. In the potash case, we have seen the continuation of the global potash market's negotiated benchmark pricing regime, with China as the benchmark price setter. However, China's emergence also led to the breakdown of the Russia-Belarus export marketing arrangement, to the weakening of Canpotex, Canada's marketing and logistics export company, and to some increased global competition. In sum, in the potash case, for almost twenty years until 2020, the trends were in the direction of a mixture of stability and gradual liberalization in China's advantage: stability in terms of the negotiated pricing regime, as Chinese consumers wanted it, and some level of increased competition among global potash producers, something Chinese consumers also favored.

At the time of China's emergence as dominant potash consumer at the turn of the twenty-first century, the coordination capacity of market stakeholders in the global potash market was high, at similar levels or higher than in the global iron ore market. China faced essentially two export and marketing organizations (some would say cartels) controlling the vast majority of potash resources.

At the domestic level, there were sharp divergences between the iron ore and potash cases. Whereas in the iron ore case, key Chinese domestic market players were unable to coordinate procurement, in the potash case, Chinese domestic market players have demonstrated a continued ability to coordinate procurement strategy. Chinese domestic potash consumers consisted essentially of two large players: Sino-Agri and Sinofert (a subsidiary of Sinochem). This placed Chinese domestic market players in a position of market power symmetry vis-à-vis global market players. This symmetry of market power translated into a tug of war and in bargaining patterns between producers and consumers and eventually in moderate and incremental liberalization of the global market, much of it in favor of Chinese consumers, until recently. The symmetry of market power also played a role in the resilience of the international potash market's benchmark pricing regime, which survives until today. This overall pattern is characteristic of that formulated in the model presented in this book (Table 3.1) for cases where there is near symmetry in coordination capacity.

Yet, China found itself in a more vulnerable position in the 2022 global potash market than in the early 2010s. Indeed, something started shifting in 2018–2019, with the emergence of Brazil as an increasingly dominant potash importer. Since then, the stability of global potash market institutions has been shaken, and China's position as dominant consumer and benchmark price setter has weakened. In an ironic turn of events, it appears as though Brazil's rapid rise as key consumer and the lack of coordination among its importers has led to the emergence of an increasingly significant global potash spot market in a fashion that mirrors China's impact on the global iron ore market ten years prior.

And here again we find a tension between China's size, its resource security ambitions, its market power, and its capacity to affect change at the global level. China is in some ways the victim of its own successful coordinated negotiation strategy. As lead benchmark price negotiator, wielding critical market power with three large importers presenting a strong united front to the world, China has been able to negotiate prices that are significantly lower than those prevailing on the spot market (in 2022 at times prices were close to twice as low). As a result, with sanctions imposed on Belarus in 2019, and the disruptions caused by Russia's invasion of Ukraine, in the 2022 tightly supplied global fertilizer market, potash producers have little incentive to send volumes to China and much more incentive to supply Brazil.

This chapter highlights details of China's domestic market dynamics that are key to explaining its behavior internationally and to tracing its impact on institutional change in the global market. But an inside-out perspective only tells half of the story. To get the full picture, we must study the interactions between domestic and international market players, specifically as it concerns their relative positions of market power. To do so, this chapter unveils interactions among Chinese domestic potash market players, these key importers' international procurement behaviors, their interactions with global potash producers, interactions among global potash producers, and the impact of the resulting market power dynamics on global potash market institutions.

The rest of this chapter is organized as follows. The first section provides an overview of the nature of potash as a global commodity as well as China's size as dominant consumer. The following section characterizes the global potash market and its pricing regime prior to China's emergence as dominant consumer. The third section provides a characterization of China's domestic potash industry, including the process-tracing of the regulatory environment that led to high levels of coordination at China's interface with the global industry. Finally, the fourth section provides an analysis of the evolution of global potash market institutions over the past fifteen years, including significant price concessions obtained by Chinese negotiators at various points over the past decade, the fall of the Russia-Belarus producers' cartel in July 2013 and China-led adjustments in the frequency of the benchmark negotiations.

## China and the Global Potash Market

Potash (containing potassium, chemical symbol K) is one of three essential plant nutrients, alongside phosphate (phosphorous, chemical symbol P) and nitrate (nitrogen, chemical symbol N). It is indispensable to agriculture, as it has a significant impact on plant yields and their overall health.[2] There are no substitutes for potassium as an essential plant nutrient and an essential nutritional requirement for animals and humans. Potash cannot be manufactured; it must be extracted from natural origins.

Historically, China has tended to use less potash compared to the two other fertilizer groups. Chinese potash deposits had not been developed until the late 1990s, and potash nutrients were obtained using less-efficient small-scale methods.[3] Starting in the 1980s, with clear acceleration in the 1990s, China started using chemical potash fertilizers and went from a minor share of global agricultural use of potash to the world's number one consumer in 2002, with 21 percent of global consumption, or 4.9 million tonnes (see Figures 5.1 and 5.2). It now consumes 10.4 million tonnes of potash annually, well above Brazil, the United States, and India, the three next largest potash consumers globally (FAO 2019).

Starting in the 2000s, China started ramping up its domestic potash production. Since 2014, China has produced close to or above 6 million tonnes of potash annually. Despite its rapidly increasing domestic production, the gap between its agricultural use and production has remained significant (see Figure 5.3). This gap has to be filled with imports.

In 2001, China's import dependence stood at 90 percent, according to FAO data.[4] Import dependence levels started declining in the 2000s, following the rise in domestic production, and stabilized at between 40 percent and 50 percent

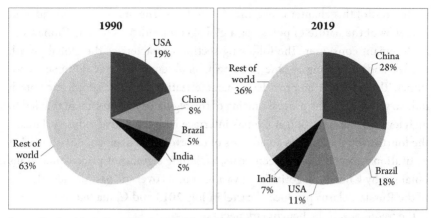

Source: Food and Agriculture Organization of the United Nations (FAO), K$_2$O total (HS 3104).

*Figure 5.1*  Agricultural use of potash, 1990 and 2019

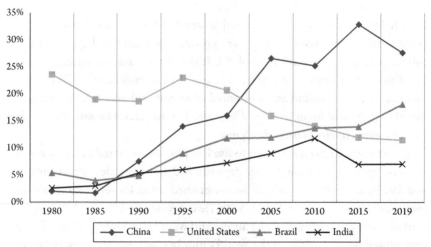

Source: Food and Agriculture Organization of the United Nations (FAO), K$_2$O total (HS 3104).

*Figure 5.2*  Agricultural use of potash for top four consumers (share of world total), 1980–2019

during the 2010s (see Figure 5.4). In 2011, "Feng Mingwei, the deputy general manager of Sinofert Holdings Limited, the largest fertilizer importer in China, said 'our dependence on imported potash fertilizer is at a rate of above 50 percent. . . . It is a threat to our national food security'" (Cai 2011). In 2017, the *Chinese Mining Yearbook* described the situation in the following way: "For a long time now, China's dependence on foreign potash is very high. [The] Chinese domestic potash self-sufficiency rate is around 55%. The potash resource security

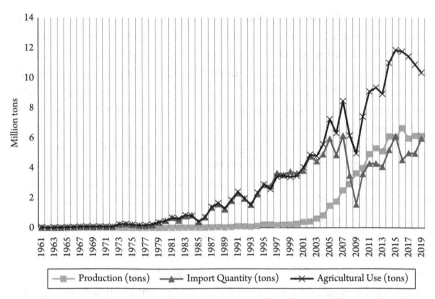

Source: Food and Agriculture Organization of the United Nations (FAO), K$_2$O total (HS 3104).

*Figure 5.3* China's agricultural use of potash, imports, and production, 1961–2019

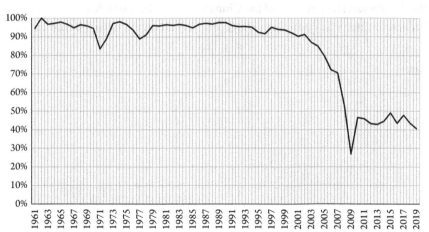

Source: Food and Agriculture Organization of the United Nations (FAO), K$_2$O total (HS 3104), share of agricultural use net of domestic production, author's calculations.

*Figure 5.4* China's potash import dependence, 1961–2019

issue remains outstanding" (*China Mining Yearbook 2016–2017* [中国矿业年鉴] 2019, 518). If we look at FAO data for 2019, Chinese import dependence levels, calculated as the share of domestic agricultural use net of domestic production, stood at 41 percent (see Figure 5.4).

Looking at UN Comtrade data by trade value, China became the world's largest potash importer in 2002, accounting for 18 percent of global potash imports. It accounted for more than 20 percent of global potash imports for the first time in 2005. China's share of global potash imports grew significantly starting in the 1990s (see Figure 5.5). The rally in potash (and other commodity) prices prior to the 2008 global financial crisis is attributed, in part, to rapid growth in Chinese demand.

As China's import dependence grew in the late 2000s and early 2010s, the Chinese government encouraged overseas investment and import diversification, with some limited success. A senior potash industry analyst explained that during the 2010s, there were encouragements from the Chinese central government to invest in small potash projects around the world: "Most of the [Canadian] projects have gone quiet. In Southeast Asia there was certainly a bit of a push and two mines got into production in Laos in the early 2010s. . . . Laos over the past couple of years has exported around 3/4 of a million tonnes of MOP globally, most of it has gone to China. . . . But obviously with the opening of the Laos-Kunming railway, a lot more is now moving to China" (Interview 155, Senior potash industry analyst, 2022). In 2017, in an agricultural news article exposing the difficulties of the "going out" policy in the potash industry, the deputy secretary general of the China Chemical Industry Association's fertilizer committee was quoted as saying, "There is an urgent need, but not enough

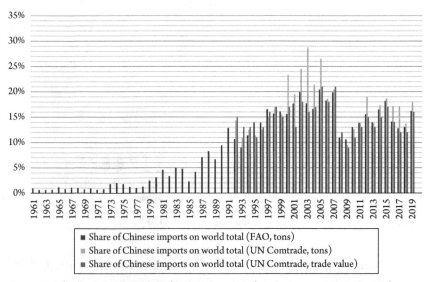

Source: FAO (total potash HS code: 3104) and UN Comtrade (Fertilizers potassic HS code: 3104), author's calculations. Note, UN Comtrade data in tons is lacking US numbers for the years 2000–2005 and Brazil numbers for the years 2012 and 2016.

Figure 5.5 China's share of global potash imports, 1961–2019

funds to build overseas potash projects" ("The Country Cannot be Short of Potassium for One Day" 2017). He Zhenwei, secretary general of the China Overseas Development Association, indicated that companies wanting to "go out" in the potash market faced many challenges: "The traditional problems of China's foreign investment still exist, it is difficult to obtain information on valuable projects, it is difficult to obtain financing for foreign investment, and it is difficult to solve problems in overseas investment.... The pressure of the international environment for Chinese enterprises to go global is increasing, and the risks of foreign investment by enterprises are increasing" ("How Potash Fertilizer Enterprises Seize the Opportunity in the Era of 'Zero Tariff'" 2019). Still, aside from the emergence of Belarus as a major global exporter of potash and the number one source of Chinese imports (by 2006, Belarus accounted for 19 percent of Chinese imports), comparing official import data, in 2001, the main suppliers (Russia and Canada) provided 81 percent of Chinese imports, and, in 2015, the main suppliers still provided 73 percent of Chinese imports (Belarus, Russia, and Canada) (see Figure 5.8).

## The Global Potash Pricing Regime Prior to China's Emergence

The global fertilizer industry had annual sales of about $175bn in 2015 (Terazono 2015). Until the 2000s, potash prices had been stable for decades, hovering between $20 and $125 per tonne from the 1960s to the 2000s (see Figure 5.7).

In the early part of the twentieth century, the potash industry was controlled by a cartel dominated by Germany as the lead producer. This arrangement came to an end around the same time as a new cohort of potash producers emerged, chief among them Canada and the former USSR. The emergence of multiple Canadian players led to the involvement of the Saskatchewan government and the creation of Canpotex in the 1970s, an organization that would coordinate all international potash sales outside of North America. Canpotex quickly displaced Germany as the dominant player on the potash market internationally. This state of affairs continued until the fall of the former USSR in the 1990s, when Russian and Belarusian producers started looking at markets beyond the former USSR and Comecon economies and, thus, entered in direct competition with Canpotex for the first time (Interview 174, Retired senior fertilizer industry analyst, 2022).

Potash reserves are distributed very unevenly across the world. In 2010, Canada harbored more than 50 percent of global potash reserves (Grant et al. 2010), whereas Canada, Russia, and Belarus together control 80 percent of the world's reserves (by comparison, OPEC's twelve members hold 70 percent of proven crude oil reserves). In 2015, these three countries controlled 80 percent of global exports (see Figure 5.7). Between 2000 and 2015, the share of potash exports by the world's top four exporting countries remained relatively stable and went from 93 percent to 88 percent over the period (UN Comtrade data, by net weight). In 2022, only sixteen countries produced potash, with an annual output of around 76 million tons KCl (Nutrien 2022). The United States Geological Survey put the annual global potash production capacity at 65 million tonnes in 2020 and estimated that in 2024, this would rise by around 5 million tonnes, mostly from production increases in Belarus, Russia, and Canada (Jasinski 2021).[5] As potash production is concentrated in so few countries, a very high percentage of global potash production is exported. In 1996, approximately 80 percent of global potash was traded (Trainor 1998) and, in 2022, that number was 78 percent (Nutrien 2022). Canada exports more than 95 percent of its potash production, 45 percent of which is shipped to the United States (Grant et al. 2010). It is important to note here that despite the United States' large share of consumption of global potash supplies, it has had a relatively minor role on the global potash market, given the fact almost all of its potash imports come directly from Canada.

Concentration among global potash suppliers is extremely high today (see Figure 5.6). In 1990, the top five potash producing companies produced 40 percent of global potash, whereas in 2010, they produced 80 percent (Ericsson et al. 2012). As we will see, there have been competing movements of consolidation and fragmentation in the potash market over the past decade. However, if the global production of potash was concentrated among eight companies in

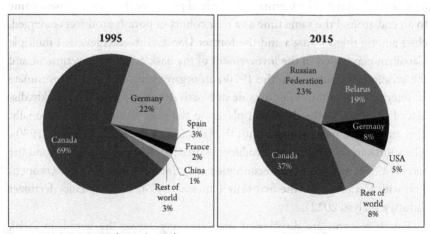

Source: UN COMTRADE (HS code 3104).

*Figure 5.6* Shares of world potash exports by country, 1995 and 2015

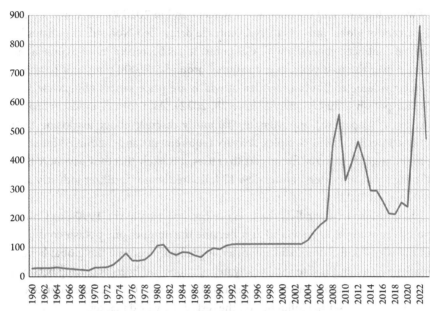

Source: World Bank Commodity Price Data (Pink Sheet), Potassium Chloride, nominal US Dollars per metric ton (2023 data is a forecast as of June 2023).

*Figure 5.7* Potash prices, 1960–2023

2010 ("Factbox: Facts about the Crop Nutrient Potash" 2010), mergers have reduced that number to six: Nutrien (from the 2018 merger of Potash Corp. and Agrium, both of Canada), Uralkali-Silvinit (from the 2010 purchase of Silvinit by Uralkali), Belaruskali, Mosaic, Israel Chemicals, and K + S.

The commodity price bubble of the late 2000s saw steep price rises (see Figure 5.7). In 2009, potash prices soared to above $600 per tonne in Canada. In 2022, potash prices climbed again following Russia's invasion of Ukraine, from $221 per tonne in January 2022 to $562.50 in March 2022 (*World Bank Commodities Price Data (The Pink Sheet)* 2022).

Prior to China's emergence as the world's number one consumer of potash, major price negotiations occurred between Canada's Canpotex and Japan's Zen-Noh, Japan's National Federation of Agricultural Co-operative Associations, a body that represents well over one thousand Japanese agricultural cooperatives. Zen-Noh was created in 1972, the same year Canada's Canpotex became operational. As the United States Geological Survey explained in 1994, "In early October, the major fertilizer importer of Japan, Zen-Noh, agreed to a $4 to $5 per ton product, muriate of potash, increase with Canpotex Ltd., the major potash exporter of Canada. The agreements between these two firms are usually trend setters for the world market" (Searls 1995). In 1988, Japan was the world's largest potash importer, with a 35 percent share globally. In 1990, Japan's share of world imports had declined to 14 percent and in 2020 its share was around 1 percent of global imports (UN Comtrade data). Zen-Noh still negotiates biannual contracts, generally with Canpotex. It has become a more marginal importer over the past years as it consumes around 500,000 tonnes of potash, a similar volume to Taiwan, neither of which are price setters (Interview 155, Senior potash industry analyst, June 28, 2022). As a former industry analyst explains, "[Japanese] importers are famously discreet about disclosing their prices. In view of their complex delivery requirements and their need for some premium-grade material for no-fertilizer uses, it is likely that they pay more than the big Asian importers" (Interview 174, Retired senior fertilizer industry analyst, August 2022).

In a pattern that parallels the iron ore case, starting in the 1990s, as China's potash consumption grew, and as it became the number one potash consumer in the world and a dominant importer, it gradually became the global benchmark price setter. Prior to that, yearly negotiations had been occurring between Chinese potash importers and international exporters, but the agreed price did not have a price-setting influence on the rest of the world market.

> China turned to Canada to supply MOP [muriate of potash] and Canpotex delivered its first cargo in 1972, starting a long-term relationship with Sinochem that continues to this day. This trade expanded in the following years and the Canadians also provided exports to assist in the promotion of potash fertilizer use at the farm level. The success of this program stimulated the demand for imports which, at this time, Canada was best placed to supply on the scale required by China. Price negotiations were something of a formality: Canpotex proposed a price for the next delivery period and, after some haggling, agreed on a small discount. The frame contracts between Canpotex and China included an MFN [Most Favored-Nation] clause which meant that China was to be given the lowest price that Canpotex offered to its customers. Canada's position as the principal supplier of MOP to the Chinese market came to an end at the start of the 1990s, when IPC [International Potash Company] emerged to supply similar volumes of MOP from Russia and Belarus. . . . Prices remained firm for the rest of the decade, despite the entry to world markets of this important new exporter. (Interview 174, Retired senior fertilizer industry analyst, August 2022)

As a former potash industry executive characterized it, "Once China's imports went over one million tonnes a year, that was basically about twenty years ago, then basically Japan's importance was not there anymore. It happened at roughly the same

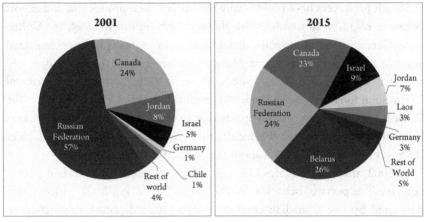

Source: China Mining Yearbooks, 2002 and 2016–2017.

*Figure 5.8* China's potash imports by country, 2001 and 2015

time as in the iron ore market. Whoever has the biggest import volumes is the leader, naturally" (Interview 157, Former potash industry executive, 2022).

In the 2000s, Russia and Belarus dealt with Sino-Agri Group (Zhongnong, 中农), one of the two major Chinese potash importers, while Canada's Canpotex sold potash exclusively to Sinofert (a subsidiary of Sinochem, 中化), the other major Chinese importer. In the late 2000s, the Chinese government spearheaded a broadening of potash import licenses, which led to minimal pluralization of Chinese potash importers, with three firms establishing themselves as dominant importers: Sino-Agri, Sinochem, and the China National Offshore Oil Corporation (CNOOC), which remains the case until today. Although China has been working to diversify its import sources, these efforts have had limited success (Figure 5.8).

## Global Potash Market Players: Coordination Capacity

Following a significant fall in prices in the 1980s, the global industry saw important structural changes in the 1990s. "The industry changed structurally from a state-owned, broad-based, specialized industry to a mostly privatized, consolidated, and integrated industry" (Trainor 1998).

Two large exporting blocs have historically controlled the global potash market: Russia and Belarus, and Canada. Canadian potash exports are handled via the Canadian export, logistics, and marketing group Canpotex. Similarly, from 2005 to 2013, BPC, the Belarusian Potash Company, was the sole marketing agent for Russian and Belarusian potash.

Potash producers have traditionally modulated their production and export targets in response to trends in the global potash supply. In 1994, the United States Geological Survey explained that "The world's potash producers remained in overcapacity for another year. Most producers around the world operated at partial capacity to maintain prices. Using an estimated world capacity of 29.9 million tons of capacity, the world produced at about 75% of capacity. The Canadian potash industry again operated at about 70% capacity, 55% for Potash Corp. of Saskatchewan and 90% for all other Canadian producers... The former U.S.S.R. producers operated at about 60% capacity" (Searls 1995, 2).

In 2002, the United States Geological Survey described Canadian potash exporters' respective behavior in the following way: "MOP prices were supported by two Canadian companies that reduced potash production to balance production with demand" (Searls 2003, 3). That same year, "[o]ne of the three Canadian potash-mining companies, Potash Corporation of Saskatchewan (PCS), operated at 53% of its annual capacity" (Searls 2003, 3). An industry analyst indicated that, in the early 2010s, before the fall of the BPC export cartel, Belaruskali and Uralkali used to operate at from 70 percent to 75 percent capacity (Interview 155, Senior potash industry analyst, August 2022).

## Canpotex

In Canada, the Potash Conservation Board (which would later become Canpotex) was established in 1969 to limit production and establish minimum prices at a time when the North American potash market was suffering from price decreases. This was a "classic cartel based on the 1938 Oil and Gas Conservation Board of Alberta. The floor price of potash was raised from $12 per ton to $33 per ton. Saskatchewan mines were to produce at 40 percent capacity while the New Mexico mines were permitted to operate at 80 percent capacity" (Warnock 2011).

Canpotex became operational in 1972. It is an international marketing and distribution company (which many call a quasi-cartel) that controls the sale of Canadian potash outside of Canadian and American markets and is owned by the North American producers Nutrien and Mosaic. Canpotex also manages the potash-specific transport infrastructure that has been built around the potash trade. Potash is water-soluble and, thus, handling it requires special care. Canpotex owns and operates a specialized rail car fleet, warehouses, and port terminals in Vancouver, Canada, and Portland, Oregon, United States. Canpotex sells its potash "delivered to the destination country," or CFR (cost and freight) and, thus, also manages the bulk cargo shipping component of its operations (Transportation Logistics, Canpotex).

In 1975, the Potash Corporation of Saskatchewan (PCS) (now Nutrien) was created as a crown corporation in the wake of the nationalization of a portion of the potash industry in the province that year. In the 1980s, Potash Corp. was required to sell potash outside of the North American market through Canpotex, where its "share of production allowed it to operate at only 67 percent capacity" (Warnock 2011). In 1989, Potash Corp. was listed on the Toronto Stock Exchange and became fully privatized by 1994 (2013).

In 2018, Nutrien was created from the merger of Potash Corp. and Agrium. It also owns 22.3 percent of Sinofert Holdings Ltd., a subsidiary of Sinochem and the largest fertilizer importer and distributor in China (*Annual Report 2020: Nurturing China's Agriculture Sector*). This company is the largest producer of potash worldwide (it controls 22 percent of world potash capacity) and continues to conduct out-of-North-America potash sales through Canpotex (*Nutrien Fact Book* 2018).

In the 2000s and early 2010s, Canpotex's position as the sole marketing and logistics agent for Canadian potash exporters was very strong. In 2012, when asked whether new North American potash producers could bypass Canpotex to sell their production abroad, a high-level potash industry insider responded, "Sure, you could replicate all the infrastructure that Canpotex has, but it wouldn't be efficient or productive, and it would end up costing you more. Infrastructure costs are just too high. Why would you duplicate wagons, port facilities, etc.? You wouldn't be able to sell at the same price. [Companies] don't need to go through Canpotex, but if they don't, they wouldn't be competitive" (Interview 85, Potash industry executive, 2012).

This started to change since at least 2020. First of all, K + S started selling outside of Canpotex. Mosaic also started opening more offices and building a distribution network in China, Brazil, and India. So, "on paper, Mosaic China buys from Canpotex, but in reality, . . . Mosaic sells on behalf of Canpotex and . . . Mosaic China distributes the product to Chinese customers", which has reduced Canpotex's role as a marketing agent (Interview 157, Former potash industry executive, 2022). With BHP planning to bring another mine into operation in Canada over the coming years, and consistently having taken the position that it would not sell product via Canpotex, more than one interviewee has qualified the future of Canpotex as uncertain and as resembling more and more a logistics firm than a marketing agency.

Even in the 2000s and early 2010s, the extent of coordination that occurred among Canadian potash exporters had been disputed. One high-level industry insider argued that "When they meet (Potash Corp, Agrium, Mosaic), they bring their lawyers, and they are not otherwise seen together. The result is the meeting of supply and demand. There is no communication on production. Each company announces how much they want to produce and then tells Canpotex their numbers" (Interview 86, Senior potash industry insider, 2012). In 2000, however, a group of American potash consumers sued North American potash producers in court for "conspiracy in restraint of trade":

> The class's price-fixing claim [was] based on a theory of conscious parallelism. Conscious parallelism is the process "not in itself unlawful, by which firms in a concentrated market might in effect share monopoly power, setting their prices at a profit-maximizing, supracompetitive level by recognizing their shared economic interests." . . . The class points out that the producers' prices were roughly equivalent during the alleged conspiracy, despite differing production costs. It further points out that price changes by one producer were quickly met by the others. This establishes only that the producers consciously paralleled each other's prices. [However,] evidence that a business consciously met the pricing of its competitors does not prove a violation of the antitrust laws. . . . [The court must find] that the plaintiff's evidence tends to exclude the possibility of independent action. (203 F.3d 1028 [8th Cir. 2000], 2000)

This condition was not met and the U.S. Court of Appeals for the Eighth Circuit dismissed the suit. However, "[b]oth parties agree that the North American potash industry is an oligopoly. Prices in an oligopolistic market tend to be higher than those in purely competitive markets and will fluctuate independently of supply and demand" (203 F.3d 1028 [8th Cir. 2000], 2000). Another class action suit against global potash producers was filed in Chicago in 2008, dismissed and then revived again in July 2012. The plaintiffs pointed to the 600 percent jump in prices between 2003 and 2008, which could not be justified by demand. This time around, Uralkali, a Russian producer, agreed to settle for $12.75 million in September 2012 (Koven 2012), and PotashCorp and Mosaic settled for $43.75 million each in 2013 ("Potash Corp. Settles" 2013).

Junior potash mining firms continued to view the behavior of major global potash suppliers, including Canpotex, as cartelized, throughout the 2010s. When a senior (non-Canpotex member) potash firm executive was asked for his thoughts on Canpotex, he replied, "Canpotex is a cartel" (Interview 115, 2013). When an industry watcher was asked how Canpotex works, he replied, "The ratios are known and the companies are aware of the situation. They wouldn't actually need to speak much; they know the global situation and whether they need to [cut production]. Canpotex first goes out and signs contracts, and then the quantities are divided according to the size of production" (Interview 120, 2013).

More recently, it has become clear that Canpotex is going through a transition. Recent interviews indicate that the organization is perceived as having weakened. A former CEO of a junior potash company and longtime industry player noted the following: "I think that Canpotex has weakened dramatically, because of the creation of Nutrien basically. It was a 'three group' oligopoly, and now it is a 'two group,' and that is significant, I think. Mosaic will feel eventually that it needs to market on its own and leave the logistics to Canpotex" (Interview 159, Former junior potash company CEO, July 2022).

### Belarusian Potash Company

Russia and Belarus, the second and third largest potash producers worldwide, went through periods of closely coordinating their international potash sales. In the 1990s, the International Potash Company (IPC) managed exports from the two countries (Searls 1995). As a former potash industry analyst explained, "The three producers in Russia and Belarus were pressed by the Canadians to establish a joint selling organization to handle their sales, and International Potash Company (IPC) was founded for this purpose in 1992. In its early years it was largely successful in eliminating internal competition and protecting prices. The Canadians conceded market share to IPC in order to maintain price stability" (Interview 174, Retired senior fertilizer industry analyst, August 2022). In 2005, IPC folded and was replaced by the Belarusian Potash Company (BPC), another producer-owned structure or quasi-cartel. At the time, BPC was created as the sole marketing agency for potash produced by Belaruskali (the Belarusian producer) and Uralkali-Silvinit (the Russian producer). "Uralkali got 60 per cent of the production quota and Belaruskali, 40 per cent. According to a senior Uralkali executive, it was very profitable for all producers. Maybe less so for consumers" (Weaver and Cienski 2013). The fall of the Belarusian Potash Company at the end of the summer of 2013 is covered below.

### Coordination between the Two Groups

The two major potash producing regions are large enough to be price makers. According to one industry analyst, "if the Canadian and Russian producers are aggressive in matching supply and demand, it shouldn't matter very much what other producers do" (Kayakiran 2012). Coordination between the two regions has stopped short of being formal, but indications are that the two groups have, at certain times, seen fit to limit their rivalry and informally coordinate production, whereas at other times competition was more intense. "Potash has almost always been in oversupply and many producers have adjusted their production levels and operated below capacity" (Ericsson et al. 2012). In 2012,

> Uralkali (URKA), Russia's biggest fertilizer maker, [was] ready to cut production to prevent potash prices from falling after Potash Corp. of Saskatchewan Inc. announced reductions this year. "Our strategy is that price is much more important than volumes," Chief Financial Officer Victor Belyakov said in an interview.... "It's a strategy for most of the big players in the market. We usually cut some production to come up with a fair price."... Uralkali pared its 2012 production target by about 8 percent to between 10.5 million metric tons and 10.8 million tons to bolster prices, Belyakov said.... Potash Corp., which announced temporary cuts at two mines in Canada last month, has since unveiled a four-week halt at its Allan mine and an extension of the shutdown at its Rocanville operation. (Kayakiran 2012)

Global producers were in oversupply during the 1990s and early 2000s and, consequently, were operating below capacity. The United States Geological Survey described a period of oversupply in 2003 as follows:

> The world's leading potash producers operated up to 40% below capacity for another year to prevent oversupply to the market or excessively large producer stocks, which could result in downward price pressures from the potential buyers. At the end of 2003, North American producer stocks were more than 12% of annual production (1.3 million [metric] tons, $K_2O$ equivalent, of 10.4 million [metric] tons) resulting in a slow increase in potash prices that started in the fall of 2003. (Searls 2005)

Chinese industry insiders have often commented on this situation. "According to Li Qiang, a spokesperson for Sinochem Group, the international price rise of potash fertilizer is partly caused by the international price rise of raw materials and resources. However, 'the most important and fundamental reason is the intensified monopoly of the international suppliers in this field,'... In a bid to cope with the price rises and potash fertilizer shortages, China [needs] to... strengthen the 'negotiation mechanism of potash fertilizer imports'" (Cai 2011). A Chinese government official corroborated this view when he said, "the question of the potash market is not about restricted supply: supply is abundant. It is a market structure and political problem" (Interview 37, Senior China industry association official, 2012). Chinese experts routinely discuss ways to break the global potash monopoly and price-setting power (Chen 2013). As recently as 2020, Sinochem issued a note summarizing the current situation and commenting on "the high monopoly of international potash fertilizer resources and production capacity" and using an "Art of War" metaphor to illustrate the appropriate posture to take in international negotiations: "If you know yourself and your enemy, you will never lose a hundred battles" (Zhu 2020).

## The Domestic Chinese Potash and Fertilizer Markets

China is self-sufficient in two out of three key fertilizer groups, phosphate and nitrate, but it is heavily import-dependent on potash, despite having brought domestic production levels from almost nonexistent in the twentieth century to a little above 50 percent of agricultural use since the 2010s. Indeed, domestic Chinese potash production went from below 50,000 tonnes in 1990 to 300,000 tonnes in 2000 to above 6 million tonnes annually in 2014. Production has since plateaued at a little above 6 million tonnes (FAO data). However, since about 2018, China stopped any further expansion of domestic potash production. "There are no further expansions planned and this is essentially because China is running out of potash ... because resources are depleting in Qinghai, it's only a matter of time before things start to fall quite noticeably.... So, it is now going to become potentially increasingly dependent on imports" (Interview 155, Senior potash industry analyst, August 2022).

The Chinese domestic potash market suffers from structural fragilities that are specific to the fertilizer industry (Bao et al. 2010). One complication in this mineral's transport logistics is due to the fact potash is water-soluble and must be transported in custom-made containers; add to this the difference in rail gauges between Russian and Chinese railways, which necessitates switching trains at the border; then there is the fact China's domestic potash production is located in isolated inland mining sites, which means, for many provinces, it is more efficient to procure potash internationally through China's seaports than to procure it domestically.

China's high level of potash import-dependence has led to an historically low use of potash. Over the past twenty years, as imports grew, potash use across provinces has been uneven, with overuse increasingly being reported, especially in more economically developed areas (Wang et al. 2015). Other idiosyncratic dynamics in the domestic potash market are notable, such as farmers' lower familiarity with potash compared with nitrate- and phosphate-based fertilizers.[6]

To deal with fertilizer overuse (mostly phosphate and nitrate), in 2015, the Chinese Ministry of Agriculture announced the implementation of a zero-growth action plan by 2020 for chemical fertilizer use across the country (Wang and Liu 2015). China's agricultural use of potash peaked in 2015, at 11.8 million tonnes (FAO data) (see Figure 5.3). However, a senior potash industry analyst indicated that "even as the use of chemical fertilizers has come under increasing environmental scrutiny in China over the past years, on the whole this has been more targeted towards nitrogen and phosphate." He argued that there is some further growth potential on the potash side, admittedly at a reduced rate from what we have seen over the past twenty years (Interview 155, Senior potash industry analyst, August 2022).

This being said, it seems fair to say that the growth we have seen in China's agricultural use of potash over the past forty years is not sustainable over the long term, and that we will see more modest rates of growth in both imports and agricultural use than what we have seen between the 1980s and the 2000s.

The Chinese domestic potash industry is quite consolidated. In 2015, there were twenty-one potash mining companies in China, nineteen operating in the province of Qinghai and two in the Xinjiang Autonomous Region, with Qinghai accounting for 81 percent of domestic production (*China Mining Yearbook 2016–2017*, 118). That year, there were seventy-nine potash processing enterprises, twenty-nine of which were located in Qinghai and Xinjiang (*China Mining Yearbook 2016–2017*, 515). In 2007, large- and medium-sized enterprises controlled 73.3 percent of the Chinese potash industry, compared to 5.4 percent in the Chinese iron ore industry and 7.8 percent on average in the Chinese mining industry (see Table 5.1).

For our purposes, however, consolidation levels are most important at the import interface with the global potash market. There, two key potash firms in China dominate imports: Sinofert (a subsidiary of Sinochem) and Sino-Agri Group. Feng Mingwei, Sinochem's deputy general manager quoted earlier, described the company's fertilizer subsidiary (Sinofert) in an interview with a state-owned Chinese media group, as being

Table 5.1 **Comparative fragmentation of the iron ore and potash industries in China, 2007**

| | Potash | Iron ore | Chinese minerals: industry average |
|---|---|---|---|
| Proportion of large- and medium-scale enterprises | 73.3% | 6.4% | 7.8% |
| Proportion of small enterprises and small mines | 2.67% | 93.6% | 92.2% |

Source: *Chinese Mineral Statistical Yearbook 2008*, author's calculations

the largest fertilizer distribution company in China, the main importer of potash, spread all over the country, except in the Tibet Autonomous Region, with 17 branches in agricultural provinces, 2106 sales outlets connected to marketing networks, 583 inland warehouses, and 12 major ports with long-term potash logistics agreements. Sinochem's warehousing and logistics capabilities ensure it can cover all major agricultural production in the country. (Li 2011)

Sinofert also owned 20.5 percent of the Qinghai Salt Lake Industry Co., the largest potash producer in China until 2017 (Ng 2017). Sino-Agri Group (the China National Agricultural Means of Production Group Corporation, or CNAMPGC)[7] is a wholly owned enterprise of the China CO-OP Group,[8] with annual sales revenue of 76 billion Chinese yuan ("Company Profile" 2015).

Looking at Chinese customs data at the firm level, since 2000, the total share of imports by Sinochem and Sino-Agri went from a little above 60 percent in 2000 to a little below 50 percent in 2014. Sinochem's share went from 36 percent in 2000 to 25 percent in 2014; and Sino-Agri went from 28 percent to 22 percent over the same period (see Figure 5.9). All things considered, these are impressively high

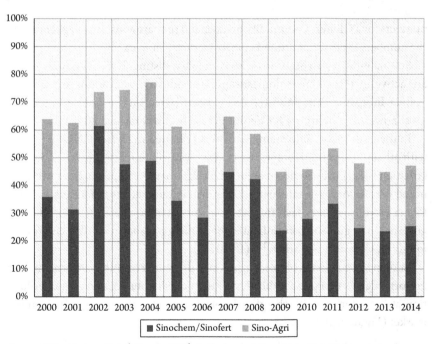

Source: China Customs Data (HS code: 3104). Author's calculations. Note: Firm IDs have changed over the years. I have done my best to trace Firm ID changes for Sinofert and Sino-Agri. Some subsidiaries or affiliated companies to Sinochem and Sino-Agri may be missing from the illustrated share of imports.

*Figure 5.9* Share of potash imports from the top two Chinese importers, 2000–2014

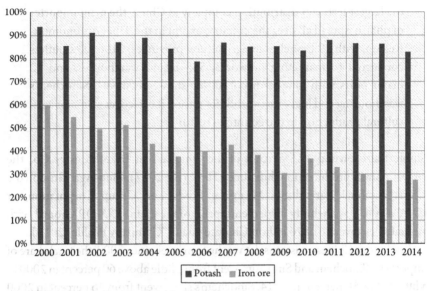

Source: China Customs Data. Author's calculations.

*Figure 5.10* Share of potash and iron ore imports of the top ten Chinese importers, 2000–2014

numbers for a Chinese commodity market, and they are considerably higher than the numbers for the iron ore and copper markets, for instance.

Several industry associations with somewhat distinct but overlapping duties are active in the Chinese domestic potash industry. Indications are that the "China Inorganic Salts Industry Association [which has a potash branch] is most powerful" (Interview 86, Senior potash industry insider, 2012).

In the mid-2000s, Sinochem, Sino-Agri (Zhongnong), and CNOOC, along with other potash import enterprises (with more minor roles), formed a joint negotiation small group to negotiate with foreign market suppliers. Feng Mingwei noted that "in order to safeguard the fundamental interests of farmers, in 2005 China established a potash imports joint negotiation mechanism, 'under the government's guidance, coordinated by industry associations, by enterprises jointly facing foreign [markets]'" (Li 2011).

Looking at the share of potash and iron ore imports of the top ten Chinese importers gives us a good indication of the potash industry's level of coordination at the interface with the global potash market, compared to the iron ore market (Figure 5.10).

## Potash Importing Licenses—A Short History

One of the key differences between the iron ore and potash cases lies in China's successful coordination dynamics at the interface with global market stakeholders. One key component of Chinese potash consumers' successful coordination capacity, beyond the successful consolidation of its domestic potash mining industry, has been the consolidation of their access to the import interface, including via import licenses.

Starting in 1993, Sinochem/Sinofert was granted the sole license in China to import potash as well as the right to be the sole negotiator with Canada's Canpotex.[9] Immediately thereafter, the Sino-Arab Chemical Fertilizer Co.[10] was granted import rights from 1993 onward (Liu 2016). Sino-Arab was created in 1985, in the spirit of the South-South cooperation that took place under Deng Xiaoping, and was one of China's biggest such projects at the time. Sino-Arab could negotiate its contracts but it had to use Sinochem as its importing agent. However, it was not permitted to sell its imported potash on the Chinese domestic market (Li 2008). Until 1998, Sinofert (Sinochem) effectively functioned as China's sole importer.

In 1998, the State Council issued a notice granting the Sino-Agri Group the right to import potash ("State Council Issues Notice 39" 1998).[11] At the time, it was agreed that the Sino-Agri Group would be responsible for 60 percent of imports from Eurasia (Russia and Belarus) and Sinofert/Sinochem would be responsible for the other 40 percent, which meant the latter would maintain its exclusive access to the Canadian market (Li 2008).

Following China's entry into the World Trade Organization (WTO) on December 11, 2001, the Chinese Ministry of Foreign Trade and Economic Cooperation released its twenty-eighth notice, which included a catalog that listed goods subject to "the Administration of Imported State Trade." This included the three fertilizer families: nitrate, phosphate, and potash (List of State Trading Import Enterprises 2001). The twenty-eighth announcement also included a catalog that listed state-controlled companies with authorization to import these products. The companies listed under the fertilizer category were Sinochem[12] and Sino-Agri (List of State Trading Import Enterprises 2001). This import management system did not impose quantity restrictions (*Potash Import Qualification Reform* 2015).

On November 25, 2002, the Chinese Ministry of Foreign Trade and Economic Cooperation released its fiftieth notice ("Ministry of Foreign Trade and Economic Cooperation of the People's Republic of China Notice 50" 2002). The announcement conferred the authority to import potash to two non-state-controlled entities, in addition to Sinochem and Sino-Agri. The first was the China National Chemical Construction Corporation (CNCCC, later a subsidiary of the CNOOC),[13] which at the time was one of the central enterprises under the State-owned Assets Supervision and Administration Commission (SASAC). The second entity was Huaken International Trading Co. (People's Republic of China Ministry of Foreign Trade and Economic Cooperation 2003), also managed by SASAC, which prior to 1992 was under the Ministry of Agriculture ("About Zhongken, Company Overview" 2019). These two companies were permitted to sell potash on the Chinese domestic market; however, their access to global suppliers was mainly limited to Jordan and Germany. Quantities of potash imports were predetermined and allocated between state-controlled and non-state-controlled enterprises (Foreign Trade and Economic Cooperation 2002). By 2007, the CNCCC was only importing 270,000 tonnes of potash, which was more than Huaken International, coming in fourth place (Li 2008).

In 2004, following the enactment of the Foreign Trade Law (2004),[14] the Ministry of Commerce issued its fifty-second notice, through which it announced that five additional Chinese compound fertilizer manufacturers would each be granted a self-managed (自营) license to import potash. Shandong Luxi Chemical Ltd.,[15] Western Liaoning Xiyang Special Fertilizer Ltd.,[16] Shandong Lubei Group,[17] Hubei Yangfeng Ltd.,[18] and PetroChina International,[19] the last of which being the listed arm of the China National Petroleum Corporation, were added to the number of companies allowed to import potash, for a total of ten (Liu 2010). However, these companies could only use these imports to fulfill their own manufacturing needs and were not allowed to sell imported potash beyond those levels on the Chinese domestic market ("Ministry of Commerce Announces Notice 52" 2004) (confirmed in Interview 99, Chinese industry insider, 2012). Only four enterprises were allowed to sell imported potash in China: Sinofert, Sino-Agri, CNCCC/CNOOC, and Huaken International (Li 2008).

Quite separate from the nine main potash import licenses, which are effectively "seaport" import licenses, the Ministry of Commerce granted licenses to twenty-five Chinese companies to import potash across land borders (which, in practice, has meant Russia), including the Suifenhe Longsheng Trading Co. Ltd. and the Suifenhe Guangcheng Economic and Trade Co. Ltd.[20] Since at least the 1990s, China has carved out preferential space and flexibility in managing its border trade, with the aim of encouraging trade between border areas and neighboring countries (*Prospect of China's Potash Fertilizer Import Qualification Reform* 2015).[21] "There are twenty-six licenses to import potash by rail, but not all companies use them" (Interview 99, 2012). The licensed rail-import enterprises also coordinate their procurement strategy. In fact, in 2012, a new association called the "Cross-Border Potash Imports Coordination Commission"[22] was created to help with the coordination of procurement (Interview 109, Chinese industry journalist, 2012). The border trade accounted for up to 30 percent of total potash imports (*Prospect of China's Potash Fertilizer Import Qualification Reform* 2015), but it does not set prices. Potash imported by rail is priced in relation with the sea import contract price, although in the past Russian exporters have been known to dump excess potash via rail trade. Rail imports are less important in terms of numbers of tonnes than sea imports and constituted around 1 and 2 million tonnes on average annually in the early 2010s (Interview 86, Senior potash industry insider, 2012). In 2022, a potash industry analyst explained that Russian railway potash sales were "never above 2.5 million tonnes, and that since then they have never been above 1.6 million tonnes" (Interview 155, Senior potash industry analyst, August 2022).

At the time, these companies complained that this again granted the two main firms a monopoly on imports. By June 2007, representatives of license holders petitioned the Standing Committee of the National People's Congress for fairer regulations regarding the potash import situation. Until then, they asserted, none of the companies had been able to directly sign one potash import contract. Many more such complaints were made (Li 2008). The champion of those efforts was Wu Sihai, a CPPCC representative and former chairman of the International Fertilizer Association. In 2006, he sent a letter to Premier Wen Jiabao entitled "Emergency Response and Recommendations on the Current Potash Import Situation." The premier agreed to further investigate. At the annual meeting of the CPPCC, in 2008, at the height of potash price increases, Wu Sihai made a speech entitled "Breaking the Potash Monopoly, Protecting Farmer's Interests."[23] In it, he noted that "on the one hand, you have an international resource monopoly, on the other hand, you have a domestic sales monopoly system as well, including in terms of price, it controls the resource, so it controls the price levels. This has led to the accumulation of vast monopoly profits for the interest groups in question."[24] As per the interview, Wu Sihai was referring to Sinochem and the Sino-Agri Group on the domestic side (Gu 2008).

On November 8, 2007, the Ministry of Commerce issued a notice granting the ten holders of potash import licenses the right to equal importing (that is, no limits on the quantity imported) and negotiating rights. However, only four companies would be allowed to sell the imported potash domestically; the other importers would have to use it for their own consumption. One private sector insider in the Chinese potash industry said that, in practice, "there are ten licenses, but really only four or five use it. The others don't, and buy from big firms [who are licensed]" (Interview 107, 2012). In 2012, a senior Chinese official with intimate knowledge of the matter confirmed that "[o]nly three companies really import potash, Sinochem, Sino-Agri, and CNOOC" (Interview 95, Senior Chinese official, 2012). The Chinese government also allowed up to six companies to attend other global negotiations, although until 2012, only the China National Offshore Oil Corporation (CNOOC) had been known to formally participate and take part in negotiations, playing a particularly active role in negotiations with Israel (Interview 95, Senior Chinese official, 2012).

As a Chinese government official explained: "China's entry in the WTO had a big impact on the way China is seen to manage imports and exports. So, the various licenses were probably given in this frame of mind, to fulfill China's WTO obligations, but in actual fact, it may be that the companies that were given the licenses do not have the warehouses, the distribution networks, the logistical power, etc. So, it is too early for them, and they are not ready to use them" (Interview 102, Representative of a foreign enterprise in China, 2012).

Regarding domestic price controls, in 2009, the National Development and Reform Commission (NDRC) issued a notice—approved by the State Council—that canceled their "fertilizer price control policies," and issued the 368th "[n]otice on how to improve potash price management policy."[25] This notice aimed to "give the potash import price and process adequate supervision" (National Development and Reform Commission 2009). The NDRC stipulated that importing enterprises could not increase the benchmark price by more than 3 percent to cover operating costs; their subsidiaries, no more than 1 percent (National Development and Reform Commission 2009). The notice sought to improve monitoring. It asked that companies report the following to the NDRC's price bureau every month: import quantities, production costs, the import benchmark price, and their sales prices, signed contracts, and import receipts. It also asked that companies report every year their import quantities, main customers, sales volumes, and sales prices.

Finally, the notice also asked, in strong language, that at each level of price control, the department must continue to increase its inspections of the potash port import price policy and seriously investigate and handle[26] potash import companies that do not respect the national pricing policy or port import prices, do not report as directed, or that collude to increase prices or to artificially inflate prices (National Development and Reform Commission 2009). In 2008, the State Council announced that, despite measures to increase the role of the market in fertilizer allocation, the country needed to continue supervising high prices in the relatively concentrated potash import market ("State Council's 6 Measures" 2008).

The final category of China's authorized potash importers includes foreign-invested enterprises and joint ventures, which were first allowed to import raw materials (in this case, potash) for their own use (*Prospect of China's Potash Fertilizer Import Qualification Reform* 2015). In 2013, the Ministry of Commerce issued a "Work Notice on Implementing Online Applications for Automatic Import Licenses of Chemical Fertilizers," which rolled out online applications for foreign enterprises and, at the same time, included further provisions for the import of potash fertilizer by foreign-invested enterprises, for the purposes of "general trade" ("Work Notice on Implementing Online Applications for Automatic Import License of Chemical Fertilizers" 2013) (see Table 5.2).

The introduction of permissions regarding imports by foreign-invested enterprises led Canadian producers to open offices in China. In 2014, Canpotex

*Table 5.2* **A short history of potash import licenses**

| Type of license | Company (date license awarded) | Legal framework |
|---|---|---|
| State trading fertilizer import enterprise | 1. Sinofert (Sinochem) (1993)<br>2. Sino-Agri (1998) | Sino-Agri: State council notice 39, 1998. Sinochem and Sino-Agri: Confirmed in Chinese Ministry of Foreign Trade and Economic Cooperation (now MOFCOM) notice 28, 2001. Permitted to sell potash on the domestic market, privileged access to global producers. |
| Non-state trading fertilizer import operation enterprise | 3. Sino-Arab Chemical Fertilizer Co. (1993)<br>4. China National Chemical Construction Corporation (CNOOC) (2002)<br>5. Huaken International (2002) | For CNCC and Huaken: Chinese Ministry of Foreign Trade and Economic Cooperation (now MOFCOM) notice 50, 2002. Permitted to sell potash on the Chinese domestic market; limited access to global producers. |
| Non-state trading potash import self-operated management rights | 6. Shandong Luxi Chemical Ltd. (2004)<br>7. Western Liaoning Xiyang Special Fertilizer Ltd (2004)<br>8. Shandong Lubei Group (2004)<br>9. Hubei Yangfeng Ltd. (2004)<br>10. PetroChina International (CNPC) (2004) | Chinese Ministry of Commerce (MOFCOM) notice 52, 2004. Imports strictly to fulfill their own manufacturing needs and are not permitted to sell potash on the Chinese domestic market. |
| Small-scale border fertilizer imports enterprises | Ministry of Commerce approved enterprises for fertilizer imports from Heilongjiang, Inner Mongolia, Xinjiang and other border areas. | Article 42 of the Foreign Trade Law of 1994 (Article 68 as amended in 2004): flexible measures and preferential treatment for trade between border areas and bordering countries. |
| Fertilizer imports for fertilizer producing foreign-invested enterprises | Foreign-invested enterprises can import raw materials (compound fertilizer, potash, and other chemicals) for their own use and for production, but not for sale.[a] This has included China-Arab Chemical Fertilizer and Jiangsu Chemical. | Article 7, Sino-Foreign Equity Joint Venture Law of 1979 (updated in 2001 under the Chinese-Foreign Joint Venture Enterprise Law). See notice 19, 2002, Ministry of Foreign Trade and Economic Cooperation. |

[a] For "distribution operations other than self-use, it is still necessary to entrust an import business enterprise authorized or approved by the Ministry of Commerce of China to act as an agent" (2015, #1789).

Source: China Fertilizer Network 2015, #1789, author's summary, translations, and addition.

opened an office in China, with the purpose of diversifying its export relationships beyond Sinofert (Sinochem) (Interview 157, Former potash industry executive, 2022). Mosaic also expanded its operations in China, including opening an office in Beijing, on top of two fertilizer blending plants it had acquired earlier in China (in Yantai and Qinhuangdao) ("Mosaic Co Form 10-K (Annual Report)" 2005). The full impact of these developments remains to be seen.

Incremental government regulations over the 2000s gradually increased the number of Chinese enterprises that have access to global potash imports, but only modestly. These efforts led to some changes in terms of import shares by firm (Figure 5.9), in an incremental fashion. In 2015, an official of the China Inorganic Salts Industry Association Potash Branch commented that "the number and structure of the overall potash import qualification enterprises have remained almost unchanged for more than a decade" (*Prospect of China's Potash Fertilizer Import Qualification Reform* 2015). In 2022, an industry executive confirmed the established position of the two largest importers compared with other, smaller domestic potash market stakeholders: "[A]t the macro level, people realize the Chinese government is supporting the big state-owned companies and the small companies do not want to challenge the system too loudly" (Interview 157, Former potash industry executive, June 29, 2022), describing a pattern opposite to that of the iron ore market. This also suggests, and this is confirmed by interviews, that the licensing system was more effectively implemented than in the iron ore case.

According to trade transactions data collected by the Customs Administration of China, the Chinese domestic environment has continued to liberalize somewhat: in 2014, there were fourteen Chinese firms importing more than 100,000 tonnes of potash (HS code 3104).[27] However, Figures 5.9 and 5.10 show that Chinese government efforts to increase the number of companies with access to the import interface have not really changed the structure of the domestic market power enjoyed by the main importers.

The number and size of domestic Chinese potash importers is important. The import licensing system has allocated access to potash imports over the years. Crucially, however, a separate mechanism has been established to regulate which companies negotiate the annual benchmark price. The two import institutions overlap but are distinct.

To this point, a Chinese central government official explained that "[t]he rationale for opening up the licenses was to increase competition [or marketization (市场化)], but *not in terms of competition against each other overseas*, . . . the aim was to relax the presence of the two big companies [domestically]" (Interview 101, Chinese central government ministry official, 2012, emphasis added). The following section delves into the potash import negotiating mechanism established in the mid-2000s.

## Negotiating Small Group

Since 2005, Chinese potash sea importers have operated under a *small group*,[28] where the major importers formally came together under the guidance of the Chinese Ministry of Commerce and the China Chamber of Commerce of Metals, Minerals & Chemicals (CCCMC), to coordinate their strategies before going out and negotiating with international suppliers (2019).

Shortly thereafter, at a meeting in 2006, a compromise was negotiated among the ten existing license holders and the Ministry of Commerce, which was formalized by Vice Premier Wu Yigao, shortly thereafter, in the "Joint Negotiation Rules for Potash Fertilizer Imports" (Jiang 2011). The more commonly known "Two Eight Split" meant that the negotiations would still be led by the two main importers, Sinofert (Sinochem) and Sino-Agri, which would be the only ones with contract-signing authority, while the other eight firms with import licenses were only permitted to sign contracts with those firms' overseas subsidiaries. It was agreed that Sinofert (Sinochem) and Sino-Agri would each send one representative to international negotiations with Russia and Belarus (for 80 percent of the share of imports),[29] and the other eight companies would also send only one representative to represent them all (for 20 percent of the share of imports), although at the beginning, that representative was not allowed to formally propose pricing strategies or to veto decisions made by the two main negotiators (Li 2008). As for the negotiations with Canpotex, Sinochem would maintain its exclusive access until 2007, after which access would be expanded. When the small group was created in 2005, it consisted of three members: Sinofert/Sinochem, Sino-Agri, and the China National Petroleum Corporation. CNOOC replaced CNPC in 2008 (Shi 2011).

As the main channel of domestic potash fertilizer imports, Sinochem Group has played an outsize role since the establishment of the mechanism. Sinochem explained this in a notice published in 2020:

> The security of potash supply is directly related to China's agricultural security. Due to the intense monopoly of international potash fertilizer resources and production capacity, in order to ensure domestic potash supply and price stability, and enhance China's foreign procurement bargaining power, at the instruction of the State Council, the Ministry of Commerce established in 2005 a potash import price joint negotiating mechanism,[30] which is "guided by the government, coordinated by industry associations and presents a united outward front by enterprises." Under the unified leadership of the Ministry of Commerce, the Chamber of Commerce for

Import and Export of Minerals and Chemicals took the lead in coordinating domestic potash importers to negotiate prices with a united outward front, to achieve the purpose of "one voice to the outside world" and to strive for maximum national benefits. (Zhu 2020), author's translation

Among other tasks, they coordinate who will negotiate with which international supplier. A Chinese government official with intimate knowledge of the matter explained how this works:

> There is a negotiating small group [谈判小组], and they all discuss together before negotiations. It is very heated. Whoever gets a deal first, the other ones follow. It used to be that Sino-Agri (Zhongnong) would settle first with BPC. But very recently, the first deal has been signed with Canpotex. . . . CNOOC didn't use to import but they bought a potash firm. They participate in the Israeli negotiations. They get the Israeli part, Zhongnong gets the Russia-Belarus part, and Sinochem gets the Canadian part. They negotiate this among themselves. It is [officially] the Ministry of Commerce that deals with that, the negotiations and allocation of who deals with which foreign markets. But to be honest, the companies decide that among themselves. The other seven companies [who have a licence], they really do not import [基本上不进口], they have to buy from the three big ones, or some of them will buy from Russian rail imports. (Interview 95, Senior Chinese official, 2012)

Since 2006, this has resulted in a global context of sharply raising potash prices, in a situation in which China has benefited from a "depressed price status" (Li 2011) (Author's translation). I asked a senior Chinese official whether there is competition among Chinese potash importing enterprises on the international stage. The official noted the following: "The point of the small group [小组] is to split things, so that there is no international competition in terms of who imports from whom!" (Interview 96, Senior Chinese official, 2012). An interview with a Chinese industry insider from the private sector also confirmed this: "Indeed, the companies do not compete against each other" (Interview 99, Senior potash industry analyst, 2012).

As a senior foreign China-based journalist explained, "The pressure is not about when the SOEs [state-owned enterprises] go into negotiations, but prior to that. There are price controls in China, by the Price Control Department of the NDRC, and the companies must know what the situation is domestically prior to when they go out and negotiate" (Interview 104, 2012). Phrased a little differently by a Chinese journalist, "Of course the negotiators have to think of both government plans and farmers' well-being. They are a state company, but they do not get direct directives. Of course, they could 'mess up' and then that would be bad for their careers. But they more have to think about getting their product out in the domestic market and making money" (Interview 109, Chinese industry journalist, 2012). All in all, once the Chinese state-owned firms go out to negotiate with their foreign counterparts, they have quite a bit of leeway in these negotiations (Interview 102, Representative of a foreign enterprise in China, 2012), but this leeway remains framed within the broader context described above, including by prior "small group" agreements and high-level state policy frames and priorities.

In 2012, a Chinese official confirmed that the two top companies are really the ones that played the dominant role: "CNOOC has no negotiation power in the sense that they accept either the BPC or Canpotex price. They never get to set the price" (Interview 96, Senior Chinese official, 2012). On January 4, 2013, the Sino-Agri Group issued a press release where it confirmed that the negotiators had reached a benchmark contract price for the first half of the year. On the Chinese side, the members of the "China potash import joint negotiation small group"[31] were Sino-Agri, Sinochem, and CNOOC, whereas the international negotiators consisted of Canpotex, BPC, and Israel Chemicals Group (ICL) ("China Concludes Potash Price Negotiations" 2013).

This situation has detractors in the Chinese domestic fertilizer market. In 2011, an expert was quoted in the news as commenting that

> there are currently 10 domestic companies that have import licenses for potash fertilizers. However, only Sinochem Fertilizer and Zhongnong Group have real import rights, and the other eight can only be purchased by overseas subsidiaries of Sinochem and Zhongnong. Similar to the current iron ore negotiation mechanism, where the Baosteel family is the representative, in the field of potash fertilizer, Sinochem is the representative of potash fertilizer import negotiation, and the contract price of potash fertilizer import negotiation is also highly confidential. As any business knows, this includes members of the joint negotiating team. Because the negotiated price is confidential, it is difficult for the outside world to know how much money was added after importing. Such a situation has created opportunities for Sinofert to seek high monopoly profits. (Shi 2011)

In the same article, Wu Shitai, the former chairman of the China International Fertilizer Industry Association, is quoted as having said the following in a speech entitled "Breaking the Monopoly of Potassium Resources and

Protecting the Interests of Farmers" at the annual "Two Sessions" meeting, in 2008: "Sinochem and Zhongnong have formed a monopoly on the right to import potash fertilizers. At the same time, it also creates a monopoly on domestic sales as a whole. They can control the price and obtain huge monopoly profits."

The lead Chinese potash importers are keenly aware of the market power afforded them. In 2008, when the eight other license holders demanded independent negotiations, Sinochem and Sino-Agri opposed this by saying that "concentrated bargaining helps increase the cohesion among importers, whereas if we were fragmented, we would be crushed one by one, and this would lead to higher import prices"[32] (Li 2008).

Today, the small group continues to coordinate negotiation strategies for the global price benchmark prior to annual or biannual negotiations. In December 2017, Sinofert (Sinochem) signed a three-year memorandum of understanding (MOU) confirming that "Sinofert will continue to be the exclusive agency for distributing Canadian red standard potash in China for the next three years. The MOU covers a total of around 3 million metric tonnes of potash.... The price and other terms and conditions are to be determined by the Chinese seaborne potash import joint negotiation every year" ("New MOU between Sinofert and Canpotex" 2017). In 2018, Sino-Agri issued a press release where it announced that, after long negotiations, a benchmark contract price for half a year had been reached between the "China potash import joint negotiation small group" and the Belarusian producers (Sino-Agri Press Release 2018).

The continued role of the small group is clearly one of the most determining factors in the continued stability of the annual potash benchmarking regime internationally.

## China's Impact on the Global Potash Pricing Regime

### Price Benchmark Negotiations

The global potash market functions under a benchmark pricing regime, where the first large contract between a leading producer (usually Canpotex, Uralkali, or BPC) and a leading consumer (since the turn of the century, usually China) sets the price for the year. The growth of China, but also that of Brazil and India as agricultural giants, coupled with growth in potash-intensive food crops, led to a sharp increase in potash prices in the latter half of the 2000s. As Chinese imports grew in importance, negotiations between Chinese purchasers and global suppliers became dominant globally, and Chinese purchasers established themselves as the lead negotiators in benchmark-setting, similar to what had occurred in the international market for iron ore from 2006 onward. Indeed, in 2000, the agreed contract price between BPC and Sino-Agri became the benchmark price for the following year (prices for Canadian potash are usually slightly higher to allow for higher transportation costs; see Table 5.3). In the early 2000s, Sino-Agri (Zhongnong) negotiated with its Russian and Belarusian counterparts, and Sinofert (Sinochem) negotiated with Canpotex. This was relaxed in the 2010s and, in recent years, Sinochem has also purchased potash from the Russian and Belarusian producers.

In the first half of the 2000s, the annual contracts with the Russian/Belarusian producers were price setters (Interview 109, Chinese industry journalist, 2012). In the latter half of the 2000s, the Canpotex-Sinochem negotiations slowly became more dominant. In April 2008, Sinochem signed what would become the 2008 benchmark deal with Canada's Canpotex before Sino-Agri had reached an agreement with BPC (Stone 2009). The first group to come to a pricing agreement sets the global benchmark price for the period at hand. For instance, and as a result, Indian consumers usually waited for the first Chinese contract to proceed and have usually signed at a higher price than China (to take into account longer shipping distances and smaller, more frequent deliveries);[33] in 2021, however, they were the first to sign the benchmark. India also has a single importer who negotiates the price, India Potash Ltd. The annual potash benchmarking regime has continued up to now and has been led by Chinese negotiators; however, it has been showing signs of strain over the past few years, as we will see below.

Table 5.3 **Chinese potash imports and prices paid, 2001**

| Country | Quantity (tonne) | Share of total (%) | Total dollar amount (USD) | Share of total amount (%) | Price per tonne |
|---|---|---|---|---|---|
| Russian Federation | 3,104,296 | 57.22 | 355,142,900 | 54.92 | 114.40 |
| Canada | 1,328,477 | 24.49 | 162,267,110 | 25.09 | 122.15 |
| Jordan | 407,098 | 7.5 | 48,140,697 | 7.44 | 118.25 |
| Israel | 287,369 | 5.3 | 34,207,074 | 5.29 | 119.04 |
| Four top countries | 5,127,239 | 94.51 | 599,757,781 | 92.94 | 116.97 |
| Total countries | 5,425,547 | 100 | 646,700,708 | 100 | 119.20 |

Source: *China Mining Yearbook 2002*, author's calculations

## China's Refusal to Sign a Procurement Contract with the Global Potash Producers

To illustrate the impact of Chinese market players' coordination levels on the global market, it is useful to look at one concrete example. In 2011, the Chinese-led negotiations concluded with an increase in the Chinese-established benchmark price of $70/tonne, or 17.5 percent, over the 2010 price. The potash branch of the Chinese Fertilizer Industry Association published a document that referred to these negotiations as "a great victory" (Li 2011). Feng Mingwei attributed "this 'victory' . . . to the Chinese potash imports joint negotiation small group"[34] (Li 2011). "The Chinese-negotiated contract price for potash imports was $470 a tonne, whereas Brazil and other Asian countries were paying more than $550 a tonne CIF. China was, thus, paying around $80 per tonne less, and since the estimated total imports contracted were around 2 million tonnes, this led to a total savings of at least $160 million USD" (Li 2011) (Author's translation).

At the beginning of 2012, Sinofert, Sinochem's subsidiary, agreed to a benchmark price of $470 a tonne with Canpotex, the same price as the benchmark agreed to the prior year, which was also a success. Shortly afterward, India followed suit and signed at $490 a tonne. Unusually, a second pricing negotiation was scheduled for the summer of 2012.

Up to then, there had been striking similarities between the potash and the iron ore cases (prior to the fall of the benchmarking regime). Then, for what an interviewee characterized as the first time in the history of the benchmark system, the Chinese refused to sign a contract. The Chinese negotiators asked for huge price markdowns from the global stakeholders and then held firm.

The key difference with the iron ore case is that when the Chinese negotiators (Sinofert and Sino-Agri) told global potash producers, "we are not buying" and asked for a price reduction, all of the other Chinese companies with import licenses held the line, including CNOOC and the smaller subsidiaries or parent companies of the two large SOEs.[35] Other companies were easily co-opted and did not go abroad to purchase potash, as was done in the iron ore case, with or without official importing licenses. Interestingly, India also waited to see the results of the standoff before going ahead with its own purchases. The standoff lasted almost six months. Eventually, the benchmark contract was signed in December 2012, at $400 a tonne, down from $470 six months earlier. This was a reduction of 15 percent and a huge win for Chinese consumers (Munson 2013). A specialized analysis in *China Chemical News* mentions the 2012 negotiation process as being one that saw a boycott by large potash customers, China among them, leading to a huge drop in the price (Chen 2013).[36]

The success of the Chinese negotiators in obtaining a sizable markdown from global potash suppliers was the result of specific dynamics between Chinese domestic market stakeholders on one side, global market stakeholders on the other, and their interaction. On both sides, negotiators held the line and refrained from "breaking rank." The key difference between the potash and iron ore cases, despite striking similarities in their opening negotiation tactics, was China's successful coordination at the import interface with the global potash market. There is no indication that the Chinese negotiators were interested in destabilizing the benchmarking system per se. On the contrary, key Chinese SOE import license holders gained huge advantages from their gatekeeping position—a position of privileged access to the global resource—and their ability to resell potash on the domestic market. One Chinese government official noted that "[a]s long as Sinochem is able to sell its fertilizer onward, it has no issues with the price" (Interview 68, Chinese central government ministry official, 2012).

## China's Impact on the Frequency and Timing of Benchmark Pricing Negotiations

Strong coordination on the Chinese and global sides of the market—or relative market power symmetry—led to bargaining dynamics, as predicted in the model developed in Chapter 3 (Quadrant 4, Table 3.1). This led to the doubling of the frequency of the negotiations, which occurred for the first time in 2010, as well as from repeated China-led modifications to the timing of the benchmark negotiations.

An early example of China-led modifications to the timing of the benchmark negotiations occurred in 2006, following two years of steep price increases, when the annual benchmarking negotiations became deadlocked in a development that was not without its parallels in the iron ore case. An agreement was reached only in July of that year.

> Contract negotiations between major potash importers in Brazil, China, and India, and major potash suppliers in Belarus, Canada, and Israel, were deadlocked for the first half of 2006 causing concerns about growing potash inventories. To alleviate the potential oversupply situation, some producers curtailed production. This included the mines in Allan, Cory, Lanigan, and Rocanville, Canada, and four mines in Belarus. . . . The stalemate between major world potash consumers and producers was broken in late July 2006 with the new base price rising by an average $25 per [metric] ton over the 2005 contract price. (Kostick 2007)

Up to 2010, price benchmarking negotiations had been settled once a year. The annual benchmarking system was referred to in announcements such as these, in 2003: "Canpotex Limited . . . signed a three-year Memorandum of Understanding (MOU) with Sinochem, China's largest potash importer. The MOU states that over the next three calendar years Canpotex will ship a minimum of 1.5 million tonnes annually (plus a 10-percent option) *at a price to be negotiated each year based on market circumstances.* . . . Canpotex will supply the Chinese market through Sinochem exclusively during the period" (emphasis added) ("PotashCorp Announces" 2003). The announcement of the annual benchmark price is usually made in a press release such as this one, in April 2008:

> Potash Corporation of Saskatchewan Inc. (PotashCorp) announced today that Canpotex Limited (Canpotex), the offshore marketing company for Saskatchewan potash producers, and Sinofert Holdings Limited (Sinofert), a leading fertilizer enterprise in the People's Republic of China (PRC), have reached agreement on 2008 potash pricing at US $400 per tonne higher than in 2007. ("PotashCorp Announces" 2008)

For the first time, in October 2010, the benchmark system transitioned from an annual to a biannual pricing system, announced via a three-year memorandum of understanding signed between Canpotex and Sinofert. The MOU stipulated that "pricing [was] to be negotiated every six months (January to June and July to December)" ("Canpotex and Sinofert Sign New MOU" 2010).

Interviews with industry insiders suggest that if Chinese stakeholders had originally pushed for the change, then both the international and Chinese negotiators had supported the increase in the benchmarking frequency. On the Chinese side, interviewees argued that consumers needed more flexibility to deal with the biannual crop planting seasons and domestic pricing difficulties. A senior Chinese official suggested that this change was, at the very least, fully supported (if not instigated) by the Chinese side, which wanted more flexibility in purchasing fertilizer and for it to be tailored to their cropping patterns (Interview 96, Senior Chinese official, 2012). An industry journalist confirmed this by saying, "The impetus behind the move from annual to biannual contract negotiations came from China. It wasn't comfortable with one year, as it was too long and prices domestically are difficult to predict, so it was easier to deal with biannual pricing" (Interview 109, Chinese industry journalist, 2012).

Global potash market stakeholders also argued that "Canpotex actually wanted this," and that it "takes some pressure off" of the negotiations, "not all the pressure, but some of the pressure" (Interview 85, Potash industry executive, 2012). Both Canpotex and BPC agreed to double the frequency of the potash benchmark negotiations. In 2015[37] and, subsequently, in 2017, Canpotex and Sinofert signed an MOU confirming the biannual nature of the negotiations: "On 28 December 2017, Sinochem Macao and Canpotex entered into the MOU, pursuant to which Sinochem Macao agreed to purchase an annual volume of 500,000 tonnes of red standard grade potash from Canpotex for each of the three years ending 31 December 2020. . . . Under the MOU, prices will be determined on a six-month basis through mutual negotiations between the parties" (*Annual Report 2018: Nurturing China's Agriculture Sector* 2018).

This pattern of interaction between key producers and consumers about a key institution of the global potash pricing regime—its negotiation frequency—was telling in that it consisted of incremental change, prompted by the Chinese side—but eventually agreed to by both—and aligned with Chinese interests. These kinds of bargaining dynamics were not present in the case of the iron ore benchmark pricing regime.

In the latter part of the 2010s, the three lead Chinese negotiators started to use their dominance over the benchmark negotiations and the fact that they commanded price leadership over around 7 million tonnes of potash annually to try to "time the market" and wait it out for prices to lower. This has led to uneven periods of time between price negotiations. "At times and more recently it has become more difficult to predict the frequency at which the settlements occur. Ultimately there have been longer gaps in recent years between the settlements. I think the longest gap we have seen is about twenty months between settlements" (Interview 155, Senior potash industry analyst, August 2022). The Chinese importing consortium draws on domestic reserves as much as possible until global market conditions favor lower prices.

This pattern had already been developing in 2012, when a potash industry executive noted the following: "The Chinese are holding off, trying to sell off their domestic potash stocks and production, and trying to get prices to go down, but it is not good! If they wait too long, they will be in a bad position and will need the potash, [so] prices will be higher. At worst, the biannual negotiations system will be relaxed, and there will be more instability in the market, just as it happened in the iron ore market, and the Chinese will lose" (Interview 86, Senior potash industry insider, 2012).

However, in contrast to the iron ore benchmark pricing regime, and despite Chinese market stakeholders' behavior and disturbances to the frequency of the pricing negotiations, the benchmark pricing regime negotiations and long-term contracts, led by China, survive today.

## Breakdown of the Russia-Belarus Cartel (BPC)

China is wary of further consolidation in the global potash industry. In 2010, it saw momentum in the industry's consolidation, with the merger of the two largest Russian exporters, Uralkali and Silvinit, which created the world's second largest potash producer. The almost $US24 billion merger caused much concern on the Chinese side.

> China's concern is about Russia's current position as the second largest producer of potash in the world and its recent consolidation of Russia's major potash producers, Uralkali and Silvinit, under a single company.... China raised these concerns to Russia in an attempt to prevent this Uralkali-Silvinit deal, which ultimately went forward and resulted in the creation of the second largest potash producer in the world. Of course, Russia already has disproportionate influence over Bela, and the Russia/Canada combo is already a concentration of power over the commodity that China is concerned about. (Interview 138, Senior East Asia analyst, 2011)

The year 2011 saw the merger between K + S, the world's sixth largest producer, and Canada's Potash One. Then, in 2018, Potash Corp. and Agrium merged to form Nutrien, the world's largest potash company.

During the same period, China continued to express deep concern about industry consolidation. BHP Billion, the largest mining company in the world by stock market capitalization, already head a dominant position in the global iron ore market. In August 2010, the company mounted a $US38.6 billion hostile takeover bid for Canada's Potash Corp (now Nutrien).[38] The likelihood of BHP Billiton's increasing its negotiating position vis-à-vis China was seen with much wariness, as confirmed in an interview with one high-level Chinese government official in the fertilizer industry: "BHP is already too powerful" (Interview 95, Senior Chinese official, 2012).

The fertilizer giant Sinochem envisioned making a counteroffer and held talks to this effect with various potential international partners (Grant et al. 2010; Massot 2011). Interviews indicate that the Chinese State Council was not ready to give the state-owned giant the go-ahead and that Sinochem could not get the approvals it needed to prepare a counteroffer.

> We didn't see it as a good thing at all. When BHP made the offer in 2010, we were really concerned. There even was an emergency meeting in Beijing in September 2010, with many interested parties, to discuss the possible strategies. They wanted to put together a purchase bid, but Sinochem was too small, the price tag was so huge, they wanted to look

and did look for partners, including in Canada, but the time pressure was huge, and they couldn't put something together in such a short time. (Interview 95, Senior Chinese official, 2012)

On November 3, 2010, in a move that shocked the global investment community, the Canadian Minister of Industry blocked the BHP Billiton bid, under the "net benefit to Canada" provision of the Canada Investment Act. This was only the second time an investment had been blocked in the history of this legislation. When the Canadian government blocked the deal, the relief of the Chinese potash importers was immediate: "The Canadian government did a good thing, actually!" (Interview 95, Senior Chinese official, 2012).

It is against this backdrop that, on July 30, 2013, Uralkali shocked the world by issuing a press release that effectively ended the cartel arrangements between it and Belaruskali.

> Unfortunately, we should state that our cooperation with our Belarusian partners within [the] BPC framework has come to a deadlock. It has always been Uralkali's position that [the] export activities of both producers should go through the unified sales network. This fundamental principle of partnership was violated by the Decree No. 566 issued by the Belarusian President on 22 December 2012, which cancelled the exclusive right of BPC to export Belarusian potash. Following the issue of the Decree, Belaruskali has made a number of deliveries outside BPC.
>
> We have repeatedly informed our Belarusian partners that such actions were unacceptable and they have ultimately destroyed the fundamentals of our prolonged fruitful cooperation. In this situation we have to re-direct our export deliveries through our own trader.
>
> Still, we thank our Belarusian partners for cooperation within the BPC framework and do not exclude the possibility of cooperation on a mutually beneficial basis in future. (Baumgertner 2013)

The Belarusian side reacted with what the *Financial Times* qualified as "rage" (Cienski and Kuznetsov 2013) over Uralkali's decision to pull out of BPC. The chief executive of Uralkali (and chairman of BPC), Vladislav Baumgertner, was detained in Belarus on his way back from a meeting with the Belarusian prime minister and was charged with abuse of office, while some argued "the Belarusians [were] trying to force the Russians to reinstate the price-fixing scheme" (Weaver and Cienski 2013). "Belarus's Investigative Committee said . . . that they suspect Baumgertner of planning to cause a drop in the potash market by quitting the joint venture 'in order to gain material benefits'" ("Uralkali CEO Arrested"

2013). The case was eventually handed over to Russia and the charges were dropped.

"'My first thought was disbelief,' said Ms. Kudryavets, director general of BPC, the sales and marketing arm of giant potash miner JSC Belaruskali" (MacDonald 2015). Among the reasons listed for the breakup of BPC, the biggest potash export agency in the world, was the fact that Belaruskali had recently sold potash to China, which meant it had stepped outside of the marketing cartel.

"It was Uralkali choosing to exit it. These were very acrimonious circumstances. Uralkali was becoming increasingly frustrated with BPC's seeming preference toward Belaruskali. Given that BPC was and is headquartered in Minsk." The analyst explained that the effect of the fall of BPC was that the two members of the marketing cartel, who were the second and third largest producers in the world, "collaborated on production and exports, which meant that overall, their operating rates were quite low, they were controlling supply. Pretty much overnight they went into direct competition with each other. Their capacity utilization... [went from] 70–75 percent... to 90 percent in the space of a year. So, they really started competing very hard" (Interview 155, Senior potash industry analyst, 2022).

As one potash industry insider explained, "Both sides have accused the other of bypassing BPC, but we haven't had any evidence of this on a large scale. All the seaborne shipments to China should have been within the BPC contract, though both sides may have been negotiating future deals independently" (Interview 130, Senior industry consultant, 2013). "Baumgertner (Uralkali CEO) and four other Uralkali executives for whom Belarus has issued arrest warrants are accused of conspiring to cut Belaruskali out of decision-making at Belarus Potash and causing $100 million of damages" (Kudrytski and Kravchenko 2013).

Many analysts thought the breakup would be short-lived. "Exiting the cartel never made sense. It didn't make sense then and it doesn't make sense now," says Joseph Dayan, head of markets at BCS Financial Group. "It was such a perfect set-up for producers. People don't tend to self-destruct intentionally" (Weaver and Cienski 2013).

Uralkali remained confident of its global comparative advantage, as it is a lower-cost producer and has direct rail links with China. Further, it argued it could increase profits by working with lower potash prices and ramping up production instead of remaining within BPC and working within higher price conditions and controlled production. Various media outlets have quoted Vladislav Baumgertner, Uralkali's chief executive, as having said that global potash prices were likely to drop to a range of $300 a tonne as early as late 2013. The contracts that were signed in early 2014 confirmed the impact that the breakup of the cartel had on prices. Indeed: "Russian... Uralkali OAO agreed on Jan. 20 to a six-month deal to sell Chinese buyers 700,000 tonnes of potash at

$305 per tonne" ("UPDATE 1—Canpotex Signs Potash Contract with China's Sinofert" 2014).

Such a drop in prices advantages lower-cost producers (such as Uralkali and ICL), although potash prices remain well above Saskatchewan's (Canada) production costs of around $100 a tonne. However, China was one of the most direct beneficiaries of this event. Interestingly, the Chinese Investment Corporation, a Chinese sovereign wealth fund, had acquired Uralkali options six months prior to this event. "Billionaire Suleiman Kerimov and his partners in OAO Uralkali (URKA), the largest potash producer, sold bonds to China's sovereign wealth fund and VTB Capital that can be exchanged for shares valued at about $3.2 billion" (Fedorinova and Corcoran 2013).

One potash industry insider commented, "I don't know how much CIC [China Investment Corp.] knew about this—the news has devalued their stake in Uralkali, but of course they hope that China will benefit from lower prices. I can't imagine CIC had the leverage to influence Uralkali's decision" (Interview 130, 2013). Another analyst explained the following:

> Were the Chinese willing to part with their money in November at a billion dollars more than their stake is now worth, because they were assured that potash would become significantly cheaper for China to buy when the bond conversion into shares falls due in a year's time? . . . The thinking in Minsk is that Lukashenko made his own deal with the Middle Kingdom when he visited Beijing on July 16. . . . I can only speculate that Belarus President Lukashenko's visit to China resulted in a contract signed outside of BPC, and this was the last stroke that broke Uralkali's patience. The Belarus theory isn't taking into account CIC's stake in Uralkali. So unless the Chinese miscalculated that their deal with Lukashenko and Belaruskali would not have the costs Uralkali has now inflicted, the Chinese are now calculating that they will gain if they play both sides against the middle. The Chinese win with this strategy in the short term because potash will cost them $200 less per tonne. (Helmer 2013)

In the short term, the China Investment Corporation lost out on the value of its investment in Uralkali, as shares went down following the news of a decrease in contract prices. But in September 2013, the CIC converted its options to a 12.5 percent equity stake in Uralkali, which came with one seat on the company's board of directors (Weaver et al. 2014). As the *Financial Times* put it, the CIC's move "should increase the probability that Uralkali will stick to its guns and resist any temptation to get back into bed with Belaruskali" (Wheatley 2013). Chinese importers overall gained as prices came down.

In 2014, the Chinese side did not invite Belaruskali to bid for the first contract of the year, which Uralkali won at 24 percent below 2013 prices, or $US305 a tonne, to become the price setter (Fedorinova and Yun 2014). In 2015, two Chinese banks, the Industrial Commercial Bank of China and the China Construction Bank, participated in a $US530 million loan agreement with Uralkali ("UPDATE 1—Russia's Uralkali Signs $530 mln Loan" 2015).

At the time, many potash industry insiders and analysts continued to think that future cooperation between Uralkali and Belaruskali remained possible. "Potash Corp of Saskatchewan chief executive officer Bill Doyle said . . . it was 'logical' to expect potash rivals Uralkali OAO of Russia and Belaruskali to reunite at some point in a move that could bolster the struggling potash industry. 'It would appear to be in their own self-interest,' he said, 'so I think it's logical to presume that they will at some point in time get back together'" (Nickel 2014). As the years went by, this did not materialize. Since 2013, there has been no indication of Uralkali's returning to the BPC marketing arrangement. Some would add that China's clear interest in a more competitive pricing regime is making this difficult. As a former potash industry executive explained, "Business-wise, the Uralkali BPC split, that increased the supplies to China. Sinofert was happy but also Uralkali and Belaruskali can choose their customers. So, a lot of Chinese customers who were not buying in the past got new opportunities" (Interview 157, Former potash industry executive, 2022).

By 2015, the relationship between Belaruskali and Chinese buyers had been re-established when Belaruskali won the price-setting contract with Chinese importers for the first time (MacDonald 2015; Kudrytski and Fedorinova 2015). At $US315 a tonne, the agreed price, which became the benchmark for the first half of the year, was significantly lower than other producers had expected ("only" $10 above the 2014 price) (Kudrytski and Fedorinova 2015). Meanwhile, Belaruskali and Uralkali continued to undercut each other and, for some, the benchmark system began to show signs of difficulty. Although the first contracts were usually signed early in the year, the 2015 contract had not been signed until March. An analyst at Bloomberg Intelligence said that "the delay is 'one more step toward dissolving the traditional patterns' in the potash market" (Hill et al. 2015).

So why did the benchmark system not collapse, as it did in the iron ore market, when, in the words of a senior potash industry analyst, "the producers would be pretty happy with that" (Interview 155, Senior potash industry analyst, 2022)? As another interviewee explains, "everybody wants the free market except for the three [Chinese] buying committee members, because that gives them the privilege to protect their market, to the cost of all the others. . . . [Other Chinese companies] just complain quietly, because they don't want to make the big guys angry, because politically, commercially, these people are by far more powerful, so you cannot fight with them" (Interview 157, Former potash industry executive, 2022). Another interviewee put it this way, "that 'trio' of importers, they have a collective willingness to continue with it and based on history they should, because their margins have been much better with it than it would have been without, almost certainly. Then [the benchmark] will continue to exist in some form" (Interview 155, Senior potash industry analyst, 2022).

## The Emergence of a Global Potash Spot Market

The 2010s were eventful for both the global potash market and the Chinese domestic potash market. The 2013 Uralkali-Belaruskali split meant that both companies could now look for new customers. At around the same time, in 2014, Canpotex was opening a China office to develop that market. Interviews suggest that the goal was to broaden relationships outside of Sinochem. "At that time Sinochem was happy about the Uralkali-BPC split, but on the other side, BPC, Uralkali and Canpotex are all looking for new customers. So really that impact a time when the potash market was moving toward a market economy" (Interview 157, Former potash industry executive, 2022).

In recent years, China's dominance on the global potash market has started to wane. The influence of the annual negotiated benchmark has diminished. In fact, various market patterns that were established since China's emergence as dominant consumer have started to break down, slowly, over the past five years. At the same time, a few dynamics have come to a head, and some of these disruptions have been amplified by the consequences on the global potash market of international sanctions imposed on Belarus in 2020 as well as the Russian invasion of Ukraine in 2022.

First, there are increasing tensions around the annual benchmark pricing negotiations. For instance, following the settlement of the benchmark, we saw very public disagreement between producers. In recent years, BPC-China negotiations had generally been the price setter. This meant that it was the first to negotiate annual contracts with Chinese consumers. But in February 2021, the sole Indian importer, India Potash Ltd., agreed to a contract with BPC for a price of $247 a tonne (CFR). Immediately thereafter, "other producers put out public statements saying that the price agreed upon was too low, that they disagreed with it, and that they were going to start sending more volumes to Brazil instead.... It has become a more bitter, more acrimonious event in the potash industry than it used to be" (Interview 155, Senior potash industry analyst, 2022).

Second, we see a weakening of Canpotex. "Canpotex is in a weaker position.... They represent two big suppliers. Today, one of these big suppliers is building up their own company in Brazil, in China, in India. In Brazil, the majority of Canpotex volumes goes to Mosaic; in China, it goes to Mosaic. Basically, Canpotex is not a marketing company anymore; it has become a logistics company" (Interview 157, Former potash industry executive, 2022). In 2015, Joc O'Rourke was appointed president and CEO of the Mosaic Company. This management change is said to have spearheaded a new period of growth for the fertilizer giant and an expansion strategy into downstream fertilizer businesses in China, Brazil, and India. "Canpotex sells to Mosaic, . . . Mosaic China buys from Canpotex. . . . Mosaic China distributes all the product to Chinese customers. . . . In the very beginning, Mosaic was very small in China, Canpotex did the majority [of the sales]. Today, Canpotex gives the majority of the volumes to Mosaic and Mosaic sells on behalf of Canpotex, or even sells by themselves. The system itself has not changed, but if you look at the perception from the Chinese customers, ten years ago, Canadian potash was Canpotex, today, they think, 'we can buy Canadian potash from Mosaic, from Canpotex, from K + S.'" (Interview 157, Former potash industry executive, 2022).

Compounding the disruptions in the global potash market were two shocks to the Eurasian market. First, sanctions were imposed on Belarus, in 2020. "Belarus has essentially been cut off from exporting potash. Even if you wanted to, you can't get anything out. It is getting some small volumes out, mostly by rail which is then re-exported" (Interview 155, Senior potash industry analyst, 2022). Then, Russia invaded Ukraine. This "sent some markets into complete panic. Brazil was of particular note because it relies on imports for around 96 percent of its annual consumption" (Interview 155, Senior potash industry analyst, 2022). As the potash industry analyst explained, Russia is still sending bulk cargoes to a number of downstream markets by sea, but Uralkali had not officially settled on a contract with either Indian or Chinese consumers by the summer of 2022. This is causing issues in terms of how they are getting product into those markets. Russia can send some potash to China by rail, but there are constraints at cross-border points because of the change in the rail gauge.

However, the major structural change to the global potash market on the side of the consumers in the past five years has been the emergence of Brazil. Citing Integer and International Fertilizer Industry data, a former Brazilian executive explained that the share of developing countries' potash demand went from 1.5 percent of global demand in 1961 to 53 percent in 2017 (Interview 173, Former senior mining industry executive, 2022). Brazil's share of global potash imports went from 3 percent in 1970 to 18 percent in 2019 (Figure 5.11). A former mining industry executive explained that, at one point, Brazil produced up to 30 percent of its potash needs but that its existing potash mine, which started producing 1 million tonnes per year in the mid-1980s, is now producing less than 300,000 tonnes per year today and will probably be depleted

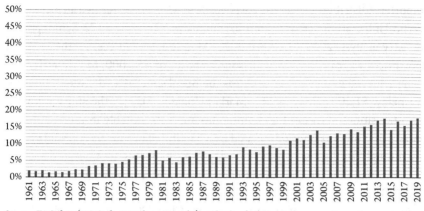

Source: FAO data (HS Code 3104, by net weight), author's calculations.

*Figure 5.11* Brazil imports as share of world imports, 1961–2019

in the next two or three years (Interview 173, Former senior mining industry executive, 2022). As a result, Brazil's domestic potash production is down to almost 0 percent today. A potash industry analyst explained that, in the 1990s, Brazil's consumption was about a quarter that of the United States, or a similar size to France. However, "[s]ince 2017, Brazil has accounted for 16–20 percent of all global demand and has become by far the world's largest single importer of potassium chloride, overtaking the US consistently in the early to mid-2010s. Indeed, in 2021 and 2022, the country's potassium chloride consumption is not far behind that of China. As a result, its influence on pricing globally has become far more significant" (Interview 172, Potash industry analyst, 2022).

Brazil's growth in potash consumption is the result of broader applications of fertilizer in Brazil but also of the emergence of Brazil as a global food exporter, especially of corn and soybean, which has led to new agricultural frontiers being pushed across the country.

According to two different observers of the global potash market, two different characteristics of Brazilian consumers are worth noting, at this point. One former Brazilian mining executive explained that a key characteristic was the Brazilian consumers' fragmentation: "With new agricultural frontiers spreading in different areas of Brazil, fertilizer demand also spread and fragmented from global producers and distributors to trading companies and farmers" (Interview 173, Former senior mining industry executive, 2022). However, the other potash industry analyst explained that "a key change in the functionality of the industry in Brazil has been the acquisition of a number of large Brazilian importers/distributors by the fertilizer producers themselves. For example, Mosaic is now a major distributor of fertilizer in Brazil, and EuroChem owns Fertilizantes Tocantins. A range of producers have also purchased stakes in Brazilian fertilizer importers/distributors over the past decade in what's been termed an increase in 'vertical integration' across the fertilizer industry" (Interview 172, Senior potash industry analyst, 2022). In April 2022, Mosaic reported the Southeast Asian spot prices as "catching up with some reports of ~$1,000/MT [metric ton] being achieved in the region," whereas the Brazil spot price "delivered" hovered just below $1,200 ("May 2022—Market Update" 2022). "The shifts in potash echo transitions seen in other commodity markets, notably iron ore. . . . Like potash, iron ore was once dominated by a handful of producers and sold primarily through fixed-price contracts. Today, iron ore prices are tracked daily, and that information is typically used to negotiate long-term sales agreements" (Hill et al. 2015).

In a fascinating turn of event that mirrors China's impact on the global iron ore market over ten years prior, in 2010, you have the coming together of two key ingredients that, as this book argues, have increased the likelihood of global market change in times of market power disruptions: the arrival of a fragmented consumer and incentives on behalf of global producers to go along with the financialization of the market pricing regime. When I put this argument to the former Brazilian mining industry executive, he said, "The shrinking of internal production and [the] fragmentation of demand countered by [an] oligopolistic supply side structure was the main driver of spot market emergence. A similar trend as happened in [the] iron ore market in China. But the size of Brazilian demand is not big enough to drive all [the] market to spot basis pricing" (Interview 173, Former senior mining industry executive, 2022).

## Conclusion

The potash and iron ore cases make for a fascinating comparison. Both markets were structured in strikingly similar ways at the outset, not only in terms of their global structure and pricing regimes but also in terms of China's import dependence on them. However, following China's emergence as the dominant consumer in both markets, their global pricing institutions evolved in significantly different ways.

To understand why China's impact on the global potash market differs from the iron ore case, we need to understand the differences in the market power asymmetries Chinese stakeholders faced in the two markets over the past twenty years. The fall of the iron ore benchmarking system was driven by the fragmented behavior of Chinese iron ore market players in the face of coordinated global iron ore producers. In the potash case, China is home to much higher levels of coordination capacity at the domestic level, especially at the interface between the domestic and the global potash market. Chinese potash consumers were thus able to maintain a high level of coordination, and they wielded this market power to influence the global market more effectively, at least until recently. For a little less than twenty years following the emergence of China as the dominant consumer of potash, Chinese consumers pursued a strategy of coordination at home and institutional stability globally in maintaining the benchmarking system, all the while bending global markets towards more competition and lower negotiated prices. Among other things, we saw the breakdown of the export marketing arrangement between the Belarusian and Russian potash exporters, which eroded their market power, and we also saw the emergence of smaller producers, such as Laos, which were encouraged by Chinese investment. This led to more competitive behavior among Eurasian producers and a favorable environment for Chinese negotiators.

At the domestic level, the Chinese domestic potash industry features a domestic entente between powerful Chinese fertilizer giants Sinochem, Sino-Agri, and newcomer CNOOC and their successful efforts to preserve the privileged position of market power they had established in their own domestic arena.

In the late 2000s, the Chinese government tried to introduce more competition into the potash import process. These attempts to increase competition at the Chinese import interface with the global potash industry have seen a modest increase in import licenses and the added role of CNOOC in international benchmark negotiations. But the continued dominance of the "Chinese potash imports joint negotiation small group" has been a critical element of market power and stability in the Chinese domestic potash market. Taking note of the fall of the benchmark in the iron ore case, Chinese potash market players have displayed keen awareness that an overly fragmented interface with global producers would weaken China's hand and shift the balance of market power in favor of global producers.

If these three giants maintain their entente and continue, with the support of the government, to coordinate prior to benchmarking negotiations and extract rents from other Chinese fertilizer market players, such as distributers and fertilizer manufacturers, the Chinese will continue to present a coordinated front to the world. As these three consumers favor the continuation of the global potash market benchmarking regime, the benchmarking system could survive a while longer. If they fail, the potash market may be the next commodity market to push the frontier of marketization.

This is a case where until the mid-2010s, China had achieved movement toward the best of both worlds: continued domestic coordination at its interface with the global market and increased fragmentation in the global market. For Chinese consumers, this represented China's movement toward the most advantageous position of market power asymmetry (Quadrant 3). However, development spearheaded by Brazil's rise as significant consumer, especially since the late 2010s, and the penchant of its consumers for spot pricing have weakened the dominance of the benchmark system and of Chinese importers in the global market.

Just as in the iron ore market, the gradual dissolution of the dominance of the potash benchmark pricing regime is occurring despite contrary preferences from the largest Chinese importers. And as in the iron ore case, marketization trends in the global potash market are occurring at a time when Chinese market stakeholders are in an increasing position of weakness vis-à-vis global market stakeholders.

# 6

# China's Impact on the Global Uranium and Copper Markets

## Market Power, Market Vulnerability, and Market Change

> With Rio and BHP, I can see how they [the Chinese iron ore importers] felt like they were pushed around a little bit, whereas in the uranium market, they [the Chinese uranium importers] are probably feeling like they have a pretty good hold on things and nobody has got the power to make problems for them. (Interview 129, Senior uranium industry executive, 2013)

> The Chinese play a bigger role, but I wouldn't say that the market dynamics [in the global copper market] have changed dramatically because of that.... It was a big industry already, they have been joining the industry, becoming a more significant player. They had to learn how to play within the rules that were already in place. (Interview 164, Executive at global commodities consultancy, 2022)

This chapter will look at the political economy of China's impact on the global commodity markets of uranium and copper, following China's emergence as dominant importer. China became the number one importer of natural uranium in 2010 and of copper in 2008. Chinese patterns of behavior in the uranium and copper markets differed from those in the iron ore and potash markets in ways that are analytically significant and can help us refine the framework developed in this book.

At first glance, in the uranium market, given the levels of import dependence, the centrality of the resource to China's civilian nuclear program and energy needs, and the general sensitivity of the resource given its dual-use scenarios, one might have expected more disruptive behavior on the part of Chinese market stakeholders, either in terms of actions or rhetoric. As discussed more at length in Chapter 3, in the literature, there are prevalent understandings that associate China's market size with its potential to disrupt global markets.

In fact, China's procurement behavior in the global uranium market has included continued support for the existing long-term pricing mechanisms (there are no international benchmarking negotiations per se in the uranium market, but long-term contracts and privileged relationships between consumers and producers dominate pricing). In addition, China has not used accusatory rhetoric against global uranium producers, as it has in other commodity markets, even while it has tripled its uranium imports (up to more than three times its annual needs), massively increasing its import-dependence levels along the way. Third, China has successfully implemented a strategy of investment in mining projects abroad in exchange for procurement access, and this led to Kazakhstan's rise as the number one uranium exporter in the world. This is a strategy that China found more difficult to meaningfully implement in the potash, the iron ore and, to some extent, the copper market. Finally, China has shown a willingness and has made high-level commitments to being a meaningful participant in various international civilian nuclear safety and security initiatives, including its full participation in the International Atomic Energy Agency. Indeed, following the 2011 Fukushima disaster in Japan, China showed an openness to international safety reviews and it has allowed teams of international safety inspectors into the core of its civilian nuclear program. China's behavior in the global uranium market stands in contrast to its behavior in other commodity markets reviewed in this book.

These findings are counterintuitive. China is highly import-dependent and is facing a global market that is relatively concentrated with powerful global firms, yet it has shown little of the frustrations, acerbic rhetoric, or even significant impact on market institutions it has in the iron ore market, for instance. China's favorable position of market power in the uranium market has also not led to major disruptions in global market pricing institutions. How can we make sense of these patterns of behavior and impacts on global commodity market institutions?

I argue that an important key to understanding the general patterns of Chinese uranium procurement behavior and impacts on global uranium market institutions lies in the relative positions of market power experienced by Chinese uranium consumers vis-à-vis their global counterparts.

Relative positions of market power matter in at least two ways. First, in the uranium market Chinese importers are in a strong position of market power at the interface with the global market, relative to global market stakeholders. Consequently, they are able to more easily develop coherent objectives regarding uranium procurement as well as to influence global market institutions. Indeed, the domestic political economy of Chinese uranium consumers is characterized by high levels of concentration and coordination. Only two entities—one a former ministry—are responsible for most of China's uranium imports. The global uranium market is characterized by lower levels of coordination—it is segmented into regional blocks that are relatively independent of each other. The combination of a favorable position of market power for China and the international conjuncture resulting from the Fukushima accident in 2011 has created more room for China to maneuver internationally in the global uranium market.

The copper market presents a case where market stakeholders on both the Chinese domestic consumer side and the global producer side were in a more fragmented position. The Chinese domestic copper industry is more similar to its domestic iron ore industry in that sense, with over 800 mining enterprises in 2010 (*China Mining Yearbook* 2011). The two largest importers of copper in China accounted for 32 percent of total imports in 2010. This proportion went down to 20 percent in 2014 (Chinese Customs data, copper concentrates). It is higher than that in the iron ore market (where the top two importers were responsible for 8 percent of total imports in 2014) but much lower than that in the potash and uranium markets (where the top two importers were responsible for, respectively, 47 percent and 100 percent of total imports in the same year). This has led to a lack of clear positions of market power on either side of the ledger. As a result, Chinese copper market stakeholders have had difficulty exerting influence on global market institutions.

Second, in the uranium market, the relative position of market power China finds itself in is a continuation of the market power relations that preceded its rise as the number one consumer. In other words, other dominant consumers of uranium, France and the United States, also found themselves in a situation of favorable market power vis-à-vis global market stakeholders, albeit with some differences. As elaborated in Chapter 3, a transition within the same quadrant (where market power relations are maintained) is more likely to lead to stability in global market institutions than a transition between quadrants. This can help explain the relatively slow market institutional change at the global level, but it doesn't explain it all. This chapter further investigates the relationship between China's additional room to maneuver in the uranium market and its relative lack of institution-disruptive behavior here. As in other cases explored in this book, we look to relative positions of market power, or lower vulnerability, and whether these have played a role, via heightened perceptions of domestic control and resource security, in informing China's willingness to act within existing global market institutions, including the relevant international nuclear safety regimes, as some of the interviews suggest.

In the case of copper, the impact of China on global market institutions has also been modest but for different reasons. The transition between Japan and China consisted of a movement between Quadrants 3 and 1 (Table 3.1), or a transition from a position of relative market power on the side of (Japanese) consumers, to a position of market power symmetry (fragmentation on both sides). As per Chapter 3, although a transition between quadrants can be disruptive, a transition toward a more symmetrical position of market power is less likely to lead to global market change than a transition toward an asymmetrical position of market power. In the early moments of transition between Japan and China as the number one consumer, the lack of coordination of Chinese copper importers, compared to their Japanese counterparts, had an initial disruptive effect on the global copper market and pushed the dynamics somewhat further in the direction of liberalization (in the context of an already financialized market), with more short-term contracts and arm's-length relationships. In this sense, the Chinese copper story shows some limited parallels with that of the iron ore market. Indeed, it is pretty clear that the disruption that amounted to a slight movement toward liberalization was not a stated aim per se of major Chinese copper market stakeholders.

In fact, since then, Chinese copper market stakeholders, including state-owned enterprises and government agencies, have attempted to build their coordination capacity—or positions of market power—vis-à-vis the global market and to bring the situation back toward Quadrant 3 (or a situation of consumer dominance). A case in point is the creation of the China Smelters Purchase Team (CSPT), which is meant to provide Chinese smelters (and consumers of copper ores) more negotiating power. The extent to which this has been successful is debated. The Chinese have been able to perpetuate the annual benchmark pricing negotiations that have existed on the margin of the global copper market, regarding treatment and refining charges (or TC/RC, which are the fees global miners pay to smelters for refining copper ores into refined copper). Interviewees tell me that prices have been hugely volatile and that CSPT members continue to undercut each other.

By expanding the empirical cases under study, this chapter seeks to evaluate the outcomes, given different values on the explanatory variables. The first two cases covered in this book investigated situations where the global market stakeholders were both highly coordinated and zeroed in on the variation in Chinese domestic coordination levels: one case, in the potash market, where the Chinese domestic market stakeholders' coordination levels were high, and another case, in the iron ore market, where the Chinese domestic market stakeholders' coordination levels were low. This chapter investigates situations where global market stakeholders were not as coordinated as were those in the cases of iron ore and potash, in other words, the two quadrants on the left-hand side of Table 3.1, Quadrants 1 and 3. This chapter looks at one market where relative global fragmentation is paired with Chinese domestic market stakeholders that are highly coordinated (uranium) and one market where relative global fragmentation is paired with Chinese domestic market stakeholders that are much less coordinated (copper).

In addition, both the global uranium and copper markets offer different starting points for our inquiry. The global copper market had already evolved toward a highly liquid global spot market prior to China's emergence as the number one consumer, with copper being traded in major exchanges such as the London Metal Exchange and the Chicago Mercantile Exchange. As a result, traders had already been playing a much bigger role in the global copper market compared to the three other markets investigated in this book. The global uranium market presents an interesting case where market institutions fell short of a global benchmarking system but were still very far from the liquid and financialized spot market situation found in the global copper market. In the uranium market, at the time of China's emergence, dominant patterns included long-term contracts, stable relationships, low volatility, and a low percentage of trades conducted on the spot market.

Investigating these further two cases allows us to refine and reaffirm some of the insights developed up to here in the book. Fundamentally, it is important to understand the domestic political economy of both markets to understand Chinese market stakeholders' behavior abroad. But it is in understanding the specific patterns of how they met global market stakeholders or, what I label in this book, their market power differentials that we can better explain the formation of Chinese stakeholders' preferences, procurement behavior, and capacity to actualize their preferences and effect change at the global level.

## China and the Global Uranium Market

China's growth in uranium consumption has been just as formidable as it was in the iron ore market. This has led to an increase in its share of global uranium consumption, from 1 percent of global imports in 2001 to 31 percent in 2010, the year it became the number one importer, to 36 percent in 2020 (see Figure 6.1). China has remained the number one importer of uranium globally since 2010.

At the international level, prior to China's emergence as the world's number one uranium consumer, the uranium market exhibited high levels of industry concentration. Indeed, global uranium market production is highly concentrated, with four countries responsible for 73 percent of global uranium production in 2009 and 75 percent in 2015, these countries being Kazakhstan, Canada, Australia, and Namibia (see Table 6.1).

China's known uranium resources are vastly insufficient for its needs. At most, it possesses 1 percent of the world's known recoverable uranium resources

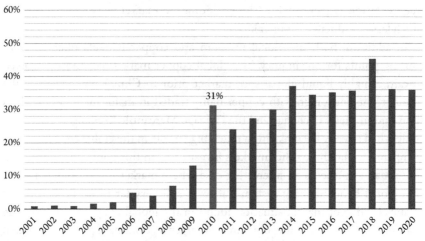

Source: UNCOMTRADE (Trade Value, USD), HSCODE: 284410, author's calculations.

*Figure 6.1* China's share of world uranium imports, 2001–2020

*Table 6.1* **Global natural uranium production, 2009–2015**

| Country | Production 2009 (tU) | Production 2015 (tU) | Share in 2009 (%) | Share in 2015 (%) | Change in production 2015/2009 (%) |
|---|---|---|---|---|---|
| Kazakhstan | 14,020 | 23,607 | 28% | 39% | 68% |
| Canada | 10,173 | 13,325 | 20% | 22% | 31% |
| Australia | 7,982 | 5,654 | 16% | 9% | −29% |
| Namibia | 4,626 | 2,993 | 9% | 5% | −35% |
| Niger | 3,243 | 4,116 | 6% | 7% | 27% |
| Russia | 3,564 | 3,055 | 7% | 5% | −14% |
| Uzbekistan | 2,429 | 2,385 | 5% | 4% | −2% |
| USA | 1,453 | 1,256 | 3% | 2% | −14% |
| Ukraine | 840 | 1,200 | 2% | 2% | 43% |
| China | 750 | 1,616 | 1% | 3% | 115% |
| South Africa | 563 | 393 | 1% | 1% | −30% |
| Others | 1,025 | 704 | 2% | 1% | −31% |
| **Total** | **50,772** | **60,304** | | | **19%** |

Source: World Nuclear Association.

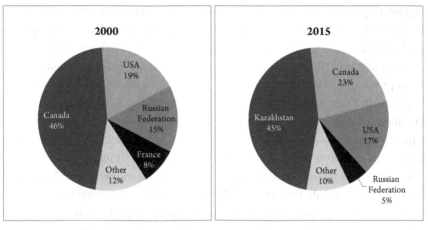

Source: UNCOMTRADE (HSCODE: 284410).

*Figure 6.2* Shares of world uranium exports by country, 2001 and 2015

or about 68,000 tonnes (Weitz 2011a). The country's uranium output in 2015, at 1,616 tonnes, was about 3 percent of global production (Table 6.1).

Global uranium exports are even more concentrated than global uranium production. In 2000, fully 88 percent of natural uranium exports came from four countries—Canada, the United States, Russia, and France—compared to 74 percent for iron ore and 86 percent for potash (UN Comtrade, by trade value). Since then, concentration among exporting countries has remained high, with the top four exporters of natural uranium accounting for 90 percent of global exports in 2015, these countries being Kazakhstan, Canada, the United States, and Russia (see Figure 6.2). The top four firms controlled 59 percent of exports in 2013 (see Chapter 2, Table 2.1).

## The Uranium Pricing Regime Prior to China's Emergence

Despite high levels of concentration, industry coordination between global uranium players is lower than it was in the potash and iron ore markets in the early 2000s. The uranium market lacks a producers' marketing cartel (such as the ones active in the potash market) or benchmark pricing negotiations (such as in the case of the iron ore market until 2010 and the potash market until now).

The only producers' cartel in the uranium market was created in the 1970s and it has since been disbanded (Stewart, 1981). In the 1960s, the American Energy Agency banned the use of foreign uranium in its domestic reactors and aggressively cut prices of its own uranium exports. This was a period of oversupply in the rest of the world. The Canadian government decided to support its domestic uranium industry while stockpiling its inevitable surplus of uranium production. It was then that Canada and the world's other major uranium producers (Australia, France, South Africa, and Rio Tinto Zinc Ltd., an Anglo-Australian multinational), in the absence of the United States, sought to mitigate the impacts of the American policy and resorted to the covert manipulation of the world market (Stewart 1981). In June 1972, the secret international uranium cartel was formally established (arrangements included price fixing, bid rigging, and market sharing). The cartel was referred to as the Société d'Études et de Recherches d'Uranium. In 1976, Westinghouse filed an antitrust action against the cartel members, including a Canadian company, and the cartel was subsequently dismantled. No other producers' cooperation initiatives have emerged since then. Historical legacies have influenced global uranium market stakeholders' behavior, particularly their reticence toward coordination. As one uranium market industry insider explained, "They haven't seen any coordination among uranium players, I can tell you that! That is absolutely the case.... Nobody will touch it with a ten-foot pole. You mention the cartel in the 1970s, those were different days" (Interview 129, Senior uranium industry executive, 2013).

In a fashion that recalls other commodity markets that have evolved into regional markets for physical reasons, such as the global liquefied natural gas (LNG) market, the global uranium market is fragmented into distinct regional markets. As one international uranium industry insider explained:

> Of course, if you think about Francophone-speaking Africa, it really means Niger, and for them, yes, Areva is the main company, apart now from a small Chinese mine in Niger that is just starting to produce.... They have also done work in DRC and in Mali, etc. When I think of Cameco, I think of Canada, I think of the US, I think of Kazakhstan, and I think more of Australia these days. It is the same with the others. Traditionally, you had Rio Tinto producing out of Africa and Australia, and you had BHP producing out of Australia, not really a traditional producer but just happened to have bought it... and then there are the Kazaks and then the Russians and the Uzbeks and the Ukrainians.... So this is really their backyard.... So, when I think about the global uranium market, it is a very diverse market. The uranium and nuclear industry are a very small little industry and very diversified globally.... If you look at certain companies, they have their regional biases. (Interview 129, Senior uranium industry executive, 2013)

As an example, in the West, smaller firms complained to me about the dominance of Cameco: "[Cameco] effectively acts as a price maker, everyone follows their price" (Interview 116, Executive at a private junior mining company, 2013). On the African continent, however, one uranium industry expert and government official from Niger explained that, from their perspective, before China's arrival, the French company Areva really controlled the uranium market (Cameco, of Canada, is not even mentioned) (Interview 122, Government official from Niger, 2013). The official from Niger indicated that China's arrival as a consumer has allowed them to diversify their export targets. For their part, Chinese analysts conceive of the global uranium market as consisting of three large regions: the developed world, Africa, and Central Asia (Xiao et al. 2009). Despite the dominance of Cameco and Areva, Chinese importers have been able to avoid dependence on these two companies. In summary, the global uranium market is relatively concentrated, thinly institutionalized, highly regionalized, and home to relatively low levels of coordination among market participants.

During the 1980s and 1990s, there was a lull in the construction of new power plants globally for several reasons. This includes the end of the Cold War and, thus, the increased availability of secondary sources of uranium; the Three Mile Island and Chernobyl disasters, the consequences of which led to a reduction in the expected growth of electricity demand from nuclear power; and the fall of the 1970s uranium producers' cartel. The result of all of this was a drop in the uranium spot price and, consequently, of mining investment. Indeed, from the early 1980s until 2001, uranium prices trended downward and remained between US$7 and US$10 a pound. The uranium market reflected a persistent buyers' market over the fifteen-year period from 1980 to 1994 and again over the five years from 1998 to 2003 (see Figure 6.3). Consequently, the uranium industry fell under the radar.

Beginning in 2001, the price of uranium began to rebound from its historic lows and continued to rise through 2007. The bubble that occurred during that year was triggered by shrinking weapons stockpiles (and thus the decreased availability of secondary sources), a flood at the Cigar Lake Mine in Canada, an undersupply due to a slew of reactors coming online, compounded by the relatively recent news of an extensive nuclear program expansion in China, as well as, many argue, speculative pressures. As the uranium price shot to historical highs, the extent of the previous twenty years of underinvestment in uranium production became all the more obvious.

Two events strongly affected the price of uranium in subsequent years: the global financial crisis of 2008 and the Fukushima triple disaster in 2011. The global financial crisis brought uranium (spot) prices down to US$42 a pound. The rally in prices to US$58 a pound in 2011 was short-lived as the Fukushima

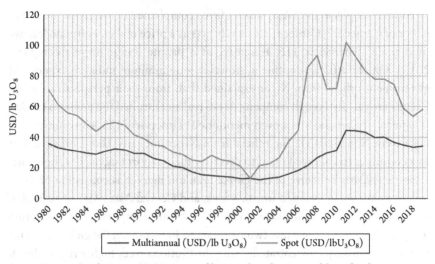

Source: Euratom Supply Agency. U3O8 prices paid by EU utilities for uranium delivered under spot or multiannual contracts during the reference year. *EU natural uranium price: ESA indices since 1980.* 2020. Euratom Supply Agency. Accessed March 25, 2020. https://euratom-supply.ec.europa.eu/eu-natural-uranium-price-esa-indices-1980_en.

*Figure 6.3* Uranium prices, 1980–2019

disaster hit in early 2011 (see Figure 6.3). Global attention on the nuclear meltdown at Fukushima led to plants being decommissioned in Germany, Japan, Belgium, Italy, and Switzerland and a fall in the spot price to around US$20 a pound by 2018.

In the 2000s, the uranium market lacked a liquid spot market and uranium was not widely traded on commodities exchanges, such as the London Metal Exchange (this has started to change more recently). During 2008, about 48 million pounds of $U_3O_8$ (or less than 22,000 tonnes) changed hands in spot auctions (Bi 2012). This is a relatively small quantity compared to the 250 million pounds of uranium (a little less than 115,000 tonnes) contracted by world utilities in 2005, or less than 20 percent of the global uranium trade. "One thing . . . that I think is very crucial to understanding the uranium price is how little material actually changes hands in the spot market" (Interview 125, Senior global uranium industry insider, 2013). This is still the case, with spot transactions amounting to between 15 percent and 25 percent of global annual uranium sales in the years leading to 2020 (*Uranium 2020: Resources, Production and Demand* 2020).

> Nuclear fuel trade is dominated by the long-term market. . . . There are two prevalent pricing mechanisms for deliveries under long-term Uranium contracts: [1] Specified pricing may comprise of either a fixed price, a series of fixed prices or a base price plus adjustment for

inflation to the date of delivery.... The long-term prices have traded at a premium to the spot price. [2] Market-related pricing is based on the Uranium market price at or near the time of delivery, and/or some other published market index, such as the average US import price. Market-related price mechanisms nearly always include a floor price... [and] a ceiling price above which the contract price may not rise. (Sinha et al. 2011)

## The Domestic Chinese Uranium Market and Civilian Nuclear Industry

In 1991, China connected its first nuclear reactor to its electricity grid (Zhou 2010). By 2002, only two nuclear reactors had been built, but the country was already firmly looking toward a future in which nuclear energy would play a central part in its energy production ("Nuclear Power in China" 2012). China's emphasis on rapidly expanding its electricity production, diversifying its energy mix, and ensuring environmental protections have contributed to the country's rapid emergence as a civilian nuclear power that has gone well beyond its capacity for self-sufficiency in uranium (Boey 2012).

In 2020, China had 49 reactors in operation, second only to the United States and France. It has by far the most ambitious civilian nuclear power plant development plan in the world, with 14 reactors under construction, 41 more nuclear reactors planned, and 168 reactors proposed in the coming years (see Table 6.2). China accounts for 27 percent of the reactors under construction in the world, 41 percent of planned reactors, and 52 percent of proposed reactors (World Nuclear Association).

Under the Two Markets, Two Resources framework and the One Third, One Third, One Third policy (see Chapter 3), the Chinese government has invested a lot of energy in finding sources of domestic uranium production (Zha 2006). According to a paper published in the journal *China Energy Power*, in 2010, China was home to ten uranium mines at the time, for a total production of around 1,200 tonnes annually (see Table 6.3). Despite high hopes, China's uranium output rose from 700 tonnes in 2000 to only 1,885 tonnes in 2020. In 2020, China's domestic uranium production amounted to 19 percent of its annual requirements, which stood at 9,834 tonnes (World Nuclear Association data; see Figure 6.4).

Some estimated that domestic production may eventually rise to 2,500 tonnes a year (Ding and Liu 2012). But even in such a scenario, this would only amount to around 25 percent of China's annual uranium needs and around 10 percent of its annual imports as of 2020.

*Table 6.2* **Reactors operable, under construction, planned, and proposed, and uranium requirements, 2007, 2015, and 2020**

| Country | Reactors operable | Reactors under construction | Reactors planned | Reactors proposed | Uranium requirements (tonnes U) |
|---|---|---|---|---|---|
| **China (2007)** | 10 | 5 | 13 | 50 | 1,454 |
| **China (2015)** | 21 | 23 | 45 | 142 | 8,161 |
| **China (2020)** | 49 | 14 | 41 | 168 | 9,834 |
| **France (2007)** | 59 | 0 | 1 | 1 | 10,368 |
| **France (2015)** | 58 | 1 | 1 | 1 | 9,230 |
| **France (2020)** | 56 | 1 | 0 | 0 | 8,936 |
| **Japan (2007)** | 55 | 2 | 11 | 1 | 8,872 |
| **Japan (2015)** | 48 | 2 | 9 | 3 | 2,549 |
| **Japan (2020)** | 33 | 2 | 1 | 8 | 2,000 |
| **Russia (2007)** | 31 | 3 | 8 | 18 | 3,777 |
| **Russia (2015)** | 34 | 9 | 31 | 18 | 4,206 |
| **Russia (2020)** | 38 | 2 | 21 | 23 | 4,834 |
| **South Korea (2007)** | 20 | 1 | 7 | 0 | 3,037 |
| **South Korea (2015)** | 24 | 4 | 8 | 0 | 5,022 |
| **South Korea (2020)** | 24 | 4 | 0 | 2 | 4,903 |
| **United Kingdom (2007)** | 19 | 0 | 0 | 0 | 2,021 |
| **United Kingdom (2015)** | 16 | 0 | 4 | 7 | 1,738 |
| **United Kingdom (2020)** | 15 | 2 | 2 | 2 | 1,820 |
| **United States (2007)** | 103 | 1 | 2 | 21 | 20,050 |
| **United States (2015)** | 99 | 1 | 5 | 17 | 18,692 |
| **United States (2020)** | 94 | 2 | 3 | 18 | 19,746 |
| **World (2007)** | 435 | 28 | 64 | 158 | 66,529 |
| **World (2015)** | 443 | 66 | 165 | 331 | 66,883 |
| **World (2020)** | 442 | 52 | 100 | 326 | 68,240 |

Source: World Nuclear Association.

*Table 6.3* **Uranium mines in operation in Mainland China (2010)**

| Mine | Province | Type | Production tonnes/year | First year of operation |
| --- | --- | --- | --- | --- |
| *Fuzhou* [抚州] | Jiangxi | Underground and open-pit | 300 | 1966 |
| *Chongyi* [崇义] | Jiangxi | Underground and open-pit | 120 (Expanding to 270) | 1979 |
| *Yining* [伊宁] | Xinjiang | Solution mining | 300 | 1993 |
| *Lantian* [蓝天] | Shaanxi | Underground mining | 100 | 1993 |
| *Benxi* [本溪] | Liaoning | Underground mining | 120 | 1996 |
| *Qinglong* [青龙] | Liaoning | Underground mining | 100 | 2007 |
| *Shaoguan* [韶关] | Guangdong | Underground mining | 160 | 2008 |
| Total | | | 1,200 | |

Source: Hou, Jianchao [候建朝] et al. 2010. "Risks in uranium supply of nuclear power development in China and its solutions [我国核电发展的铀资源供应风险及对策]." *China Electric Power* 43, no. 12: 1–4. All mines affiliated with CNNC.[a]

[a] A search of online open-source information indicates that all mines listed were affiliated in one way or another with the China National Nuclear Corporation.

Considering the country's poor uranium resources, China has had no choice but to develop a strong foreign procurement strategy (Xiao 2012). Chinese imports went from 656 tonnes in 2001 to 17,136 tonnes in 2010, when it became the world's number one importer, to 23,693 tonnes in 2020, a more than thirty-six-fold increase (UN Comtrade data). In anticipation of a continued steep increase in its uranium demand, since 2009 China's uranium imports have been considerably higher than its annual requirements (the uranium it actually needs annually to run its civilian nuclear program) (see Figure 6.4). For instance, in 2020, despite China's uranium requirements standing at 9,834 tonnes per year, it imported 23,693 tonnes of the ore (UN Comtrade data). This was more than the United States' annual requirement, which stood at 19,746 tonnes per year (the United States had 94 reactors in operation in 2020, compared to China's 49 (Table 6.2).

In addition to China being poor in uranium resources, these resources are also low in quality and, thus, expensive to mine (Guang and Wenjie 2010). Therefore, continued and increasing dependence on imports is unavoidable. China's civilian nuclear program has led to a very high import-dependency ratio, at 81 percent in 2020 (see Figure 6.5).

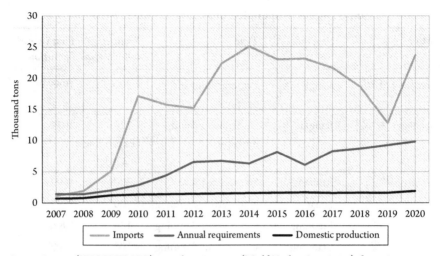

Source: Imports (UNCOMTRADE), annual requirements (World Nuclear Association), domestic production (Nuclear Energy Agency and International Atomic Energy Agency data–Resources, Production and Demand reports or the "Red Book").

*Figure 6.4* Uranium imports, requirements, and production in China (tonnes), 2007–2020

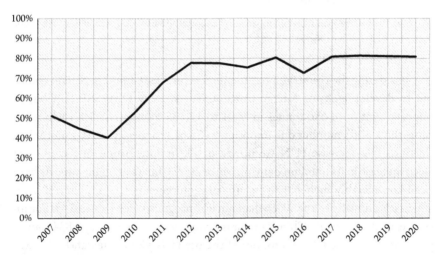

Source: World Nuclear Association; UNCOMTRADE, share of annual requirements net of domestic production (China imports more uranium than it needs annually to run its reactors), author's calculations. To note that data for 2019 are missing.

*Figure 6.5* China's uranium import dependence, 2007–2020

The earthquake, tsunami, and consequent severe damage to a nuclear reactor at Fukushima, Japan, in March 2011 had an impact on China's nuclear program. In China, "five days after the earthquake and tsunami, the State Council suspended approval of new nuclear projects and started conducting comprehensive safety inspections of all nuclear projects—those in operation as well as those under construction. It also decided to halt four approved projects due to start construction in 2011" (Liu 2012). In 2007, the National Development and Reform Commission (NDRC) outlined a target to have 40GWe (gigawatt-electric) online by 2020 (Wang 2009), which was upgraded to 70–80GWe in 2010 and revised downward to 60–70GWe in the aftermath of the nuclear accident at Fukushima ("Nuclear Power in China" 2012).

However, if there were any doubts as to whether China would press ahead with its ambitious civilian nuclear program following the yearlong safety review, these doubts were dispelled in 2012. In his speech at the Nuclear Security Summit in Seoul, in March 2012, President Hu Jintao underlined the "irreplaceable role of nuclear energy in ensuring energy security and climate change" ("President Hu Jintao Delivers a Speech" 2012). This was a signal that echoed Wen Jiabao's comments of a couple of months earlier in Abu Dhabi, where he said that "nuclear power is a safe, reliable, mature technology providing clean energy. The safe and efficient development of nuclear power is the solution to future energy supply strategy" (Wen 2012). This confirmed that China would be going ahead with its extensive program of expanding its civilian nuclear power plants, albeit at a slower rate than originally planned. In 2014, in his own remarks to the Nuclear Security Summit, Xi Jinping said that "The horrific nuclear accidents of the past few years have rung the alarm bell for all of us" and that "China has tightened nuclear security measures across the board." He then affirmed that "China will continue to take an active part in nuclear security activities, and invite IAEA to conduct International Physical Protection Advisory Service [sic]." At the same time, he confirmed his belief that "The peaceful use of nuclear energy is important to ensuring energy security and tackling climate change" ("Statement by H.E. Xi Jinping President of the People's Republic of China at the Nuclear Security Summit" 2014).

## Interface with the Global Uranium Market

The Chinese domestic uranium industry is very concentrated, partly because uranium is conceived of as a strategic resource and only selected companies can mine it (Interview 33, Chinese state-owned enterprise employee, 2012). One interviewee commented that "Uranium companies control the upstream businesses. They are concentrated there and they have control there" (Interview 64, Chinese state-owned enterprise employee, 2012). Both the Chinese uranium mining industry and civilian nuclear industry are overwhelmingly controlled by two state-owned enterprises that report directly to the State Council—the China National Nuclear Corporation (CNNC, the former Chinese Ministry of Nuclear Industry) and the China General Nuclear Power Group (CGNPG) (Weitz 2011a). In 2007, the National Nuclear Safety Administration (NNSA) permitted three state-owned enterprises to own and operate nuclear power plants in China: the CNNC, the CGNPG, and the State Power Investment Corporation (SPIC).[1,2] As one industry insider commented, "There is nowhere else in the world like China, nowhere else in the world where [companies] ship to that country strictly for that country's demand. They want concentrates shipped in there and they want to process them all ... and at the end of the day, they hold the key! They hold the key to the import licenses" (Interview 129, Senior uranium industry executive, 2015).

CNNC, formerly the Ministry of Nuclear Industry, was founded in 1988, is under the supervision of the State-owned Assets Supervision and Administration Commission (SASAC), and constitutes China's most central and largest state-owned enterprise engaged in the civilian nuclear industry. It is the only exporter of Chinese nuclear power plants ("China National Nuclear Corporation [CNNC]" 2019). The CGNPG (named the China Guangdong Nuclear Power Group until 2013) was founded in 1994, is under the supervision of the SASAC, and is headquartered in Shenzhen ("China General Nuclear Power Corporation [CGN]" 2019). By 2017, it had been managing twenty nuclear reactors ("China General Nuclear Power Corporation [CGN]" 2019).

A government official from a central government agency said the NDRC did not really take care of uranium procurement strategies. "The one in charge is really CNNC [中核]" (Interview 57, Former Chinese government official, 2012). This was confirmed by a Chinese academic who noted that "Zhonghe is a ministry. It used to be one and it still is one. The head of Zhonghe has ministerial status. It behaves like a ministry" (Interview 60, Academic at a Chinese University, 2012). A Chinese official from a large SOE explained the following:

> Following Western logic, we would think that strong concentration, for instance, with CNNC, leads to more independence, whereas weak concentration, such as in the steel industry, would be weak companies that would have to follow the central government's lead. But it is the total opposite in China. You see, the strong, concentrated companies are so close to the government that they are much closer to its thinking; CNNC is a former ministry as well, which makes it all the more clear. CNNC has little leeway. (Interview 64, Chinese state-owned enterprise employee, 2012)

As for CGNPC, a senior uranium industry insider explained the following:

> CNNC's background is different from CGNPC ..., they have been on the ground forever, and they are also the owner and operator of most of the facilities. They are the old guard in China, CGNPC is the newcomer.

They operate a little bit differently. CGNPC is a little bit more driven by pure economics and pure commercialism, whereas CNNC is coming more from a government entity's perspective ... and they feel a little more powerful in the whole situation than CGNPC. (Interview 129, Senior uranium industry executive, 2013)

The small number of domestic actors and the history of the China National Nuclear Corporation have prevented the emergence of a powerful industry association. One Chinese official noted that "Industry associations exist because they group an industry together, but in the nuclear industry there are no companies to group together! There are only a couple or a few big ones ... so no industry association" (Interview 51, Chinese government official, 2012).[3] Another official remarked that "In the steel market, there is CISA [the China Iron and Steel Association], ... in the nuclear case, there is no middleman" (Interview 65, Senior researcher at Chinese state-backed institution, 2012).

More important for the purposes of this study, levels of coordination by Chinese uranium market stakeholders at the import interface with the global uranium industry are high. At least until 2014, only CNNC and CGN had been allowed to import uranium (Figure 6.6), and only these two firms had ventured abroad to invest in uranium mining (Xie et al. 2011).

Most of the uranium that the leading Chinese nuclear SOEs have been procuring abroad has been finding its way back to China (whereas Chinese National Oil Companies, for example, are actively selling the oil they procure abroad on the international market). Some Chinese researchers have argued that because of a lack of clear legal frameworks and support for the Going-Out

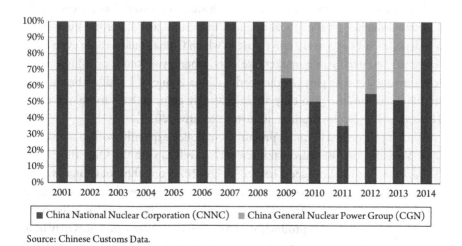

Source: Chinese Customs Data.

Figure 6.6 Share of China's total uranium imports by company, 2000–2014

policy in the uranium industry, other players have refrained from joining in (Xie et al. 2011).

This may have facilitated more overlap between the two large SOEs and the objectives of Chinese state planners. Interviewees signaled that there is high overlap between the state-owned enterprises and the government's priorities in this sector. As a Chinese academic explained, "Uranium is a special strategic resource. It isn't like iron ore. The company may lead the negotiations, but actually, you need a signature from above, very high. For instance, when China signed a big contract with Australia, Wen Jiabao [the Chinese Premier at the time] signed it" (Interview 60, Academic at a Chinese University, 2012).

Despite CNNC's power, other interviewees pointed to the emergence of competition between it and CGNPC: "[CNNC and CGNPC] have a healthy competition going, every once in a while" (Interview 129, Senior uranium industry executive, 2013).

## China's Impact on the Global Uranium Market

China has been able to comfortably fulfill and surpass its uranium procurement needs in the international uranium market and to avoid excessive dependence on dominant global uranium producers, such as Cameco and Areva. A few external dynamics in the global uranium market have contributed to creating more room for maneuver for the Chinese importers. Importantly, the Fukushima accident has had a lasting impact on the global civilian nuclear industry. The drop in demand following the accident left the global market open to Chinese consumers before the projected growth in other emerging countries materialized.

When a senior global uranium industry insider was asked about the future of Chinese influence on the global uranium market in 2013, after the Fukushima accident, he foresaw a near-term future in which China could wrestle even more influence, "especially in a market like ours, where, you know, post-Fukushima it is slowing in other parts of the world. China is one of a sudden bright spot in the nuclear industry, so they are increasingly going to have more influence" (Interview 129, Senior uranium industry executive, 2013).

China's planners in uranium procurement policy explicitly worked within the Two Markets, Two Resources framework, as well as with the One Third, One Third, One Third policy (see Chapter 3): "By 2020, one third of China's supply of natural uranium will come from domestic uranium production, one third from direct procurement from foreign suppliers, and one third from the overseas holdings of uranium production" (Xiao 2012). Chinese planners may have pursued this frame in other commodity markets, but they have encountered many difficulties, whereas the overall approach has been more successfully carried out in the uranium market (although domestic production is simply not adequate to amount to a third of China's uranium needs). A Chinese uranium industry expert argued that China initially sought to emphasize overseas holdings and investments in neighboring countries, such as Kazakhstan and Mongolia, while continuing to procure directly from developed countries, such as Canada and Australia (Xiao and Gao 2009). As the Chinese continued to build confidence, they looked to Africa for further diversification. This strategy has spread out the risk associated with a high import-dependency ratio.

The first and perhaps largest impact China's rise as the number one uranium consumer has had on the global uranium market is the emergence of Kazakhstan as the number one uranium producer in the world, whereas it had been all but absent from the global uranium trade in the early 2000s ("Uranium Market Outlook—Second Quarter 2011" 2011). To fulfill China's rapidly growing uranium needs, Chinese firms invested in Kazakhstan and this directly contributed to its rise as the world's number one producer. One industry consultant confirmed that "Kazakhstan has seen major changes and an important reason is Chinese investment" (Interview 30, Consultant at a Chinese consulting firm, 2012). Central Asia has been described by Chinese experts in uranium procurement as a region where China has "strong geopolitical advantages" (Xiao and Gao 2009). Kazakhstan is in China's backyard. The fact that China has ongoing long-term relationships with its close Central Asian neighbors, such as Kazakhstan and Uzbekistan, has played a part in its ability to invest and sign long-term procurement agreements with them. In 2005, China procured 91 percent of its uranium from Kazakhstan. In 2015, uranium imports from Kazakhstan and Uzbekistan accounted for 78 percent of total imports. Over the course of the last decade, China has worked to diversify its import sources. In 2015, imports from Canada, Russia, and Namibia accounted for 18 percent of total imports (see Figure 6.7).

Beyond Kazakhstan, China has also continued to invest in uranium production internationally and was able to get a foothold in major sites, arguably more successfully than in the three other markets studied in this book. Since 2008, China is one of only four countries in the world that have reported non-domestic exploration and development expenses in the uranium market, alongside France, Japan, and Russia. In 2012, it spent 44 percent of total global non-domestic uranium exploration and development dollars; in 2015 this figure was 90 percent, and in 2018, 57 percent (*Uranium 2020: Resources, Production and Demand* 2020, 39). In terms of overseas holdings and joint ownership, beyond Kazakhstan, China has sought equity in Namibia, among other sources of uranium. Chinese companies have invested in the three biggest uranium producers in Namibia: Husab, Langer Heinrich, and Rossing. In 2018, for instance, the China National Uranium Corporation Limited (CNUC) bought a majority

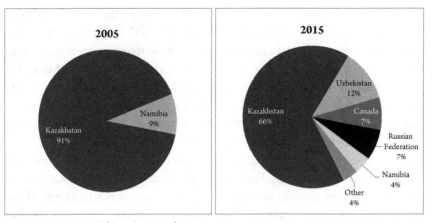

Source: UNCOMTRADE (Hs code: 284410).

*Figure 6.7* China's uranium imports by country, 2005 and 2015

stake in Rossing[4] from Rio Tinto, which resulted in the Chinese company's accumulating a 68.6 percent equity stake ("Uranium in Namibia" 2022).

Beijing has also used creative ways to engineer procurement contracts. In November 2006, two Chinese firms established a joint venture with Kazakhstan's state-owned Kazatomprom in a uranium mining project (a 49 percent stake), in exchange for Kazatomprom acquiring stakes in either Chinese nuclear power plants or fuel reprocessing facilities (Komesaroff 2007). China also "provided interest-free soft loans to the governments of Uzbekistan, Niger and other uranium-rich countries" (Weitz 2011b). A subsidiary of the China National Nuclear Corporation bought a 25 percent joint venture equity stake in the Namibian mine Langer Heinrich "for $190 million, entitling it to that share of output" ("Uranium in Namibia" 2022). China Guangdong Nuclear Power Uranium Resources Co (CGN-URC) and the China-Africa Development Fund jointly own 90 percent of the Husab mine (60 percent and 40 percent, respectively), one of Namibia's largest. This results in most of the production being shipped to China, while 20 percent is sold on international markets by CGN Global Uranium Ltd ("Uranium in Namibia" 2022).

A leading uranium executive explained that, as a rule, Chinese consumers continue to prefer long-term contracts and large volumes. Over the years, they have adapted their approach to include more foreign direct investments and some trading on the spot market. But this executive hastens to add that Chinese consumers trade and sell through firms (not traders) (Interview 139, Uranium industry executive, 2022). When I asked him whether, in his view, the Chinese consumers caused major disruptions in the global uranium market, he responded that they have not, not in the sense that I describe. "They do have the biggest [civilian nuclear] program in the world. They are a valued partner because of the way they dealt with their program."

In sum, Chinese importers, themselves in a strong position of market power, have been able to implement a multipronged strategy of procurement in the uranium market, in a global market that has afforded them more room for maneuver than in other commodity markets such as the iron ore or potash markets. This allowed the country to increase its total uranium imports thirty-six times between 2001 and 2020 and to forge ahead with the world's most ambitious civilian nuclear power development plan.

As China developed a multipronged procurement strategy in the global uranium market, a parallel development was taking place, with the emergence of global investment firms offering exposure to the global uranium market by purchasing and holding physical uranium and providing investment opportunities in major commodity markets. The two leading companies in this space are the Sprott Physical Uranium Trust, a Canadian company that holds physical uranium in Canada, the United States, and France and is listed on the TSX ("Sprott Physical Uranium Trust"), and Yellow Cake PLC, a Jersey company that holds physical uranium in Canada and France and is listed on the London Stock Exchange ("About Us"). The arrival of these new players, in recent years, on the global uranium market has had an impact on global market dynamics, including by increasing the volatility of uranium prices on the spot market. The uranium executive explained that what he called "recent financialization trends" were clearly "not caused by China" (Interview 139, Uranium industry executive, 2022). He added that global utilities, which number around forty to fifty on the consumer side of things, dislike this development. To give an idea of the scale, in 2021, "Sprott's trust [held] about 26 million pounds of uranium, equal to about 14% of the annual consumption from the world's nuclear reactors" (Li and Deaux 2021). S&P Global went as far as saying that in 2021, "Sprott's activity has single-handedly moved the price of uranium" ("Sprott Fund Transforms Uranium Spot Market" 2021). These new players have brought new dynamics to and increased financialization levels to the global uranium market. Until 2008, spot pricing represented a negligible proportion of overall uranium trading, but since then, the proportion has increased to about 25 percent of all uranium trades ("Uranium Markets" 2022). What we observe for now is that the impact of these new players has been felt on prices and volatility levels, but other aspects of the global uranium pricing system remain stable, with the market continuing to function under a mixture of "2-to-4-year contracts and the 5-to-10-year contracts" (Interview 139, Uranium industry executive, 2022), "with producers selling directly to utilities at a higher price than the spot market, reflecting the security of supply. The specified price in these contracts is, however, often related to the spot price at the time of delivery" ("Uranium Markets" 2022).

## Civilian Nuclear Multilateral Initiatives

Given uranium's special status as a core resource for civilian nuclear power plants, China's behavior regarding the international initiatives and organizations related to this industry, such as the International Atomic Energy Agency, is of interest. In the context of international civilian nuclear security and safety initiatives, China is arguably seen as being a constructive participant, and its behavior has been characterized as conciliatory (Xu 2012). It is a full-fledged member of the International Atomic Energy Agency and it is committed to cooperating on issues of civilian nuclear technology with France (Areva), Canada (Atomic Energy of Canada–CANDU), and the United States (Westinghouse), among others, as well as to participating in other related international frameworks.

Even though sovereignty concerns and economic and technological differences hinder the establishment of binding safety standards across the board, China has demonstrated a willingness to work in cooperation with other developed nations in the context of the Nuclear Security Summit. China has also made noticeable efforts to reach out regarding nuclear safety, as it has done with the United States. This was highlighted, in 2006, in a memorandum of understanding that granted Westinghouse a contract to build four commercial nuclear reactors in China. The MOU affirmed "the United States government's support of the Chinese expansion and use of safe, emissions-free nuclear power and the related technology transfer" (U.S.-Chinese Agreement, 2006).

Enhanced cooperation on issues of nuclear security at the global level had already started with the Washington Nuclear Security Summit in 2010, but the Fukushima accident the following year brought to the fore the need to fully address issues of nuclear safety. The second Nuclear Security Summit held in Seoul, in March 2012, did this by broadening its agenda to include nuclear safety issues. China showed a willingness to take the issue seriously and learn from the Japanese accident. At the 2012 Nuclear Security Summit in Seoul, President Hu Jintao said that "China has increased its investment in nuclear safety, improved its nuclear safety regulatory system, and made efforts to improve its nuclear safety management. China has conducted comprehensive inspections of the safety of [its] nuclear facilities nationwide" ("President Hu Jintao Delivers a Speech" 2012). A senior researcher in China later explained that "The speech by Hu Jintao at the Seoul Summit was not merely a diplomatic exercise. It was very meaningful. It shows that the leadership has put a lot of thought, a lot of research into this" (Interview 14, Senior researcher at Chinese state-backed institution, 2012).

A foreign industry expert (a scientist with access to the Chinese nuclear industry) confirmed in an interview that the safety review following the Fukushima accident had been thorough. The expert said that common myths about insufficient security in the nuclear sector in China were wrong and that the safety review was comprehensive, from mining, to every step along the way (he also said that one of CNNC's 100,000 employees told him he had been working fourteen-hour shifts doing reviews) (Interview 90, Western government expert, 2012). "In July 2010, a 22-strong IAEA team from 15 countries carried out a two-week integrated regulatory review service mission to review China's regulatory framework for nuclear safety. The IAEA made a number of recommendations but said that the review had provided 'confidence in the effectiveness of the Chinese safety regulatory system and the future safety of the vast expanding nuclear industry'" ("Nuclear Power in China" 2012). China also "requested and hosted 12 operational safety review team (OSART) missions from IAEA teams to October 2011" ("Nuclear Power in China" 2012). China subsequently affirmed that it would be going ahead with an extensive expansion of its civilian nuclear power plant program, albeit at a slower rate.

China continued to signal the highest level of attention to civilian nuclear safety and security issues by having President Xi Jinping personally attend the Nuclear Security Summit in The Hague in March 2014. There, the Chinese Minister of Information and Technology, Miao Wei, reiterated China's commitments to nuclear safety and international cooperation: "China remains an active supporter of international cooperation in nuclear security and it supports the central role of the International Atomic Energy Agency (IAEA) in international nuclear security architecture" ("China Committed to Global Nuclear Security" 2014). Among other initiatives, Miao Wei highlighted the China Center of Excellence on Nuclear Security, which opened in Beijing in 2015 and had been built in collaboration with the United States, as likely to become "the biggest nuclear security international exchange, training and demonstration centre in the Asia-Pacific region." Also highlighted were continued Chinese efforts to help developing countries, including Ghana, fulfill their IAEA commitments ("China Committed to Global Nuclear Security" 2014).

Large Chinese state-owned enterprises as well as key Chinese state ministries (such as the NDRC) have also developed a relatively transparent engagement strategy with global civilian nuclear multilateral institutions, including the International Atomic Energy Agency.

China clearly does not exhibit conciliatory behavior across the full range of global policy issues. Given the sensitivity of uranium as a resource, certainly compared to the other cases in this book, one might have expected Chinese behavior to be less conciliatory in the global spheres directly related to civilian nuclear power. Some argue that China only participates in such initiatives when it has "little to lose." But the nuclear security and safety initiatives China participates in include self-imposed constraints, including on the export of dual-use technologies, and expose Chinese regulators to public scrutiny.

In recent years, in a trend that was compounded by the Fukushima disaster but which had started earlier, Chinese citizens have become increasingly mobilized over civilian nuclear safety issues. One example is the opposition to the Gaozhuang power plant in Nanyang, Henan province, in 2011 ("The Reason Why Nanyang Is Not Suitable for the Construction of a Nuclear Power Plant" 2011). The government has been responsive to public pressure, to some extent, over the safety of its nuclear program. In fact, this dimension of public salience may have encouraged Chinese government officials' willingness to engage in international safety and security initiatives.

## China and the Global Copper Market

Copper is one of the world's most critical industrial minerals. It has been central to any electricity-related technology because of its incomparable high conductivity and low potential for substitution. Its value is proving ever more fundamental to the green economy as it is one of the key energy transition minerals, alongside cobalt, lithium, and nickel, among others.[5] Clean energy technologies are set to become responsible for over 40 percent of copper demand in the coming years ("The Role of Critical Minerals in Clean Energy Transitions" 2022). Copper has always been essential to traditional power-generating technologies, including nuclear power, and traditional technologies for vehicles, but copper intensity is even higher in wind and solar technologies as well as electric vehicle technologies. The International Energy Agency estimates that the rise in green technologies will lead to a near tripling of global copper demand over the next twenty years ("The Role of Critical Minerals in Clean Energy Transitions" 2022).

The global copper industry has historically been geographically concentrated in a few countries. Over the past two decades, concentration has remained relatively high, although less so than in the global market for iron ore, potash, and uranium. In 2000, the four top exporters of copper by country accounted for 63 percent of global exports; in 2015, their share had decreased to 53 percent (see Figure 6.8). Whereas the geographic concentration of many mineral commodities is set to remain high over the near future, current planned production growth for copper in the United States, the Democratic Republic of Congo, and Indonesia should somewhat dampen geographic concentration ("The Role of Critical Minerals in Clean Energy Transitions" 2022).

Concentration by company is lower in the copper market than in the three other commodities studied in this book. In 2012, Magnus Ericsson, a leading commodities expert, calculated the global copper market's Herfindahl-Hirschman index at 428 (HHI, where below 1,000 is identified as low concentration, between 1,000 and 1,800 as medium concentration, and above 1,800

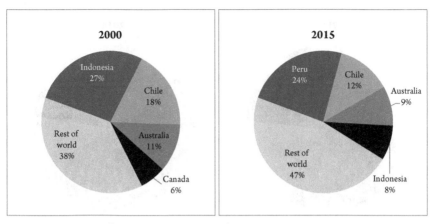

Source: UNCOMTRADE (HS Code: 2603, by net weight), author's calculations.

*Figure 6.8* World shares of copper exports by country, 2000 and 2015

as high concentration). For comparison purposes, the gold market, which is regarded as very fragmented, scored 266, and the niobium market, which is regarded as heavily concentrated, scored 5,884 (Ericsson 2012). In 2001, 75 percent of China's copper imports came from three countries. In 2015, China's three top suppliers accounted for 59 percent of total imports (see Figure 6.9).

> Regarding industry structure copper is more fragmented, you've got smaller producers who don't have significant marketing apparatus, it's cheaper for them to sell it to Glencore or Dreyfus rather than setting up a marketing department. Because it's more fragmented, because there are smaller producers, because there are producers in parts of the world which don't have very sophisticated infrastructure, it meets those requirements better. With more suppliers, more producers, you get a different form of trade, but the homogeneity of the product is also a factor in determining how much traders can be involved. (Interview 152, Former mining industry executive, June 2022)

For our purposes, there are two stages that are critical to copper processing, which seeks to bring the concentration levels of copper from lows of 1–2 percent (copper ores) up to 99.99 percent (refined copper). First, we have the mining of raw copper ores. These typically contain extremely low percentages of copper (below 2 percent). Copper ores are then often processed into copper concentrates at the mining site. This can bring the copper concentration levels to between 25 percent and 40 percent. Global trade in copper ores and concentrates constitute an approximately $US62.4 billion global industry

212        CHINA'S VULNERABILITY PARADOX

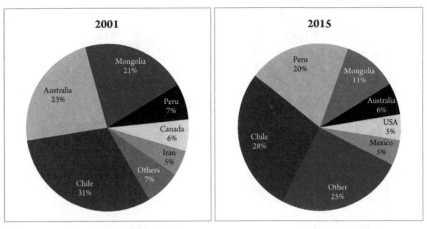

Source: China Mining Yearbook, 2002 and 2016.

*Figure 6.9*  China's copper imports by country, 2001 and 2015

(UN Comtrade 2020, HS code: 2603). China is heavily import dependent on copper ores and concentrates and is the number one importer in the world, with 57 percent of global imports (UN Comtrade 2020, by net weight). Most statistics presented in this chapter will focus on copper ores and concentrates (HS code 2603).

Second, we have the smelting and refining process. This itself comprises multiple phases. Through the smelting process, copper concentrates will be processed into copper anodes at 99.5 percent purity. Through the refining process, copper cathodes/plates (or refined copper) will be produced with 99.99 percent purity. Many smelters were traditionally built in the vicinity of large copper mines, and the geographic distribution of smelters has contributed to the copper market's distinctive structure. In recent years, however, China has positioned itself as a key player in the copper smelting and refining industry, with 40 percent of global copper processing volumes ("The Role of Critical Minerals in Clean Energy Transitions" 2022). The total value of global refined copper imports stands at around $US 65.4 billion (UN Comtrade, HS code: 7403). Refined copper usage stood at 25 million tonnes in 2020, with China responsible for 14.4 million tonnes (*The World Copper Factbook* 2021). Despite its processing capacity, China remains import dependent on refined copper and China is the number one importer of refined copper in the world, with 48 percent of global imports (UN Comtrade 2020, by net weight). China has, in parallel, established a dominant position in the downstream deployment of electric vehicle and other clean copper intensive technologies.

In a story that is by now becoming familiar, China rose to replace Japan as the number one copper (ores and concentrates) importer in the world, in 2008 (see Figure 6.9). In the space of a decade, between 2000 and 2010, Chinese imports as

China's Impact on Global Uranium and Copper 213

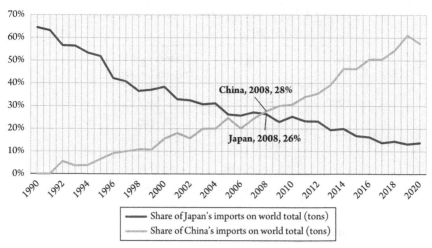

Source: UNCOMTRADE (HS Code: 2603), author's calculations.

Figure 6.10  China's and Japan's share of world copper imports, 1990–2020

a share of global imports rose from 16 percent to 31 percent, as Japan's declined from 38 percent to 25 percent (see Figure 6.10 and Table 6.4). "Obviously, for copper, China is so incredibly important, and that wasn't the case twenty years ago. It has become the biggest player by far. Fifty percent of all consumption takes place in China. Refined copper consumption is more than 50 percent from China. After that, it does get exported in products that contain copper but that's the size of China's demand" (Interview 164, Executive at global commodities consultancy, 2022).

## The Global Copper Pricing Regime Prior to China's Emergence

The global copper market has been one of the most commodified and financialized of the commodity markets for decades.[6] Even back in 1982, Rodrik explained that "copper is the closest one that comes to a competitive industry: whether long- or short-term, all copper contracts are priced at some LME [London Metals Exchange]-related value over which the trading partners rarely have an impact" (Rodrik 1982, 543). In 1978, concentration levels in the copper mining industry for the top four producers (among non-socialist states) was 37.6 percent; as Rodrik explains, vertical integration mostly took place at the national level and international trade mostly occurred between independent entities (Rodrik 1982).

*Table 6.4* **Top four copper importers (1990, 2000, 2010, 2020)**

| Year | Country | Share of world copper imports |
|---|---|---|
| **1990** | Japan | 64% |
| | Germany | 9% |
| | Spain | 7% |
| | South Korea | 7% |
| | Rest of world | 13% |
| **2000** | Japan | 38% |
| | China | 16% |
| | South Korea | 10% |
| | Germany | 6% |
| | Rest of world | 30% |
| **2010** | China | 31% |
| | Japan | 25% |
| | India | 10% |
| | South Korea | 8% |
| | Rest of world | 26% |
| **2020** | China | 57% |
| | Japan | 14% |
| | Zambia | 5% |
| | South Korea | 5% |
| | Rest of world | 18% |

Source: UN Comtrade, author's calculations (HS code: 2603, by net weight)

In 1970, Japan had a "near-monopsony" in the global copper market and imported the equivalent of 73 percent of global copper exports (in the non-socialist world) (Rodrik 1982, 542). Whereas the United States had tended to adopt a strategy of vertical integration, the Japanese importers relied on "long-term contracts, frequency of more than 10 years duration, provided a powerful incentive for US firms signed with independent mines" (Rodrik 1982, 544). With time, "the Japanese importers . . . [turned] the long-term contracts to their advantage through the exercise of monopsony power and improvements in chipping technology and associated transport-cost reductions." On the domestic side of things, "[o]n the one hand, the relatively high levels of domestic protection shielded metals processors from foreign competition. On the other, the more relaxed Japanese atmosphere with regard to anti-trust allowed the formation of import cartels by the largest firms, thus enhancing their bargaining leverage vis-à-vis ore-exporting countries" (Rodrik 1982, 545).

It thus appears that the Japanese era of dominance in the global copper market had been located just within the boundaries of Quadrant 3 (see Table 3.1), where a more coordinated Japanese industry faced a more fragmented global market. However, Rodrik hastened to add that "[t]o a large extent because their copper contracts were linked to LME prices, the Japanese have had the least opportunity to translate their superior bargaining position into favourable prices" (compared to their success in the iron ore market, for instance) (Rodrik 1982, 553). As the Japanese were wrestling with their difficulties in wielding market power via the negotiation of long-term contracts, despite their favorable position, Japanese copper market stakeholders turned their sights on foreign direct investment. Japan's experience with overseas investment in commodities started with the copper market, with investments and loans directed at projects in the Philippines, Canada, Indonesia, and Chile, among others. As the Japanese era progressed, we saw a transition from more short-term to more long-term contracts and increasing involvement of long-term investment and other financial relationships between Japanese consumers and global producers. Japan was never able to modify the global copper market's reliance on spot pricing, but over the course of its tenure as dominant consumer, it pulled the global copper market moderately in the direction of de-liberalization. In the copper market, as in the iron ore market, the Japanese domestic industry stakeholders demonstrated "a remarkable degree of common sense of purpose" and an unmatched ability to undertake colossal projects in direct government-to-government deals" (Rodrik 1982, 555–556).

Before China's emergence as the number one consumer, "copper . . . was an established market. Similar to iron ore, the main destinations for export were Europe and Japan, it had been for thirty years, and suddenly China starts coming through" (Interview 161, Executive at leading financial institution, 2022).

When China emerged as the number one consumer, the global copper market displayed a mixture of long-term arrangements between producers and consumers established by Japanese market stakeholders and employed by other consumers around the world, yet it had also remained one of the most financialized, liquid commodity markets in the world. Copper continues to be traded on the LME (which was acquired by the Hong Kong Exchanges and Clearing Limited [HKEX] in 2012) and is also traded on the COMEX (the Commodity Exchange Inc., which is part of the New York Mercantile Exchange, NYMEX) and, more recently, the Shanghai Futures Exchange (SHFE). In 2015, the LME was responsible for 59.9 percent of copper transactions, the SHFE, for 28.1 percent, and the remainder, on the COMEX (*GFMS Copper Survey* 2016). A senior industry consultant described the global copper market as "a very competitive market, very visible" (Interview 164, Executive at a global commodities consultancy, 2022).

Copper's physical characteristics have certainly played a role in the market's financialization. It is impossible to distinguish the origin of copper once it is refined, or whether it was recycled or mined, contrary to iron ore, which remains a differentiated product (therein comes the saying "copper is copper is copper").

## The Domestic Chinese Copper Market

China's copper import dependence is high. In 2001, taking into account copper ores, refined copper, and scrap copper, Chinese consumption stood at more than 2.4 million tonnes of copper, of which only 29–30 percent was supplied with domestic raw materials (*China Mining Yearbook 2002* [(中国矿业年鉴] 2002). The Chinese domestic copper mining industry bears some resemblance to the iron ore mining industry in terms of the proportion of small enterprises and small mines on the total number of mining enterprises. This proportion has been historically high (94 percent in 2001), with little change over the years (88 percent in 2015) (see Figure 6.11). We can see that at the interface with the global copper market, the share of imports by the top two Chinese importers has gone from a total of 29 percent in 2000 to 20 percent in 2014, a downward trajectory like the markets of iron ore and potash (see Figure 6.12). The copper imports by the two largest importers consist of a higher proportion of total imports than the equivalent numbers for the iron ore market, but a much lower proportion than equivalent numbers for the potash (53 percent in 2014) and uranium (100 percent in 2014) markets.

Describing the evolution of the domestic Chinese copper industry, an executive at a global consultancy explained that

> China has changed the ways in which it imports copper because it doesn't have a big copper mining industry. It has grown a bit in parts of China, in Tibet, in parts of southern China, they have a few more modern, large-scale mines there. Most of the rest of Chinese production comes from old mines, small-scale mines, often integrated operations

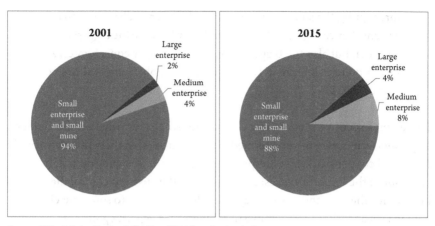

Source: China Mining Yearbook (2002 and 2016), author's calculations.

*Figure 6.11* Share of copper mining enterprises in China by enterprise size, 2001 and 2015

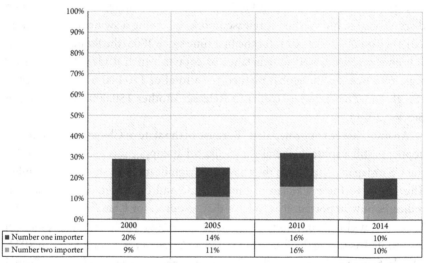

Source: China Customs Data (author's calculations). The number one importer in 2000, 2005, and 2010 was Jinling Copper Co. and in 2014, Tongling Nonferrous Metals Group. The number two importer in 2005 was Tongling Nonferrous Metals Group; in 2010, Jiangxi Copper; and in 2014, Yanggu Xiangguang Copper Co.

*Figure 6.12* Share of copper imports by the top two Chinese importers, 2000, 2005, 2010, and 2014

and sometimes not integrated, but even smaller. All the new production has come from the projects in the south of China, but it is not enough to fill the requirements that China has. So, they don't have the resources, and they have this huge demand. But they have developed, and growing more rapidly, the smelting industry. So, the intermediate step. That has been another change. So, they have not only become the biggest copper consumer, but also the biggest consumer of copper concentrates. And this is a policy. (Interview 164, Executive at global commodities consultancy, 2022)

I asked the executive who is also a copper industry expert whether the Chinese importers were trying to cut intermediaries (or traders) in their interaction with the global copper market. He responded as follows: "Yes, they do try. They try and control the import licenses; in the old days they used to control the import licenses for the concentrates so the traders had to sell on to someone else, they couldn't get a foothold in the domestic Chinese market... it's gone now. Because the Chinese traders ... the Chinese entities got enough control effectively, I would say" (Interview 161, Executive at leading financial institution, 2022).

China's National Food and Strategic Reserves Administration (NFSRA, formerly the State Reserve Bureau, under the NDRC) has as a mandate to stockpile strategic resources and to intervene in the market, sparingly, to avoid disruptions (as it did when it released pork, following a swine flu outbreak in 2019) (Kuo 2019). In 2021, for the first time since 2005, the Strategic Reserves Administration released four batches of copper, which it identifies as a strategic resource, on the global market, for a total of 110,000 tonnes of copper (Singh and Zhang 2021; "China to Release Another 150,000t of Base Metal Stocks" 2021).

An interviewee confirmed that "Because of the state of Chinese development, copper is still a strategic metal ... it's like what copper was many years ago for the US or Japan ... in China they have very significant large strategic stockpiles. They come to the market from time to time and buy more copper, and that indicates how important it is to have that resource, for China" (Interview 164, Executive at global commodities consultancy, 2022). An NDRC spokesperson was quoted as saying the following at a State Council press conference in 2021, "The last auctions have basically achieved our expected goals, and it has reflected the government's determination and confidence to ensure supplies and price stability of the bulk commodity markets" ("China to Release Another 150,000t of Base Metal Stocks" 2021). The spokesperson continued, "[o]ur auction is targeted at processing and manufacturing enterprises and excluding traders and other intermediate links as much as possible to prevent hoarding, so that it can directly benefit entity enterprises" ("China to Release Another 150,000t of Base Metal Stocks" 2021). In 2005, following large losses from bad Chinese government futures trading positions and rapidly raising prices, China's State Reserve Bureau at the time had also released 80,000 tonnes of copper (Lague 2005; Singh and Zhang 2021). Citigroup estimates that China's NFSRA holds upward of 2 million tonnes of copper, amounting to about one-sixth of the refined copper China consumes annually (Zhang and Daly 2021).

Another key player in the Chinese copper refining industry and, as a result, in the global copper concentrates market is the China Smelters Purchase Team (CSPT). CSPT members include the top players in the domestic Chinese copper mining, smelting, and refining industry (among which are the large state-backed Jiangxi Copper, Tongling Nonferrous, and Jinchuan Group). In 2020, the CSPT brought their membership base from ten to twelve members, in order to increase their market share ("CSPT Considers Taking In New Members"), ostensibly in order to provide a stronger position of power in negotiations. In 2020, the CSPT consisted of the following twelve members: "Tongling Nonferrous, Jiangxi Copper, Daye Nonferrous, China Gold, Baiyin Nonferrous, Gansu Jinchuan, Yunnan Copper, Zhongtiaoshan, Yantai Guorun, Zijin Mining, Fuye Heding, and Huludao Zinc's subsidiary copper smelter. The 12 smelters contribute over 85pc of China's copper production" ("China Leading Cu Smelters Cut Price Floor for 1Q TC/RCs" 2020). "In terms of the smelters, Jiangxi Copper is always viewed as the one that controls the CSPT" (Interview 161, Executive at leading financial institution, 2022).

## China's Impact on the Global Copper Market

At the time of China's emergence as the number one consumer of copper, the global copper market was the most financialized out of the four commodity markets studied in this book. In practice, this means that copper was and still is broadly traded on commodity exchanges, now chiefly the LME and the SHFE, and that spot prices, which adjust throughout the day and form the basis of copper contract negotiations, are publicly available. As a result, commodities traders and merchants play a larger role in the market. No matter how financialized a market is, there are always battles for market power. For instance, starting in 2012, as the LME started losing market share to the Shanghai Futures Exchange (SHFE), it developed plans to build warehouses directly in China, to which many were opposed, including the SHFE (*GFMS Copper Survey* 2016).

Even if the global copper market had already been financialized before China's emergence as the number one importer in 2008, long-term contracts still prevailed between large copper producers and major copper importers, Japanese and European importers (chiefly Germany), and the global copper market had seen decades of stability in production and consumption levels.

When China emerged, its domestic copper industry had been very fragmented and this had an impact on its capacity to organize its copper procurement, much in the way it had experienced in the iron ore market (the meaningful difference here was the nature of the global pricing system in both markets). An executive and copper industry expert explained that

> [t]he one thing about China relative to Japan and Europe is that term contracts, so contracts for volume, were less important. Partly because it was growing so quickly.... Suddenly that was the growth area, China was investing hard in copper. So, you didn't just have one dominant buyer, you had all these companies trying to compete to be the leader in the industry, in China.... They were competing against each other for raw materials because they wanted to be bigger. It was very similar in the steel industry, when China emerged as iron ore buyer in those days, and even if you look now at the Chinese market and levels of consolidation, [they] are still very low relative to peers. There are still a lot of players and this is something the Chinese government will have to work on in the next five years and consolidate these industries. (Interview 161, Executive at leading financial institution, 2022)

In the copper case, we witnessed a movement from Quadrant 3, in the era of Japanese dominance, a space where market power was more heavily skewed toward consumers, to Quadrant 1, a space where more fragmented Chinese importers faced a fragmented global market. As a result, the capacity for China to purposefully shape global market institutions was small. But still, impacts were being felt. In fact, the initial impact of China's rise as the number one importer on global copper market pricing institutions, in terms of the nature of the contracts and long-term relationships between producers and consumers, was being felt in the direction of the liberalization of existing market institutions. Indeed, the fragmented and disorganized nature of domestic Chinese copper importers played in ways not unlike what had happened in the iron ore market, moving the needle away from strategic interactions.

Despite this initial impact in the direction of liberalization, the overall impact of Chinese copper consumers on the global copper market has been relatively small. When I asked a leading industry consultant whether China had changed the way in which copper is being sold globally, his answer was that

> [t]he main copper market has changed to some extent, but it still works basically in the same way. Obviously now the big players are Chinese players, and you didn't have the SHFE (Shanghai Futures Exchange), ... [the] LME (London Metals Exchange) now has Chinese owners.... Their presence in the smelting industry is quite big, and they had a big impact. But the copper market is really a global market. It cannot be dominated by China, except from the fact that they are the

biggest consumer.... Until very recently, I would say that globalization was the general view. So, it didn't really matter who was buying the copper, it was a global market, nobody really cared where that copper was going. Probably that is starting to change, but only very recently. (Interview 164, Executive at global commodities consultancy, 2022)

When I asked him what had started to change, he explained that in the concentrates market, some of the exporters, Chile in particular, have started to express concerns about an overreliance on China as a customer.

In recent years, Chinese stakeholders have sought to build their market power and influence within global copper market institutions, including via acquisitions and by taking over the TC/RC negotiations in the smelting industry. There has also been a tug of war between different Chinese market stakeholders about the potential lifting of domestic restrictions on the import of copper concentrates for the purpose of blending concentrates in China. All of these have had mixed results.

In terms of acquisitions, a respected copper industry consultant explained that

> from the Chinese perspective what has really changed is that initially they were not very active in investing outside of China but that has slowly been changing over time. They now have a big presence in Africa. They moved to Peru at some time, but that slowed down very quickly. Obviously, they acquired the biggest acquisition in the history of copper mining, Las Bambas, and they built Toromocho at the same time, they had two or three other projects . . . but because Peruvian mining has not been developing as fast as expected, we haven't heard more from that. Africa is where most of the investment has taken place, and it is very strategic because it's associated with cobalt as well. So, they also acquired other companies, they have a big investment in Rio Tinto. (Interview 164, Executive at global commodities consultancy, 2022)

Another executive explained that

> Chile has always been a little more cautious about Chinese involvement, so if you look, no copper mine in Chile is owned by a Chinese entity, whereas the Japanese have been down there for years. Now Peru is different, we see a lot of Chinese investment in Peru over the last decade, Las Bambas being the prime example. You have seen the Chinese buying the ownership of mines in copper where they can, to try to bypass the traders that way, but for some of the raw material, especially

from Chile, they don't have any option. (Interview 161, Executive at leading financial institution, 2022)

Chinese market stakeholders have not limited themselves to foreign direct investment in mining projects, they have also proceeded to enter the global trading business.

> There are . . . very important Chinese traders. Some of the biggest companies, Louis Dreyfus for example, a big player, was bought by a Chinese [company]. . . and it is one of the biggest players in the traders' industry, and it is now called IXM. And there are other big players in China, so for example Trafigura, which is another big trader, has some investments in China in the smelting industry. So, they have a good relationship with a big player in China, they even have a share in a big smelter in South China. (Interview 164, Executive at global commodities consultancy, 2022)

The second executive added, "Some of the big traders buy for the state grid. The state grid in China is the biggest copper consumer in the world by a long way" (Interview 161, Executive at leading financial institution, 2022).

One of the ongoing battles at the interface of the Chinese domestic and global market is whether copper concentrates with higher levels of impurities can be imported in China. Copper concentrates contain a series of toxic elements such as arsenic or mercury. Different countries impose different limits on the rate of impurities metals concentrates can contain at the time of import. China's limit on arsenic content for copper concentrates was 0.5 percent from 2006 until 2022 for instance (Luk 2022). These rules create commercial opportunities for traders who buy copper concentrates with various levels of impurities and blend them to create packages that can be marketed to Chinese smelters. Giant trading company Glencore built a blending facility in Taiwan for this purpose, for instance (Singh 2019). One interviewee explained that, indeed, "One source of income on the concentrate side for traders was related to quality and the fact that there were some import restrictions in China with regards to arsenic and other impurities. So, one line of business for traders was to blend material, let's say in Taiwan, or different places and then send it to China" (Interview 164, Executive at global commodities consultancy, 2022).

Smelters can charge more to refine copper with slightly higher levels of impurities. More resource availability would also allow them to extract higher TC/RC rates and resolve supply issues. On the other hand, tighter rules on impurities would disadvantage smaller, less efficient smelters. Reports cited a source saying that "If [the Chinese] customs press ahead with these, plenty of mid-sized Chinese copper smelters will not survive" ("EXCLUSIVE: China's Customs Lobby Smelters to Impose Lower Arsenic Threshold on Copper Conc Imports" 2019). Nevertheless, even larger Chinese smelters were said to strongly oppose the tightening of regulations concerning impurities content, and they have been pressing the government to allow blending on Chinese territory. On the other hand, higher levels of impurities cause environmental headaches as toxic elements have to be extracted in greater quantities, handled, and stored.

In 2019, the Chinese government consulted copper smelters on the possibility of tightening restrictions on impurities. Jiangxi Copper, Tongling Nonferrous, and Yunnan Copper were specifically reported to having strongly opposed eventual tightening ("EXCLUSIVE: China's Customs Lobby Smelters to Impose Lower Arsenic Threshold on Copper Conc Imports, 2019"). Subsequently, reports circulated in 2019 of China's Minmetals and Jinchuan Copper being in talks to open a blending facility in Guangxi ("China's Minmetals, Jinchuan Eye Copper Concentrate Blending Plant in Guangxi—Sources" 2020). Later reports in 2022 mentioned Glencore being in talks with a Chinese smelter for the opening of a blending facility in Qingdao (Hunter and Biesheuvel 2022).

Then, in 2022, the China Nonferrous Metals Industry Association announced that the level of impurities allowed in copper concentrates imports were going to be tightened, after all. Sometime in 2023, arsenic thresholds were to go down from 0.5 percent to 0.4 percent, levels of lead from 0.7 percent to 0.6 percent (Luk 2022). An interviewee had indicated to me that there were constituencies in China that wanted to allow blending on Chinese territory to "move the market a little closer to China" (Interview 164, Executive at global commodities consultancy, 2022). Should the tightened regulations come into force in 2023, market stakeholders pushing for environmental considerations or, perhaps, market stakeholders pushing for industry consolidation, would prevail.

As mentioned earlier, the Chinese copper smelting industry has rapidly built an imposing presence globally, with 40 percent of global refining capacity. This growth has happened relatively recently. When China emerged as a major copper consumer and importer in the early 2000s, China did not possess refining capacity and thus relied more heavily on the import of refined copper. As a reminder, there are roughly two types of copper sold internationally, raw copper ore/concentrates and refined copper (99.9 percent), or copper cathode. Copper anode (99 percent), an intermediate product, represents a smaller share of the market.

In 2000, the share of the value of China's imports of copper ores and concentrates of the total value of China's imports (ores and concentrates and refined copper) was 39 percent. In 2005, it was 45 percent. The year 2016 was the first one in which China's imports of copper concentrates (by value) surpassed its imports of refined copper, at 54 percent of the total value (UN Comtrade).[7]

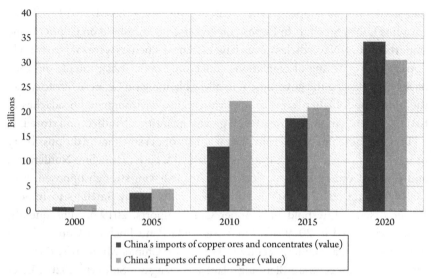

Source: UNCOMTRADE (HS codes 2603 and 7403), by trade value (USD), author's calculations.

*Figure 6.13* China's imports of raw copper and refined copper, 2000–2020

In 2020, China's imported copper amounted to 57 percent of global imports of copper ores and concentrates and 48 percent of global refined copper imports. Figure 6.13 illustrates the increasing share of copper concentrates in the mix of China's overall imports of copper over time.

> Cathode [refined copper] is an easy thing to get, you just go out and buy it, when you are going through rapid demand growth. Then because this demand growth was expected to be sustained, China started investing in copper smelting. And building, quite frankly, very good copper smelters. . . . I think last year was the first time China got more than 50 percent of its copper units from imported copper concentrates. (Interview 161, Executive at leading financial institution, 2022)

I asked this longtime copper industry expert why it took so long for China to build copper refining capacity. His reply was as follows:

> I actually like to compare copper to an industry like steel, in steel China was moving up the curve very quickly in the 2000s and in copper it took a little bit longer. . . . I don't think anyone had built a copper smelter for ten to fifteen years. So, there were very few people that knew how, there wasn't even the engineering. In steel you could go out there and get yourself a Danieli to build you a steel mill, no problem at all, they would

send their engineers to China.... In copper, that just took a little bit longer. There is a little bit more technical expertise involved in building an optimized copper smelter.... That was just part of it. Second, there were these long-term contract relationships and because the mine supply wasn't really growing, and couldn't react very quickly, no one had free material to sell to China. So, it just took a little bit longer to get the raw material flowing... they wanted the raw material, but it just wasn't available in copper as much as it was in other markets. Iron ore was dead easy: go to Australia, dig some rocks, put them on a ship, send it to China. Whereas in copper it takes a lot more capex investment in order to bring raw materials to market. (Interview 161, Executive at leading financial institution, 2022)

Unlike in other metals, China does not export copper, so it has not necessarily "displaced," as it were, refining capacity from elsewhere. One could say that it has added less refining capacity than it has added to global copper demand.

Still, there are many ways in which China's refining industry has had an impact on the global refining industry. For a start, China's arrival in the copper refining business has brought down the returns on smelting, so that it is "at a level that allows operating but that is not enough to justify investing in another smelter. You haven't seen any development in the smelting industry outside of China. The reason for that is that it is not a good business" (Interview 164, Executive at global commodities consultancy, 2022). One way of seeing this is that China's arrival has rendered the smelting industry very competitive. The only other space where building new smelting capacity has been profitable is in Africa, since distance from markets and logistical challenges make building smelters close to mines the most profitable choice. Another way of seeing this is that

[f]or other regions which have a competitive smelting industry such as Europe, there is a feeling that this is not fair competition, so to speak.... Contracting and building smelters in China is cheaper than anywhere else in the world. It is cheaper to operate it because of lower energy prices and lower labor costs, etc. But the feeling is that it is also to some extent subsidized.... So, if you look at where the growth has taken place in China, it mostly has been big state-owned companies. Those are the ones that have been growing and growing systemically, even acquiring some of the smaller private players. A lot of medium-sized smelters and refiners in Shandong province which were private basically have been acquired by state-owned companies, because they couldn't survive and one of the explanations has been that the access to

finance was completely different for private players than for state-owned players. That is the situation. The market is not structured so that you cannot make money, it is that you cannot justify investing in capacity outside of China. (Interview 164, Executive at global commodities consultancy, 2022)

The price that is reflected on global metal exchanges is the price of refined copper. The way the copper smelting industry works is that copper miners generally sell their copper ores or concentrates to copper smelters/refiners for a little less than 100 percent of the value of the actual copper content in the concentrate (remember copper concentrates contain between 25 percent and 40 percent of copper), which corresponds to what is called treatment and refining charges (TC/RCs) (Pistilli 2022). For the smelters, "[m]ost of the earnings come from treatment and refining charges, and sulfuric acid sales, and a few by-product sales. But the TC/RC charges are the main component of earnings, and that really depends on the balance between copper concentrates demand and copper concentrates supply" (Interview 164, Executive at global commodities consultancy, 2022). TC/RC rates move in the opposite direction from copper ores and concentrates. In other words, when the supply of copper ores and concentrates is tight and the price rises, smelters and refiners' leverage goes down and TC/RC rates go down along with it. On the other side, when the supply of copper ores and concentrates is more plentiful, the leverage favors smelters and refiners and TC/RC rates tend to go up. As an example, in 2021, when copper supply was tight, TC/RC (term supply contract) rates fell to the lowest level in ten years, at US$59.50/tonne ("The Copper Market, Treatment and Refining Charges" 2021). As supply eased, Chinese smelters negotiated a raise in TC/RC (term supply contract) rates to $65/tonne in December 2021, valid for 2022. In April 2021, spot TC/RC rates fell to $28.70/tonne ("Chinese Copper Smelters Raise TC/RCs for 2022 Term Contracts in Benchmark Deal" 2021).

TC/RC rates have historically been negotiated annually in a ritual not unlike the benchmark pricing system in the iron ore or potash markets. An executive consultant explained that these negotiations occur on an annual basis, leading to a benchmark agreed upon by the biggest miner and the biggest smelter. "Until not so long ago, for example, the Japanese were the leaders in the negotiations that take place each year between the mining industry and the smelting industry. And now probably five or six years ago, could be more, the Chinese basically became the largest player, and the main party in these annual negotiations that take place between the biggest players of the industry" (Interview 164, Executive at global commodities consultancy, 2022).

The China Smelters Purchase Team (CSPT), the group comprising the largest Chinese smelters, holds quarterly meetings to agree on a "floor TC/RC rate," which then guides the lead copper smelters in negotiating with global copper producers. The CSPT appoints a revolving leader, which in 2022 was Jinchuan Group (after China Copper and, prior to that, China Dongling) ("China's Top Copper Smelters Appoint New Leader—Sources" 2022). All members then have to stick to this floor in their subsequent copper concentrates contracts. TC/RC rate negotiations have been held between a representative on the side of the global miners, which in recent years has been Freeport-McMoRan and, recently, four smelters on the Chinese side, Chinalco China Copper Co. Ltd., Jiangxi Copper Corp. Ltd., Jinchuan Group, and Tongling Nonferrous Group ("Chinese Copper Smelters Raise TC/RCs for 2022 Term Contracts in Benchmark Deal" 2021). It is important to reiterate that these negotiations are not negotiations for the price of copper itself, as they were in the case of iron ore, or as they are in the case of potash, but rather for the treatment and refining charges the smelting industry will charge miners to refine copper concentrates. Nevertheless, patterns of coordination and market power relations can be observed in ways not entirely dissimilar to those of the main benchmark pricing systems in the iron ore and potash markets.

During the Japanese era, in a pattern reminiscent of that in the iron ore market, the negotiations were held with BHP Billiton. The executive consultant explained that BHP Billiton is no longer the lead negotiator on the producer side because it "does not want to be involved" with those TC/RC benchmark negotiations.

> They want to sell it in a different way. They have been doing it differently for some time. But the rest of the industry prefers this system. It's simpler, it has worked well for decades. . . . They [BHPB] have been trying to move, probably following the changes that took place on the iron ore side. . . . They prefer a system based on frequent contracts, or monthly sales, quarterly sales. Creating an index and selling their contracted tonnage based on those prices, rather than an agreed price. (Interview 164, Executive at global commodities consultancy, 2022)

I asked another executive to explain what he thought the Chinese smelters were trying to achieve with the CSPT grouping and its coordination attempts. He replied as follows:

> They are trying to go back to the old school bilateral negotiations, but at the end of the day though, the problem is, the first thing you negotiate on is where the spot price is . . . the problem is that the spot price is set by the others and then the spot price is what gets used to negotiate the contracts, so the CSPT is an effort to try and do two

things: control the price that gets paid, so you don't have people stepping too far over the line. Are they fully disciplined? No, but they all sit down and . . . agree on a floor . . . but they try to get an edge over each other. The second thing they do, though, is that they try to secure the quality that they want. Copper concentrates come in all sorts of different qualities, levels of impurities, so they make sure they get the Los Pelambres concentrates from Antofagasta, which is probably the premium concentrate out there. So, they make sure that that's going to the CSPT smelters. (Interview 161, Executive at leading financial institution, 2022)

In the end, whereas the TC/RC benchmark had been stable for many years under the Japanese tenure, it has not been the case since China took over: "[T]hey have fluctuated a lot. They were let's say $120/tonne and now they've reached below $60/tonne last year, they went up a bit this year, the benchmark has" (Interview 164, Executive at global commodities consultancy, 2022).

## Conclusion

The uranium case may seem counterintuitive at first sight. This is the case where Chinese market stakeholders had perhaps the clearest position of market power. One might have assumed either a large impact on global market institutions or more assertive behavior on behalf of Chinese stakeholders. This should perhaps especially be the case, given that the uranium market is related to civilian nuclear security concerns.

There are two reasons the model presented in this book help us think differently about this case. First, the framework presented here makes the case that preferences for global market institutions are not necessarily shared across markets or stakeholders. The specific configuration of relative market power has an impact on preference formation. In this case, two elements of this relative market power are noteworthy. First, the lead Chinese market uranium importers find themselves in a clearly dominant position of market power domestically, in an economic, regulatory, and political sense (although there is some degree of competition among the top two importers). I suggest, in this book, that this may lead to preferences for de-liberalization at the global level. Indeed, we have seen Chinese importers pursue procurement at the strategic end of the spectrum, with long-term investments, joint ventures, and direct long-term contracts and relationships.

Second, the model presented in this book reminds us of the importance of putting Chinese preferences and behavior in context. In this case, at the time of

China's emergence, the global market presented characteristics that were not misaligned with Chinese preferences. In the language developed in Chapter 3, because China's rise as number one consumer occurred within the same Quadrant, it was less likely to profoundly disrupt established market institutions. In other words, it was unlikely to profoundly disrupt global market institutions because it did not profoundly disrupt existing relative positions of market power between consumers and producers.

Being attuned to relative positions of market power in this case also highlights the fact that Chinese stakeholders in this case faced less resistance in the fulfillment of their procurement needs from global market stakeholders in general. China's level of coordination capacity domestically and its ability to maneuver at the global level mean that it has been able to push forward a multipronged international uranium procurement strategy relatively unimpeded. On one hand, at the domestic level, the coordinated nature of China's interface with the global uranium industry has allowed more overlap between the objectives of its major uranium consumers and those of other government entities, which in turn have led to the development and implementation of a more coherent procurement strategy. On the other hand, at the international level, the regionalized nature of the global market before China's emergence as the number one importer and the opportunity that the parallel emergence of Kazakhstan presented to China have reduced constraints and enabled it to carve out a more comfortable place in the global market. The uranium market is distinctive in this regard. In the iron ore and potash cases, China experienced heavier constraints on the development of its procurement strategy internationally. It also expressed deep dissatisfaction toward either the global market institutions that had been created prior to its recent emergence as the world's top consumer or toward the behavior of key global market stakeholders.

This was partly due to a global lack of enthusiasm for nuclear energy, as well as the Fukushima accident and the sudden drop in global uranium demand, all of which coincided with China's rapid emergence as the number one consumer. Whatever the reason, China has succeeded in carving room to maneuver in the uranium market and, as a consequence, has displayed more confidence, less frustration, and less accusatory rhetoric than it has certainly in the iron ore market but also arguably in the potash market. China has also displayed a willingness to collaborate with the International Atomic Energy Agency on issues of civilian nuclear safety in ways that stand apart from more testy behavior in other global institutions.

The uranium market is just one case, so it would not be prudent to extrapolate too much. All I can say is that I observe China's relatively seamless integration into the global uranium market and overall lack of disruption of existing global market institutions at the same time as I observe a favorable position of market power for China. I will also note that this is a case where China's procurement behavior was led by powerful SOEs and has been in alignment with key economic development and energy policies but this did not lead to revisionist behavior on the global stage or to economic conflict. This in itself yields important insights. For a start, it follows that Chinese positions of power do not necessarily lead to conflictual relationships at the global level or to global institutional disruption. In addition, it is interesting to note that expressed perceptions of market vulnerability, in the language of the Chinese uranium market stakeholders interviewed in the course of this research, were much fewer than in the iron ore or potash markets. Can it be that positions of market vulnerability undermine trust in global market institutions and are more likely to lead to disruptive behavior? This presents an avenue for future research.

In the copper case, Chinese market stakeholders found themselves in a position of relative market power symmetry with global copper producers. To re-emphasize, my assessment of the Chinese market stakeholders' position of market power is relational. It was not enough that the Chinese domestic copper industry was relatively fragmented for Chinese stakeholders to find themselves in a position of market vulnerability. The fact that at the global level, copper market stakeholders also presented relative fragmentation meant that there was a lack of clear market power on both sides and, thus, less likelihood that one side would be able to wield determining influence on global market institutions.

The situation had evolved from a Japanese era where copper consumers had been more coordinated, although perhaps to a lesser degree than they had been in the iron ore industry. Japan, as the world's number one copper importer, had been able to exert some influence on global copper market institutions, including by establishing a system of long-term contracts (whereas short-term contracts dominated the market at the onset of the Japanese era) and through the creation of various long-term financial ties with producers (Rodrik 1982). The emergence of China therefore represented a movement from a consumer-dominated scenario and a situation of market power symmetry. A movement toward symmetric positions of market power, especially fragmented ones, is, I argue, the least likely to lead to major disruptions in global market institutions. However, China's emergence did represent a level of disruption. As was the case in the iron ore market, at the time of China's emergence, Chinese copper consumers were many and they were not effectively coordinated. This led to a disruption of established market pricing norms, a slight movement in the direction of further liberalization. Since then, Chinese market stakeholders have been trying to bring China back toward a position not unlike the one Japan had been able to build, a more favorable position of market power. These efforts have been met with mixed success.

The two cases investigated in this chapter provide us with a few supplementary insights, furthering the insights drawn from the iron ore and potash cases. First, they illustrate that important clues to explaining China's behavior toward and eventual impact on global market institutions lie at the intersection of domestic and global market power configurations. The full picture comes to light when we look at the unique balance of power between domestic and global market stakeholders and how it manifests itself in each market. Fragmented Chinese copper consumers did not lead to the same kind of interactions and outcomes as in the iron ore market; the structure and subsequent behavior of global iron ore market stakeholders were distinct. Similarly, a position of market power in the uranium case did not lead to conflict and bargaining dynamics as in the potash case; Chinese market stakeholders rose to face fewer constraints in the global uranium market, which was more fragmented than the global potash market, and they used this room for maneuver in a way that satisfied their resource procurement needs more easily. This is one of the benefits of investigating two further case studies in this chapter, as they provide supplementary variation on the independent variable at the global level.

One further insight, which will need to be investigated further, is the importance of looking at the global market institutional starting point. The global copper market was already financialized at the time of China's emergence, contrary to the three other markets investigated in this book. This scenario is qualitatively different from the iron ore or potash cases, which were home to decades-old benchmark pricing regimes. There are ways in which the financialized nature of the global copper market structured Chinese market stakeholders' behaviors. But domestic concerns were also strong determinants of behavior, as seems to be the case concerning the tightening of impurities thresholds for copper concentrates imports. Further work is needed on the ways in which institutional differences among domestic markets and global markets structure behavior and how they interact to lead to distinct market outcomes.

# 7

# Conclusion

## Puzzles

The global commodity markets explored in this book unveil a fascinating range of dynamics. In the two main cases—markets that were initially similarly structured—China's rise as dominant consumer led to different outcomes: in the iron ore case, decades-old benchmark pricing institutions rapidly fell apart, yet in the potash case, they mostly survive to this day. This led to the articulation of three puzzles: a variation puzzle, a vulnerability puzzle and a liberalization puzzle.

First, the variation in outcomes requires an explanation, as the two main cases were carefully selected because they initially presented many similarities. Second, the case with the largest magnitude of change globally, the iron ore case, was also the case where Chinese market stakeholders were in a position of market vulnerability, whereas the case with the most continuity in global market institutions, the potash case, was the one where Chinese market stakeholders had the most market power. This needs to be explained. Relatedly, the fall of the benchmark pricing institutions and the emergence of spot pricing in the iron ore market was not the outcome intended by the leading Chinese domestic market stakeholders, including SOEs, the leading industry association, and key ministries. Finally, this outcome constitutes, in fact, the liberalization of market institutions. The potash case, despite the survival of the main pricing institution, also presents liberalization trends, some of them the result of China's emergence, some of them, more recently, the result of the emergence of another systemically relevant consumer, Brazil. Those outcomes taken together are counterintuitive.

To date, major variation in the behavior and impact of China's interaction with global markets has not been sufficiently empirically surveyed or theorized in the global and comparative political economy of China literatures. Important efforts have been made in the international relations or global China literatures, in an emerging body of work I call the China as heterogeneous power literature. This literature, which is based on careful empirical work, has established a practice of seeking to illustrate and explain the concurrent variation in China's behavior in distinct areas of global affairs, and there have been notable advances made (Foot and Walter 2010; Kastner et al. 2018; Weiss and Wallace 2021; Jones and Hameiri 2021; Johnston, 2019). But in the comparative political economy of China literature more effort has been devoted to study variation in "second-image reversed" effects (the global economy's impact on China's domestic political economy) than variation in "second-image" effects (China's impact on the political economy of global markets). And in the global political economy of China literature, not enough attention has been devoted to studying variation in global outcomes.

Regarding the second puzzle, vulnerability, it is noteworthy that the most important impact on global market institutions as a result of China's emergence as dominant consumer was situated in the case where Chinese stakeholders were in the weakest position of market power. Many in the global China literature, for understandable reasons, have tended to assume that the largest impacts internationally would result from a strong Chinese position of power, or at least from coherent behavior aimed at accomplishing a stated aim. What I find here is that a fragmented China in a vulnerable position of market power led to disruptive behavior and systemic change in the global iron ore market. Importantly, the fall of the iron ore benchmark pricing institution was the opposite outcome main Chinese iron ore market stakeholders were seeking. Interviews confirm that key stakeholders had a stated vested interest in the continuation of the pricing regime. This is critical for our understanding of the relationship between Chinese preferences and global outcomes, and it puts into question claims of China's coherence in strategic aims, behaviors, and impacts. At least these are not true in all cases and so need to be treated with caution. To be sure, the preferences and behaviors of global market stakeholders are a critical part of the explanation, as Chapter 4 makes clear. But the benchmark pricing system that coordinated Japanese market stakeholders had helped put in place in the decades prior was China's to lose, as it were. Without the disruptive and uncoordinated behavior of Chinese iron ore importers in the years leading up to 2010, the benchmarking system would not have collapsed so rapidly, if at all. Some of the most powerful global market stakeholders, such as Rio Tinto, did not want this outcome. Neither did the other global iron ore consumers, Japan, South Korea, and the Europeans. This holds important lessons for the study of China's impact on global institutions, to which we will return below. Among others, China's size is such that its domestic dynamics can have systemic effects abroad, whether intended or otherwise.

Regarding the third puzzle, liberalization, the fact that China's emergence and increased interaction with global commodity markets would lead to liberalization trends of varying intensity warrants an explanation no matter one's prior expectations. This is the case for at least three reasons. First, conceptually speaking, liberalization trends are always and everywhere political in that they constitute a transformation that entails distributive outcomes, creates winners and losers, and, as such, must be explained. Liberalization, as we are seeing in our post-Covid pandemic world, is not to be taken for granted. There can be reversals or pendulum movement dynamics and, as such, movement in either direction needs to be explained. Second, the liberalization trends observed in the cases studied in this book are unequal and occur via different mechanisms and at different times. Third, no matter where one comes from on the depth and nature of the market reforms conducted in China since 1978, the fact that China would lead to liberalization trends also cannot be taken as expected. There are many potential reasons for and against the expectation that China would lead to increased competitiveness or increased strategic behavior in global markets, and we have seen both trends at play in the four commodity markets studied here. The mixed picture calls us to caution in developing expectations of China as having singular unidirectional impacts on global markets. If a general insight can be derived from this liberalization puzzle, it is that the emergence of a large economy can lead to an unsettling of existing power relationships that can take the form of liberalization in specific global markets. But we know that it can also lead to strategic behavior and strategic competition. The important question is why certain patterns emerge when they do. More research is needed to refine the contributions made in this book on the particular contexts and variables that are more or less likely to lead to disruption, increased market competition, or, on the other hand, more state control and strategic behavior in global market institutions.

## Argument

In this book, I argued that relative positions of market power between systemically relevant domestic and global market stakeholders offer critical cues to behavioral patterns and the likelihood of institutional change in global markets. At the most basic level, dominant positions of market power, measured in this book as the relative capacity for coordination, provide market stakeholders with greater capacity to influence global market institutions. Market power dominance in favor of systemically relevant consumers affords them the opportunity to play determining roles in shaping global market institutions, as we saw Japan do in the iron ore case in the second half of the twentieth century with the creation of the benchmark pricing regime. The opposite scenario affords global market stakeholders this opportunity, as was the case with global iron ore producers when China emerged as the number one importer in the 2000s.

To determine relative positions of market power, careful examination of the domestic political economy of each market is necessary, with particular attention being paid to each market's interface with global markets. In the case of potash, for instance, whereas the domestic political economy of the fertilizer industry in China exhibits levels of complexity and fragmentation, the import interface is tightly controlled by three—but really two—large firms that each play a leading role in the coordinating "small group" that was created for the express purpose of more effectively wielding market power vis-à-vis global producers. It is important to devote attention to the efforts to effectively coordinate on both sides—the consumers and the producers—and to how these efforts evolved over time. In the two cases where symmetry of high-level market power was observed between Chinese domestic and global market stakeholders, in the potash case and the narrower case of iron ore shipping, I observed patterns of strategic bargaining. In both of those cases, Chinese market stakeholders were able to extract some major concessions from global market stakeholders.

In the potash case, the continued survival of the benchmark pricing institution may depend on the continuation of effective market coordination on both the Chinese consumer side and the global producer side. In a fascinating twist of fate, the emergence of Brazil as a systemically relevant potash consumer since the late-2010s and the high level of fragmentation of its own domestic fertilizer industry have created disruptions and led to the emergence of more prevalent spot pricing. As a consequence, the potash benchmark pricing regime is being slowly marginalized but could survive as long as Chinese consumers maintain high levels of coordination at the import interface. Any significant opening of import licenses or any changes on this front on the part of Chinese authorities would likely lead to the unraveling of the potash benchmark pricing system not unlike what we saw in the iron ore case in 2010. For the moment, global potash producers continue to go along with the existing benchmark pricing system, even though there are indications that they would switch to more spot pricing, given the chance. This is a scenario that resembles the iron ore case in the 2010s, the only difference being the continued effective wielding of market coordination and market power by dominant Chinese consumers.

The case study of China's impact on the global uranium market allows us to leverage supplementary variation across cases and to refine the arguments developed here. In the uranium case, it is noteworthy that China, while in a more dominant position of market power and able to operate more comfortably, faced fewer hurdles in its international procurement strategy and has been less disruptive at the global level. China's rapid rise did lead to some structural changes in the global uranium market, chiefly via the support of Kazakhstan, which emerged as the world's number one producer, and also via a continued large role for the state. But the pricing institutions have seen continuity and remain broadly unchanged (except for some activity on the spot market front that is happening quite separately from Chinese involvement). One lesson from this case is that the presence of stronger positions of market power, as well as closer ties with central government objectives on the part of Chinese market stakeholders, is not a sufficient condition for disruptive behaviour internationally. The limited number of cases studied here does not allow me to make more generalizable claims, but the least I can say is that in a case of a stronger position of market power, I do find evidence of Chinese behavior that has worked within prior existing practices and that also includes conciliatory behavior in related international civilian nuclear safety initiatives.

There is another key way in which relative positions of market power have determining impacts on global markets. If, in a static sense, relative positions of market power afford the dominant side with more leeway to influence global market institutions, it follows that a shift in the balance of market power increases the likelihood of market institutional change at the global level. I have argued in this book that the most profound the change in the relative balance of market power, the higher the likelihood of market institutional change at the global level. This book has focused on one of the most momentous events in the recent history of global commodities: the rise of China as the number one consumer and importer of many raw commodities. This rapid emergence has provided us with a quasi-experiment setup in which China's rise was conceived of as a shock to existing global market institutions. In some cases, China's rise profoundly shifted the preexisting balance of market power between consumers and producers. In other cases, it did not. The most profound transformation of market power relations between leading consumers and producers occurred in the iron ore market as a result of the transition between Japan and China as number one consumers. Whereas the Japanese tenure as lead importer placed Japan in a dominant position of market power relative to global iron ore producers, China emerged as a fragmented consumer facing an industry that had seen high levels of consolidation over the preceding years. As a result, whereas Japan had a more comfortable position of market power from which to operate, China found itself in a position of market vulnerability. Positions of market power are important in themselves, but I argue here that it is the dramatic transfer in relative market power between consumers and producers that led to higher instability and higher likelihood of change in the case of the global iron ore market pricing institutions.

A related argument is that changes of market power relations toward more asymmetric positions of market power are more likely to be disruptive than changes toward more symmetric positions of market power. This is simply because the absence of a clear dominant side leads to either competitive (both fragmented) or strategic bargaining (both coordinated) dynamics, which are arguably less prone to rapid institutional transformation, although bargaining dynamics can be conflictual and unpredictable. The case of the copper market provides insights into the former scenario, where China emerged as a relatively fragmented consumer in a global copper concentrates market that was also relatively more fragmented than the potash or iron ore markets. In this case, China's emergence has not led to profound institutional changes in global market institutions. The nature of the global copper pricing system prior to China's emergence also played a role here. Copper was already financialized and being traded on major commodity exchanges prior to China's rise as the number one importer. Interestingly, the refining industry is one aspect of the global copper industry where China has perhaps been in a slightly more advantageous position of market power (as opposed to a symmetric position of market fragmentation). Here, China is inserting itself in relative continuity with previously established Japanese practices, specifically in the case of the annual benchmarking negotiations for "treatment and refining charges," which it has led for the past few years. In all cases, we can say that China has worked hard to either create or maintain consolidation levels and coordination capacity, with varying levels of success.

There is one final, tentative argument I make about the effect of relative market power. I argue that positions of market power relative to a market stakeholders' own peers affect preferences for the liberalization of global market institutions. More evidence is needed to confirm, refine, or reject this hypothesis. For the time being, I hypothesize that at the (Chinese) domestic consumer level, positions of market vulnerability relative to their peers will lead to preferences for liberalization at the global level, and vice versa. The opposite dynamic seems to be in play at the global level; this is to say, strong positions of market power relative to their peers lead to preferences for the liberalization of global market institutions, and vice versa.

At its core, the argument developed in this book calls attention to relative positions of market power between systemically relevant players in distinct global markets and their change over time. Market stakeholders' positions of market power relative to global market stakeholders bear on their preferences for global market institutions, their capacity to organize and effect change and, combined with the nature of global market institutions and stakeholders' behaviors, produce unique outcomes across global markets.

The argument presented in this book was generated on the arguably fertile ground provided by two main case studies, the iron ore and potash cases. It was refined through investigations of within-market case studies in the iron ore case with the study of the cases of China's impact on iron ore shipping and of the Japanese era of dominance. Finally, the argument was further refined through investigations of two other commodity case studies, the uranium and copper markets. How far can the argument travel? There is early indication that it provides useful theoretical framing for an analysis of China's emergence as dominant consumer in other commodities, such as the global nickel, lithium, and cobalt markets, in which China has rapidly become a systemic player. In the global nickel market, the emergence of China has led to a reorganization of the global producer market, with the development of new refining technologies that have made certain deposits newly viable, including in Indonesia. The behavior of one Chinese nickel consumer and leading stainless-steel producer, Tsingshan, caused the LME to halt trading in March 2022 as a result of massive short positions that had proven ill-timed in the wake of the Russian invasion of Ukraine (Russia is a major exporter of nickel) ("LME Suspends Nickel Trading after Prices Surge More than 110% to Over US$100,000 a Ton" 2022). Unpacking the relative positions of market power in this market and their evolution over time would likely help us explain important changes that have occurred in the global nickel market since China's emergence and also the prospects for future (de)liberalization.

Despite the focus on commodities, the broader goal of this book were to use the cases of China's impact on global commodity markets in order to draw broader insights into how China's rise is affecting global market institutions. It remains to be seen whether the arguments generated in this book can be directly applied to cases other than commodity markets. The concept of relative market power and vulnerability is certainly operationalizable beyond commodities. It could also be adapted to the study of other areas of international relations, by focusing on relative power and vulnerability more broadly and operationalizing it in consequence. In fact, the way in which I have conceptualized this variable is compatible with Jessica Chen Weiss and Jeremy Wallace's heterogeneity variable, which they conceptualize as the "degree of domestic division and contestation over government policy regarding a given international issue" (Weiss and Wallace 2021, 651). Jones and Hameiri also focus on the Chinese state's capacity to coordinate various subnational actors in the conduct of foreign policy. They develop a variable that is very much compatible with the one developed in this book, which they label "efficacy of coordinating mechanisms" (Jones and Hameiri 2021). We have pretty good evidence that coordination capacity varies from issue area to issue area (and from market to market!) in China. Further theorizing and refining of how this variation influences China's impact on global institutions should continue to yield important insights.

## Broader Lessons

What are the broader lessons we can draw from this book to reflect on the ongoing relationship (the integration and, at times, retreat) between the Chinese economy and the global economy? Here are six: the heterogeneity of China's behavior and impacts abroad, the importance of unintended consequences, the resonance between domestic and global market institutions, market vulnerability as seen from China, the question of market fairness, and, finally, the return of market power, including via the re-emergence of economic nationalism and the attendant much-needed problematization of the concept of "open markets."

## China as Heterogeneous Power

We have already discussed the importance of considering the concurrent heterogeneity of Chinese behavior in this book. Suffice it to reiterate here that characterizations of Chinese preferences, behaviors, and impacts as unitary fall short of empirical accuracy in the cases reviewed in this book. This builds on a growing body of scholarship that has found heterogeneity in Chinese preferences, behaviors, and impacts covering a wide range of global issues and applies these insights to political economy. Some could argue that the heterogeneous nature of Chinese behavior is a transitional feature of a growing China. This to me is a question worthy of further reflection. It would be interesting to map out the heterogeneity of China's behavior over the recent past as well as to continue to track its ebbs and flows over the future. It is my sense at this point that given the deep domestic sources of variation in Chinese behavior at the global level as well as the continued variation in global market institutions and global market stakeholders' behaviors, heterogeneity will remain a feature of Chinese interactions with the world for the foreseeable future.

Understanding the ways in which the political economy of Chinese markets varies and the ways in which this variation finds its expression in international patterns of behavior should thus remain a promising area for future research. We have seen in this book that coordination capacity, or market power, varies in significant ways across industries in China. To fully understand this variation, we need to trace global behaviors back to their domestic roots and unveil the historical processes that led to current market structures.

One thing is for sure, we cannot presume countrywide patterns of behavior. In the case of the fall of the benchmarking regime, the key determinants of disruptive aggregate Chinese behavior and its impacts were issues associated with fragmentation, the presence of diverging preferences regarding global market institutions and, more important, the incapacity of powerful stakeholders to coordinate procurement behavior. In the case of the Valemax cargo saga, on the contrary, COSCO was able to successfully coordinate the behavior of multiple Chinese stakeholders at the interface with global markets, over and against the interests of some Chinese steelmakers and other state actors.

This research also shows that pitting "the state" against "the market" only goes so far in providing a comprehensive picture of the interaction between China and global market stakeholders. At times, Chinese market stakeholders, state or otherwise, have demonstrated successful coordination capacity; at other times, they have been unsuccessful. Similarly, Chinese firms have at times demonstrated behavior in line with state objectives, and at other times their behavior has been running against it. Chinese public and private stakeholders have at times demonstrated behavior in line with accepted international practices and institutions and, at times, they have pushed back against these practices and institutions.

Unitary predictions of behavior for China do not do justice to the empirical dynamics observed in the case studies presented here. The nature of Chinese stakeholders, whether they are public or private entities, does not give us sufficient information to understand their behavior.

## Unintended Consequences

A related insight yielded by this book's findings is that some of the impacts of China's rise we observe at the global level were not intended by the largest Chinese stakeholders. The outcomes of China's rise globally vary only in part according to the preferences of leading Chinese SOEs, ministries, industry associations, central planning agencies, or private firms. The difficulty we face in parsing out the intended and unintended impacts of Chinese behaviour with regard to foreign markets stems in part from the fragmentation of its domestic political economy.

It is possible to arrive at better granular understanding of the process through which domestic Chinese dynamics translate into global outcomes, via careful tracing of a variety of stakeholder behaviors, both in China and internationally. To do so, it takes broader consideration of relevant stakeholders (than just the "main ones"), attentiveness to the presence of diverging preferences and awareness of interaction effects that can lead to unintended global outcomes. If there ever was a rationale for investing in a deeper knowledge of and familiarity with China and its various subnational private, semi-private, state-led, or party entities, this is it.

This insight not only has profound implications for our understanding of Chinese impacts on the world but also of policy prescriptions in response to Chinese patterns of behavior in various global issue areas. The importance of unintended outcomes should help us reframe arguments that take for granted the tendency not only for Chinese actors to articulate coherent long-term objectives in all areas of global economic import (what "China" wants) but also for Chinese stakeholders to then deliver the behaviors that would produce the intended outcomes and, even in this case, for the intended outcomes to happen at all, given the attendant interaction effects and resulting unpredictability. The unexpected nature of global outcomes actually presents the opportunity to bring more humility to discussions of resource security, supply chain vulnerabilities, and global market institutional design.

## Resonance between Domestic and Global Market Institutions

This book demonstrates the importance of studying changes in global markets from the perspective of the deepest sort of institutional resonance and continually adjusting complementarities between global markets and their systemically significant stakeholders. The fall of the iron ore benchmark pricing regime, the blocking of Valemax's vessels from docking at Chinese ports, the fall of the Belarusian Potash Company potash export marketing cartel, or Japan's emergence and the creation of a stable iron ore pricing regime in the second half of the twentieth century are all events that cannot be explained from either an international or domestic perspective. The market power dynamics at both domestic and international levels combine to create conditions for institutional change at the global level.

The pathways through which China will continue to effect change on the global economy are complex. China is dealing with the fact that increasingly, domestic policy choices and even uncoordinated procurement behavior can have significant impacts on global markets beyond the intended policy objectives. In short, due to its size, China's domestic political economy now resonates at a global level, no matter what. This is what systemic power entails, the fact that domestic market dynamics will likely have global impacts even when these domestic dynamics have no international intent per se.

The consequences of such dynamics sometimes come back to haunt China. As a case in point, the fall of the iron ore benchmark pricing regime was not in the interest of some of China's largest iron ore market stakeholders, including leading state organs.

China's sheer size and its arrival in global market contexts that offer little room for maneuver have put it in a position in which both disorganized procurement and purposeful actions can have the effect of destabilizing the concentrated and coordinated behavioral patterns that exist among producers. It is therefore primordial that we unpack the causal pathways through which Chinese behaviors impact global markets. Looking at outcomes to derive initial intentions can provide a partial picture at best and a misleading picture at worst (see similar concerns expressed in Jones and Hameiri 2021).

Importantly, expectations in terms of the direction of global impact as a result of China's emergence should be more complex than assuming they will reflect domestic market tendencies. China's hybrid state-led economy does not necessarily have a "statist" effect on global markets. In fact, one of the most counterintuitive findings of this book is the fact that China's emergence, under certain circumstances, led to liberalization trends globally. On the other hand, the relationship between China's domestic market-oriented reforms and liberalization outcomes is not straightforward, either. Questions of timing, variation across cases, and causal mechanisms need to be answered.

## Market Vulnerability as Seen from China and Other Emerging Economies

It is at times assumed in the literature that bold behavior on behalf of China internationally comes from a position of strength. The corollary, perhaps more often implicitly invoked, would be that a position of vulnerability, or weakness, would lead to less disruptive behavior and perhaps more acceptance of global institutions or the rules of the game. Bearing in mind the limited number of cases studied in this book, we have nevertheless seen the largest magnitude of disruption of a long-lasting global market institution in the case of a position of vulnerability on behalf of China. In other words, Chinese vulnerability has enabled significant change internationally. We could say that the survival of a decades-old global iron ore pricing regime depended on the capacity for Chinese market stakeholders to effectively coordinate procurement behavior, which they failed to do. China's inability to overcome collective action problems was the ultimate enabler of the transformative change that took place at the global level.

There is a rich literature in Chinese politics where authors have theorized about the fragmentation of Chinese domestic policymaking processes (see, e.g., Oksenberg and Lieberthal 1988; Mertha 2009). Some have then extrapolated a rationale for behavior abroad based on this domestic assessment. This is critically important work. The distinction I am making here is that beyond this important domestic assessment of fragmentation or fragility, a more complete picture of Chinese behavior internationally needs to be relational, or based on "two-levels" of considerations (see also Fravel 2008). In the case of market vulnerability, I argue that the particularly relevant forms of Chinese vulnerability are those that manifest at the interface between Chinese domestic and global markets. It is, in other words, the specific configurations of domestic-international positions of vulnerability in each market that are relevant. I think about vulnerability in a relational context.

The argument about vulnerability presented in this book can help us understand current policy debates in China. Given the fact that China is facing oligopolistic, coordinated markets in many areas of the global economy and is, itself, home to markets that are more often than not complex and fragmented, it can often find itself in a vulnerable position of market power. If so, at least two options are available. The first is to attempt to consolidate its domestic economy to match the high levels of global concentration and coordination. Indeed, the Chinese government has been encouraging domestic industrial consolidation and the creation of mechanisms to better coordinate international procurement behavior, notably in the iron ore and copper markets, where its domestic markets have been more fragmented. Second, China can try to disrupt consolidation and coordination among global firms. This fits the anti-monopoly narrative, directed at global firms, that has been prominent in China. It can also try to paliate positions of market vulnerability by devoting energy to diversification of supply, as we have seen China pursue with unequal success. It can also pursue this aim by consolidating market positions, via acquisitions abroad or investments home, as it has done in the copper mining and processing segments of the global supply chain, respectively. Attention to positions of market power can help frame China's struggle with established market stakeholders as a multifaceted and not necessarily always coherent or effective attempt to deal with the power of existing oligopolies while at the same time building up coordination capacity at the domestic level in an attempt to shift from a position of market vulnerability to a more advantageous position of market power.

## Market Fairness

The question of market fairness was not directly addressed in this book, but its findings suggest this is another area of promising research. From the moment we accept that there are no neutral global markets, but different market institutional systems with different power distributions, this opens the way for a different kind of discussion about global market design, resource security or the relationship between producers and consumers of natural resources.

Notions of fairness are key to understanding China's relation to the global economy. Positions of vulnerability between domestic and global market stakeholders in specific industries matter because they impart a sense of inequality and undermine trust. This is important since the conduct of economic activity depends on high trust levels. If market institutions are perceived as being unfair, or if market players perceive their position as one of vulnerability, then trust levels will be low and behavior is affected as a result. We have seen the increased securitization of global supply chains, and this is related of course to the perception of vulnerability experienced during the Covid pandemic. Exactly how perceptions of market vulnerability influence behavior should be further investigated.

China is keenly aware of global power asymmetries, as it is operating within global institutional market environments that it largely had not taken part in establishing. In a context in which global markets are home to high levels of industry concentration, fragmented Chinese stakeholders have expressed mistrust and frustration given the perceived mismatch between China's aggregate economic weight and its market power and resultant influence (or lack thereof) on global market institutions. Perceptions of vulnerability in certain areas can perhaps help explain the unequal tendency for China to invest in initiatives that stand outside established institutional pathways (the Asian Infrastructure Investment Bank comes to mind).

Chinese stakeholders have some soul-searching to do regarding what kind of global market institutions they want to encourage globally. In interviews, many Chinese stakeholders expressed dissatisfaction with global market institutions on the grounds that they are unfair. As a response, we have seen China's attempts to diversify sources of imports and to discourage further consolidation in existing markets. We have also seen China's attempts to increase domestic consolidation and relative market power. But when I probed my interviewees further, asking, "What does a fair global market arrangement ultimately look like, to you?," few expressed clear preferences, even for those who said that purely competitive global commodity markets are not desirable or even possible.

From the point of view of international stakeholders, who often scold China for not playing by market rules, some soul-searching is also warranted. The extractive resource industries operate under extraordinary levels of industry concentration, and this has created high barriers to entry and perceptions of market vulnerability for many emerging economies. Exhortations to "liberalize" or to "open up" ring false to many around the world, as they see global markets as noncompetitive, oligopolistic institutions controlled by powerful market stakeholders.

## Market Power

This book calls for bringing the study of power back into the study of global commodity markets. Ironically, this is where the international political economy literature started in the 1970s, following the oil shock and concerns about a wave of nationalization and cartelization of commodity production (Moran 1973; Bergsten 1974; Krasner 1974; Katzenstein 1977; Zacher 1987). Power never disappeared from commodity markets, of course, despite the waning of the era of producers' cartels. Chinese stakeholders are well aware of this fact as they emerged in the early 2000s to face high levels of concentration and established positions of power that reflected the winners of the past decades of global political economic history.

Most of the Chinese market stakeholders interviewed for this project conceived of markets as being the loci of intense power relations. The perception that relations of market power are a critical part of global commodity market institutions was much less commonly shared among market stakeholders in Anglo-Saxon liberal market economies when I conducted the first round of interviews in 2012. This had changed ten years later in 2022. China's emergence as dominant consumer and its disruptive impact on established global institutions has put issues of market power in sharper relief for market stakeholders in Western economies, yet they were there all along.

## The Return of Economic Nationalism

At the time of writing in 2023, we stand in the midst of a return of economic nationalism (Helleiner 2021), industrial policy, and state-directed resource management around the world, of a kind that hasn't been seen since perhaps the heyday of resource nationalism and production cartels in the 1960s and 1970s. Governments from the United States, to Japan, to Canada, to Europe have unveiled critical minerals strategies to ensure supply chain resilience and resource security, notably in the case of rare earths and other critical minerals necessary for the green shift (e.g., lithium and cobalt).

In some ways, we are witnessing the reversal of decades of dominant neoliberal market paradigms in government policymaking about natural resources. We have not yet seen the full impacts of this paradigmatic shift on actual global market institutions and liberalization trends in the natural resources sector. As such, over the coming years, it will be interesting to track the liberalization trends I observed to varying degrees and in various forms in the four markets under study in this book. There may be reversals, or there may be the emergence of new combinations of market and strategic coordination mechanisms. Here, this book's focus on coordination capacity and broader manifestations of market power on behalf of consumers and producers of natural resources around the world takes on even more relevance. For instance, this book's framework could be used to study the one area where China has had a definite market power advantage, in rare earths. The various efforts internationally to characterize rare earths procurement as a strategic matter, to give state organs more power over procurement matters, and to diversify sources of supply may lead to a situation where a position of Chinese market power evolves into a more evenly matched scenario, which is more likely to lead to conflictual or strategic bargaining dynamics.

Chinese stakeholders see challenges in the governance of global commodity markets today coming from two opposite directions—continued liberalization and financialization *and* the (re)emergence of economic nationalism. In the case of financialization, concerns include the fading away of decades-old stable pricing institutions, increased volatility, and increased systemic risk. In the case of rising economic nationalism, concerns include the wielding of market power by dominant producers, decoupling, and deepening lack of trust.

## Problematizing the Concept of "Open Markets"

Debates about the likely impact of China on the global economy, across liberal or realist theoretical proclivities, have tended to characterize the global markets that existed at the time of China's emergence as "open." To provide but two examples, Ikenberry argues that the United States, as the "center of the liberal international order . . . provided public goods of security protection, market openness, and sponsorship of rules and regulations" (Ikenberry 2009, 82), whereas Mearsheimer argues that "creating a liberal international order involved . . . creat[ing] an open and inclusive international economy that maximized free trade and fostered unfettered capital markets" (Mearsheimer 2019, 22).

Disagreements are situated around the likely impact of China's rise—to integrate or to disrupt global markets, rather than the original diagnostic of the state of global markets at the time of China's rise. The current debate has evolved into one that is dominated by those who see China as threatening open markets, faced increasingly by some who argue that the United States is also undermining global market openness.

As this book suggests, however, this is not a terribly satisfactory way to frame the debate. First, the argument that China's rise has lead to the undermining of openness is not the best way to describe the changes that have taken place, at least not in the cases studied here. To be sure, the argument that China has integrated into existing open market institutions is also unsatisfying. In both cases, the framing falls short because the markets China has been engaging with for the past decades were not best characterized as "open" to start with. The global iron ore market of the 2000s, when China rose to face it, was not best characterized as open, or "accessible, legitimate, and durable", to borrow a phrase from Ikenberry (2008). Many global markets function under very high levels of industry concentration and coordination. When China emerged as the number one consumer in most of the commodity markets reviewed here, the top four companies controlled more than 50 percent of exports. In the case of iron ore, compared to Japan at the time of its emergence, China faced a more consolidated global market, one that was also organized in meaningfully different ways. This situation meant China had less leeway than Japan had enjoyed in shaping its global market institutions.

Characterizing global market institutions as open does not do justice to the political economy of global markets. It obscures the power relations that were present among global market stakeholders prior to China's rise, power relations that Chinese stakeholders were painfully aware of and that they rose to disrupt, in a variety of fashions, both unintended and intended, over the past decades.

This book has made the case that we gain analytical leverage when we acknowledge that global markets vary along fundamental characteristics, both concurrently and over time. The cases in this book concerned specific market pricing institutions, but global markets vary along a wide variety of characteristics, from more micro level processes, such as individual patterns of behavior, to geographical distribution, coordination capacity, governance structures, power relations, and embeddedness levels (Massot 2021). China's emergence and transformation of established market institutional systems should prompt us to re-evaluate deep-seated assumptions about what global markets are and how they function.

We also need to do a much better job of theorizing about large states' preferences for (open) global economic institutions in today's context. China's rise raises some unique sets of questions in this regard. The two most broadly studied hegemonic transitions, the rise of the UK and of the United States, occurred against a backdrop of mercantilism (the UK in the nineteenth century), or economic nationalism (the United States in the interwar period), and both oversaw, for reasons that are debated in the literature, the subsequent liberalization of global economic institutions, although to extents and in fashions that I argue can be overstated. This led some of the most acute observers of the political economy of hegemony to argue that "large dominant states possess strong preferences for free and open international exchange, and, in turn, coerce, induce or persuade other states into opening their markets to foreign trade and investment" (Krasner 1976 and Gilpin 1977, in Lake 2009, 223).

China's case offers us the opposite scenario of an illiberal economy rising at a time where the global economy was arguably at the apex of a neoliberal globalization era, while decades on, we are experiencing a return of economic nationalism at the global level. The assumptions developed via the analysis of the behavior of hegemonic Anglo-Saxon liberal economies are not well adapted to the Chinese case. How should we theorize, then, about China's global economic preferences in this situation? The variation in behavior and outcomes within the same sector of the economy suggests that a focus either on factor endowments or on industry-level characteristics is insufficient, as Llewellyn Hugues argues in his study of oil market governance (Hughes 2014, 204). A promising area of research will be to better specify the conditions under which China's (or other dominant economies') market stakeholders develop preferences for open international exchange.

There is another aspect to the framing of global markets as open that China's rise is leading us to ponder. There are normative assumptions embedded in the notion of market openness, whether openness is seen to be "good" as a means toward better outcomes, or as an end in itself. But the inescapable persistence of unequal power relations in global markets that were long touted as open poses a moral problem. The important insight is that global markets are never fully open, neutral grounds—whether prior to or following China's emergence—and that power relations matter in our thinking about China and global markets. To think of global markets as open arenas that must be protected from China's behavior frames the issue in an unproductive way, and this can have deleterious effects as we try to imagine global market institutions that have to adjust to a range of rising economies, and not just to China. Thinking about global markets and global market change in their myriad institutional manifestations helps us see global market design as a legitimate political and normative terrain, as opposed to the technical issue it is sometimes portrayed to be. In other words, bringing back market power relationships to the fore raises questions of institutional and distributive fairness, which have to be considered if (more) open global markets are to be considered an attractive proposition.

*Appendix*

DATA

The data on which this book is based include statistics, documentary evidence, and qualitative data acquired from a large number of interviews. The statistics come from various sources, including the Chinese Customs Department; Chinese statistical yearbooks; Chinese and international industry associations; industry conference presentations by government officials, state-owned enterprise representatives, and private industry insiders; and data from consultant firms, media sources, and international organizations such as UNCTAD, the FAO, and UN Comtrade. A note needs to be made regarding the use of Chinese customs data. During one of my research stays in China, in 2012, I personally purchased Chinese customs statistics, on three out of the four commodities studied in this book, directly from the Information Office of the Chinese Customs Department. This was a fairly straightforward operation that yielded precious data on Chinese imports at the firm level. Later on, when I was putting the finishing touches to the manuscript and bringing the empirical narratives up to 2022, Loren Brandt graciously provided access to a complete dataset of Chinese Customs data from 2000 to 2015 for the four commodities covered in this book, which Torsten Jaccard helped put into shape. The data aggregate to UN Comtrade data and allowed me, among other things, to build a granular picture of the share of imports by the top Chinese importers in each market at the company level, from 2000 to 2015.

Documentary analysis included official Chinese policy documents as well as Chinese news, and industry and academic literature, which for the most part have been scarcely referenced, if at all, in previous English-language publications. The documentary analysis included a systematic review of official Chinese policy documents, legal notices, regulations, official press releases from Chinese SOEs, and speeches, with particular attention being paid to the history of the import licensing process in the iron ore and potash cases as well as to the history of the global pricing regimes from the perspective of Chinese stakeholders as cited in

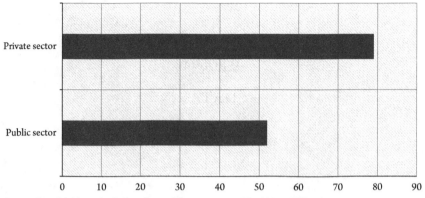

Source: Based on the author's data obtained from interviews. N = 131 workplaces.

*Figure A.1* Nature of ownership

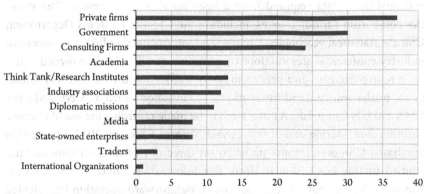

Source: Based on the author's data obtained from interviews. (N = 131).

*Figure A.2* Workplaces

the Chinese press. It also includes a review of the Chinese-language academic literature on the respective Chinese resource procurement policies more generally and on each market. Finally, the data utilized also include Chinese- and English-language business literature on the subject (corporate reports, strategic policy documents, and press releases).

A large amount of effort was placed on obtaining high-quality interviews with elite stakeholders of various backgrounds in each industry, both in China and around the world. I conducted a total of 169 interviews, of which 160 yielded relevant interview material, for a total of 141 interviewees and 131 workplaces (see Figures A.1, A.2, and Table A.1).

Interview data were collected during two main periods. The first interview collection period took place in China during three field research periods of two to four months each (for a total of over eight months) in 2011 and 2012. Part of this time was spent as a visiting scholar at the Chinese Academy of Social Sciences (World Institute of Economics and Politics) in Beijing and at Peking University's Center for International Political Economy. During that time, I attended multiple mining industry conferences, either as a participant or an invited speaker. Around 120 interviews were collected in that period. The second interview collection period took place during the summer of 2022 as I was completing revisions to the manuscript and endeavored to complete the various empirical narratives I had elaborated and to bring my various case studies up to date. Around 50 interviews were collected in that period, for a total of 169 interviews (of which 160 contained relevant material). In the second period, the majority of the interviews were conducted virtually, with interviewees from around the world. Both periods included a visit to the Toronto-based annual conference of the Prospectors and Developers Association of Canada (PDAC), in 2013 and 2022, where I was officially accredited either as a speaker or a member of the media. The PDAC holds an enormous industry conference year, which gathers together tens of thousands of mining industry participants from around the world.

Interviewees were selected using a mixture of diversity, (loose) quotas, and purposive and snowball sampling techniques (Tansey 2007). First, I established the landscape of key market stakeholders in each industry at the domestic and international levels and established a variety of organizational targets (e.g., a particular SOE, foreign company, or industry association). As my comprehension of the processes and sequencing at play deepened, I adjusted targets to include good coverage of key events. "The aim is not to draw a representative sample of a larger population of political actors that can be used as the basis to make generalizations about the full population, but to draw a sample that includes the most important political players who have participated in the political events being studied" (Tansey 2007, 765).

Using a variety of initial starting points that range from introductions, to the pursuit of a specific target via various strategies, to encounters at industry conferences, I worked to reach the identified organizational targets and cover important events in each market from a diversity of perspectives. While leveraging growing networks to deepen my knowledge of a particular sub-group's perspectives, I periodically reassessed the coverage and range of interviewees and adjusted further interview targets by either discriminating or guiding the referral process or by starting anew from a separate starting point. I worked to minimize selection bias while maximizing coverage, diversity, and relevance.

My interviews were semi-structured. In the first phase, most were in person. In the second phase, in 2022, most were conducted virtually or by email. In China, in-person interviews were conducted in Beijing, Shanghai, Nanning

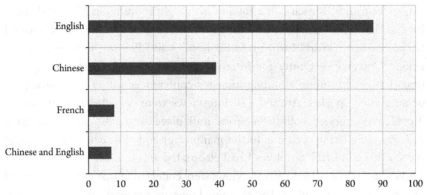

Source: Based on the author's data obtained from interviews. (N = 141 interviewees).

*Figure A.3* Language used in interviews

(Guangxi), Tianjin, and Nanjing. I also conducted interviews in Canada. Virtually I connected with interviewees from around the world, including China, Latin America, and Europe. All of my interviews were conducted, transcribed, and coded by myself, without the help of assistants. Interviews were always conducted in the interviewee's preferred language where possible, whether Mandarin Chinese, English, or French (see Figure A.3). I took great care in providing anonymity for my interviewees (very few were comfortable being identified). The interviews are numbered, and information about the interviewee is added in brackets in this format: (number, profession, and date).

*Table A.1* **Workplaces, by interview (N = 160 interviews)**

| Workplaces (non-exhaustive examples) | Number of Interviews |
|---|---|
| **Private firm** | 37 |
| - Chinese potash firm | |
| - Chinese petroleum firm | |
| - Chinese energy development firm | |
| - Junior Canadian mining firm | |
| - Junior Canadian potash firm | |
| - Junior Canadian uranium firm | |
| - Junior Australian potash firm | |
| - Large Canadian mining firm | |
| - Canadian law firm | |
| - Large global uranium firm | |
| - Large global iron ore firm | |
| - Large Japanese conglomerate | |
| **Consulting Firm** | 24 |
| - US consulting firms | |
| - Chinese iron ore consulting firm | |
| - Chinese mining consulting firm | |
| - International mining consulting firm | |
| **Trader** | 3 |
| **Government** | 30 |
| - Chinese ministry | |
| - Chinese central government agency | |
| - Canadian provincial government | |
| - Australian provincial government | |
| - Nigerian ministry | |
| **Industry Association** | 12 |
| - Chinese industry association | |
| - International industry association | |
| **Academia** | 13 |
| - Chinese university | |
| - Canadian university | |

(*continued*)

*Table A.1* **Continued**

| Workplaces (non-exhaustive examples) | Number of Interviews |
|---|---|
| **Media** | 8 |
| - Chinese media | |
| - Australian media | |
| - British Media | |
| **State-owned Enterprise** | 8 |
| - Chinese SOEs | |
| **Think Tank/Research Institute** | 13 |
| - Chinese research institute | |
| - Chinese think tank | |
| - Canadian research institute | |
| **Diplomatic mission** | 11 |
| - Brazil | |
| - Canada | |
| **International Organization** | 1 |
| - Development bank | |
| **Total: 131** | **Total: 160** |

# NOTES

*Chapter 1*

1. In this book, wherever possible I go beyond the notion of China as unitary actor to consider the multiple market stakeholders, state or otherwise, active in any commodity market. At times I do use "China" to point to the collective, state actors or otherwise. Thus, "China's impact abroad" really means the aggregate global impact of Chinese market stakeholders. However, the very fact that different market stakeholders have distinct positions of market power, distinct preferences, and distinct behavior is at the core of the framework developed in this book.
2. Potash levels of import dependence are calculated as the share of agricultural use, net of domestic production (FAO), and iron ore levels of import dependence are calculated as the share of imports on the sum of imports and domestic production (UNCTAD).
3. It must be said that this is bound to change with the end of the era of US-led hyperglobalization and the return of state capitalism around the world.
4. Looking at agricultural use data (share of global consumption), China's agricultural use of potash stood at 2 percent in 1985, 16 percent in 2000, and continued to increase to 28 percent of global agricultural use of potash in 2019. China started using more than 20 percent of global potash in 2002, at 21 percent.
5. As per John Stuart Mill, "[i]f an instance in which the phenomenon under investigation occurs, and an instance in which it does not occur, have every circumstance in common save one, that one occurring only in the former, the circumstance in which alone the two instances differ, is the effect, or the cause, or an indispensable part of the cause, of the phenomenon" (Mill 1868, 429). Mill explains that "The two instances which are to be compared with one another must be exactly similar, in all circumstances except the one which we are attempting to investigate.... And in the case of most phenomena we learn at once, from the commonest experience, that most of the coexistent phenomena of the universe may be either present or absent without affecting the given phenomenon, or, if present, are present indifferently when the phenomenon does not happen and when it does.... We choose a previous state of things with which we are well acquainted, so that no unforeseen alteration in that state is likely to pass unobserved, and into this we introduce, as rapidly as possible, the phenomenon which we wish to study" (Mill 1868, 430).
6. "The name [potash] comes from the ancient practice of obtaining potassium by leaching wood-ash in large iron pots" (Simmons 2011). Potassium (K) is found in nature, combined with other elements. The term "potash" is used to describe a variety of mineral compositions containing K (potassium), which are used as fertilizers (Searls 1994). Examples include potassium chloride (KCl), or muriate of potash (MOP), and potassium sulfate ($K_2SO_4$). Because of the variety of forms it can take, potash fertilizer is usually measured in terms of "its oxide, or $K_2O$ equivalent content" (Production and Use of Potassium 1998), although $K_2O$ is never found in this particular state in nature.
7. UN COMTRADE.

## Chapter 2

1. Mordecai Kurz (2017), for instance, measured "monopoly wealth" (levels above which profits or stock values are not purely chance events but rather reflective of monopoly power) at 82 percent of total stock-market value.
2. This section draws from the article: "The State of the Study of the Market in Political Economy: China's Rise Shines Light on Conceptual Shortcomings," *Competition & Change* 25, no. 5: 534–560, published by the author in 2021.
3. Exceptions to this are the early IPE of resources literature, which identified distinct dynamics across a variety of resource markets, as well as the literature on global value chains (GVCs) and global production networks (GPNs).
4. These include the Bloomberg Commodity Index, the Goldman Sachs Commodity Index, the Thomson Reuters/CoreCommodity CRB Index, and the Deutsche Bank Liquid Commodity Index. Among other commodities, the Bloomberg Commodity Index includes natural gas, Brent crude oil, corn, soybeans, wheat, sugar, cotton, copper, aluminum, zinc, nickel, gold, and silver.
5. The work of Llewelyn Hughes is also informative in this regard. In his book, Globalizing Oil (2014), he discusses the liberalization of oil market governance in France, Japan and the U.S., by tracking liberalization trends along ownership and trade openness variables at the national level. Here, I am interested in liberalization trends at the global level, in market institutions that sit outside of (or across various) national polities.
6. This section draws from the article: "Market Power and Marketisation: Japan and China's Impact on the Iron Ore Market, 50 Years Apart," *New Political Economy* 25, no. 4: 511–534, published by the author in 2020.
7. I thank Louis W. Pauly for his useful comments on this section.
8. On the rise of China as dominant resource consumer, see Economy and Levi (2014), Kong (2011), Zweig and Bi (2005), Garnaut and Song (2006), Song and Li (2009), Rosen and Houser (2007), Moran (2010), and Streifel (2006).
9. Van de Graaf and Colgan (2016) argue, in their review of the literature on global energy governance, that scholars have only recently rediscovered energy as a research endeavor and call the field "nascent," although it is currently "thriving."
10. To illustrate, a search in JSTOR for "potash" in "item title" for articles and books, across all disciplines, between 2000 and 2022, yields only one result that could be broadly conceived as belonging to the IPE of resources, and this covers an analysis of fertilizer demand in Pakistan (Quddus et al. 2008).

## Chapter 3

1. Krasner, for instance, listed the following variables as having an impact on the likelihood of firm collusion taking place: "price inelastic demand, high barriers to entry, high market concentration, shared experience among producers, lack of consumer resistance, ability to work with an extended time horizon, and shared values" (Krasner 1974, 72). Here, I am theorizing not about the likelihood of collusion but about preferences for competitive or strategic (negotiated) pricing regimes, which is different. There can be firm collusion in both types of pricing regimes. This is just an illustration of the kinds of variables that influence firm behavior at the global level.
2. See Susan Strange's definition of power: "Power is simply the ability of a person or group of persons so to affect outcomes that their preferences take precedence over the preferences of others" (Strange 1996, 17). Power is also conceived, as Baldwin and Dahl have suggested, as a matter of degree (Baldwin 1980; Dahl 1957).
3. I thank Herman Mark Schwartz for his comments.
4. I thank Loren Brandt for his comments to this effect.
5. 两个市场两种资源.
6. UN Comtrade data.
7. FAO data.

8. Indeed, as A. Iain Johnston pointed out to me, some realists have argued that China is a status quo power, and some liberals have argued that China is threatening the liberal international order.
9. Johnston's 2015 book *Social States: China in International Institutions, 1980–2000* also merits a mention here, for its important theorization of China's socialization into international security institutions, which could form the basis of an evaluation of variation across domains, although its focus is more on the presence of these socialization processes across institutions, and in the two decades prior to 2000 (Johnston 2015).
10. I thank A. Iain Johnston for his thoughtful comments on this section.
11. See Manjari Chatterjee Miller's *Why Nations Rise* for a discussion of *active* and *reticent* rising powers (Miller 2021).
12. I thank Kevin McMillan for suggesting this.
13. I thank Mark Salter for directing me to this literature.
14. But Weiss also argues that a strong state that allows such protests to occur will be perceived by foreign interlocutors as having more "resolve." Protest under weak or strong states may lead to different mechanisms, but the end result, if protests do occur, will probably lead to a less-compromising stance (2014, 38).
15. As Quek and Johnston have argued, the extent to which the Chinese regime is truly constrained by public opinion remains an open debate (Quek and Johnston 2018).
16. Here, it is worth pondering Baldwin's comment: "the possibility of unintended or undesired influence should be noted. . . . Concepts of power that allow for the possibility of unintended influence may be more useful to the student of dependency and autonomy than other power concepts" (Baldwin 1980, 499).
17. "Writing in 1976, Peter Katzenstein called for an end to the division between the study of international politics and domestic politics. A decade later, Stephan Haggard and Beth Simmons renewed the call. 'We suggest,' they wrote, 'a research program that views international [politics] not only as the outcome of relations among states, but of the interaction between domestic and international games and coalitions that span national boundaries'" (Bates 1997, 3).

## Chapter 4

1. Either small-scale enterprises (小型) or small mines (小矿).
2. One interviewee formulated the hypothesis that the high levels of industry fragmentation were, if not caused, at least deeply aggravated by the Great Leap Forward launched by Mao Zedong in the late 1950s (Interview 160, Former senior mining industry executive, 2022).
3. This followed the introduction, in 2004, of the Foreign Trade Law, where Article 15 stipulates that the Foreign Trade Department of the State Council can implement automatic import licenses in order to be able to monitor the country's import situation. At around the same time, in December 2004, the Chinese Ministry of Commerce and the General Administration of Customs issued a notice that introduced an automatic import license management system that was to be implemented on January 1, 2005 ("Provisional Procedures" 2005).
4. The three notices were titled "2010 Iron Ore Importing Enterprises Qualifying Standards and Application Process" [2010 年铁矿石进口企业资质标准及申报程序], "Regarding the Implementation of Regulations on Iron Ore Import Representatives" [关于进口铁矿石代理制实施细则], and "Imported Iron Ore Contract Information Reporting, Registration, and Flow Registration Guidelines" [进口铁矿石合同信息上报登记及其流向登记备案规定] (Li 2010), author's translation
5. Original text: 由于具备进口铁矿石资质的企业固定，不仅没有达到中钢协曾推行铁矿石代理制的目标，反而催生了"倒卖资质"的现象.
6. The Stern Hu affair, in which a dual citizen from Australia and China and a Rio Tinto employee who was convicted for bribery in China, in 2010, were directly linked to the domestic difficulties surrounding the iron ore import license system. At the time, Chinese companies, including Sinochem and China National Building Materials Group, along with twenty others,

were exposed in the Rio Tinto bribery scandal. As discussed in the Chinese media, mostly private Chinese companies were suspected of conspiring with Rio Tinto employees and licensed Chinese companies to import iron ore (in exchange for a bribe) and then reselling it on the Chinese market for a large profit (Xie 2011).
7. Original text: 规范铁矿石市场秩序联合会议.
8. Original text: 进口铁矿石联合办公室.
9. Original text: 打击炒矿行为.
10. BHP Billiton, Vale, Rio Tinto, and Fortescue.
11. A price and energy reporting company headquartered in London but founded in the United States over 100 years ago, which grew over the years from a focus on the oil market to encompass commodities such as iron ore. The platform provides price information on a range of physical commodities including, famously, oil, but also coal, natural gas, and metals. Via its own networks, it compiles as broad a range as possible of offers and trades on commodities to generate an industry benchmark price every day in the various commodities it monitors.
12. After failing to offer a strong response to the Japanese negotiating position in the 1960s, the Australian government had developed a stronger position by the early 1970s. As a result, in the mid-1970s, Australian producers were able to extract price increases from the Japanese. This shows the emergence of bargaining patterns as coordination improved on the producers' side. However, Japan followed suit with government-supported proactive foreign investment policies regarding global iron ore projects, especially in Brazil, and was able to maintain its dominant position vis-à-vis the Australian producers (Hurst 2015b).
13. CRVD (Companhia Vale do Rio Doce) at the time.
14. Rodrik continues, "This has on occasion elicited complaints that Japan was deliberately attempting to maintain excess supply in the iron ore market by financing more new capacity than was warranted by the incremental growth in demand. These complaints appear not to have much validity. The total volume of Japanese finance was quite limited and, besides, until the early 1970s Japanese steel mills generally kept to the upper ceilings of contract volumes from mines they had helped finance" (Rodrik 1982, 551).

## Chapter 5

1. In 1995, the top four exporters of potash accounted for 63 percent of global exports, and in 2000 the three largest producers, BHP Billiton, Rio Tinto, and Vale, controlled almost 70 percent of the world's exports (see Table 2.1, Chapter 2).
2. Potash deposits are salt deposits resulting from the evaporation of salt water, a process sometimes millions of years old. There are three forms of potash deposits. The first and most common one is found in "underground bedded deposits" (Better Crops 1998). In this case, potash is mined from deposits found most often hundreds of meters below ground (this is the case in North America, including in the famous Williston Basin, an ancient bed of mineral salts). The second method is solution mining, in which potash is still extracted from underground deposits, but instead of building mine shafts and sending machinery underground, heated water solutions are injected deep into the deposits and potassium is then extracted from the solution, which is brought to the surface, mostly through the use of evaporation ponds. Solution mining is also used in North America. Underground potash mining accounts for 90 percent of global KCl capacity (Ericsson et al. 2012). The third method of harvesting potash is through the surface harvesting of marine evaporates in salt lakes such as the Dead Sea. Chinese potash mining mainly takes this form, with the main deposit located in Qinghai Province's Qarhan Salt Lake.
3. "Manure and glauconite are low-potassium-content sources that can be profitably transported only short distances to the crop fields" (Kostick 2007).
4. The Chinese Ministry of Land and Resources put the number at 81 percent in 2012.
5. These projections will need to be adjusted following Russia's invasion of Ukraine, but they are included here to highlight the continued global importance of the potash deposits in Russia, Belarus, and Canada, compared to the rest of the world.
6. Feng Mingwei, Sinochem's deputy general manager, said, in 2011, that "China's agricultural department recommended a ratio of nitrogen, phosphorus and potassium fertilizer of

1: 0.4: 0.3. By this calculation, the actual annual demand for potash should be more than 20 million tonnes. Due to the rising international potash prices, however, China's domestic demand is suppressed" (Li 2011). To some extent, farmers can decide to reduce the amount of fertilizer they use in a given year. It is still possible to grow crops without an optimal level of potash application; however, crop yield, strength, and quality will be affected.
7. 中国农业生产资料集团公司.
8. 中国供销集团有限公司.
9. China had imported potash from Canada before then, as the US Potash Annual Mineral Yearbook from 1980 confirms. "In 1980, China released official potash production figures for the first time in 20 years. Actual production is nearly an order of magnitude smaller than past estimated figures.... Canpotex Ltd. of Canada signed an agreement to export to China at least 650,000 tons per year for 3 years" (Searls 1980).
10. 中国-阿拉伯化肥有限公司.
11. The China National Offshore Oil Corporation (CNOOC) became a major shareholder of Sino-Agri in 2008.
12. 中国化工进出口总公司.
13. In October 2006, CNOOC acquired CNCCC to deepen its competitiveness in the chemical industry, especially in fertilizers. At the same time, it also acquired CNCCC's import license.
14. Article 15 stipulates that the Foreign Trade Department of the State Council can implement automatic import licenses so it can monitor the country's import situation.
15. 山东鲁西化工股份有限公司.
16. 辽宁西洋特肥股份有限公司.
17. 山东省鲁北企业集团总公司.
18. 湖北洋丰股份有限公司.
19. 中国石油国际事业有限公司.
20. A group of companies formerly under Heilongjiang Agricultural Production Company, Suifenhe Longsheng Economic and Trade Co., was the fifth largest importer of potash in the country and ranked first among importers of potash by land, in 2014, according to official Chinese customs data.
21. See Article 42 of the Foreign Trade Law of the People's Republic of China, which was implemented on July 1, 1994 (*Prospect of China's Potash Fertilizer Import Qualification Reform* 2015).
22. 边贸钾肥进口协调委员会.
23. 突破钾资源垄断，保护农民利益.
24. Original: "一个是对国外资源的垄断，同时对国内销售整体上的垄断，包括价位，他拿着资源了，他能左右价位，造成了巨额的垄断利润，给这些利益集团" (Author's translation).
25. 关于完善钾肥价格管理政策的通知.
26. 严肃查处.
27. Many thanks to Loren Brandt, from the University of Toronto, for graciously sharing his dataset of trade transactions data collected by the Customs Administration of China. Many thanks also go to Torsten Jaccard, for his help. These data aggregate to UN Comtrade data.
28. In this case, small groups are cross-cutting committees of relevant political, bureaucratic, and SOE staff, which serve as a connecting organ between the Party and key stakeholders. They are absent from official organizational charts and often deal with sensitive issues. One Chinese government official explained that "when BHP tried to buy Potash Corp. in 2010, there was a special meeting in Beijing, a small group (小组), an ad-hoc meeting group was created for the occasion" (Interview 102, Representative of a foreign enterprise in China, 2012).
29. One industry insider confirmed that although it is true that "Sinofert is the single negotiator with Canpotex, [both] Sino-Fert and Sino-Agri can import from BPC" (Interview 99, Senior industry consultant, 2012).
30. Original: 钾肥进口价格联合谈判机制.
31. Original: 中国进口钾肥联合谈判小组. See discussion below.
32. "中化、中农...认为集中谈判有助于增加凝聚力，一旦分散可能被各个击破，进口价格将会更高" (Author's translation).

33. It is likely that, after taking account of any discounts and other special terms, the two countries will end up paying similar prices for their MOP imports (Interview 174, Retired senior fertilizer industry analyst, 2022).
34. More on the small group below.
35. The railway trade is excluded here, as it is considered separate from the seaborne trade and does not have price-setting weight.
36. The mention of large potash consumers is likely a reference to the fact that India was waiting for the outcome, rather than collaborating with China per se.
37. "Canpotex Limited (Canpotex) has entered into a new three-year Memorandum of Understanding (MOU) with Sinochem Fertilizer Macao Commercial Offshore Ltd. (Sinofert) to supply a minimum of 1.9 million metric tons of red standard-grade potash during the term of the MOU.... Pricing will be negotiated every six months (January to June and July to December), based on market conditions" (Canpotex Reaches Agreement with Sinofert 2015).
38. Some of the only Canadian interest groups to support the takeover were Canadian farm organizations (Warnock 2011), which argued it would bring the price of fertilizer down, since BHP had publicly stated it would seek to increase production.

## Chapter 6

1. Formerly the China Power Investment Corporation.
2. Other companies were allowed to own above 25 percent of equity in such projects only after eight years of experience being minority partners below 25 percent (*Nuclear Power in China* 2022).
3. Another interviewee explained that there is an industry association in the nuclear industry but that it does not have a lot of power. It acts more like a consultancy company (Interview 67, Chinese central state agency researcher, 2012).
4. The Rossing mine produced 2,444 tonnes of uranium in 2021, or 5 percent of global uranium production ("World Uranium Mining Production" 2019).
5. There are roughly four types of copper raw materials: copper ores and concentrates, copper anodes (99 percent copper, a smaller share of the global market) and refined copper, or copper cathodes (99.9 percent copper), and scrap copper. In this chapter, we mainly use data for copper ores and concentrates (HS 2603) as well as some data for refined copper (HS 7403).
6. In 1967, four major copper exporters, Zaire (now the Democratic Republic of Congo), Zambia, Chile, and Peru, had attempted to form a cartel, the Intergovernmental Council of Copper Exporting States (CIPEC) (Krasner 1974). In 1969, CIPEC briefly reached an agreement to support declining prices, but it mostly failed to coordinate effectively and was eventually disbanded. Krasner explains that the member states attempted to agree on open market purchases and to target prices, but lack of trust and enforcement mechanisms as well as ideological differences made it difficult to surmount collective actions problems (Krasner 1974).
7. HS code 2603 for copper ores and concentrates and HS 7403 for refined copper, author's calculations.

# REFERENCES

203 F.3d 1028 (8th Cir. 2000). 2000. United States Court of Appeals for the Eighth Circuit, February 17. Accessed May 14, 2015. https://law.resource.org/pub/us/case/reporter/F3/203/203.F3d.1028.97-1330.html.

"About Us." Yellow Cake PLC. Accessed November 27, 2023. https://www.yellowcakeplc.com/about/.

"About Zhongken, Company Overview." 2019. China Agricultural Reclamation Group Co. (中国农垦). Accessed October 25, 2022. https://csfa.cnadc.com.cn/gsgk/10612.jhtml.

Ahmed, Ishtiyaque, and Shantanu Rai. "India's Static Red Treasure, It's Time to Make It Dynamic." National Portal of India. Accessed November 6, 2022. https://www.niti.gov.in/indias-static-red-treasure-its-time-make-it-dynamic.

Alden, Chris, and Martyn Davies. 2006. "A Profile of the Operations of Chinese Multinationals in Africa." *South African Journal of International Affairs* 13, no. 1: 83–96.

Al-Moneef, Majed. 1998. Vertical Integration Strategies of the National Oil Companies. *The Developing Economies* (June):203-222.

Andrews-speed, Philip, et al. 2004. "The Strategic Implications of China's Energy Needs." *The Adelphi Papers* 42, no. 346: 71–97.

Annual Report 2018: Nurturing China's Agriculture Sector. 2018. Sinofert Holdings Ltd. http://www.sinofert.com/Portals/54/Uploads/Files/2019/7-25/636996719049523759.pdf.

*Annual Report 2020: Nurturing China's Agriculture Sector.* 2020. Sinofert Holdings Ltd. Accessed August 31, 2022. https://www1.hkexnews.hk/listedco/listconews/sehk/2021/0416/2021041600321.pdf.

Asariotis, Regina, et al. 2011. *Review of Maritime Transport*. New York: UNCTAD. http://unctad.org/en/docs/rmt2011_en.pdf.

Baldwin, David A. 1980. "Interdependence and Power: A Conceptual Analysis." *International Organization* 34, no. 4: 471–506.

Baldwin, David A. 2020. *Economic Statecraft*. New ed. Princeton, NJ: Princeton University Press.

Banks, Ferdinand E. 1979. "The 'New' Economics of Iron and Steel." *Resources Policy* 16, no. 2: 95–103.

Bao, Ronghua [鲍荣华], et al. 2010. "Distribution of Global Potash Resources and Necessary Chinese Strategic Response [世界钾盐资源分配态势及我们的应对争略]." *Land and Resources Information* [国土资源情报] no. 8: 44–47.

"Baosteel, Vale Agree on 2008 Iron Ore Benchmark Price." 2008. Xinhua News Agency, February 23.

Barndon, Karma. 2016. "A Pilbara History." *Australia's Mining Monthly*. Accessed August 2, 2017. http://www.miningmonthly.com/insight/50-years-of-iron-ore-in-the-pilbara/a-pilbara-history/.

Basov, Vladimir. 2013. Top 10 copper companies in 2012. *Mining.com*. Accessed November 24, 2022, https://www.mining.com/top-10-copper-companies-in-2012-85961/

Bates, Robert H. 1997. *Open-Economy Politics: The Political Economy of the World Coffee Trade*. Princeton, NJ: Princeton University Press.

Baumgertner, Vladislav. 2013. "Uralkali Board Meeting Decisions," July 30. Accessed May 14, 2015. http://www.uralkali.com/press_center/company_news/item300713/.

Bergsten, C. Fred. 1974. "The Threat Is Real." *Foreign Policy* 14 (Spring): 84–90.

Bergsten, C. Fred, et al. 2008. *China's Rise: Challenges and Opportunities*. Washington, DC: Peterson Institute for International Economics, Center for Strategic and International Studies.

Best, Jacqueline. 2004. "Hollowing Out Keynesian Norms: How the Search for a Technical Fix Undermined the Bretton Woods Regime." *Review of International Studies* 30, no. 3: 383–404.

Bi, William. 2012. "Cameco Seeing 'Strong' Growth in China, Chief Executive Says." Bloomberg, February 9. Accessed March 29, 2015. http://www.bloomberg.com/news/2012-02-09/cameco-seeing-strong-growth-in-china-chief-executive-says.html.

Blanchard, Jean-Marc F. 2011. "Chinese MNCs as China's New Long March: A Review and Critique of the Western Literature." *Journal of Chinese Political Science* 16, no. 1: 91–108.

Blas, Javier. 2010. "Annual Iron Ore Contract System Collapses." *Financial Times*, March 30. Accessed October 11, 2022. https://www.ft.com/content/e8a78a74-3c21-11df-b40c-00144feabdc0.

Blas, Javier. 2011. "Quarterly Pricing Model Buckles under Spot Pressure." *Financial Times*, October 25. Accessed May 14, 2015. http://www.ft.com/intl/cms/s/0/2c49991e-ff1e-11e0-9b2f-00144feabdc0.html#axzz1c2C9vZET.

Blas, Javier, and Peter Smith. 2010. "Steel Prices Set to Soar after Iron Ore Deal." *Financial Times*, March 30. https://www.ft.com/content/d15d7758-3bad-11df-a4c0-00144feabdc0.

Boey, Augustin. 2012. "Nuclear Power and China's Energy Future: Limited Options." *Asia-Pacific Journal* 10, no. 9: 1–10.

Boliden Annual Report. 2002. Upplands Väsby, Sweden. http://investors.boliden.com/files/press/boliden/Boliden_Annualreport2002_en.pdf

Brandt, Loren, et al. 2022. "Ownership and Productivity in Vertically-Integrated Firms: Evidence from the Chinese Steel Industry." *Review of Economic and Statistics* 104, no. 1: 101–115.

Brantley, F. E. 1966. "Iron Ore." In *Minerals yearbook 1965: Metals and minerals (except fuels)*. Washington D.C.: USGS (*United States Geological Survey*), United States Department of the Interior, 475–507.

Breaking New Ground: Mining, Minerals and Sustainable Development. 2002. International Institute for Environment and Development (IIED): London. https://www.iied.org/sites/default/files/pdfs/migrate/9084IIED.pdf

Bremmer, Ian. 2010. *The End of the Free Market: Who Wins the War between States and Corporations*. New York: Portfolio.

Bunker, Stephen G., and Paul S. Ciccantell. 2007. *East Asia and the Global Economy: Japan's Ascent, with Implications for China's Future*. Baltimore: Johns Hopkins University Press.

Büthe, Tim. 2014. "Commitments across Borders: The Role of Institutions." The UBC Political Science Department's Distinguished Speaker Series, conference paper, Vancouver, Canada, April 16.

Buzan, Barry, and Michael Cox. 2013. "China and the US: Comparable Cases of 'Peaceful Rise'?" *Chinese Journal of International Politics* 6: 109–132.

Cai, Muyuan. 2011. "Fertilizer Costs Threaten China's Food Security." *China Daily*, July 25. Accessed May 14, 2015. http://www.chinadaily.com.cn/bizchina/2011-07/25/content_1 2979049.htm?utm_source=twitterfeed&utm_medium=twitter.

Calder, Kent E. 1996. "Asia's Empty Tank." *Foreign Affairs* 75, no. 2: 55–69.

Cang, Alfred. 2022. "How and Why China Is Centralizing Its Billion-Ton Iron Ore Trade." Bloomberg, July 24. https://www.bloomberg.com/news/articles/2022-07-25/china-wants-to-rewire-its-billlion-ton-iron-ore-trade-quicktake.

"Canpotex and Sinofert Sign New MOU." 2010. Canpotex, October 20. Accessed May 14, 2015. http://www.potashcorp.com/news/1016/.

"Canpotex Reaches Agreement with Sinofert." 2015. Canpotex, January 12. Accessed November 26, 2022. https://www.canpotex.com/news/canpotex-reaches-agreement-sinofert.

Cao, Kaihu [曹开虎]. 2009. "China's Iron Ore Import Chaos Traced Back to the Import Licences for Starving Small Steel Mills [中国铁矿石进口乱局溯源 进口许可为饿死小钢厂]." Sohu.com. Accessed November 26, 2022. http://news.sohu.com/20090717/n265275360.shtml.

Carr, Edward Hallet. 1939. *The Twenty Years' Crisis, 1919–1939*. New York: Harper & Row.

Chang, Ha-Joon. 2002. *Kicking Away the Ladder: Development Strategy in Historical Perspective*. London: Anthem Press.

Chen, Danjiang [陈丹江]. 2013. "Looking Forward to Find the Path towards the Missing Third of the Global Potash Market, but the Road Is Long [期待三分天下有其一海外找钾路漫漫]." *China Chemical News* [中国化工报], November 21. Accessed May 14, 2015. http://www.ccin.com.cn/ccin/6298/6301/index.shtml.

Chin, Gregory T. 2007. "Between Outside-in and Inside-out: The Internationalization of the Chinese State." In *China's Reforms and International Political Economy*, edited by D. Zweig et al. New York: Routledge. 177–192.

"China: Lessons Not Learned in Iron-Ore Talks." 2009. Stratfor Analysis, December 28. Accessed November 2, 2011. http://search.ebscohost.com/login.aspx?direct=true&db=bth&AN=47454561&site=ehost-live.

"China—Measures Related to the Exportation of Various Raw Materials." 2010. First Written Submission of the United States of America to the WTO. https://www.worldtradelaw.net/document.php?id=wtodisputesubmissions/us/DS394_USFirstWrittenSubmission.pdf&mode=download#page=24.

"China Blocks Large Ore Carriers from Ports." 2012. Stratfor, February 3. Accessed March 1, 2012. http://www.stratfor.com/analysis/china-blocks-large-ore-carriers-ports.

"China CBMX Transfers Iron Ore Trading Platform Ownership to JV of Mill, Miners, Traders." 2014. S&P Global. Accessed June 19, 2023. https://www.spglobal.com/commodityinsights/en/market-insights/latest-news/metals/090314-china-cbmx-transfers-iron-ore-trading-platform-ownership-to-jv-of-mill-miners-traders.

"China Committed to Global Nuclear Security: Official." 2014. *Xinhua*, March 25. http://www.china.org.cn/world/Off_the_Wire/2014-03/26/content_31907233.htm.

"China Concludes Potash Price Negotiations for the First Half of 2013 [2013年上半年中国钾肥进口协议价格确定]." 2013. CNAMPGC Holding Limited Corporation (Sino-Agri Group).

"China General Nuclear Power Corporation (CGN)." 2019. *China Daily*. Accessed November 4, 2022. https://govt.chinadaily.com.cn/s/201904/23/WS5cbe84d0498e079e6801ec16/china-general-nuclear-power-corporation-cgn.html.

"China Iron and Steel Association Plans Domestic Iron Ore Pricing Mechanism, Resists Platts Pricing Index [中钢协谋划国内铁矿石定价机制 普氏指数遭抵制]." 2013. China.com [中国网], March 22. http://finance.china.com.cn/industry/energy/gtys/20130322/1343989.shtml.

"China Leading Cu Smelters Cut Price Floor for 1Q TC/RCs." 2020. Argus Media, December 24. Accessed November 29, 2022. https://www.argusmedia.com/es/news/2172094-china-leading-cu-smelters-cut-price-floor-for-1q-tcrcs?amp=1.

*China Mining Yearbook 2002* [中国矿业年鉴]. 2003. Edited by China Mining Yearbook Editorial Department. Beijing: Seismological Press [地震出版社].

*China Mining Yearbook 2007* [中国矿业年鉴]. 2008. Edited by China Mining Yearbook Editorial Department. Beijing: Seismological Press [地震出版社].

*China Mining Yearbook 2008* [中国矿业年鉴]. 2009. Edited by China Mining Yearbook Editorial Department. Beijing: Seismological Press [地震出版社].

*China Mining Yearbook 2010* [中国矿业年鉴]. 2011. Edited by China Mining Yearbook Editorial Department. Beijing: Seismological Press [地震出版社].

*China Mining Yearbook 2011* [中国矿业年鉴]. 2012. Edited by China Mining Yearbook Editorial Department. Beijing: Seismological Press [地震出版社].

*China Mining Yearbook 2016–2017* [中国矿业年鉴]. 2019. Edited by China Mining Yearbook Editorial Department. Beijing: Seismological Press [地震出版社].

"China National Nuclear Corporation (CNNC)." 2019. *China Daily*. Accessed November 4, 2022. https://govt.chinadaily.com.cn/a/201904/19/WS5cb99801498e079e6801e9c5.html.

*China Steel Yearbook 2001* [钢铁工业年鉴]. 2002. Edited by: China Steel Yearbook Editorial Board. Beijing: Seismological Press [地震出版社].

*China Steel Yearbook 2002* [钢铁工业年鉴]. 2003. Edited by: China Steel Yearbook Editorial Board. Beijing: Seismological Press [地震出版社].

*China Steel Yearbook 2004* [钢铁工业年鉴]. 2005. Edited by: China Steel Yearbook Editorial Board. Beijing: Seismological Press [地震出版社].

*China Steel Yearbook 2005* [钢铁工业年鉴]. 2006. Edited by: China Steel Yearbook Editorial Board. Beijing: Seismological Press [地震出版社].

*China Steel Yearbook 2006* [钢铁工业年鉴]. 2007. Edited by: China Steel Yearbook Editorial Board. Beijing: Seismological Press [地震出版社].

*China Steel Yearbook 2008* [钢铁工业年鉴]. 2009. Edited by: China Steel Yearbook Editorial Board. Beijing: Seismological Press [地震出版社].

*China Steel Yearbook 2010* [钢铁工业年鉴]. 2011. Edited by: China Steel Yearbook Editorial Board. Beijing: Seismological Press [地震出版社].

*China Steel Yearbook 2011* [钢铁工业年鉴]. 2012. Edited by: China Steel Yearbook Editorial Board. Beijing: Seismological Press [地震出版社].

"China to Release Another 150,000t of Base Metal Stocks." 2021. Argus Media, September 28. Accessed November 1, 2022. https://www.argusmedia.com/en/news/2258198-china-to-release-another-150000t-of-base-metal-stocks.

"China's Minmetals, Jinchuan Eye Copper Concentrate Blending Plant in Guangxi—Sources." 2020. Reuters, August 10. Accessed December 7, 2022. https://www.reuters.com/article/us-china-copper-blending-idUSKCN25706D.

"China's Top Copper Smelters Appoint New Leader—Sources." 2022. *Financial Post*, January 4. Accessed November 29, 2022. https://financialpost.com/pmn/business-pmn/chinas-top-copper-smelters-appoint-new-leader-sources.

"Chinese Copper Smelters Raise TC/RCs for 2022 Term Contracts in Benchmark Deal." 2021. S&P Global, December 16. Accessed June 22, 2022. https://www.spglobal.com/commodityinsights/en/market-insights/latest-news/metals/121621-chinese-copper-smelters-raise-tcrcs-for-2022-term-contracts-in-benchmark-deal.

"Chinese Dependence on Foreign Iron Ore: A Special Report." 2011. Stratfor Analysis, March 3. Accessed November 9, 2011. http://www.stratfor.com/memberships/186619/analysis/20110302-chinese-dependence-foreign-iron-ore-special-report#ixzz1SDXkWfJh.

Chinese potash import qualification reform outlook [中国钾肥进口资质改革展望]. 2015. *China Fertilizer Network/Sina.com*, July 4. Accessed August 1, 2019, news.sina.com.cn/c/2008-08-07/101716078337.shtml

Cienski, Jan, and Sergei Kuznetsov. 2013. "Uralkali's Russian chief arrested in Belarus." *Financial Times*, August 26.

Colgan, Jeff. 2021. *Partial Hegemony: Oil Politics and International Order*. Oxford: Oxford University Press.

Colgan, Jeff D., et al. 2012. "Punctuated Equilibrium in the Energy Regime Complex." *Review of International Organizations* 7: 117–143.

Commodity Prices and "Pink Sheet" Data. In *The World Bank* [Data set]. https://www.worldbank.org/en/research/commodity-markets

"Company Profile." 2015. Sino-Agri Group. Accessed April 13, 2015. http://www.sino-agri.com/intro.php?cid=3.

Copeland, Dale C. 2015. *Economic Interdependence and War*. Princeton, NJ: Princeton University Press.

"The Copper Market, Treatment and Refining Charges." 2021. *Metso*. Accessed June 22, 2022. https://www.mogroup.com/insights/blog/mining-and-metals/the-copper-market-treatment-and-refining-charges/.

"CSPT Considers Taking In New Members." 2019. *SMM News*. Accessed June 22, 2022. https://news.metal.com/newscontent/100974074/cspt-considers-taking-in-new-members/.

"The Country Cannot Be Short of Potassium for One Day. How Can the Potash Industry Survive and How to 'Go Out' in the Future? [国不可以一日缺"钾"，钾肥行业如何活下去，如何走出未来？]." 2017. *China Agricultural Media* [中国农资传媒]. Accessed August 31, 2022. https://www.sohu.com/a/197746253_676151.

Craze, Matthew, and Jeb Blount. 2006. "CRVD, Baosteel Agree to Benchmark Iron-Ore Price Rise." Bloomberg, December 21. Accessed May 14, 2015. http://www.bloomberg.com/apps/news?pid=newsarchive&sid=aFjPvh.7fFis.

Cuddington, John T., and Daniel Jerrett. 2008. "Super Cycles in Real Metals Prices?" *IMF Staff Papers* 55, no. 4: 541–565.

Dahl, Robert A. 1957. "The Concept of Power." *Behavioral Science* 2, no. 3: 201–215.

Dai, Suping, et al. 2018. "Focus: Chinese Steelmakers Get Foreign Miners' Agreement to Introduce Domestic Iron Ore Price Index in 2018 Contracts [焦点：中国钢厂获外资矿商同意在2018年合约中引入国内铁矿石价格指数]." Reuters (Chinese version), January 26. Accessed October 11, 2022. https://www.reuters.com/article/china-steelmills-iron-ore-pricing-0125-t-idCNKBS1FF0I0.

de Graaff, Nana, and Bastiaan van Apeldoorn. 2017. "US Elite Power and the Rise of 'Statist' Chinese Elites in Global Markets." *International Politics* 54, no. 3: 338–355.

Ding, Qingfen, and Yiyu Liu. 2012. "Nation Plans to Import More Uranium." *China Daily*, March 13. Accessed September 14, 2012. http://www.chinadaily.com.cn/bizchina/2012-03/13/content_14820002.htm.

Dore, Ronald, and Susan Berger, eds. 1996. *National Diversity and Global Capitalism*. Ithaca, NY: Cornell University Press.

Dreher, Axel, et al. 2022. *Banking on Beijing: The Aims and Impacts of China's Overseas Development Program*. Cambridge: Cambridge University Press.

Dubash, Navroz K., and Ann Florini. 2011. "Mapping Global Energy Governance." *Global Policy* 2 (September): 6–18.

Duina, Francesco. 2011. *Institutions and the Economy*. Cambridge: Polity Press.

Eaton, Sarah. 2015. *The Advance of the State in Contemporary China: State-Market Relations in the Reform Era*. Cambridge: Cambridge University Press.

Ebner, Alexander, and Nikolaus Beck. 2008. *The Institutions of the Market: Organizations, Social Systems, and Governance*. Oxford: Oxford University Press.

Economy, Elizabeth. 2010. "The Game Changer: Coping with China's Foreign Policy Revolution." *Foreign Affairs* 89, no. 6: 142–152.

Economy, Elizabeth, and Michael Levi. 2014. *By All Means Necessary: How China's Resource Quest Is Changing the World*. Oxford: Oxford University Press.

Ellis, Evan. 2009. "Strategic Implications of Chinese Aid and Investment in Latin America." *China Brief* 9, no. 20: 9–12.

Epstein, Gerald A. 2005. *Financialization and the World Economy*. Cheltenham: Edward Elgar.

Ericsson, Magnus. 2002. "Mining M&A Reaches Record Levels in 2001." *Minerals & Energy* 17, no. 1: 19–26.

Ericsson, Magnus. 2003. "Squeeze for Iron Ore?" *Metal Bulletin Monthly*, no. 392: 10–11.

Ericsson, Magnus. 2004. Iron ore breaks new records. *Mining Journal* (July 2):18–20.

Ericsson, Magnus et al. 2012. "Phosphate and potash as examples for non-metallic raw material markets." Polinares (EU Policy on Natural Resources) Working paper 21. 1–9. Accessed October 31, 2022. http://pratclif.com/2015/mines-ressources/polinares/chapter9.pdf

# REFERENCES

Ericsson, Magnus, et al. 2011. "Iron Ore Review: High Prices and Tight Markets to Continue Until 2013?" *World of Mining Professionals* 9 (November).

Ericsson, Magnus. 2012. "Mining Industry Corporate Actors Analysis." Polinares (EU Policy on Natural Resources) Working Paper 16. Accessed October 31, 2022. https://goxi.org/sites/default/files/2019-06/Mining%20industry%20corporate%20actors%20analysis.pdf.

Esping-Andersen, Gøsta. 1990. *The Three Worlds of Welfare Capitalism*. Princeton, NJ: Princeton University Press.

*EU natural uranium price: ESA indices since 1980*. 2020. Euratom Supply Agency [Data set]. Accessed March 25, 2020. https://euratom-supply.ec.europa.eu/eu-natural-uranium-price-esa-indices-1980_en

"EXCLUSIVE: China's Customs Lobby Smelters to Impose Lower Arsenic Threshold on Copper Conc Imports." 2019. Fast Markets, August 2. Accessed December 7, 2022. https://www.fastmarkets.com/insights/exclusive-chinas-customs-lobby-smelters-to-impose-lower-arsenic-threshold-on-copper-conc-imports.

Fabi, Randy, and Ruby Lian. 2011. "Analysis: Damaged Ship Threatens to Sink Vale's China Hopes." Reuters, December 8. Accessed May 14, 2015. https://www.reuters.com/article/us-shipping-vale-china/analysis-damaged-ship-threatens-to-sink-vales-china-hopes-idUSTRE7B70LH20111208.

"Factbox: Facts about the Crop Nutrient Potash." 2010. Reuters. Accessed August 22, 2022. https://www.reuters.com/article/cbusiness-us-potashcorp-nutrient-idCATRE67G2UI20100817.

Facts and Figures. In *World Nuclear Association* [Data set]. https://world-nuclear.org/information-library/facts-and-figures.aspx

Fedorinova, Yuliya, and Jason Corcoran. 2013. "China Fund, VTB Capital Invest in Kerimov's Uralkali." Bloomberg, November 9. Accessed May 14, 2015. http://www.bloomberg.com/news/2012-11-09/kerimov-said-seeking-china-s-cic-to-invest-in-uralkali.html.

Fedorinova, Yuliya, and Michelle Yun. 2014. "Uralkali Agrees to 24% Cut in Potash Price for China." Bloomberg, January 21. Accessed July 31, 2019. https://www.bloomberg.com/news/articles/2014-01-20/uralkali-agrees-on-24-lower-china-potash-price-researchers-say.

Fligstein, Neil. 1996. "Markets as Politics: A Political-Cultural Approach to Market Institutions." *American Sociological Review* 61, no. 4: 656–673.

Fligstein, Neil. 2001. *The Architecture of Markets: An Economic Sociology of Twenty-First Century Capitalist Societies*. Princeton, NJ: Princeton University Press.

Fligstein, Neil. 2008. "Myths of the Market." In *The Institutions of the Market: Organization, Social Systems and Governance*, edited by A. Ebner et al. Oxford: Oxford University Press. 131–156.

Flynn, Matthew. 1999. "PRC Maritime and the Asian Financial Crisis." *Maritime Policy & Management* 26, no. 4: 337–347.

Food and Agriculture Statistics. In *Food and Agriculture Organization of the United Nations (FAO)* [Data set]. https://www.fao.org/food-agriculture-statistics/en/

Foot, Rosemary, and Andrew Walter. 2010. *China, the United States and Global Order*. Cambridge: Cambridge University Press.

Foreign Trade and Economic Cooperation, Notice No. 27, 2002. "Pilot Scheme for the Management of State-Run Imports of Crude Oil, Refined Oil and Fertilizer [对外贸易经济合作部令2002年第27号 "原油、成品油、化肥国营贸易进口经营管理试行办法]." 2002. Ministry of Commerce of the People's Republic of China [中华人民共和国商务部], March 27. Accessed May 14, 2015. http://www.mofcom.gov.cn/article/b/c/200404/20040400207891.shtml.

Fravel, Taylor M. 2008. *Strong Borders, Secure Nation: Cooperation and Conflict in China's Territorial Disputes*. Princeton, NJ: Princeton University Press.

Frieden, Jeffry A., and Ronald Rogowski. 1996. "The Impact of the International Economy on National Policy." In *Internationalization and Domestic Politics*, edited by R. Keohane et al. Cambridge: Cambridge University Press. 25–47.

Fung, Courtney. 2016. "China and the Responsibility to Protect: From Opposition to Advocacy." *Peace Brief*, United States Institute for Peace. https://www.usip.org/publications/2016/06/china-and-responsibility-protect-opposition-advocacy.

Garnaut, Ross, and Ligang Song. 2006. "Rapid Industrialization and Market for Energy and Minerals: China in the East Asian Context." *Frontiers of Economics in China* 1, no. 3: 373–394.

Gereffi, Gary, et al. 2005. "The Governance of Global Value Chains." *Review of International Political Economy* 12, no. 1: 78–104.

Gerschenkron, Alexander. 1962. *Economic Backwardness in Historical Perspective*. Cambridge, MA: Harvard University Press.

*GFMS Copper Survey 2016*. 2016. London: Thomson Reuters. https://miningpress.com/media/briefs/gfms-annual-copper-survey-de-thomson-reuters_1751.pdf.

Gill, Bates. 2007. *Rising Star: China's New Security Diplomacy*. Washington, DC: Brookings Institution Press.

Gilpin, Robert. 1977. "Economic Interdependence and National Security in Historical Perspective." In *Economic Issues and National Security*, edited by K. Knorr et al., 19–65. Lawrence, KS: Allen Press.

Gilpin, Robert. 1987. *The Political Economy of International Relations*. Princeton: Princeton University Press.

Gilpin, Robert. 2000. *The Challenge of Global Capitalism: The World Economy in the 21st Century*. Princeton, NJ: Princeton University Press.

*Global coal production, 2018-2021*. 2022. International Energy Agency [Data set]. Accessed November 25, 2022. https://www.iea.org/data-and-statistics/charts/global-coal-production-2018-2021

Global Steel Market Overview. 2019. "World Steel Association: Tokyo." Accessed November 28, 2022. https://www.steelforum.org/stakeholders/gfsec-october-2019-worldsteel.pdf.

Goh, Brenda, and Matthew Miller. 2017. "China's COSCO Shipping Offers $6.3 Billion for Orient Overseas Ltd." *Reuters*, July 9. https://www.reuters.com/article/us-china-cosco-oil-idUSKBN19U0F4.

Goldthau, Andreas, and Jan Martin Witte. 2009. "Back to the Future or Forward to the Past? Strengthening Markets and Rules for Effective Global Energy Governance." *International Affairs* 85, no. 2: 373–390.

Gourevitch, Peter A. 1977. "International Trade, Domestic Coalitions, and Liberty: Comparative Responses to the Crisis of 1873–1896." *Journal of Interdisciplinary History* 8, no. 2: 281–313.

Gourevitch, Peter. 1978. "The Second Image Reversed: The International Sources of Domestic Politics." *International Organization* 32, no. 4: 881–911.

Gourevitch, Peter Alexis, and James J. Shinn. 2005. *Political Power and Corporate Control: The New Global Politics of Corporate Governance*. Princeton, NJ: Princeton University Press.

Grant, Michael, et al. 2010. "Saskatchewan in the Spotlight: Acquisition of Potash Corporation of Saskatchewan Inc.—Risks and Opportunities. The Conference Board of Canada." Accessed May 14, 2015. www.gov.sk.ca/adx/aspx/adxGetMedia.aspx?mediaId=1245&PN=Shared.

Gries, Peter. 2020. "Nationalism, Social Influences, and Chinese Foreign Policy." In *China and the World*, edited by David Shambaugh. New York: Oxford University Press. 63–84.

Gu, Ping [顾平]. 2008. "Economic Half-Hour: Sinochem, Sino-Agri and Others Are Pushing Fertilizer Prices Up [经济半小时：中化中农等企业推高化肥价格上涨]." CCTV.com, April 18. Accessed May 14, 2015. http://business.sohu.com/20080418/n256374390.shtml.

Gu, Ying [顾颖]. 2009. "Iron Ore Negotiations: Bad News? Not Cecessarily [铁矿石谈判,坏消息?不一定]." Industry Research, Donghai Securities (东海证券). Accessed May 14, 2015. http://www.simuwang.com/bencandy.php?fid=12&id=7553.

Gu, Zhongmao [顾忠茂], and Naiyan Wang [王乃彦]. 2005. "The Sustainable Development of China's Nuclear Energy [我国核裂变能可持续发展战略研究]." *Research and Approach* [研究与探讨] 27, no. 11: 5–10.

Guang, Yang, and Huang Wenjie. 2010. "The Status Quo of China's Nuclear Power and the Uranium Gap Solution." *Energy Policy* 38, no. 2: 966–975.

Hall, Peter A., and Daniel W. Gingerich. 2004. "Varieties of Capitalism and Institutional Complementarities in the Macroeconomy: An Empirical Analysis." MPIfG Discussion Paper 04/5, Max-Planck Institute for the Study of Societies Cologne. http://citeseerx.ist.psu.edu/viewdoc/download?doi=10.1.1.515.451&rep=rep1&type=pdf.

Hall, Peter, and David Soskice. 2001. *Varieties of Capitalism: The Institutional Foundations of Comparative Advantage*. Oxford: Oxford University Press.

Hall, Peter A., and Rosemary C. R. Taylor. 1996. "Political Science and the Three New Insititutionalisms." *Political Studies* 44: 936–957.

Hancock, Kathleen J., and Vlado Vivoda. 2014. "International Political Economy: A Field Born of the OPEC Crisis Returns to Its Energy Roots." *Energy Research and Social Science* 1: 206–216.

Heap, Alan. 2005. "China—The Engine of a Commodities Super Cycle." Citigroup Global Markets Paper, Citigroup. http://www.fallstreet.com/Commodities_China_Engine0331.pdf.

Hearn, Denise, and Jonathan Tepper. 2018. *The Myth of Capitalism: Global Implications of Market Concentration*. Hoboken, NJ: John Wiley & Sons.

Helleiner, Eric. 1994. *States and the Reemergence of Global Finance: From Bretton Woods to the 1990s*. Ithaca, NY: Cornell University Press.

Helleiner, Eric. 2021. *The Neomercantilists: A Global Intellectual History*. Ithaca, NY: Cornell University Press.

Helleiner, Eric, and Jennifer Clapp. 2012. "International Political Economy and the Environment: Back to the Basics?" *International Affairs* 88, no. 3: 485–501.

Helmer, John. 2013. "Kremlin's Potash War Picks Its Prisoners." *Asia Times*, August 8. Accessed May 14, 2015. http://www.atimes.com/atimes/Central_Asia/CEN-01-080813.html.

Hertz, John H. 1950. "Idealist Internationalism and the Security Dilemma." *World Politics* 2, no. 2: 157–180.

Hill, Liezel, et al. 2015. "Potash Price System Faces 'Collapse' as Chinese Talks Stall." *Bloomberg*, March 17. Accessed May 14, 2015. http://www.bloomberg.com/news/articles/2015-03-18/potash-price-system-faces-collapse-as-china-negotiations-stall.

Hiscox, Michael J. 2001. "Class versus Industry Cleavages: Inter-Industry Factor Mobility and the Politics of Trade." *International Organization* 55, no. 1: 1–46.

Holman, Jacqueline. 2022. "Massive Copper Supply Required for Electrification of Global Economy: Friedland." *S&P Global*. Accessed May 11, 2022. https://www.spglobal.com/commodityinsights/en/market-insights/latest-news/energy-transition/051122-massive-copper-supply-required-for-electrification-of-global-economy-friedland.

Hou, Jianchao [侯建朝], et al. 2010. Risks in uranium supply of nuclear power development in China and its solutions [我国核电发展的有资源供应风险及对策]. *China Electric Power* 43 (12):1–4.

Houser, Trevor. 2008. "The Roots of Chinese Investment Abroad." *Asia Policy*, no. 5: 141–166.

*How China Should Deal with Overseas Uranium Dependence* [中国如何应对海外铀依赖]. 2012. *Yicai* [第一财经日报]. Accessed September 20, 2022. https://www.yicai.com/news/1654156.html.

"How Potash Fertilizer Enterprises Seize the Opportunity in the Era of 'Zero Tariff' ['零关税'时代钾肥企业如何把握机遇]." 2019. *China Industry News* [中国工业新闻网]. Accessed August 31, 2022. http://www.cinn.cn/gongjing/201904/t20190424_211159.html.

Huang, Yukon. 2017. *Cracking the China Conundrum: Why Conventional Economic Wisdom Is Wrong*. Oxford: Oxford University Press.

Hughes, Llewelyn. 2014. *Globalizing Oil: The Politics of Oil Market Governance in France, Japan, and the United States*. Business and Public Policy. Cambridge: Cambridge University Press.

Hughes, Llewelyn, and Philip Y. Lipscy. 2013. "The Politics of Energy." *Annual Review of Political Science* 16: 449–469.

# REFERENCES

Hughes, Llewelyn, and Austin Long. 2014. "Is There an Oil Weapon? Security Implications of Changes in the Structure of the International Oil Market." *International Security* 39, no. 3: 152–189.

Humphreys, David. 2013. "New Mercantilism: A Perspective on How Politics Is Shaping World Metal Supply." *Resources Policy* 38: 341–349.

Humphreys, David. 2015. *The Remaking of the Mining Industry*. London: Palgrave Macmillan.

Hunter, Archie, and Thomas Biesheuvel. 2022. "Glencore Talking to Chinese Copper Smelter on Blending Plant." Bloomberg, January 14. Accessed December 7, 2022. https://www.bloomberg.com/news/articles/2022-01-14/glencore-in-talks-with-chinese-copper-smelter-on-blending-plant?leadSource=uverify%20wall.

Hurst, Luke. 2015a. "Assessing the Competitiveness of the Supply Side Response to China's Iron Ore Demand Shock." *Resources Policy* 45: 247–254.

Hurst, Luke. 2015b. "The Development of the Asian Iron Ore Market: A Lesson in Long-run Market Contestability." *Resources Policy* 46: 22–29.

Hurst, Luke. 2016. *China's Iron Ore Boom*. New York: Routledge.

Ikenberry, G. John. 2008. "The Rise of China and the Future of the West." *Foreign Affairs* 87, no. 1: 23–37.

Ikenberry, G. John. 2009. "Liberal Internationalism 3.0: America and the Dilemmas of Liberal World Order." *Perspectives on Politics* 7, no. 1: 71–87.

Ikenberry, G. John. 2012. *Liberal Leviathan: The Origins, Crisis, and Transformation of the American World Order*. Princeton Studies in International History and Politics. Princeton, NJ: Princeton University Press.

*Iron Ore 62% Fe, CFR China (TSI) Swa*. 2022. Financial Times [Data set]. Accessed November 6, 2022. https://markets.ft.com/data/commodities/tearsheet/charts?c=Iron+ore

"Iron Ore: A History of Iron Ore Pricing." 2012. *Mining Journal Online*, September 28. Accessed March 13, 2014. http://www.mining-journal.com/reports/iron-ore-a-history-of-iron-ore-pricing?SQ_DESIGN_NAME=print_friendly.

Iron Ore Industry Trends and Analysis. 2009. *Baffinland Iron Mines Corporation*.

"Iron Ore Price Talks Reach a Crossroads: Can China Get What It Wants?" 2009. Knowledge at Wharton, November 11. Accessed October 11, 2022. https://knowledge.wharton.upenn.edu/article/iron-ore-price-talks-reach-a-crossroads-can-china-get-what-it-wants/.

Jacques, Martin. 2009. *When China Rules the World: The End of the Western World and the Birth of a New Global Order*. New York: Penguin.

Jasinski, Stephen. 2021. "Potash." U.S. Geological Survey, Mineral Commodity Summaries. https://pubs.usgs.gov/periodicals/mcs2021/mcs2021-potash.pdf.

Jia, Dashan. 2012. "The Development of Ports and Iron Ore Seaborne Trade." In 12th China International Steel and Raw Materials Conference. Dalian, China: China Iron and Steel Association and Metallurgical Council of CCPIT.

Jiang, Yunzhang. 2011. "Sinochem Leads Second Half of Potash Import Price Hike of 17.5% and Was Questioned [中化主导下半年钾肥进口价涨17.5%遭质疑)]." *Tencent Finance* [腾讯财经]. Accessed February 14, 2022. https://finance.qq.com/a/20110806/001326.htm.

Johnson, Chalmers. 1982. *MITI and the Japanese Miracle: The Growth of Industrial Policy 1925–1975*. Stanford, CA: Stanford University Press.

Johnston, Alistair Iain. 2003. "Is China a Status Quo Power?" *International Security* 27, no. 4: 5–56.

Johnston, Alastair Iain. 2015. *Social States: China in International Institutions, 1980–2000*. Princeton, NJ: Princeton University Press.

Johnston, Alistair Iain. 2019. "China in a World of Orders: Rethinking Compliance and Challenge in Beijing's International Relations." *International Security* 44, no. 2: 9–60.

Jones, Lee, and Shahar Hameiri. 2021. *Fractured China: How State Transformation Is Shaping China's Rise*. Cambridge: Cambridge University Press.

Jorgenson, John D., and William S. Kirk. 2004. "Iron Ore." In *Minerals Yearbook 2003: Metals and Minerals*. Washington D.C.: USGS (United States Geological Survey), United States Department of the Interior, 1–22.

Jun, Pu. 2013. "Vale's Ship Enters Chinese Port, Unclear if Ban Was Lifted." *Caixin*. Accessed May 14, 2015. http://english.caixin.com/2013-04-18/100516001.html.

Kane, Thomas M., and Lawrence W. Serewicz. 2001. "China's Hunger: The Consequences of a Rising Demand for Food and Energy." *Parameters* (Autumn): 63–75.

Kastner, Scott L., et al. 2018. *China's Strategic Multilateralism: Investing in Global Governance.* Cambridge: Cambridge University Press.

Katzenstein, Peter J. 1976. "International Relations and Domestic Structures: Foreign Economic Policies of Advanced Industrial States." *International Organization* 30, no. 1: 1–46.

Katzenstein, Peter J. 1977. "Domestic and International Forces and Strategies of Foreign Economic Policy." *International Organization* 31, no. 4: 587–606.

Katzenstein, Peter. 1985. *Small States in World Markets.* Ithaca, NY: Cornell University Press.

Katzenstein, Peter J., et al. 1998. "International Organization and the Study of World Politics." *International Organization* 52, no. 4: 645–685.

Kayakiran, Firat. 2012. "Uralkali Ready to Cut Potash Output to Shield Price: Commodities." Bloomberg, January 25. Accessed May 14, 2015. http://www.bloomberg.com/news/2012-01-25/uralkali-ready-to-cut-potash-output-to-protect-45-price-gain-commodities.html.

Kennedy, Scott, and Shuaihua Cheng. 2012. "From Rule Takers to Rule Makers: The Growing Role of Chinese in Global Governance." Shanghai: Research Center for Chinese Politics and Business (RCCPB), International Center for Trade and Sustainable Development (ICTSD). https://www.files.ethz.ch/isn/154720/the-growing-role-of-chinese-in-global-governance.pdf.

Keohane, Robert O. 1980. "The Theory of Hegemonic Stability and Changes in International Economic Regimes, 1967–1977." In *Change in the International System*, edited by O. R. Holsti et al. Boulder, CO: Westview Press. 131–162.

Keohane, Robert. 1989. "Theory of World Politics: Structural Realism and Beyond." In *International Institutions and State Power: Essays in International Relations Theory*, edited by R. Keohane. New York: Routledge. 35–73.

Keohane, Robert, and Helen Milner. 1996. *Internationalization and Domestic Politics.* Cambridge: Cambridge University Press.

Keohane, Robert, and Joseph S. Nye. 1977. *Power and Interdependence: World Politics in Transition.* Boston: Little, Brown.

Kirkby, R W. 2001. Steel Making Raw Materials: Opportunities and Challenges (BHP Billiton). AJBCC/JABCC Joint Business Conference, October. http://www.bhpbilliton.com/home/investors/reports/Documents/SteelMakingRawMaterialsOpportunitiesChallenges.pdf

Kirshner, Jonathan, ed. 2003. *Monetary Orders: Ambiguous Economics, Ubiquitous Politics.* Ithaca, NY: Cornell University Press.

Komesaroff, Michael. 2007. "Energy: China Goes Nuclear." *China Economic Quarterly* (Q4): 10–13.

Komesaroff, Michael. 2010. "Death of the annual mating ritual". *China Economic Quarterly* June: 10–11.

Komesaroff, Michael. 2013. "A Potash Romance." *China Economic Quarterly Metals Man* (December).

Kong, Bo. 2011. "Governing China's Energy in the Context of Global Governance." *Global Policy* 2 (September): 51–65.

Kostick, Dennis S. 2007. "Potash." In *Mineral Commodity Summaries 2007*. Washington D.C.: USGS (United States Geological Survey), United States Department of the Interior, January: 124–125.

Koven, Peter. 2012. "Russian Potash Firm Settles Price-Fixing Suit." *Financial Post*, September 24. Accessed May 14, 2015. http://business.financialpost.com/legal-post/russian-potash-firm-settles-price-fixing-suit.

Krasner, Stephen D. 1974. "Oil Is the Exception." *Foreign Policy* 14: 68–84.

Krasner, Stephen D. 1976. "State Power and the Structure of International Trade." *World Politics* 28, no. 3: 317–347.

Krasner, Stephen. 1978. *Defending the National Interest: Raw Materials Investments and U.S. Foreign Policy*. Princeton, NJ: Princeton University Press.

Krasner, Stephen. 1984. "Review: Approaches to the State: Alternative Conceptions and Historical Dynamics." *Comparative Politics* 16, no. 2: 223–246.

Kudrytski, Aliaksandr, and Yuliya Fedorinova. 2015b. "Belarus Potash Contract with China Disappoints Competitors." Globe and Mail/Bloomberg, March 19. Accessed July 31, 2019. https://www.theglobeandmail.com/report-on-business/international-business/belarus-potash-contract-with-china-disappoints-competitors/article23542722/.

Kudrytski, Aliaksandr, and Stepan Kravchenko. 2013. "KGB Offers Tolstoy as Russia Presses Belarus to Free Potash CEO." Bloomberg, August 30. Accessed May 14, 2015. http://www.bloomberg.com/news/2013-08-30/kgb-offers-tolstoy-as-russia-presses-belarus-to-free-potash-ceo.html.

Kuo, Lily. 2019. "China to Auction 10,000 Tonnes of Pork from State Reserves." *The Guardian*, September 18. Accessed November 1, 2022. https://www.theguardian.com/world/2019/sep/18/china-auction-pork-reserves.

Kupchan, Charles A. 1994. *The Vulnerability of Empire*. Cornell: Cornell University Press.

Kurz, Mordecai. 2017. "On the Formation of Capital and Wealth: IT, Monopoly Power and Rising Inequality." Stanford Institute for Economic Policy Research (SIEPR) Working Paper, Stanford University. https://siepr.stanford.edu/sites/default/files/publications/17-016_0.pdf.

Lague, David. 2005. "China to Sell Some Copper to Battle Rising Price." *New York Times*, November 15. Accessed November 1, 2022. https://www.nytimes.com/2005/11/15/business/worldbusiness/china-to-sell-some-copper-to-battle-rising-price.html.

Lake, David A. 1993. "Leadership, Hegemony, and the International Economy: Naked Emperor or Tattered Monarch with Potential?" *International Studies Quarterly* 37, no. 4: 459–489.

Lake, David A. 2009. "Open Economy Politics: A Critical Review." *Review of International Organizations* 4, no. 3: 219–244.

Leonard, Mark. 2013. "Why Convergence Breeds Conflict: Growing More Similar Will Push China and the United States Apart." *Foreign Affairs* 92, no. 5: 125–135.

"Leverage the Two Markets and Two Resources to Cultivate New Advantages in Cooperation and Competition [利用两个市场两种资源培育合作和竞争新优势]." 2022. National Development and Reform Commission/Xinhua News Agency. Accessed September 20, 2022. https://www.ndrc.gov.cn/fggz/lywzjw/jwtz/202204/t20220429_1324007.html?code=&state=123.

Li, Hanzhang [李含章]. 2008. "The Import Monopoly behind the Surge in Potash [钾肥暴涨背后的进口垄断]." Sina.com, July 8. Accessed May 14, 2015. http://news.sina.com.cn/c/2008-08-07/101716078337.shtml.

Li, Jinqian [李金千], and Yongzhi Li [李咏知]. 2011. "Discussion on China's Iron Ore External Dependence Status [中国铁矿石对外依存状况刍议]. *Modern Mining* (现代矿业) August (508):1–4."

Li, Ruoxin [李若馨]. 2010. "Establishment of the 'Joint Office of Iron Ore Imports,' as the Two Associations Seriously Investigate Iron Ore Reselling [成立"进口铁矿石联合办公室 两协会严查炒矿"]." *China Securities Journal* [中国证券抱], April 6. Accessed May 14, 2015. http://www.chinanews.com/cj/cj-gncj/news/2010/04-06/2208150.shtml.

Li, Ruoxin [李若馨]. 2011. "Commerce Department Appointed to Reestablish the Order in the Iron Ore Import Market [商务部受命整顿进口铁矿石市场秩序]." *China Securities Journal* [中国证券报], March 18. Accessed May 14, 2015. http://finance.sina.com.cn/chanjing/cyxw/20110318/04549552925.shtml.

Li, Xinmin [李新民]. 2011. "60% Dependence Ratio on Foreign Potash Puts Food Security in Peril [国内钾肥对外依存度高达60% 危及粮食安全]." *Xinhua*. Accessed May 14, 2015. http://info.chem.hc360.com/2011/07/250842284601.shtml.

Li, Ying. 2019. *Report on the Special Work of the Industry Economic Index of China Iron and Steel Association in 2018* [2018年中国钢铁工业协会行业经济指数专项工作情况汇报].

China Iron and Steel Association. Accessed April 27, 2022. http://www.sasac.gov.cn/n4470048/n10286230/n10888519/n10888544/c10948607/content.html.

Li, Yue Yivonne, and Joe Deaux. 2021. "As Uranium Soars, Top Trust Sees Hedge Funds Fueling Demand Lift." Bloomberg. Accessed November 29, 2022. https://www.bnnbloomberg.ca/as-uranium-soars-top-trust-sees-hedge-funds-fueling-demand-lift-1.1652825.

Liang, Caiheng [梁彩恒]. 2007. "Imminent Iron Ore Negotiations: Qualified Iron Ore Importers Reduced by 6 Companies [铁矿石谈判在即 具备进口资质企业再减6家]." *China Business News* [第一财经日报], October 15. Accessed May 14, 2015. http://mnc.people.com.cn/GB/54849/69894/105281/105307/6380149.html.

List, Friedrich. 1909. *The National System of Political Economy*. Translated by S. S. Lloyd. London: Longmans, Green, and Co. (Original work published 1841)

"List of State Trading Import Enterprises [进口国营贸易企业名录)]." 2001. Ministry of Commerce of the People's Republic of China Department of Foreign Trade (National Mechanic and Electronic Import and Export Office) [中华人民共和国商务部对外贸易司 (国家机电产品进出口办公室], December 11. Accessed May 14, 2015. http://wms.mofcom.gov.cn/article/zcfb/e/v/200209/20020900039659.shtml.

Liu, Fangbin [刘方斌]. 2010. "Chinese Potash Fertilizer Import Negotiations: Everybody Has a Say [中国钾肥进口谈判大家谈]." China Chemical Fertilizer Network [中国化肥网], November 8. Accessed May 14, 2015. http://www.ccin.com.cn/ccin/news/2010/11/08/150530.shtml.

Liu, Yanmei [刘艳梅]. 2016. *Researching the International Pricing Power Contest in Bulk Agricultural Products* [大宗农产品国际定价权博弈问题研究]. Beijing, China: Xinhua Publishing House [新华出版社].

Liu, Yiyu. 2012. "New Nuclear Projects Ready to Power Ahead." *China Daily*, May 18. Accessed September 14, 2012. http://www.chinadaily.com.cn/cndy/2012-05/18/content_15325518.htm.

Llewellyn-Smith, David. 2013. "A Brief History of Iron Ore Markets." *Macrobusiness*, August 16. Accessed November 6, 2022. https://www.macrobusiness.com.au/2013/08/a-brief-history-of-iron-ore-markets/.

"LME Suspends Nickel Trading after Prices Surge More than 110% to Over US$100,000 a Ton." 2022. *South China Morning Post*, March 8. Accessed November 22, 2022. https://www.scmp.com/business/commodities/article/3169700/lme-suspends-nickel-trading-after-prices-surge-more-110-cent?module=inline&pgtype=article.

Löf, Anton, and Magnus Ericsson. 2016. *Iron Ore Market Report*, E&MJ Engineering and Mining Journal. Accessed April 20, 2022. https://www.e-mj.com/features/iron-ore-market-report-2016/

Lof, Anton, and Magnus Ericsson. 2017. "Iron Ore Market Report 2017." *E&MJ Engineering and Mining Journal* (November): 32–37.

Lof, Anton, and Magnus Ericsson. 2018. "Iron Ore Markets Improve in Most Regions." *E&MJ Engineering and Mining Journal* (October): 48–54.

"The Lore of Ore: The Most Important Commodity after Oil Deserves More Attention than It Gets." 2012. *The Economist*, October 13. Accessed May 14, 2015. http://www.economist.com/node/21564559.

Lu, Feng, and Yuanfang Li. 2009. "The China Factor in Recent Global Commodity Price and Shipping Freight Volatilities." *China Economic Journal* 2, no. 3: 351–377.

Luk, Julian. 2022. "China to Tighten Import Thresholds for Impurities in Metal Concentrates, Sources Say." *Fastmarkets*, October 31. Accessed December 7, 2022. https://www.fastmarkets.com/insights/china-to-tighten-import-thresholds-for-impurities-in-metal-concentrates-sources-say.

MacDonald, Alistair. 2015. "How a Potash Cartel Collapsed." *Wall Street Journal*, December 14. Accessed July 31, 2019. https://www.wsj.com/articles/how-the-belarusian-potash-company-re-gained-its-footing-1450098821.

# REFERENCES

"Major Potash Contract Price Successfully Reached for China at Crucial Moment in 2018 [2018中国钾肥大合同价格在关键时刻顺利达成]." 2018. Sino-Agri Press Release, September 18. Accessed August 1, 2019. http://www.sino-agri.net/article/detail/id/1678.html.

"Management's Discussion and Analysis of Financial Condition and Results of Operations for the Six Months Ended June 30, 2011." 2011. US Securities and Exchange Commission. Accessed April 4, 2022. https://www.sec.gov/Archives/edgar/data/1243429/000119312511204761/dex991.htm.

Massot, Pascale. 2011. "Chinese State Investments in Canada: Lessons from the Potash Saga." Canada-Asia Agenda, Asia Pacific Foundation of Canada: Vancouver. Accessed May 25, 2023. https://www.asiapacific.ca/sites/default/files/filefield/chinese_state_investments_in_canada_v4.pdf.

Massot, Pascale. 2021. "The State of the Study of the Market in Political Economy: China's Rise Shines Light on Conceptual Shortcomings." *Competition & Change* 25, no. 5: 534–560.

"May 2022—Market Update." 2022. Mosaic. https://s1.q4cdn.com/823038994/files/doc_financials/2022/q1/1Q22-Market-Update-Final.pdf.

Mayfield, Callum. 2013. *The Chinese Iron Ore Industry and What Lies Ahead*. London: CRU Group.

Mazarr, Michael J., et al. 2018. "China and the International Order." In *Building a Sustainable International Order*. Santa Monica, CA: RAND Corporation. https://www.rand.org/pubs/research_reports/RR2423.html.

Mearsheimer, John J. 2001. *The Tragedy of Great Power Politics*. New York: W. W. Norton.

Mearsheimer, John J. 2010. "The Gathering Storm: China's Challenge to US Power in Asia." *Chinese Journal of International Politics* 3: 381–396.

Mearsheimer, John J. 2014. "Can China Rise Peacefully?" *National Interest*. Accessed September 21, 2022. https://nationalinterest.org/commentary/can-china-rise-peacefully-10204.

Mearsheimer, John J. 2019. "Bound to Fail: The Rise and Fall of the Liberal International Order." *International Security* 43, no. 4: 7–50.

Mertha, Andrew. 2009. "Fragmented Authoritarianism 2.0: Political Pluralization in the Chinese Policy Process." *China Quarterly* 200 (December): 995–1012.

Schatzker, Adam et al. 2011. Uranium Market Outlook—Second Quarter 2011.*Metal Prospects*, RBC Capital Markets.

Mill, John Stuart. 1868. *A System of Logic*. London: Longmans.

Miller, Manjari Chatterjee. 2021. *Why Nations Rise: Narratives and the Path to Great Power*. New York: Oxford University Press.

Ministry of Commerce Notice 52, 2004, on the Allocation of Self-Managed Potash Import Rights to 5 Non-State-Run Enterprises [商务部公告2004年第52号 赋予5家企业钾肥非国营贸易自营进口经营权]. 2004. 年第200452号 赋予5家企业钾肥非国营贸易自营进口经营权. Ministry of Commerce of the People's Republic of China [中华人民共和国国商务部], August 26. Accessed May 14, 2015. http://www.mofcom.gov.cn/article/b/c/200409/20040900276287.shtml.

"Ministry of Foreign Trade and Economic Cooperation of the People's Republic of China Notice 50, 2002—Crude Oil, Refined Oil, Fertilizer Non-State Trade Import Business List (First Batch) [中华人民共和国对外贸易经济合作部公告2002年第50号—原油、成品油、化肥非国营贸易进口经营备案企业名单（第一批）]." 2002. Ministry of Commerce of the People's Republic of China [中华人民共和国国商务部], March 10. http://www.mofcom.gov.cn/article/b/c/200403/20040300192984.shtml.

Mo, Jongryn. 1994. "The Logic of Two-Level Games with Endogenous Domestic Coalitions." *Journal of Conflict Resolution* 38, no. 3: 402–422.

Moran, Theodore H. 1973. "Transnational Strategies of Protection and Defense by Multinational Corporations: Spreading the Risk and Raising the Cost for Nationalization in Natural Resources." *International Organization* 27, no. 2: 273–287.

Moran, Theodore H. 2010. *China's Strategy to Secure Natural Resources: Risks, Dangers, and Opportunities*. Washington, DC: Peterson Institute for International Economics.

Mosaic Co Form 10-K (Annual Report). 2005. United States Securities and Exchange Commission: Washington D.C. https://d18rn0p25nwr6d.cloudfront.net/CIK-0001285785/7c5d3d5e-fef1-4349-ac3c-2373ffb2cd12.pdf

Munson, James. 2013. "Reading the Tea Leaves of China's Resource Purchases." *iPolitics*, March 7. Accessed May 14, 2015. http://www.ipolitics.ca/2013/03/07/reading-the-tea-leaves-of-chinas-resource-purchases/.

Murphy, Colum. 2012. "Beijing Wields Big Stick against Megaships: How China Closed Its Ports to Brazilian Miner Vale's Huge Iron-Ore Vessels." *Wall Street Journal*, November 13. Accessed May 14, 2015. http://online.wsj.com/article/SB10001424127887324595904578116702590372508.html.

Musgrave, Paul, and Daniel H. Nexon. 2018. "Defending Hierarchy from the Moon to the Indian Ocean." *International Organization* 72, no. 3: 591–626.

Nathan, Andrew J. 2016. "China's Rise and International Regimes: Does China Seek to Overthrow Global Norms?" In *China in the Era of Xi Jinping: Domestic and Foreign Policy Challenges*, edited by R. S. Ross et al. Washington, DC: Georgetown University Press. 165–195.

"National Development and Reform Commission's Notice on Improving Potash Price Management Policy [国家发展改革委关于完善钾肥价格管理政策的通知]." 2009. National Development and Reform Commission [中华人民共和国国家发展和改革委员会): 发改价格]. Accessed May 14, 2015. http://www.sdpc.gov.cn/fzgggz/jggl/zcfg/200902/t20090218_261792.html.

Nem Singh, Jewellord Torentino. 2013. "Towards Post-neoliberal Resource Politics? The International Political Economy (IPE) of Oil and Copper in Brazil and Chile." *New Political Economy* 19, no. 3: 329–358.

"New MOU between Sinofert and Canpotex." 2017. Sinofert News Release. http://www.sinofert.com/en/s/5635-15450-115741.html.

Ng, Eric. 2016. "Baosteel-Wisco Marriage Sets Stage for Faster Steel Industry Consolidation." *South China Morning Post*, October 4. https://www.scmp.com/business/companies/article/2025028/baosteel-wisco-marriage-sets-stage-faster-steel-industry.

Ng, Eric. 2017. "China's Largest Fertiliser Maker Sinofert Sells Stake in Key Production Asset to Parent to Fund Major Restructure." *South China Morning Post*, October 25. https://www.scmp.com/business/companies/article/2116909/chinas-largest-fertiliser-maker-sinofert-sells-stake-key.

Nickel, Rod. 2014. "UPDATE 1—Potash Corp CEO says Uralkali-Belaruskali Reunion 'Logical.'" *Chicago Tribune*, February 25. Accessed May 14, 2015. http://articles.chicagotribune.com/2014-02-25/news/sns-rt-potashcorp-russia--20140225_1_potash-corp-belarusian-potash-company-canpotex-ltd.

Nolan, Peter. 2012. *Is China Buying the World?* Cambridge: Polity Press.

Norris, William J. 2016. *Chinese Economic Statecraft: Commercial Actors, Grand Strategy, and State Control*. Ithaca, NY: Cornell University Press.

"Nuclear Power in China." 2012. World Nuclear Association. Accessed September 14, 2012. http://www.world-nuclear.org/info/inf63.html.

"Nuclear Power in China." 2022. World Nuclear Association. Accessed November 6, 2022. https://world-nuclear.org/information-library/country-profiles/countries-a-f/china-nuclear-power.aspx.

*Nutrien Fact Book*. 2018. Nutrien. https://www.nutrien.com/sites/default/files/uploads/2018-01/Nutrien%20Fact%20Book%202018.pdf.

*Nutrien Fact Book*. 2022. Nutrien. https://nutrien-prod-asset.s3.us-east-2.amazonaws.com/s3fs-public/uploads/2022-06/Nutrien%202022%20Fact%20Book.pdf.

Nye, Joseph. 2019. "China Will Not Surpass America Any Time Soon." *Financial Times*. https://www.ft.com/content/7f700ab4-306d-11e9-80d2-7b637a9e1ba1.

Oksenberg, Michel, and Kenneth Lieberthal. 1988. *Policy Making in China: Leaders, Structures, and Processes*. Princeton, NJ: Princeton University Press.

Olson, Mancur. 1965. *The Logic of Collective Action: Public Goods and the Theory of Group*. Cambridge: Harvard University Press.

OPEC Annual Statistical Bulletin. 2016. Organization of the Petroleum Exporting Countries: Vienna, Austria [Data set]. https://www.opec.org/opec_web/static_files_project/media/downloads/publications/ASB2016.pdf

Organski, A. F. K. 1958. *World Politics*. New York: Knopf.

Ostrom, Elinor. 1997. "A Behavioral Approach to the Rational Choice Theory of Collective Action: Presidential Address." *American Political Science Review* 92, no. 1: 1–22.

Park, Gayoung. 2011. "China Launches Iron Ore Spot Price Index to Better Reflect Local Market." July 5. *Global Times*.

"People's Republic of China Ministry of Foreign Trade and Economic Cooperation, Notice No. 50, 2002—List of Filing Non-State Trading Enterprises in Crude Oil, Refined Oil, and Fertilizer Imports [中华人民共和国对外贸易经济合作部公告2002年第50号——原油、成品油、化肥非国营贸易进口经营备案企业名单（第一批）]." 2003. People's Republic of China Ministry of Foreign Trade and Economic Cooperation [中华人民共和国对外贸易经济合作部]. Accessed May 14, 2015. http://www.mofcom.gov.cn/article/b/c/200403/20040300192984.shtml.

PIW's Top 50: How the Firms Stack Up. 2016. *Petroleum Intelligence Weekly* (November 15). https://www.energyintel.com/0000017b-a7d0-de4c-a17b-e7d2729b0000

Pistilli, Melissa. 2022. "Copper Refining: From Ore to Market." *INN Investing News*. Accessed June 22, 2022. https://investingnews.com/daily/resource-investing/base-metals-investing/copper-investing/copper-refining-from-ore-to-market/.

Pnovolos, Theophilos. 1987. "An Econometric Model of the Iron Ore Industry." World Bank Staff Commodity Working Papers. Washington, DC: The World Bank. http://documents.worldbank.org/curated/en/974851468183562922/pdf/SCP019.pdf.

Polanyi, Karl. 1944. *The Great Transformation*. Boston: Beacon Press.

Porter, Patrick. 2018. "A World Imagined: Nostalgia and Liberal Order." *Cato Institute Policy Analysis*, no. 843: 1–21.

"PotashCorp Announces New China Potash Memorandum of Understanding." 2003. PotashCorp news release, August 7. Accessed May 14, 2015. http://www.potashcorp.com/news/225/.

"PotashCorp Announces Significant Potash Price Increase in 2008 Canpotex, Sinofert Agreement." 2008. PotashCorp news release, April 16. Accessed May 14, 2015. http://www.potashcorp.com/news/365/.

"Potash Corp. Settles 8 Antitrust Cases for $43M." 2013. *Chicago Tribune*, January 30. Accessed May 14, 2015. http://articles.chicagotribune.com/2013-01-30/business/chi-potash-corp-settles-8-antitrust-cases-for-43m-20130130_1_potash-corp-global-potash-potash-prices.

"President Hu Jintao Delivers a Speech at the Nuclear Security Summit in Seoul [胡锦涛在首尔核安全峰会上的讲话]." 2012. *Xinhua News*, March 27. Accessed May 14, 2015. http://news.xinhuanet.com/politics/2012-03/27/c_111708025.htm.

"Production and Use of Potassium." 1998. *Better Crops* 82, no. 3: 6–8.

"Prospect of China's Potash Fertilizer Import Qualification Reform [中国钾肥进口资质改革展望]." 2015. *Sina Finance* [新浪财经]. Accessed August 31, 2022. http://finance.sina.com.cn/money/future/20150711/103522659106.shtml.

"Provisional Procedures for the Automatic Import License of Iron Ore [铁矿砂自动进口许可证申领暂行办法]." 2005. General Administration of Customs of the People's Republic of China. Accessed May 14, 2015. http://www.customs.gov.cn/publish/portal0/tab637/info38576.htm.

Putnam, Robert D. 1988. "Diplomacy and Domestic Politics: The Logic of Two-Level Games." *International Organization* 42, no. 3: 427–460.

Quddus, M. Abdul, et al. 2008. "The Demand for Nitrogen, Phosphorus and Potash Fertilizer Nutrients in Pakistan." *Pakistan Economic and Social Review* 46, no. 2: 101–116.

Quek, Kai, and Alastair Iain Johnston. 2018. "Can China Back Down? Crisis De-escalation in the Shadow of Popular Opposition." *International Security* 42, no. 3: 7–36.

Radetzki, Marian. 2006. "The Anatomy of Three Commodity Booms." *Resources Policy* 31: 56–64.

Radetzki, Marian. 2012. "The Perseverance of the Ongoing Metal and Mineral Boom." *Mineral Economics* 25, no. 2: 83–88.

Radetzki, Marian. 2013. "The Relentless Progress of Commodity Exchanges in the Establishment of Primary Commodity Prices." *Resources Policy* 38: 266–277.

Radetzki, Marian, et al. 2008. "The Boom in Mineral Markets: How Long Might It Last?" *Resources Policy* 33: 125–128.

Rapp, William V. 2002. "Steel: Nucor, Tokyo Steel, Nippon Steel." In *Information Technology Strategies: How Leading Firms Use IT to Gain an Advantage*, edited by W. V. Rapp. Oxford: Oxford University Press. 92–127.

"The Reason Why Nanyang Is Not Suitable for the Construction of a Nuclear Power Plant [南阳不适合建核电站理由]." 2011. *Tianya* [天涯社区]. http://bbs.city.tianya.cn/tianyacity/content/506/1/10108.shtml.

"Rio Tinto Joins Steel Reform as Local Costs Mount." 2010. *Construction Week*, April 11. Accessed October 11, 2022. https://www.constructionweekonline.com/products-services/article-8019-rio-tinto-joins-steel-reform-as-local-costs-mount.

Rodrik, Dani. 1982. "Managing Resource Dependency: The United States and Japan in the Markets for Copper, Iron Ore and Bauxite." *World Development* 10, no. 7: 541–560.

Rogowski, Ronald. 1989. *Commerce and Coalitions*. Princeton, NJ: Princeton University Press.

"The Role of Critical Minerals in Clean Energy Transitions." 2022. World Energy Outlook Special Report, International Energy Agency. https://read.oecd-ilibrary.org/energy/the-role-of-critical-minerals-in-clean-energy-transitions_f262b91c-en#page2.

Rosen, Daniel H., and Trevor Houser. 2007. "China Energy: A Guide for the Perplexed." Center for Strategic and International Studies and the Peterson Institute for International Economics. Accessed May 14, 2015. http://www.iie.com/publications/papers/rosen0507.pdf.

Ross, Robert S. 2011. "Chinese Nationalism and Its Discontents." *National Interest*, no. 116: 45–51.

Rosser, Andrew. 2006. "Escaping the Resource Curse." *New Political Economy* 11, no. 4: 557–570.

Rudra, Nita, and Nathan M. Jensen. 2011. "Globalization and the Politics of Natural Resources." *Comparative Political Studies* 44, no. 6: 639–661.

Ruggie, John Gerard. 1982. "International Regimes, Transactions, and Change: Embedded Liberalism in the Postwar Economic Order." *International Organization* 36, no. 2: 379–415.

Rust, Bob. 2014. "Valemax Ban 'Here to Stay' Says China Shipowner Group." *TradeWinds*. Accessed September 30, 2014. http://www.tradewindsnews.com/weekly/332806/valemax-ban-here-to-stay-says-china-shipowner-group.

Seabrooke, Leonard. 2007. "Everyday Legitimacy and International Financial Orders: The Social Sources of Imperialism and Hegemony in Global Finance." *New Political Economy* 12, no. 1: 1–18.

Searls, James P. 1980. "Potash." In *Minerals yearbook: Metals and minerals*. Washington D.C.: U.S. Bureau of Mines, United States Department of the Interior: 651-661.

Searls, James P. 1995. "Potash." In *Minerals yearbook 1994: Metals and minerals (except fuels)*. Washington D.C.: USGS (United States Geological Survey), United States Department of the Interior: 1–9..

Searls, James P. 2003. "Potash." In *Minerals yearbook 2002: Metals and minerals (except fuels)*. Washington D.C.: USGS (United States Geological Survey), United States Department of the Interior: 1–10..

Searls, James P. 2005. "Potash." In *Mineral Commodity Summaries 2005*. Washington D.C.: USGS (United States Geological Survey), United States Department of the Interior: 126–127..

Serapio, Manolo, Jr. 2012. "RPT—Rival to China Iron Ore Platform to Launch Wednesday." Reuters, May 28. Accessed October 11, 2022. https://www.reuters.com/article/globalore-idUKL4E8GS1Z620120528.

Shambaugh, David. 2011. "Coping with a Conflicted China." *Washington Quarterly* 34, no. 1: 7–27.

"Shandong Valemax Secrets Slipping Out." 2014. *TradeWinds*, January 14. Accessed August 29, 2018. https://www.tradewindsnews.com/weekly/shandong-valemax-secrets-slipping-out/1-1-330421.

Sheng, Yu, and Ligang Song. 2012. "China's Iron Ore Import Demand and Its Determinants: A Time-Series Analysis." In *The Chinese Steel Industry's Transformation*, edited by L. Song et al. Cheltenham, UK: Edward Elgar Publishing. 145–161.

Shepherd, Christian. 2016. "China Deal to Create World's Second-Largest Steelmaker." *Financial Times*, September 21. https://www.ft.com/content/b01a1d28-7fbf-11e6-bc52-0c7211ef3198.

Shi, Tao [石涛]. 2011. "Questioning the Monopoly Mechanism of Potash Fertilizer Imports [质疑钾肥进口垄断机制]." Agricultural Supply and Sales Network [农资供销网]. Accessed August 31, 2022. http://nzgx.org/html/XinWenZiXun/NongZiDongTai/20110314/228959.html.

Singh, Shivani. 2019. "Glencore Starts Copper Concentrates Blending Facility in Taiwan." Reuters, July 26. Accessed December 7, 2022. https://www.reuters.com/article/us-copper-glencore-blending-idUSKCN1UL19L.

Singh, Shivani, and Min Zhang. 2021. "China's Sales and Purchases of State Metal Reserves." Reuters. https://www.reuters.com/world/china/chinas-sales-purchases-state-metal-reserves-2021-08-05/.

Sinha, Rajesh, et al. 2011. "World Trade in Uranium." SML 820 Global Business Environment, Indian Institute of Technology, Delhi. Accessed May 14, 2015. http://www.academia.edu/6525820/WORLD_TRADE_IN_URANIUM.

Song, Yuhua, and Feng Li. 2009. "How Can China Build Purchase Alliances in the World Market of Resource Commodities?" *Journal of Chinese Economic and Foreign Trade Studies* 2, no. 2: 121–130.

"Sprott Fund Transforms Uranium Spot Market." 2021. S&P Global, October 19. Accessed November 29, 2022. https://www.spglobal.com/marketintelligence/en/news-insights/latest-news-headlines/sprott-fund-transforms-uranium-spot-market-67100457.

"Sprott Physical Uranium Trust." Sprott. Accessed November 29, 2022. https://sprott.com/investment-strategies/physical-commodity-funds/uranium/.

Staff, Policy Planning. 2020. "The Elements of the China Challenge." Office of the Secretary of State, Washington, DC. Accessed October 28, 2022. https://www.state.gov/wp-content/uploads/2020/11/20-02832-Elements-of-China-Challenge-508.pdf.

Stanway, David. 2015. "Iron Ore Slump Set to Shrink China's Mining Capacity (UPDATE 2)." Reuters, March 27. Accessed March 31, 2015. http://www.reuters.com/article/2015/03/27/china-ironore-idUSL3N0WT18J20150327.

"State Council Issues Notice 39 on 'Deepening the Reform of the Fertilizer Circulation System' [国务院关于深化化肥流通体制改革的通知]." 1998. State Council [中华人民共和国国务院], November 16. Accessed May 14, 2015. http://faolex.fao.org/docs/pdf/chn23908.pdf.

"State Council's 6 Measures to Promote the Healthy Development of the Fertilizer Industry [国务院6项措施促化肥行业健康发展]." 2008. Quota & Licence Administrative Bureau Ministry of Commerce of the People's Republic of China [中华人民共和国商务部配额许可证事务局]. http://www.licence.org.cn/rdgz2008/3468.htm.

"Statement by H.E. Xi Jinping President of the People's Republic of China at the Nuclear Security Summit." 2014. Ministry of Foreign Affairs of the People's Republic of China. Accessed November 26, 2022. https://www.fmprc.gov.cn/mfa_eng/wjdt_665385/zyjh_665391/201403/t20140325_678144.html.

Steinfeld, Edward S. 2010. *Playing Our Game: Why China's Rise Doesn't Threaten the West*. New York: Oxford University Press.

Stewart, Larry R. 1981. "Canada's Role in the International Uranium Cartel." *International Organization* 35, no. 4: 657–689.

Stigler, George J. 1947. "The Kinky Oligopoly Demand Curve and Rigid Prices." *Journal of Political Economy* 55, no. 5: 432–449.

Stiglitz, Joseph E. 2017. "America Has a Monopoly Problem—and It's Huge." *The Nation*, October 23. https://www.thenation.com/article/america-has-a-monopoly-problem-and-its-huge/.

Stone, Kevin. 2009. "Potash." In *Canadian Minerals Yearbook 2008 Review and Outlook*. Ottawa, Canada: Natural Resources Canada Minerals and Metals Sector, Chapter 36: 1–12.

Strange, Susan. 1996. *The Retreat of the State: The Diffusion of Power in the World Economy*. Cambridge Studies in International Relations. Cambridge: Cambridge University Press.

Streeck, Wolfgang. 2009. *Re-Forming Capitalism: Institutional Change in the German Political Economy*. Oxford: Oxford University Press.

Streifel, Shane. 2006. "Impact of China and India on Global Commodity Markets: Focus on Metals & Minerals and Petroleum, Background Paper for *Dancing with Giants: China, India, and the Global Economy*." Institute for Policy Studies and the World Bank: Washington, DC. Accessed August 29, 2018. http://www.tos.camcom.it/Portals/_UTC/Studi/ScenariEconomici/39746563551035393/ChinaIndiaCommodityImpact.pdf.

Su, Bo [苏波], ed. 2012. *Steel Industry Development Report* [钢铁产业发展报告]. Beijing: Chemical Industry Press [化学工业出版社].

Sukagawa, Paul. 2010. "Is Iron Ore Priced as a Commodity? Past and Current Practice." *Resources Policy* 35, no. 1: 5–63.

Sweezy, Paul M. 1939. "Demand under Conditions of Oligopoly." *Journal of Political Economy* 47, no. 4: 568–573.

Tan, Keith. 2012. Iron ore pricing: A review of recent developments (Platts). *Presentation delivered at the China Mining Congress, Tianjin, China*, November 4.

Tan, Yeling. 2021. *Disaggregating China, Inc.: State Strategies in the Liberal Economic Order*. Cornell Studies in Political Economy. Ithaca, NY: Cornell University Press.

Tang, Xiangyang. 2011. "Chinese Steel Supremo Rues Weak Position in Ore Negotiations." *Economic Observer*, February 28. http://www.eeo.com.cn/ens/2011/0602/202732.shtml.

Tansey, Oisin. 2007. "Process Tracing and Elite Interviewing: A Case for Non-Probability Sampling." *PS: Political Science and Politics* 40, no. 4: 765–772.

Terazono, Emiko. 2015. "Fertiliser Market Looks for Return of Higher Growth in 2016." *Financial Times*, December 7. https://www.ft.com/content/e80c7ee0-9cfa-11e5-8ce1-f6219b685d74.

Tiberghien, Yves. 2007. *Entrepreneurial States: Reforming Corporate Governance in France, Japan and Korea*. Ithaca, NY: Cornell University Press.

Tiberghien, Yves. 2020. "Asia's Rise and the Transition to a Post-Western Global Order." In *Contending Views on the Decline of Western-Centric World and the Emerging Global Order in the 21st Century*, edited by Y.-h. Chu et al. London: Routledge. 357–378.

Tordo, Silvana, et al. 2011. "National Oil Companies and Value Creation." World Bank Working Paper Series #218. http://siteresources.worldbank.org/INTOGMC/Resources/9780821388310.pdf.

Trade transactions data. 2000-2015. In *General Administration of Customs of the People's Republic of China* [中华人民共和国海关总署] [Data set].

Trainor, Cynthia. 1998. "Industry & Trade Summary: Fertilizers." US International Trade Commission. https://www.usitc.gov/publications/docs/pubs/industry_trade_summaries/pub3082.pdf.

"Transportation Logistics." Canpotex. Accessed May 25, 2023. https://www.canpotex.com/how-we-move-potash/transportation-logistics.

UN Comtrade Database. In *United Nations Department of Economics and Social Affairs, Statistics Division* [Data set]. https://comtradeplus.un.org/

UNCTADstat. In *United Nations Conference on Trade and Development (UNCTAD)* [Data set]. https://unctadstat.unctad.org/datacentre/dataviewer/US.IronOreTrade

"UPDATE 1—Canpotex Signs Potash Contract with China's Sinofert." 2014. Reuters, January 24. Accessed November 26, 2022. https://www.reuters.com/article/potash-china-canpotex-idUSL2N0KZ02620140125.

"UPDATE 1—Russia's Uralkali Signs $530 Mln Loan Deal with Global Banks." 2015. Reuters, April 20. Accessed July 31, 2019. https://uk.reuters.com/article/russia-uralkali/upd

ate-1-russias-uralkali-signs-530-mln-loan-deal-with-global-banks-idUKL5N0XH3WR2
0150420.
"Uralkali CEO Arrested in Belarus amid Potash Dispute." 2013. Canadian Broadcasting Corporation, August 26. Accessed July 31, 2019. https://www.cbc.ca/news/business/uralk ali-ceo-arrested-in-belarus-amid-potash-dispute-1.1346471.
*Uranium 2020: Resources, Production and Demand.* 2020. OECD Nuclear Energy Agency (NEA) and International Atomic Energy Agency (IAEA). https://www.oecd-nea.org/jcms/pl_52 718/uranium-2020-resources-production-and-demand.
*Uranium Enrichment.* 2013. World Nuclear Association. Accessed February 19, 2013. http://www.world-nuclear.org/info/inf28.html
"Uranium in Namibia." 2022. World Nuclear Association. Accessed March 25, 2022. https://world-nuclear.org/information-library/country-profiles/countries-g-n/namibia.aspx.
"Uranium Markets." 2022. World Nuclear Association. Accessed November 29, 2022. https://world-nuclear.org/information-library/nuclear-fuel-cycle/uranium-resources/uranium-markets.aspx.
Uranium Resources, Production and Demand (Red Book). In *Nuclear Energy Agency and International Atomic Energy Agency joint NEA/IAEA Uranium Group* [Data set]. https://www.oecd-nea.org/jcms/pl_28569/uranium-resources-production-and-demand-red-book
"U.S.-Chinese Agreement Provides Path to Further Expansion of Nuclear Energy in China." 2006. Department of Energy, December 16. https://www.energy.gov/articles/us-chinese-agreem ent-provides-path-further-expansion-nuclear-energy-china.
"Vale Mega Ship Enters China Port, First Time since Ban." 2013. Reuters, April 18. Accessed May 14, 2015. http://www.reuters.com/article/2013/04/18/vale-china-valemax-idUSL3N0D5 2FD20130418.
Valiante, Diego. 2013. "Global Commodities Markets after Financialization." EconoMonitor. Accessed July 30, 2013. http://www.economonitor.com/blog/2013/07/global-commodit ies-markets-after-financialisation/?utm_source=contactology&utm_medium=email&utm_ campaign=EconoMonitor%20Highlights%3A%20Detroit%20What%20Next%21.
Van de Graaf, Thijs, and Jeff Colgan. 2016. "Global Energy Governance: A Review and Research Agenda." *Palgrave Communications* 2: 1–12.
Vance, Robert E. 2000. Uranium. In *Canadian Minerals Yearbook*: Natural Resources Canada: 1–14.
Viner, Jacob. 1948. "Power and Plenty as Objectives of Foreign Policy in the Seventeenth and Eighteenth Centuries." *World Politics* 1, no. 1: 1–29.
Vivoda, Vlado. 2009a. "China Challenges Global Capitalism." *Australian Journal of International Affairs* 63, no. 1: 22–40.
Vivoda, Vlado. 2009b. "Resource Nationalism, Bargaining and International Oil Companies: Challenges and Change in the New Millennium." *New Political Economy* 14, no. 4: 517–534.
Waldmeir, Patti, and William MacNamara. 2010. "Rio Tinto Case Highlights Risks in China." *Financial Times*, April 5. https://www.ft.com/content/fdd1e036-40d4-11df-94c2-00144 feabdc0.
Waltz, Kenneth N. 1959. *Man, the State and War*. New York: Columbia University Press.
Wang, Hongying, and Erik French. 2014. "China in Global Economic Governance." *Asian Economic Policy Review* 9, no. 2: 254–271.
Wang, Lu, and Yangyang Liu. 2015. "Ministry of Agriculture: Strive to Achieve Zero Growth in Fertilizer Use by 2020 [农业部：力争到2020年实现化肥使用量零增长]." Xinhua News Agency. Accessed June 8, 2022. http://www.gov.cn/xinwen/2015-03/17/cont ent_2835461.htm.
Wang, Mark Yaolin. 2002. "The Motivations behind China's Government-Initiated Industrial Investments Overseas." *Pacific Affairs* 75, no. 2: 187–206.
Wang, Qiang. 2009. "China Needing a Cautious Approach to Nuclear Power Strategy." *Energy Policy* 37, no. 7: 2487–2491.
Wang, Yu, et al. 2015. "The More Fertilizer You Use, the More You Need—China's Fertilizer Use Accounts for 30% of the World's Total, Highlighting 'Fertilizer' Troubles

[肥越用越多地越吃越馋—我国化肥使用量占全球三成凸显"肥"之烦恼]." *Xinhua*. Accessed June 8, 2022. http://www.gov.cn/xinwen/2015-03/17/content_2835486.htm.
Warnock, John W. 2011. "Exploiting Saskatchewan's Potash: Who Benefits?" Canadian Centre for Policy Alternatives, January: 1–37.
Washburn, Donald Arthur. 1978. "Price Leadership." *Virginia Law Review* 64, no. 5: 691–734.
Watson, Matthew. 2005. *Foundations of International Political Economy*. New York: Palgrave Macmillan.
Watson, Matthew. 2018. *The Market*. New York: Columbia University Press.
Weaver, Courtney, et al. 2014. "CIC Chinese Fund Obtains 12% Equity Stake in Uralkali." *Financial Times*, September 24. https://www.ft.com/content/6eb1eed6-24e8-11e3-bcf7-00144feab7de.
Weaver, Courtney, and Jan Cienski. 2013. "Mining: Gone to Potash." *Financial Times*, September 17. Accessed July 31, 2019. https://www.ft.com/content/b59b0d0c-1eba-11e3-9636-00144feab7de?siteedition=uk.
Weiss, Jessica Chen. 2014. *Powerful Patriots: Nationalist Protests in China's Foreign Relations*. Oxford: Oxford University Press.
Weiss, Jessica Chen, and Jeremy Wallace. 2021. "Domestic Politics, China's Rise, and the Future of the Liberal International Order." *International Organization* 75, no. 2: 635–664.
Weitz, Richard. 2011a. "China's Uranium Quest Part 1: Domestic Shortages Fuel Global Ambitions." *China Brief* 11, no. 15: 6–10.
Weitz, Richard. 2011b. "China's Uranium Quest Part 2: The Turn to Foreign Markets." *China Brief* 11, no. 16: 12–15.
Wen, Jiabao. 2012. "China Firmly Set on a Path towards Green and Sustainable Development [中国坚定走绿色和可持续发展道路]." *Economic Daily* [经济日报], January17. Accessed May 14, 2015. http://paper.ce.cn/jjrb/html/2012-01/17/content_186609.htm#.
Wheatley, Jonathan. 2013. "Uralkali and CIC—Will China Call the Shots?" *Financial Times*, September 25. https://www.ft.com/content/9b264d22-9941-3f53-9f97-d0904be0fb2b.
Wildau, Gabriel. 2017. "China Prepares Fresh Round of State-Orchestrated Megamergers." *Financial Times*, July 9. https://www.ft.com/content/e3972f54-62e2-11e7-91a7-502f7ee26895.
Wilson, Ernest J., III. 1986. "The Petro-Political Cycle in World Oil Markets." In *Energy Resource Development: Politics and Policies*, edited by R. L. Enders et al. Westport, CT: Greenwood Press: 1–20.
Wilson, Jeffrey D. 2012. "Chinese Resource Security Policies and the Restructuring of the Asia-Pacific Iron Ore Market." *Resources Policy* 37: 331–339.
Wilson, Jeffrey D. 2013. *Governing Global Production: Resource Networks in the Asia-Pacific Steel Industry*. Edited by T. M. Shaw. International Political Economy Series. Basingstoke: Palgrave Macmillan.
Wilson, Jeffrey D. 2015. "Resource Powers? Minerals, Energy and the Rise of the BRICS." *Third World Quarterly* 36, no. 2: 223–239.
"Work Notice on Implementing Online Applications for Automatic Import License of Chemical Fertilizers [关于化肥自动进口许可证实行网上申领的工作通知]." 2013. The Ministry of Commerce of the People's Republic of China Quota Licensing Bureau. Accessed August 30, 2022. http://xkzj.mofcom.gov.cn/article/ggl/202107/20210703178629.shtml.
World Bank Commodities Price Data (The Pink Sheet). 2022. The World Bank. Accessed April 11, 2022. https://thedocs.worldbank.org/en/doc/5d903e848db1d1b83e0ec8f744e55570-0350012021/related/CMO-Pink-Sheet-April-2022.pdf.
*The World Copper Factbook*. 2021. Lisbon: International Copper Study Group.
"World Uranium Mining Production." 2019. World Nuclear Association. Accessed July 29, 2019. https://www.world-nuclear.org/information-library/nuclear-fuel-cycle/mining-of-uranium/world-uranium-mining-production.aspx.
Wright, Brian. 2014. "Global Biofuels: Key to the Puzzle of Grain Market Behavior." *Journal of Economic Perspectives* 28, no. 1: 73–97.

Wright, Robert, et al. 2012. "Mining Giant Vale Docks First Ship in China." *Globe and Mail*, January 30. Accessed May 14, 2015. http://www.theglobeandmail.com/report-on-business/international-business/mining-giant-vale-docks-first-ship-in-china/article4197555/.

Wu, Jimin [吴吉民], and Jinhe Wu [吴金和]. 2009. "Chinese Steel Enterprises' Lack of Iron Ore Pricing Power: Difficulties and Policy Responses [我国钢铁企业铁矿石定价话语权缺失的困境与对策]." *Economic Forum* [经济论坛] 466, no. 18: 74–76.

Wu, Jing. 2011. "COSCO to Open World's Largest Bulk Carrier." *Caixin*. Accessed May 14, 2015. https://www.caixinglobal.com/2011-12-07/101016224.html.

Wuthnow, Joel. 2012. *Chinese Diplomacy and the UN Security Council*. London: Routledge.

Wyatt, Stephen. 2010. "Baosteel Concedes Pricing Changes Are Overdue". *Financial Review*, March 29. Accessed October 11, 2022. https://www.afr.com/markets/baosteel-concedes-pricing-changes-are-overdue-20100329-ivskh.

Xiao, Xinjian. 2012. "Chinese Nuclear Energy Development in 2011: Future Trends and Policy Suggestions" [2011年中国核电发展状况, 未来趋势及政策建议]." *China Energy* 34, no. 2: 18–23, 47.

Xiao, Xinjian [肖新建], and Shixian Gao [(高世宪]. 2009. "Securing China's Nuclear Energy Resources [我国核能资源保障研究]." *Research and Approach* [研究与探讨] 29, no. 12: 35–38.

Xie, Lan [谢岚]. 2011. "Sinochem, China National Building Materials Group, and 20 Other Firms Exposed in Rio Tinto Bribery [中化国际、中建材集团等20家企业行贿力拓被曝光]." *Xinhua* [新华网], February 21. Accessed May 14, 2015. http://www.cibeicn.com/a/201102/20110221092658.ht.

Xie, Qingxia, et al. 2011. "China's Uranium Industry 'Going Out' Policy: Opportunities and Challenges [我国铀矿业'走去出'所面临的机遇与挑战]." *China Mining Magazine* 20, no. 12: 16–19, 27.

Xu, Yi-chong. 2012. "Nuclear Power in China: How It Really Works." *Global Asia* 7, no. 1: 32–43.

Yang, Limei. 2010. *Chinese Steel Industry and Sustainable Development Research under Constraints of Iron Ore Procurement* [铁矿石资源约束下的中国钢铁行业可持续发展研究]. Beijing: Metallurgical Industry Press.

Yin, Jianfeng [阴剑锋]. 2015. "Potash Negotiations, Where Is the Win? [钾肥谈判, 赢在哪里]." Sinochem Press Room. Accessed February 18, 2022. http://www.sinochem.com.cn/s/1375-4638-16105.html.

Zacher, Mark W. 1987. "Trade Gaps, Analytical Gaps: Regime Analysis and International Commodity Trade Regulation." *International Organization* 41, no. 2: 173–202.

Zacher, Mark W., ed. 1993. *The International Political Economy of Natural Resources*. The Library of International Political Economy Series, Vol. 2. Aldershot: Edward Elgar.

Zha, Daojiong. 2006. "China's Energy Security: Domestic and International Issues." *Survival* 48, no. 1: 179–190.

Zhang, Fan [张帆]. 2009a. "International Pricing System for Iron Ore and China's Negotiation Position [论国际铁矿石定价模式及我国的谈判地位]." *Practice in Foreign Economic Relations and Trade* [对外经贸实务] 10, no. 1: 90–92.

Zhang, Min, and Tom Daly. 2021. "Explainer: What We Know about China's Metals Reserves Release." Reuters. https://www.reuters.com/world/china/what-we-know-about-chinas-metals-reserves-release-2021-06-17/.

Zhang, Qi. 2009b. "Ministry Rejects Steel Lobby Proposal." *China Daily*, July 16. Accessed May 14, 2015. http://www.chinadaily.com.cn/business/2009-07/16/content_8434860.htm.

Zhang, Qi, and Lan Lan. 2010. "Commerce Ministry Studies Foreign Anti-Monopoly Probes." *China Daily*, April 16. http://www.chinadaily.com.cn/business/2010-04/16/content_9739994.htm.

Zhao, Pu [赵普]. 2013. "Background on the Repeal of the Iron Ore License System [铁矿石进口资质废止背后]." *China Times* [华夏时报], June 15. Accessed May 14, 2015. http://finance.sina.com.cn/roll/20130615/012615796860.shtml.

Zhong, Zhimin [钟志敏]. 2013. "NDRC: Four Factors Contributing to Short-Term Iron Ore Prices Skyrocketing [发改委：四因素令铁矿石价格短期暴涨]." *China Securities News*. Accessed May 14, 2015. http://finance.sina.com.cn/money/future/fmnews/20130307/011014743074.shtml.

Zhou, Yun. 2010. "Why Is China Going Nuclear?" *Energy Policy* 38, no. 7: 3755–3762.

Zhu, Keming [朱克明]. 2020. "2020 Sinochem Potash Fertilizer Import Negotiation Chronicle [2020中化钾肥进口谈判纪实]." Sinochem. Accessed February 18, 2022. http://www.sinochem.com.cn/s/17751-51246-140544.html.

Zhuang, Hongtao. 2006. "Iron Ore Negotiations Still Deadlocked, China Steel Association Tightens Import Management System [铁矿石谈判仍僵持 中国钢协收紧进口贸易管理]." *People's Daily*, June 12. Accessed May 14, 2015, http://finance.people.com.cn/GB/1038/4460296.html.

Zweig, David, and Jianhai Bi. 2005. "China's Global Hunt for Energy." *Foreign Affairs* 84, no. 5: 25–38.

Zysman, John. 1983. *Governments, Markets, and Growth*. Ithaca, NY: Cornell Univeristy Press.

# INDEX

*For the benefit of digital users, indexed terms that span two pages (e.g., 52–53) may, on occasion, appear on only one of those pages.*
Note: Tables and figures are indicated by *t* and *f* following the page number

Africa, uranium market, 195
Agrium, 153, 176
"area of entanglement" concept, 64
Australia and iron ore
   as exporter, 131, 132–33, 135
   in iron ore market, 98
   shipping, 122–23, 129

Baosteel, 102–3, 107, 109, 114, 118
Bates, Robert H., 88
Baumgertner, Vladislav, 177–78
Beijing Iron Ore Trading Center Corporation (COREX), 118
Beijing Olympics, 110
Belarus and potash
   in potash market, 147, 151, 155, 177–78
   in pricing negotiations, 167, 170–71
   reserves, 147–48
   sanctions, 182
Belarusian Potash Corporation (BPC)
   benchmark pricing regime – negotiations, 170–71, 174–75, 181, 185
   breakdown, 176–81
   in potash market, 12–13, 151, 155–56
Belaruskali, 152, 155, 177, 178, 179–80, 181
Belt and Road Initiative (BRI), 88–89
benchmark pricing regime. *See* pricing regime – iron ore and iron ore market; pricing regime – potash and potash market
*Berge Everest*, 124–25
BHP Billiton
   coking coal pricing system, 116–17
   hostile takeover attempt for Potash Corp, 11–12, 176–77

   in potash market, 176–77
   pricing regime change in iron ore, 66–67, 70
   spot trading platform, 118
   TC/RC rates for copper, 227
   transition to spot price, 111–12
   *See also* Big Three
Big Three (BHP Billiton, Rio Tinto, and Vale)
   benchmark pricing negotiations for iron ore, 92–93, 100, 109–10
   in iron ore market, 98–99, 100
   prices for iron ore, 100, 101
   spot trading platform, 118
   transition to spot price, 110, 111–13, 114–15, 116
Brazil
   and iron ore, 98, 122–23, 129
   and potash, 13, 142, 182–84, 183*f*, 235
building blocks (in argument for this book)
   heterogeneity, 14–15, 78–83
   markets as institutional systems, 13–14
   resonance, 15–17
   vulnerability, 1–4, 83–87

Cameco, 195
Canada
   and BPC, 155–56
   offices in China for potash enterprises, 164–66
   potash capacity, 152
   potash industry, 152–54
   in potash market, 147, 150, 151, 155–56
   potash reserves, 147–48
   uranium industry and market, 193–94
Canadian government, and hostile takeover attempt for Nutrien, 11–12, 177

Canpotex
  benchmark pricing regime – negotiations, 170–71, 172, 174–75
  description and role, 152–53
  office in China, 164–66, 181
  in potash market, 12–13, 147, 150, 151, 152–55
  in pricing negotiations, 149–50, 167
  weakening, 181–82
case selection and methodology. *See* methodology and case selection
CBMX trading platform, 117–18
Cheng, Shuaihua, 79
China
  international postures, 14–15
  revisionist power, 76–77
  rise and impact (debate on), 76–78
  status quo power, 77
  unintended consequences of rise, 240–41
China as heterogeneous power, 14–15, 78–83, 239–40
  across issues areas, 15
  characteristics, 15, 78
  concurrent variation in Chinese behavior, 15, 78–80
  definition, 78–79
  impact of China on institutions, 82–83, 232–33
  other variation in Chinese behavior, 80–82
  this book's contribution to, 82–83, 90–91
  *See also* heterogeneity
China Beijing International Mining Exchange spot trading platform (CBMX), 117–18
China Chamber of Commerce of Metals, Minerals & Chemicals Importers & Exporters (CCCMC), 106, 107, 113, 117–18, 167
China General Nuclear Power Group (CGNPG), 201–3, 204
China Iron and Steel Association (CISA)
  benchmark pricing regime – fall of, 114, 115, 137
  benchmark pricing regime – negotiations, 92–93, 109–10, 113–14, 116, 122
  description, 92, 101
  iron ore licenses reduction, 106, 107
  iron ore price indices, 119
  and price-setting by Big Three, 101
  spot trading platform, 117–18
China Iron Ore Price Index (CIOPI), 118
China Mineral Resources Group (CMRG), 1, 49–50, 120–21
China National Chemical Construction Corporation (CNCCC), 161–62
China National Nuclear Corporation (CNNC), 201–3, 204
China National Offshore Oil Corporation (CNOOC), 151, 162, 163, 167, 169
China National Petroleum Corporation, 167
China National Uranium Corporation Limited (CNUC), 205–6

China Nonferrous Metals Industry Association, 223
China Ocean Shipping Company (COSCO), 94, 123–25, 126–27, 128–29, 130
China Shipping, 123–24
China Smelters Purchase Team (CSPT), 190, 219, 226–28
Chinese Investment Corporation, 179
Christmas, Ian, 116
Clapp, Jennifer, 53
coffee market, 88
coking coal, pricing system, 116–17
Colgan, Jeff, 59, 64–65, 78
comparative political economy (CPE) literature, use in this book, 43–44
competitive market
  "competitive-strategic" continuum, 44–45, 45$t$, 47$t$, 48$t$
  and liberalization, 45, 46
  liberalization indicators in pricing regimes, 45$t$
  and pricing regimes, 9–10
coordination capacity
  description and role, 8, 63
  in domestic and global markets, 64
  and hypotheses for this book, 95–96
  and institutional change, 63–64
  and market concentration, 63–64
  in market power, 8, 63–64, 234
  in variation of Chinese behavior, 79–80, 238, 239–40
copper and copper market
  asymmetrical and symmetrical power, 189–90, 230
  concentration, 35–38, 75$t$, 210–11, 213
  cooperation, 75$t$
  domestic market coordination in China, 27$t$, 28–29, 190–91
  domestic market in China, 189, 216–20, 222
  exports, 210, 211$f$
  financialization of market, 213, 215–16, 219, 231
  global market, 210–13, 215–16
  global market coordination, 28–29, 190–91
  in hypotheses for this book, 62
  impact of China, 26–27, 190–91, 219–28
  importance as product, 210, 218–19
  imports (*see* copper and copper market – imports)
  impurities in, 222–23
  inclusion in case studies, 26–27, 28
  and institutional change, 62, 189–90, 236–37
  liberalization, 5, 189–90
  market characteristics at emergence of China, 27–28
  market power of China, 187, 189–90, 221, 230, 231, 236–37
  processing and concentrates, 211–12, 219, 222, 223–24, 224$f$, 226
  raw, refined, cathode, and anode, 223–26, 224$f$

share of large, medium, small enterprises in China, 216, 217f
smelting and refining process, 212
TC/RC rates (treatment and refining charges), 190, 226–28
traders on market, 218, 222
vulnerability paradox for China, 83
*See also* pricing regime – copper and copper market
copper and copper market – imports
by China, 189, 210–13, 212f, 213f, 214t, 216–18, 217f, 224f
China as number one importer, 21, 22t, 187
dependence of China, 27–28, 216
exceeding 20 percent, 21, 22t
globally, 214t
COSCO Bulk Carrier Co. Ltd., 123–24
"Cross-Border Potash Imports Coordination Commission," 162–63
CSI Index, 118
Custeel, 118, 119

Dayan, Joseph, 178
de-liberalization
as argument, 246–47
definition and concept, 45, 46, 51, 94
and market power, 59, 60–61
of pricing regime of iron ore, 61, 137
and pricing regimes, 10, 69–70
domestic and global markets
approach in this book, 87–88
coordination capacity, 64
dynamics, 54
framework for institutional change, 7–8, 7t
impact of China, 9, 49–50
impact of emerging economies, 6
power differentials, 3, 6–7, 57–58, 83
resonance between, 7, 9, 87–89, 96, 241–42
scholarship on, 88–89
variation in, 138
and vulnerability, 138–39, 242–43
domestic market (for commodities) in China
concentration, 71, 72f
coordination, 71–75, 73t
fragmentation, 3, 83, 242–43
fundamental market conditions, 71f, 71, 72t
number of extractive enterprises, 72t
overview and state of affairs, 35–39
policies and regulations of Chinese government, 73–74
power asymmetries, 56–57, 57t
power relations hypotheses, 60–61
pricing regime, 67
procurement policies, 73, 74
variation in/across, 4, 34–35, 39
variation in coordination, 28–29, 30, 190–91

economic nationalism, return of, 245–46

economy (global economy)
assertive behavior by countries, 83–85
and great powers, 89
literature on China's impact, 75–90
market concentration, 38
and nationalism, 245–46
preferences in, 68–69
rise and impact of China, 15–17, 19, 34, 50, 241
statist effect of China, 50
Economy, Elizabeth, 76–77
electricity in China, 197
Ericsson, Magnus, 36t, 98–99, 100, 114–15, 148–49, 155–56, 210–11
Europe, 130–31, 133

Feng Mingwei, 143–45, 158–59, 160, 172
fertilizers, 23–24, 143, 157–70
Fligstein, Neil, 38, 41, 63–64
Foot, Rosemary, 15, 80–81, 232–33
Fravel, Taylor, 85–86
freight sharing (pricing system), 135
French, Eric, 15, 79

Gaozhuang power plant (Henan province), 210
General Office of the State Council, and iron ore licenses in China, 106
Germany, and potash, 147
Gilpin, Robert, 38, 41–42, 63–64, 68, 89, 247
global commodities
China's place in procurement, 3, 83
consumption increase in China, 34
definition and differentiation, 18
in methodology of this book, 18
share of imports for China, 18
variation in Chinese behavior, 82–83, 187
global commodity markets
China as number one importer, 21–23, 22t
"competitive–strategic" continuum, 10
coordination in, 71–75
definition and boundaries, 18
features investigated, 42
financialization, 51–52, 246
impact of China, 16–17, 18–19, 49, 55–56, 64–65, 241–42
impact of China – divergent or opposite, 1–2, 9, 39–40, 49
market concentration, 35–38, 36t
overview and state of affairs, 35–39
paradox of China, 1–2, 6
political economy of, 39–42
power of China, 90
revisionist argument on China, 76–77
rise of China, 1, 8–9, 55
share of market for China, 18
transitions in, 52–53
variation in, 4–5, 34–35, 38, 39–40
and vulnerability, 9, 49, 55
*See also* domestic and global markets

global market institutions. *See* institutions
global markets
  change in, 13, 14
  concentration, 75, 75t
  cooperation, 75t
  coordination, 28–29, 75, 93–94, 190–91
  as creation, 41
  definition and concept, 41, 65–66
  as disputed or contested, 41–42
  as distinct markets, 43–44
  divergence in, 42
  as embedded, 41
  framework for institutional change, 7–8, 7t
  as institutional systems, 13–14
  institutions (*See* institutions)
  as "one," 13–14
  as "open," 246–47, 248
  as plural, 42
  power asymmetries, 56–57, 57t
  preferences and behaviors of China, 17
  propositions for, 41–42
  regulation over prices, 100–1
  spaces in, 41
  variation in, 42, 247
  *See also* domestic and global markets
GlobalOre, 118
Gourevitch, Peter, 87

Hall, Peter, 44
Hameiri, Shahar, 8–9, 14, 77, 81–82, 238
Hancock, Kathleen, 52, 53
Hayashida, Eiji, 136
hegemonic stability theory (HST), 89
Helleiner, Eric, 50–51, 90, 245
heterogeneity, 15, 66, 78–83, 238–39
  *See also* China as heterogeneous power
He Zhenwei, 146–47
Huaken International Trading Co., 161–62
Hughes, Llewelyn, 53, 63–64, 247–48
Hu Jintao, 201, 208
Hurst, Luke, 54, 98–99, 100, 109, 131, 133, 135

Ikenberry, G. John, 77, 246
imports by China
  and consumption, 1, 2f
  dependence on, 2, 83
  share of global commodities, 18
  *See also* copper and copper market – imports;
    iron ore and iron ore market – imports;
    potash and potash market – imports;
    uranium and uranium market – imports
India, 110, 171, 172
India Potash Ltd., 171, 181
"infant industry" theory, 89
insecurity of states, and vulnerability, 84–86
institutions (global market institutions)
  argument and hypotheses for change in this
    book, 56–63
  as building block, 13–14
  change in – overview, 55–56
  and coordination capacity, 63–64
  framework for change, 7–8, 7t
  global markets as, 13–14
  impact of China, 6–7, 9, 20, 34–35, 238
  impact of one country, 20
  and market fairness, 243–44
  and market power, 7–8, 7t, 16, 58–60, 58t, 59t,
    95, 231, 233, 234, 235–37
  as "open," 246–47, 248
  outcomes of Chinese behavior, 82–83, 232–33
  and patterns of exchange, 3, 83
  power asymmetries, 56–58, 57t, 58t, 60, 95–96
  power symmetries, 56–57, 57t, 58, 59t, 60, 95
  and preferences, 68–71, 247–48
  and price levels change, 66
  and prices, 64–71
  pricing institutions, 1–2, 20, 34–35
  starting point in scenarios, 231
international political economy (IPE). *See* political
  economy – global
International Potash Company (IPC), 155
IODEX, 118
iron ore and iron ore market
  additional strategy in case studies, 29–30, 29t
  asymmetric and symmetric positions of power,
    95, 96, 130, 137
  candidate for comparison with, 11, 12
  China as number one consumer, 92, 93–94, 122
  and CMRG, 1
  concentration and cooperation, 75t
  consolidation in China, 104–5, 120–21
  consumption and production by China (supply
    and demand), 2, 10–11, 83
  coordination capacity, 132, 136–37
  domestic and global markets
    coordination, 49–50
  domestic market coordination in China, 26, 27t,
    28–29, 93–94, 190–91
  domestic market coordination in Japan, 131–33
  domestic market in China, 101–9
  exports, 98–99, 99f, 110
  fragmentation in China, 102, 103–5, 104f,
    108, 158t
  global market coordination, 28–29, 93–94
  global production, 12
  history before China's emergence, 97–99
  impact of China, 12–13, 54, 55–56, 138–39, 236
  impact of Japan fifty years earlier, 130–36
  importance as product, 23
  imports (*see* iron ore and iron ore market
    – imports)
  industry prior to Japan's emergence, 130–31

and institutional change, 61–62, 95, 121, 136–37, 138–39
market characteristics at emergence of China, 23, 24t, 25
market concentration, 35–38, 98–99
market power – change in, 11, 93, 136–37
market power of China, 16, 93, 95–96, 136–38, 236
market power vulnerability, 86–87, 96, 236
vs. potash and potash market for China, 12–13, 140–42, 158, 158t, 160f, 172, 173, 184–85, 186, 232
procurement by CMRG, 120–21
production cuts in China, 110
production firms, 25f, 25
production in China, 101–2, 102f
qualification standards for licenses in China, 106
reserves and exports, 24t, 25
share of large, medium, small enterprises in China, 103–4, 104f
shipping regime – at time of China's emergence as top importer, 122–23, 129
shipping regime – domestic shipping, 124
shipping regime – impact of China, 29–30, 62, 94–95, 122–30, 137
traders as player on market, 119–20
transition from Japan to China, 11, 61, 96
vulnerability paradox for China, 83
See also pricing regime – iron ore and iron ore market
iron ore and iron ore market – imports
by China, 23, 97f, 97–98, 98f, 99f, 101–9, 102f, 107f, 113, 160f
China as number one importer, 21, 22t, 109
dependence of China, 25–26, 27f, 98, 99f, 101–2, 103f
exceeding 20 percent, 21, 22t
illicit imports, 107–8
importing licenses in China – history, 106–9
importing licenses in China – reduction, 106–9, 115

Japan
copper and copper market, 189–90, 212–13, 213f, 214–15, 214t, 226, 227, 230
domestic market coordination, 30, 131–33
imports of copper, 214–15
market power, 61–62, 93–94, 189–90
potash prices and imports, 149–50
transition from US to Japan, 52–53
Japan – and iron ore
domestic steel industry, 131–33
impact on market fifty years before China, 130–36
imports, 97–98, 98f

in market and benchmark pricing system, 2, 10–11, 30, 92, 93–94, 95–96, 109, 130, 133–36, 137, 236
market before emergence, 131
in move to spot price, 113
pricing regimes change after emergence, 48f, 48t
in shipping regime, 30, 94, 122, 123, 135–36
Jia Dashan, 125
Johnston, A. Iain, 76, 77, 78
Jones, Lee, 8–9, 14, 77, 81–82, 238

Katzenstein, Peter J., 42, 43, 52, 54, 87, 132, 244–45
Kazakhstan, and uranium, 188, 205, 206
Kazatomprom, 206
Kennedy, Scott, 79
Keohane, Robert O., 42, 59, 64–65, 77, 84, 89
Kloppers, Marius, 111
Krasner, Stephen, 38, 52–53
K + S, 148–49, 153, 176

Lake, David, 52, 63, 68, 89, 247
Levi, Michael, 76–77
liberalization
and case studies, 50
China's role and impact, 5–6, 44–45, 49–50, 138
and competitive market, 45, 46
definition and concept, 45, 94
and domestic market, 49–50
explanation of patterns/trends, 5–6, 46–52, 233–34, 245–46
of global commodity markets, 4–6, 44–45, 50, 51
and hierarchies, 41
measurement, 43–46
as political economic process, 50–51
and power relationships, 233–34
as puzzle, 4–6, 233–34
and relative market power, 237
in shipping pricing regime, 137
speed of, 51
tracking of trends, 245–46
See also de-liberalization
liberalization of pricing regimes, 10, 45–46, 45t, 47t, 48t, 69–70
indicators, 45–46, 45t, 47t
iron ore, 47t, 48t, 49–50, 69–70, 96
liberal market economies, 44, 68
Lipscy, Philip Y., 53
literature on China
comparative political economy, 43–44
concurrent variation in Chinese behavior, 15, 78–80
on global China, 76–78
and impact on global economy, 75–90
See also China as heterogeneous power

Long, Austin, 63–64
Luo Bingsheng, 101

market fairness, 243–44
market power
  in argument for this book, 16, 89–90, 95–96, 234–38
  asymmetric positions, 56–58, 57t, 58t, 59–60, 63, 95–96, 236–37
  balance domestic–global markets, 56
  and coordination capacity, 8, 63–64, 234
  definition in this book, 63
  description and concept, 8
  in global commodity markets, 19–20, 244–45
  hypotheses for this book, 60–63, 69
  impact of China, 6–7, 8, 15–16, 236
  impact on behavior of states, 86
  and institutions (*see* institutions)
  IPE focus, 54
  positions and interactions in methodology, 19–20
  and pricing regimes, 60–61
  role in political economy, 89–90
  symmetry in, 56–57, 57t, 58, 59t, 60, 95, 236–37
  two-level market power, 57–59, 57t
  and vulnerability (*see* market power vulnerability)
  *See also* relative market power
market power vulnerability and market vulnerability
  and copper, 230
  of China, 3, 83, 87, 138–39, 233, 243
  and disruptive behavior of China, 86
  iron ore, 86–87, 92–94, 96, 136–37, 138–39, 140–41, 236
  positions and preferences in, 8
  and potash, 140, 142
  and uranium, 229–30
"market-strategic" continuum of Hall and Soskice, 44
market vulnerability *see* market power vulnerability and market vulnerability
Martins, José Carlos, 128
Mearsheimer, John J., 14, 76, 83–84, 246
methodology and case selection
  additional strategy for iron ore, 29–30, 29t
  "emerging economy– commodity market" dyads, 20
  as framing for future work, 237–38
  inclusion of uranium and copper, 26–27, 28
  liberalization effect of China, 50
  main cases lists, 29t
  market power of China, 16, 231
  methodology, 18, 237–38
  methodology and data, 18–20

selection strategy for cases, 23–30
SOEs and non-state actors, 8–9
Miao Wei, 209
Mill's method of difference, 23
Milner, Helen, 42
mining sector in China
  number of mines, 105
  proportion or share of enterprises by size, 39f, 39, 40f, 71f, 105f, 105
  sales revenue by employee, 39, 40f
Ministry of Commerce (China), 162–63, 164, 167
Ministry of Commerce (MOFCOM) of China, 106, 108–9, 113, 116
Ministry of Foreign Trade and Economic Cooperation (China), 161–62
Ministry of Transport (China), in Valemax saga, 125, 129
Minmetals, and spot trading platform, 118
"moment of systemic significance," 20–23, 22t
Mosaic and Mosaic China, 153, 164–66, 181–82
Mysteel, 119

Namibia, uranium market, 205–6
Nathan, Andrew, 15, 78, 79
National Development and Reform Commission (NDRC), 101, 117–18, 164, 200–1, 202
National Food and Strategic Reserves Administration (NFSRA), 218–19
national markets, change in, 13
National Nuclear Safety Administration (NNSA), 201–2
nickel market, 237–38
Niger, uranium market, 195
Nippon Steel, 109, 131–32, 133, 135
non-state actors, and SOEs, 8–9
nuclear reactors, globally, 197, 198t
Nuclear Security Summit, 201, 208, 209
Nutrien, 153, 155, 176
Nye, Joseph S., 77

One Third, One Third, One Third policy, 73, 74, 197, 204–5
"open markets," problematization of concept, 246–48
O'Rourke, Joc, 181–82
Ostrom, Elinor, 8, 38, 63

Peru, copper market, 221–22
Platts, 118–19
Polanyi, Karl, 41, 51–52
political economies – national, 44, 87–89
political economy – global
  and commodity market, 16, 18–19, 39–42
  comparative study China-global, 18–19
  description and origins as field, 52
  economy and great powers, 89
  impact on/of China, 88–89

and insecurity, 84
"inside-out" and "outside-in" arguments, 87–88
market power's role in, 89–90
and national political economies, 87–89
of natural resources, 52–54
research contributions of this book, 53–54
scholarship on, 52–54, 88–89
uranium and copper, 26–27
and vulnerability of China, 86–87
political economy – of China
and commodity market, 4, 18–19
iron ore vs. potash markets, 12–13
state vs. private ownership, 10
and variation, 4, 232–33
potash and potash market
agricultural use, 144f, 145f, 157–58, 183–84 (*see also* fertilizers)
asymmetric and symmetric positions of power, 141–42, 184–85
and breakdown of BPC, 176–81
capacity and oversupply, 152, 156–57
China as number one importer and consumer, 21, 22t
concentration and cooperation, 75, 75t
consolidation in China, 158, 160–61
consolidation outside China, 176–77
coordination capacity globally, 141, 151–57
coordination capacity in China, 71, 142
coordination in China, 71, 141–42, 160–61, 172, 173, 184–85, 235
coordination outside China, 153–54, 155–57
domestic market coordination in China, 26, 27t, 28–29, 141–42, 185–86
domestic market in China, 157–70, 185
dominance weakening of China, 181–83, 184
exports, 147–48, 148f
fragmentation in China, 158t
global market coordination, 28–29
global market overview, 143–47, 151, 156–57
hostile takeover attempt, 11–12, 176–77
in hypotheses for this book, 62
impact of China, 12–13, 55–56, 142, 184–85
importance as product, 23–24, 143
imports (*see* potash and potash market – imports)
and institutional change, 62, 184
vs. iron ore market for China, 12–13, 140–42, 158, 158t, 160f, 172, 173, 184–85, 186, 232
liberalization, 5
market characteristics at emergence of China, 23–25, 24t, 141
market power of China, 16, 141–42, 184–86
market power vulnerability, 142
overseas investment by China ("going out" policy), 146–47
positioning of China, 11–12
procurement contract refusal by China, 172–73
producing countries, 12, 147–48, 151–52, 155–56
production and consumption in China, 143, 144f, 145f, 157, 158
production firms, 25, 26f, 148–49, 158
reserves and exports, 24t, 25, 26f, 147–48
system in China, 70
transport, 152, 157
vulnerability paradox for China, 83
*See also* pricing regime – potash and potash market
potash and potash market – imports
by China, 143–47, 146f, 150–51, 158–60, 159f, 160f, 171t, 185
China as number one importer, 21, 22t
by China – negotiating small group, 167–70, 172, 185
by China – regulations, 163, 166
dependence of China, 25–26, 27f, 143–45, 145f, 146–47, 157
exceeding 20 percent, 21, 22t
by foreign-invested enterprises and joint ventures, 164–66, 165t
importing licenses in China, 160–66, 165t
by land (rail imports) to China, 162–63, 182
Potash Conservation Board (Canada), 152
*See also* Canpotex
Potash Corporation of Saskatchewan (PCS), or Potash Corp. (now Nutrien), 11–12, 152, 153, 176–77
Potash One, 176
preferences
approach in this book, 68–69
in global markets, 17
and institutions, 68–71, 247–48
and power, 69–71
and prices, 65t, 66–68, 69–70
in uranium's case, 228–29
variation in, 68, 247–48
prices
and impact of China on global commodity markets, 64–65
and institutions, 64–71
levels and pricing regimes, 65, 65t
levels as indicators, 64–66
and preferences, 65t, 66–68, 69–70
price-determined logic, 66–67, 70
as principal focus of this book, 65–66
and stakeholders, 66–67
pricing institutions, 1–2, 20, 34–35
pricing regime – copper and copper market
benchmark pricing – negotiations, 190
description, 43
pricing regime – prior to China's emergence, 213–16
spot prices, 219

# INDEX

pricing regime – iron ore and iron ore market
  benchmark pricing – fall of and opposite results, 1–2, 4–5, 10–11, 49, 70, 92–93, 233
  benchmark pricing – negotiations, 10–11, 92–93, 99–100, 109–10, 113–14, 116, 122
  benchmark pricing regime – history, 10–11, 92–94, 99–100, 109–22, 133–34, 137
  CFR (cost and freight) pricing, 122–23, 135
  coordination in, 10–11
  de-liberalization, 61, 137
  FOB (free on board) pricing, 122–23, 135
  in hypotheses for this book, 61–62, 95–96
  liberalization, 47t, 48t, 49–50, 69–70, 96
  price indices, 118–19
  prices 1975–2022, 115f
  price-setting by corporations, 100–1
  pricing regime, 11, 26, 30, 69–70
  pricing regime – change/variation, 48f, 48t, 66–67, 70, 93–94
  pricing regime – history, 99–101, 130–31, 133–36
  pricing regime – prior to China's emergence, 99–101
  pricing regime – prior to Japan's emergence, 130–31
  in shipping regime, 122–23, 124–25, 129–30
  spot market – trading platforms, 117–18
  spot market – use in China, 110, 115
  spot pricing – emergence, 4–5, 92–93, 110, 122
  spot pricing – transition to, 110, 111–13, 114–15, 116
pricing regime – potash and potash market
  benchmark pricing regime, 5, 12–13, 70, 142, 170–71, 174, 235
  benchmark pricing regime – and China, 150, 170–71
  benchmark pricing regime – frequency and timing, 173–75
  benchmark pricing regime – negotiations, 170–71, 172, 173–75, 181
  price-fixing claims in North America, 153–54
  prices, 147, 149f, 149, 152, 161, 170–71, 171t, 172–73, 174, 178–79, 180
  prices – control by NDRC, 164
  pricing – negotiations, 149–50, 168–69, 170
  pricing regime, 26, 43, 141, 149–50
  pricing regime change, 48f, 48t, 70
  pricing regime – impact of China, 170–84
  pricing regime – prior to China's emergence, 147–57
  spot market emergence, 181–84
pricing regimes
  change after emergence of China and Japan, 48f, 48t
  change explanation, 9–10
  changes in market as methodology, 19
  characteristics at emergence of China, 24t

  in competitive and strategic markets, 9–10
  "competitive–strategic" continuum, 10, 44–45, 46, 48f
  definition and concept, 43
  and de-liberalization, 10, 69–70
  extent and direction of change, 48f
  in hypotheses for this book, 60–62, 63, 95–96
  and market power, 60–61
  operationalization, 46, 47t
  and price levels, 65, 65t
  variation, 43, 232
  variety in global commodity markets, 9, 43
  *See also* liberalization of pricing regimes
pricing regime – uranium and uranium market
  benchmark pricing – negotiations, 193
  prices (spot prices), 195–96, 196f, 207
  pricing mechanisms, 188, 196–97
  pricing regime – prior to China's emergence, 193–97
  spot transactions, 196–97
Putnam, Robert, 54, 64, 87–88
puzzles in this book
  liberalization as, 4–6, 233–34
  overview of results, 232–34
  solving as goal, 6, 55
  variation as, 4, 6, 232–33
  vulnerability as, 1–4, 6, 233

Qinghai Salt Lake Industry Co., 159
quasi-natural experiment approach, 20

Radetzki, Marian, 8, 63–65
rare earths, 245–46
relative market power
  and copper, 230
  description, as measure, and in argument of this book, 6–7, 8, 56, 95, 234–35, 237, 238
  relationship with institutional change, 6–7, 8, 89, 95–96, 236
  symmetry in, 173
  and uranium, 228
Rio Tinto, 66–67, 112–13
  *See also* Big Three
Rodrik, Dani, 35, 52–53, 132–33, 136, 213, 215
Russia
  invasion of Ukraine, 182
  potash benchmark pricing regime – negotiations, 170–71
  potash exports by rail, 162–63
  in potash market, 147, 151, 155
  potash market merger, 176
  potash negotiations, 167
  potash reserves/production, 147–48

Shan Shanghua, 92–93, 122
shipbuilders in China, 124

## INDEX

shipping industry of China, description and size, 123–24
Shirk, Susan, 84–85
Shouguo Zhang, 127
Silnivit, 176
Singapore, GlobalOre spot trading platform for iron ore, 118
Sino-Agri Group (Zhongnong)
 importing license for potash, 161–62, 163
 potash benchmark pricing regime – negotiations, 170–71
 in potash market, 151, 158, 159*f*, 159–60
 potash negotiations, 167, 169–70
Sino-Arab Chemical Fertilizer Co., 161
Sinochem / Sinofert
 importing license for potash, 161–62, 163
 and potash, 140–41, 151, 156–57, 159–60
 potash benchmark pricing regime – negotiations, 170–71, 172, 174
 in potash market, 151, 158–59, 159*f*, 176–77
 potash negotiations, 167–68, 169–70
Sinofert Holdings Ltd., 153
Société d'études et de Recherches d'Uranium, 193–94
Soskice, David, 44
spot pricing and market. *See* pricing regime – iron ore and iron ore market
Sprott Physical Uranium Trust, 207
stakeholders
 in China, 6–7
 impact on global market, 6–8
 and market power, 7–8, 56–57, 57*t*, 60, 70, 96
 and prices, 66–67
state, as unitary actor, 68
state-owned enterprises (SOEs)
 iron ore benchmark pricing regime fall, 114, 115
 and rise of China, 8–9
State Power Investment Corporation (SPIC), 201–2
steel and steel manufacturing
 description and size as market, 23
 domestic market in China, 101–9
 in Japan, 131–33
 production in China, 101–3, 103*f*
Strange, Susan, 8, 38, 63, 89
strategic market (or managed)
 and de-liberalization, 45, 46
 liberalization indicators in pricing regimes, 45*t*
 and pricing regimes, 9–10
Streeck, Wolfgang, 38
systemic significance
 commodity consumption in China, 34
 impact of China, 20–23
 impact on pricing institutions, 20
 imports exceeding 20 percent, 20, 21, 22*t*
 measurement, 20–21
 "moment of," 20–23, 22*t*
 temporal framing, 20–23, 22*t*
 use and relevance for other cases, 20

Taiwan, 84–85
Tan, Yeling, 88
Tiberghien, Yves, 15, 42, 80, 81, 85–86
Two Markets, Two Resources policy, 73–74, 197, 204–5

United States
 nuclear reactors and security, 208, 209
 as potash buyer, 147–48
 uranium ban policy, 193–94
 variation in behavior *vs.* China, 80–81
Uralkali, 152, 155, 156, 176, 177–80, 181, 182
uranium and uranium market
 behavior of China, 187–88, 189
 cartel in, 193–94
 civilian nuclear industry in China, 197, 198*t*, 200–2
 civilian nuclear multilateral initiatives, 208–10
 civilian nuclear safety and security, 188, 201, 208–10, 229
 concentration and cooperation globally, 75, 75*t*, 193–94
 concentration and cooperation in China, 188–89, 201–3
 domestic market coordination in China, 27*t*, 28–29, 190–91, 229
 domestic market in China, 197–204
 exploration, 205–6
 exports globally, 193*f*, 193
 fragmentation, 194–95
 global investment firms, 207
 global market, 190–94, 201–4, 205–6, 207, 229–30, 235–36
 global market coordination, 28–29, 75
 in hypotheses for this book, 63
 impact of China, 26–27, 190–91, 204–10
 imports (*see* uranium and uranium market – imports)
 inclusion as case studies, 26–27, 28
 and institutional change, 63, 189, 235–36
 liberalization, 5
 market characteristics at emergence of China, 27–28
 market power of China, 187, 188–89, 207, 228–30, 231
 nuclear power plants, 195–96, 201–2
 procurement by China, 188, 199, 203–7, 228, 229–30
 procurement policy, 74
 production globally, 191, 192*t*, 193–94, 205–6
 production in China, 197, 199*t*, 200*f*
 resources and output in China, 191–93, 199
 vulnerability paradox for China, 83
 *See also* pricing regime – uranium and uranium market

uranium and uranium market – imports
  by China, 191, 192f, 199, 200f, 203f, 203, 207
  China as number one importer, 21, 22t, 187, 191
  dependence of China, 27–28, 188, 199, 200f
  exceeding 20 percent, 21, 22t

Vale
  ban on large cargoes in China, 125–27
  move to spot price, 111–12
  pricing regime change in iron ore, 66–67
  in shipping regime, 94, 123, 124–25
  spot trading platform, 118
  See also Big Three
Vale Beijing, 125
Vale Malaysia, 128
Valemax (cargoes) saga, 62, 94, 123, 124–30, 239
Van de Graaf, Thijs, 53, 54, 59, 64–65
variation
  argument in this book, 6–13
  in China as heterogeneous power literature, 78–82
  in China market, 4–5
  concurrent variation in China, 15, 78–80
  in coordination capacity of China, 79–80, 238, 239–40
  in coordination of domestic and global markets, 28–29, 30, 190–91
  and domestic and global markets, 138
  in domestic commodity market of China, 4, 34–35, 39
  in global commodities, 82–83, 187
  global commodity markets, 4–5, 34–35, 38, 39–40
  and political economy of China, 4, 232–33
  in pricing regimes, 43, 232
  as puzzle, 4, 6, 232–33
very large ore carriers (VLOCs), 94
Vivoda, Vlado, 52, 53, 63–65, 76
VOC (variety of capitalism) literature, use in this book, 43–45
vulnerability
  and China in global economy, 87
  and China in global political economy, 86–87
  in domestic and global markets, 138–39, 242–43
  domestic variables, 84–86
  as identity for China, 3–4
  and impact of China on global commodity markets, 9, 49, 55
  insecurity and fragility of China, 84–86
  and institutional change, 233, 242
  and international behavior, 83–84
  international variables in China, 85–86
  and market fairness, 243–44
  and power assertion by countries, 84–85, 86
  as puzzle, 1–4, 6, 233
  in resource procurement, 54
  See also market power vulnerability; market vulnerability
vulnerability paradox for China
  in copper market, 83
  description and dynamics, 2–4
  four paradoxes, 2–3, 83
  in iron ore market, 83
  overview, 1, 55, 83
  in potash market, 83
  in uranium market, 83

Wallace, Jeremy, 15, 79–80, 232–33, 238
Walter, Andrew, 15, 80–81, 232–33
Wang, Hongying, 15, 79
Wei Jiafu, 127
Weiss, Jessica Chen, 15, 79–80, 85, 232–33, 238
Wen Jiabao, 163, 201
Wilson, Jeffrey, 8, 54, 63, 100, 109–10, 131
World Steel Association, 116
Wu Sihai, 163, 169–70
Wu Yigao, 167

Xi Jinping, 201, 209

Yang Jiasheng, 103–4
Yellow Cake PLC, 207

Zen-Noh, 149–50
Zhou Tao, 119

The manufacturer's authorised representative in the EU for product safety is Oxford
University Press España S.A. of El Parque Empresarial San Fernando de Henares,
Avenida de Castilla, 2 – 28830 Madrid (www.oup.es/en or product.safety@oup.com).
OUP España S.A. also acts as importer into Spain of products made by the manufacturer.

Printed in the USA/Agawam, MA
April 4, 2025

885391.007